THE NEW SOVIET FICTION

THE NEW SOVIET FICTION

Sixteen Short Stories

Compiled by Sergei Zalygin

Abbeville Press   Publishers   New York

Editor: Jacqueline Decter
Designer: Vladimir Radunsky
Production Editor: Robin James
Production Supervisor: Hope Koturo

First edition

Library of Congress Cataloging-in-Publication Data
The New Soviet fiction : 16 short stories / compiled by Sergei Zalygin.
     p.   cm.
     Translated from the Russian.
     ISBN 0-89659-881-0
     1. Short stories, Russian—Translations into English.   2. Short
stories, English—Translations from Russian.   3. Short stories,
Soviet—Translations into English.   4. Short stories, English—
Translations from foreign languages.   5. Russian fiction—20th
century.   6. Soviet fiction.   I. Zalygin, Sergei, 1913–
PG3286.N35   1989
891.73'01'08—dc19   88-39673
                                               CIP

The translation of "What Should I Tell the Crow?" is reprinted
with permission of Northern Illinois University Press, from
Siberia on Fire: Selected Stories and Essays by Valentin Rasputin,
translated by Gerald Mikkelson and Margaret Winchell (1989).

For the transliteration of Russian names, a modified version of
the New York Public Library transliteration system has been used.

CONTENTS

List of Illustrations   7

SERGEI ZALYGIN *Introduction*   9
translated from the Russian by Steven W. Nielsen

ANDREI BITOV Pushkin's Photograph (1799–2099)   15
translated from the Russian by Priscilla Meyer

ELCHIN Auto Accident in Paris   61
translated from the Russian by Stefani Hoffman

I. GREKOVA No Smiles   79
translated from the Russian by Dobrochna Dyrcz-Freeman

VALENTIN KATAEV The Sleeper   111
translated from the Russian by Catharine Theimer Nepomnyashchy

VIKTOR KONETSKY Cat-Strangler Silver   135
translated from the Russian by Steven W. Nielsen

VLADIMIR MAKANIN Antileader   163
translated from the Russian by Jamey Gambrell

REVAZ MISHVELADZE A Question Mark
and an Exclamation Point   205
translated from the Russian by Edythe C. Haber

BULAT OKUDZHAVA The Art of Needles and Sins   213
translated from the Russian by Michele A. Berdy

LYUDMILA PETRUSHEVSKAYA   Through the Fields   235
translated from the Russian by Stefani Hoffman

VALENTIN RASPUTIN   What Should I Tell the Crow?   239
translated from the Russian by Gerald Mikkelson and Margaret Winchell

MIKHAIL ROSHCHIN   The Devil's Wheel in Kobuleti   261
translated from the Russian by Michele A. Berdy

VLADIMIR SOLOUKHIN   Stepanida Ivanovna's Funeral   279
translated from the Russian by Diane Nemec Ignashev

TATYANA TOLSTAYA   Fire and Dust   297
translated from the Russian by Jamey Gambrell

ARVO VALTON   Love in Mustamägi   311
translated from the Estonian by Ritva Poom

S. YAROSLAVTSEV   The Details of Nikita Vorontsov's Life   325
translated from the Russian by Gerald Mikkelson and Margaret Winchell

SERGEI ZALYGIN   Prose   363
translated from the Russian by Catharine Theimer Nepomnyashchy

Biographical Notes   387

First Publication Information   397

LIST OF ILLUSTRATIONS

Three Soviet artists were specially commissioned to illustrate this volume. The stories they have illustrated and the pages on which the illustrations appear are given below.

LEONID TISHCOV
    Pushkin's Photograph (1799–2099)   35
    The Sleeper   123
    What Should I Tell the Crow?   247

ANDREI KOSTIN
    Cat-Strangler Silver   147
    Fire and Dust   301
    Love in Mustamägi   317

YURI VASHCHENKO
    The Details of Nikita Vorontsov's Life   345

INTRODUCTION

Sergei Zalygin

The Russian word for short story, *rasskaz*, comes from the word *skaz*, an oral narrative whose subject might be anything—all of life, any incident in life, any event, any human emotional state whatsoever, both reality and fairy tale.

It is the most universal literary form.

The novel makes much stricter demands on its material. Since it has to hold the reader's attention for a long time, it must be meaningful. It thus follows that the novelist must instill in the reader certain more or less serious thoughts, even thoughts of an edifying nature; he must introduce a meaningful "event" as well, if only from his point of view. Moreover, if there is no such event in the novel—and these days this is entirely possible, perhaps even fashionable—then the very negation of the need for a meaningful event is nothing but the author's way of expressing his own meaningfulness. In that case it is a modernist, even a revolutionary, meaningfulness, a rebellion against the canon.

The short story is much freer and more independent of theoretical literary tenets, of the canons and laws of genre. Perhaps this is precisely why literary theory has avoided too close and constant a rapport with the short story. Its idol has been and remains the novel. The short story is just as free as our everyday speech. In speaking among ourselves, after all, we do not think about the demands of literature.

But at the same time the short story, being the genre closest to conversational speech, is, if not conservative, then in any case more traditional than any other literary form, inasmuch as our everyday speech is traditional, traditional to a much greater degree than literature, than prose in general. The Russian short story, and even more so the fairy tale and the oral narrative that preceded it, is a phenomenon just as national as Russian speech itself, as the Russian language in its reality and naturalness, in its traditionalism and modernism, and, in short, in all its history and contemporaneity.

It is for this very reason that not one of the classic writers of Russian literature, not one of those who wrote novels of worldwide, undying significance and meaning, overlooked the short story in his work. Tolstoy, Dostoevsky, and Turgenev all wrote stories, and earlier still, Pushkin (although he called his stories tales—the *Belkin Tales*, for example). But certainly the greatest short-story writer was Chekhov.

No one, not a single writer before Chekhov, raised the short story to such heights as he did. No one demonstrated as persuasively that the short story not only can but should be as classical a literary form as the novel. To be sure, Edgar Allan Poe and, to a certain extent, Guy de Maupassant accomplished this in the West, but in Russia it was without doubt Chekhov who did this, and he did it in the most convincing and significant way, considering the subsequent impact of the short story on literature as a whole.

I probably can't prove it, but I am nevertheless convinced that the Chekhovian short story, that everyday discourse peculiar to him, left its mark on the work of Chekhov the dramatist and then on the rest of Russian drama as well, and even had an effect on poetry. Many of Sergei Esenin's works are nothing other than poetic short stories about himself, about those close to him, or about this or that incident in his life.

Not to speak of such writers as Bulgakov, Bunin, Gorky, Platonov, or Sholokhov—all of whom are also Chekhovian storytellers in their own way, if only because they have a Chekhovian trust in the short story and the same sense of the need for the short story in literature and in their own work. This allowed Bunin to write the story "Sunstroke" even after Tolstoy's novel *Anna Karenina* had been written, and Platonov to write the story "Fro" after Bunin's "Sunstroke."

Tracing the subsequent development of the Soviet short story is the task of literary scholars, a task that, in my opinion, is far from complete. To glance back at the past, the literary past in particular, and to note certain trends, to name this or that figure, is always much easier than to do the same with the literature of just yesterday or, even more so, of today.

In this regard one can only say that the short story has, apparently, become firmly established in Soviet literature once and for all, perhaps even more securely than in any other literature. Collections of short stories by one author or another, collections of the most diverse authors, and, finally, collections of short stories by foreign authors from all over the world are a phenomenon that surprises no one here. What would surprise us would be the *absence* of such collections and anthologies.

Therefore, the very appearance of an anthology of contemporary Soviet short stories in the United States will tell the American reader not only about our short stories as such, not only about our short-story writers, but also about our readers' literary tastes and preferences and about the world of publishing here. It is, you see, virtually impossible to publish a single issue of one of our so-called thick literary journals without including a short story.

No matter how interesting the novel published in that issue might be, no matter how good the poetry is, no matter what questions of *perestroika* are raised, an issue of a journal without a short story is, in the eyes of our readers today, an incomplete and unusual issue.

I say this on the basis of my own experience as editor of so widespread and widely read a journal as *Novy Mir*. Such an attitude on the part of the reader toward the short story is both good and bad for it. Good because it is very difficult for any genre to develop if it is not in demand among readers, if they are not interested in it or not well-disposed toward it. Bad because constant demand eases the requirements on the very object in demand.

Of course the status of literature in a society can hardly be determined by the status of one of its genres, be it poetry or the short story, but the state of affairs within literature itself certainly can be discerned—if not entirely, then at least in part—through any genre, including the short story.

It is true that the changes taking place in our country now are so rapid and, at times, so unexpected for us that even a genre as functional as the short story cannot absorb and reflect them right away. But there is something else that is no less important: It is essential for the foreign reader to know against what background, with what degree of freedom, and at what level of thought these changes began. Only then can their true sense and significance be understood.

And here I would like to voice the opinion that our literature—at its best, naturally—has, on the whole, always risen to the occasion, even during the period of stagnation. And I hope that the American reader of the collection I have compiled will share this opinion.

If that reader has heard at least something about our literature of the recent past, if he has heard of such names as Yuri Trifonov, Vasily Shukshin, or Valentin Rasputin, he will, after reading this collection, be convinced that these writers were not alone. They may have been better and more talented than others, it is true, but they did not constitute an exception to the rules that literature sets for itself, circumventing the pressure "from above," that is, from those in power, and "from below," from readers who are simply indiscriminate.

It is precisely from this independent group of independent writers (as I call them) that I made my selection, which is far from comprehensive. For a complete representation a multivolume short-story anthology would certainly be necessary.

At the same time I am sure that if any of the writers included in our collection were omitted from it, the American reader would not get even an approximate picture of this group.

This was the principle that guided my selection.

And that is all I thought necessary to say to the American reader.

I am not going to recommend every author in this book individually to you, nor am I going to evaluate their writing from the point of view of craft, social trenchancy, traditionalism, or modernism. All of that is the intellectual and emotional work that lies in store not as much for me as for you.

This, too, incidentally, is a primary and long-standing feature of Russian literature, which has never relied on diversion or sensationalism but has always depended on the reader's contemplation.

Right now, perhaps, this principle is being violated because changes and everything that we call *perestroika*, alas, can never take place without sensations, without superficial and frivolous judgments and conclusions. But this won't last for long.

Fashion and sensations will pass, but art as such will remain, a witness of its time, forever.

Translated from the Russian by Steven W. Nielsen.

THE NEW SOVIET FICTION

PUSHKIN'S PHOTOGRAPH
(1799–2099)

Andrei Bitov

And today it finally turned out that there isn't any war yet.

But the day before yesterday it had broken out, and yesterday it was still possibly going on.

And today there is still time.

But the day before yesterday I came down from the attic at dusk to turn on the light (my switch is downstairs), and everyone was already asleep. I stole by, turned it on, went out on the porch, and sat down to have a smoke. I sat there on the porch as if I were looking at myself from upstairs, from the attic, thinking out some unfinished thought up there. I gazed in front of me at this loss of clarity; it was as if everything that life had drawn for us during the day out of clouds, shadows, grass, and fences had now been completely erased; it hadn't turned out right, and life had smeared it with her eraser. But having blurred the white page of the day, life left things out in her haste: A bush stood out unrealistically, as if it were coming to meet you, carefully outlined down to the last twig, though it hadn't been outlined at all in the sunlight; the evening flowers started lighting up individually, as if they were swimming through the darkness. . . . I'll sit here like this, abandon myself to it, feeling too lazy to go back to my now-illuminated upstairs to harness myself to the reins of my attic, to drag it through the impassable text. Suddenly the already invisible gate opens, indicating its absence with a squeak, and a completely visible man tumbles in, leaning, like the fence, to one side, shaking up the dusk with his unsteady step. "I haven't seen you around here before," he says as he sits down next to me, and he asks for a glass.

Usually in our tumbledown little village (three inhabited houses out of a couple of dozen in various stages of disrepair and destruction, as in a speeded-up film) it isn't the custom to simply drop in on one another even during the daytime. I try not to give him the glass, saying that everyone's asleep, that I don't drink myself, I'm afraid of disrupting the little time I have, suddenly wanting very much to go upstairs and continue working. . . . I try not to give him a glass. Then, overflowing with grief, twitching his jaw muscles and throwing me quick glances, dropping his head as if either wiping away a tear or hiding it, he says, "So what does it mean? War again?"

And just three days ago I'd covered five hundred kilometers on our roads from Yaroslavl, Kostroma, Sudislavl, and Galich, had finally broken away from the capital, to my son, to my attic. . . . I'd gotten here quickly, without seeing any destruction or accidents in the course of twelve hours of driving. What war? What are you talking about?

Without taking offense, but with pain, he explains all the details to me as he would to a half-wit. How he took the last bus from the regional center, how one guy had a transistor radio, how all the men on the bus listened . . . how it all happened that war had started. . . . Even now that everything's over I don't want to repeat the details. "What is this—"shaking his head like a horse—"we just got ourselves grandchildren and now we won't be able to bring them up?"

I let him in, and gave him a cup. It turned out he was only asking for water. That was all he wanted. . . . But he sat down solidly, as if for life. "So," I think, "should I wake them all up now and go, or let them sleep till morning? Or maybe there's no point in going—there isn't even anything left there, and it was my fate that in trying to get to my son, I saved myself. . . . But how can this be?" Over there—you can't even think about those people who are OVER THERE. That really sobers you. Okay, enough, You've made this all up, right? Oh no, he says, if I'd made it all up . . . And again he starts in with the details. I ought to know what a detail is. It's hypnosis . . . but I'm believing it again. Because it's terrifying.

"How come I don't know you?" he says again, that's while he's sitting in my house, and I let him in! "And I don't know you," I say. "You don't know me? There isn't anyone here who doesn't know me! I'm Chistyakov! My brother works on the railway . . ." and so on.

I figured him out: The kind of guy who has either been in prison or fought in the war; he has medals or grandchildren; I'm a son to him or he's younger than I am—a lush, a poetic soul. I've seen a lot like him, not IN the village but FROM it. I figured him out, but not completely: "You don't know me, but do you know that you're sitting in MY house?" I vaguely knew the story of how my father-in-law had bought the house—maybe it was true. It wasn't hard with a bit of authorial sentimentality to fill this all in: He found out that there was war, he wasn't all there in the head, his legs brought him here by themselves . . . and there on the threshold where he had been born and bred, some unknown guy, some Jew, is sitting in his mustache and glasses ("Why do you have a mustache and I don't?" he had asked me with played-up class hostility, but didn't say anything about the glasses), is sitting on his native threshold and won't let him in the house and won't even give him a glass of water. . . . And I had let him in, and given him water (because of the war!), and he's sitting there grieving, and can't manage to finish the water: he's sitting at a permanent incline, masterfully leaning on nothing at all and not falling off his stool, while the cup in his hand is tilted in the opposite direction but also not spilling, and the sharp angle of the water in it, in accordance with physical law, defines the horizon as well as the improbable angle of both Chistyakov and the cup. We'll leave him in this pose until morning.

And in the morning the grass and the weather are the same, but there's no Chistyakov and no war. But in the three village houses they confirm with surprising calm that yes, there was something going on— we were at war; we'll wait, they'll tell us. . . . But who said so? Chistyakov said so.

We waited another day—and they didn't tell us anything, the report was not confirmed, and we weren't interested: The weather had finally turned fine and we had hay to turn.

But I didn't have hay to turn. I'm sitting in my attic. I'm creating, see. Only what I'm creating I don't know. Maybe I'll fail to describe the view from the window for the hundredth time. That's just where they're turning the hay. A peasant man and woman. They've started a campfire on one side. You can't tell who they are from here. Probably the Molchanovs—it's their corner. . . .

In the foreground a fly is crawling on the glass, and my thought crawls off after the fly. . . . Look at that, I think, it's not a painting or a photograph—there's no way to describe what was framed for me by someone who built this house long before I was around and who naturally did not think about planning the view from my window, but nonetheless sentenced me to this landscape. You couldn't photograph it to catch the frame of the window—like the frame of a painting—and the fly crawling on the picture, and a pole in the foreground with wires like a music staff lining the landscape in advance so that the fence is on the bottom line, on the middle one they're turning hay, and on the top two are the distant forest and the sky. . . .

I only had to turn away to write this down for the peasant woman to go off, the fly to fly away, and the man to disappear behind a hayrick before my eyes. Only one dog remained, who, admittedly, was not there before. And the man who had disappeared was stamping out the campfire and setting off in the direction in which the woman had disappeared.

And now I look around and there is nothing: neither smoke nor the dog. And the light has changed. A peaceful landscape, so comforting in its eternity! Where are you? What wild time whistles through it. Tachycardia. Swoosh. Not to mention the breeze and the clouds. . . . And there, hidden, on the sly, a mushroom grows, a louse crawls, a mouse rustles. The smoke broke away from the ground like a soul, by itself, without the peasant—a gust, a breeze—and it's gone. The landscape is closed for lunch. Natasha the cat is going home along the deserted landscape, also to lunch, to feed . . . now they'll call me downstairs, too, to eat my soup—and the landscape's gone.

And that's what happened. War or no war, you have to move. It's time. A living person has always just begun to live. As I'll begin now, but starting where? With this or with that? That folder of rejected beginnings and sketches is terrifying—the corners get bent, the paper turns yellow, the text fades, and nothing moves. Not this one, not that one, and I don't feel like this one either. . . . A landscape is not a landscape but a whoosh of time: two butterflies are bumping against it, knocking on the glass against some quickly drawn sheep. Maybe this one? Oh, no! How long has it lain here? Seventeen and a half. Not minutes (look at how much happened in one minute in the landscape!), not hours (see how much hay they turned this morning!), not days (I've been here a week already . . .), but years! Years, minutes— what a difference! I was thirty. . . . The difference is visible. The attic is not the same. And the view is different. There will be no continuation. Contin . . .

". . . . we have before us no more noble task than to mark appropriately on the pages of our publications the three hundredth anniversary of Alexander Sergeyevich Pushkin's birth. Pushkin's whole life, his activity, his titanic labor are near and dear to hundreds of millions of those who dwell on our planet. The name of Pushkin rings out everywhere. . . ."

Pushkin's name rang out this time under the vaults (a natural mistake, considering the grandeur of the setting, because actually there were no vaults)—or rather, within the walls, where it (the name) might readily have rung out even during the life of the culprit. . . . Even, perhaps, his voice . . . but no, imagining it makes your head spin— you begin to tremble. "The well-deserved success of the organizers of this, it would not be an exaggeration to say, forum of the chairman of the Parliament of the Mongolian SSR, our friend Albuu Serzhbudeh, and his indefatigable assistants, our friends Ivan Moskowitz and John Ivanov, merits our congratulations (stormy applause and ordinary applause). Their idea of moving the meeting of the jubilee council from the Sputnik of United Nations (SUN) to ancient Earth, where Pushkin lived, could not but have a positive effect on the atmosphere, comrades, of the meeting. Here beneath the silver sky of Petrograd, under the crystal cloud of Petersburg . . ."

Bringing his voice to a ringing pitch, the speaker himself shuddered as if at a sudden shout, lost the thread, and looked around briefly. We, too, will look around now, as if together with him but not in such a confused state, to note and clarify a few things. The silver sky of Petrograd, in the picturesque expression of the speaker, designates a gigantic dome that reflects certain hard and sharp rays and really is very silvery on the outside, but, of course, is not made of silver but of a special anti-something (by way of explanation: a kind of plastic, although, of course, not really plastic); "the crystal cloud of Petersburg" no less picturesquely refers to a dome of smaller size, concentrically located within the Petrograd dome, except completely translucent, glassy, crystal, plexiglassy, although, of course, these substances have long since become obsolete, and their names sound to our distant contemporaries as magical as the words *ether, zephyr,* and *Venetian amalgam* do to us. This Petersburg dome was the kind of dome that, in our distant times, used to be put over blue-and-gold clocks so that the careful folds of bronze would not get covered with dust and patina; these clocks are still chiming in the past tense, a sonic past perfect, and somehow remind me—and I'm already confused about which direction I'm looking in from the middle-temporal point of my Adler (that is, tapping away now on my typewriter)—"And they recall to me" . . . that on the "crystal cloud of Petersburg" from inside the dome there were also spots of pale blue enamel painted on (pinned on, plastered on) the gold spire of the Admiralty, the Peter and Paul Fortress, St. Isaac's Cathedral, resembling live, becalmed clouds. . . .

And so, while this mantel clock ticks away the time inside the dome, measuring the quarter hours, wound by my charming great-grandmother between lacemaking and glances out the window, until the ticking is joined with the clacking on the wooden pavement and the melodic striking merges with her exclamation in the front hall . . . Lord! this gives me the strange opportunity to relate things that never happened . . . and so, until the clock runs down, we will continue our explanation, for I sense (as if I could smell it) that the speaker will again bring his intonation to a ringing climax and look around in all directions, as if searching us out in the audience.

". . . At last the epoch of the successful preservation of nature and monuments has arrived!" (I was right: The speaker stopped and looked at me—actually, through me—in confusion.) And here we must explain that the epoch really had arrived. Analogous domes had been raised over Paris and Rome, Peking and Lhasa. In the Hamburg Zoo the rabbit produced progeny, and under the dome of the Tower a historic lawn was restored. The Earth looked very pretty from the cooperative sputniks: a deep black with silver bubbles of museum centers, it looked like the starry night sky—and it was a night sky—and that's how people looked at it, from the bottom up. They looked at the Earth as if they were looking at the sky. . . .

Meanwhile, on the dais new orators appeared. . . .

". . . but we, gentlemen-comrades, face an irritating lacuna"—this without excessive emotion or metaphoricalness, as befits a scholar (facts and nothing but the facts!), Academician Princeff of Russian descent was saying. "The first photograph, as is well known, appeared in Russia in the forties of the nineteenth century. Our great scientific achievements enabled us to produce photographs of Gogol, Chaadayev, and a few other of Pushkin's contemporaries. But Pushkin himself, to our great regret, did not manage to be photographed. What do we actually know objectively about the external appearance of the great poet? The iconography is extraordinarily meager and, perhaps, tells us more about the personalities of the portraitists than of the model. . . . We must correct this error of time!

> And every living tongue will name me,
> The proud grandson of the Slavs,

> The Finn, the still-wild Tungus,
> And the Kalmyk, friend of the steppes,"

intoned the Academician, as if it were one word.

Oh, Alexander Sergeyevich! You should have crossed that verse out.

They had filled the hall with every living tongue. We, too, will walk along the aisles, pushing past the correspondents and cameramen, if you can call them that, because the objects they carry are barely recognizable as what in our day we called photographic equipment. . . . In any case, these people are not obliged to look attentive or to applaud in the necessary places—they're busy. With foreshortening, catching an essential delegate—and then a new pale blue flash illumines first of all the photographers themselves, and the print of this moment will always signify that the moment has passed, but will comfort those caught in the picture with the idea that the moment allegedly existed. . . . And we, like a camera lens, will fumble in the aisles and take a close-up of this one and that one—totally arbitrarily (we might need one of them for a hero later in the story—what a clumsy maneuver!).

We find, however, so much in common among the multicolored faces that so far we are unable to single one out. And really, not everyone deserves the honor of sitting here, only the select few. Especially on such an extraordinary occasion—a congress on Earth to which you need a pass, a visa (and Petersburg—as in our distant time—is the room in the public library that requires a special pass): to get through all this you need rather to blend in than to stand out. That is understandable: Earth's gravity is now somewhat dangerous in an ideological sense. So it is hard to single out any one face. . . . We could, of course, pick someone, that is, anyone, without making a choice: an arbitrary preference, the first to come along has already slipped by. . . . But— suddenly!—a certain fineness of feature, a lowered gaze. He looks down the way some people pick at the tablecloth with a fork, although actually his hands are behaving with restraint, that is, they aren't doing anything in particular. This goes unnoticed by the colleagues of our nervous young man (unnoticed because the very suspicion of difference is already impossible; it has long since atrophied out of lack of necessity, which is the very thing that, fortunately, saves our man, which he, we suspect, takes advantage of in his own way), this quality that they don't notice makes us pick him . . . and here it is pleasant to

note that this youth is none other than a distant descendant of Lev
Odoevtsev and Faina—an illegitimate branch, Igor.*

Igor's throat tickles from the dryness of the Petersburg air, and this
descendant of the Neva floods is thirsty. Yes, how everything has
changed—it really is dry. When Igor visited the museum of Pushkin's
apartment the day the congress opened and saw the writing table
covered with a dome, and the inkstand inside covered with still another significantly smaller dome, he immediately (how did he make
it through all the screening tests?) imagined the dome over Petersburg, and over it another, a Leningrad dome. His head started to swim
from the telescoping, and for some absurd reason he palpated it, his
head. . . .

Just in time. He felt as if he had lightly taken his head from his
shoulders the way you would a nozzle, and now (it immediately shrank
to the size of an apple, very neat) he turned it in his hands with surprise, but at the same time inspected it indifferently, as if it were not his
own. . . . This would probably be the closest representation of his
lowered gaze and what he saw there in front of him on the empty reading stand, to which he was attached by a white wire (a mini-amplifier)
to his ear, occasionally switching channels from Flemish to Japanese
or to the marvelous crackling of the Hottentots, but the other ear nonetheless heard everything perfectly. . . .

". . . only one hundred and three days separate us from the great
event—the three hundredth anniversary of the birth of Alexander
SerG(G is a fricative)eyevich Pushkin. This event takes place at a moment of Great Governmental upsurGe," the fricative G was saying.
"The all-nation competition has called forth a new surGe of creative
enthusiasm amonG our people. . . ."

Igor rolled his little head in his palm like a sphere from the ball bearing of my childhood. The turning of the ball bearing also used to make
a fricative sound, maybe a G.

". . . the whole Universe is delighted by our achievements in the
field of the subjugation of time. We can say with full justification that
the first time machine was invented in Russia almost two centuries
ago. (Stormy applause.) This machine has taken us to the distant future, instantly leaving the rest of the history of the Earth in the distant
past. And it was quite natural that shortly thereafter, some century and

---

*Lev Odoevtsev is the hero of Bitov's novel *Pushkin House*, and Faina is Lev's beloved. —Trans.

a half ago, the first step was taken toward the subjugation of space—the first step into the cosmos. Now space is conquered, and it is equally natural that we have taken the first step toward conquering time. On the verge of the third millennium of our era we have launched the first manned time flight in the history of humanity! (S-tormy applause). The time flight Outlay-1, piloted by the first time traveler in the world, General Flazhko, successfully traveling almost two centuries at . . . at . . . temporarily stopped at the designated point with the astonishing accuracy of plus or minus two years! (A-pplause). A vexing lacuna in history has been filled—we have received the missing photograph—an enormous triumph. . . ."

Igor gulped convulsively; it felt as though he had tried to swallow a small brush, and he took the white amplifier out of his ear. Now he started listening with both ears: his chairman was on the dais, his consultant and director, the respected Pushkin scholar of the galaxy, John Ivanov:

". . . one is left breathless, my dear sirs, by the perspectives now opening before worldwide literary scholarship!" Igor's teacher cut a figure somewhat distinct from the rest of the meeting: He played the role of an eccentric old professor, so kind and naive; he had that eternally youthful rapture of the scholarly enthusiast who boils his watch while he holds the egg; he says "my dear sirs," willingly gives talks, displaying superb concreteness of thought and precision of observation; he doesn't let you finish your sentence, extending his very washed hand, and then his little glued-on beard, glasses in empty gold frames, and extreme rosiness are particularly conspicuous—a type that has not changed in two centuries because another reading of the role was never done, and therefore he is totally familiar to us. Now he was rolling his r's:

". . . we will be able in the future, and, gentlemen-comrades, not such a distant one, to photograph Pushkin's entire life with a hidden camera, record his voice . . . imagine how wonderful it will be when every schoolboy will be able to hear Pushkin read his own poetry! And that's not all, comrades! Our imagination is still too poor, is still not strong enough to take in this new miracle and fully conceive of all the possibilities! We will restore the whole of former culture down to the tiniest detail. . . . Homer will sing us *The Iliad*. . . . Shakespeare will finally tell us his autobiography. . . ."

Igor's little head slipped out of his palm—that shiny sphere from the ball bearing rolled along the aisle and stopped at the heels of the friend of the steppes. Igor shuddered and mentally crawled along the aisle, trying to be unnoticeable. But it was impossible to be unnoticeable: he grew terrifyingly in his own eyes, and now it would be hard for him to be unnoticeable and even, perhaps, hard to fit in the aisle. . . . Therefore he just sat there and sadly gazed at the nice shiny sphere from his great-great-grandfather's childhood and stopped worrying whether anyone had noticed him.

. . . The proposal of the presidium of the forum of the session to direct the resolution of the present meeting to the presidium of the Academy of Sciences with a request to petition the General Kommittee Beryozka* (GKB), as well as the prime minister of the Society for the Protection of Monuments and Nature, to decree that the Historical Institute and the Council of Ministers send the next time flight, Raskhod-3, to the Pushkin era in order to have in hand for the jubilee a genuine enlarged photographic portrait of Alexander Sergeyevich Pushkin, and also a recording of his voice, was unanimously approved.

They met and voted. In a closed session.

"Silence, silence, comrades!" The chairman tapped on the water decanter (the decanter had not changed). "It is now time to define clearly the boundaries of the discussion and equally clearly to pose the question—WHOM will we send into time, a PHOTOGRAPHER or a HUMANIST?"

Voices (hostile, lazy, and discordant):

"A humanist!"

"A photographer!"

Both professions aroused similar concerns.

"A Party worker!"

But this time the Party did not decide all.

They needed ONE man, but he had to be able to do not one but a minimum of THREE things: to take the pictures, record the voice, and UNDERSTAND.

The more reliable the candidates, the less they were capable of any of these things.

That is how a proposal even more fantastic than the time flight itself was made: to send Igor Odoevtsev, of that same Odoevtsev family, young and promising, who, although he had done nothing to recommend himself, had so far done nothing deserving of reproach. But he was good at recording things (from experience gained on folkloric expeditions:

*Beryozka is the name of the Soviet hard-currency stores. It means "birch tree." The birch is a traditional symbol of Russia. —Trans.

legends about meat and fish), at photography (not quite professionally, but using modern equipment), and he was a hereditary Pushkinist, furthermore almost undoubtedly of Russian origin. This really made an impression. *Hereditary*, the problem of ethnic background . . . But his great-great-Faina was apparently a quarter part . . . exactly seven times removed. If she was a quarter part, that meant it was unto the seventh generation, someone noted reasonably. But then something else came up. . . . First, as a plus: he even had ancestors in the Pushkin epoch, those same Prince Odoevtsevs, and, this was definite, they were Russian . . . and right away someone said:

"That means he has direct relatives in *that* epoch!"

There was a long silence. There had not yet been any attempt at a flight to such a *famous* epoch.

The one who had figured out the part about the seventh generation was put in charge. . . . He was such an old man that he remembered from his early childhood the funeral of Odoevtsev's great-great-Lyova, who had lived until the two hundredth anniversary of the Decembrist uprising (2025). The old man had nothing to lose by taking on this responsibility, and they risked him.

Igor's youth did its part, and the doctors had no objections.

How his heart beat! Igor was flying, and beneath him the times rustled, mushroom-shaped clouds receded as if into a funnel, and bombs flew back, unscarring the Earth; the Earth became covered with megalopolises and settled by man, it crumbled into cities, towns, and villages, grew grass and trees, was enlivened by birds and beasts. . . . Sunsets alternated with sunrises, and the sun flashed by from west to east with the frequency of bicycle spokes. We cannot comprehend how he felt when, chirping backwards (the sound was "prich-prich") the first frightened bird flew into HIS, Igor's, consciousness! Below the bird's wing the dam that had turned the city of his forefathers into a bog and emptied the reservoirs fell apart and the flooded villages surfaced, bell towers began to ring up from the depths their dongs and days ("Dong-ding" he heard the reversed chime), and became *creation*.

One should not exaggerate: For *us* it is not as hard to picture the actual *way* he flew as it is to imagine *who* was flying. His poor head! What thoughts filled it! More than a century had passed since our time, not to mention Pushkin's (figure it out yourself). It may be easier for us to calculate, but much harder to understand. For him it's even harder to understand us than it is for us to understand Pushkin. Only in this are we equal. But we won't understand either him or Pushkin, while he at least doesn't have to understand us. It's a great blessing when he flies by at this moment right above the head of his author and something squawks in this authorial head, giving rise to the inside-out and backwards thought about the meaning of being "neither dead nor alive nor beloved."

"The genuine flow of time"—I finally realized how to translate it into the present, and Igor had already long since flown by! He's flying over Apothecary Island; having fought two wars in reverse order, he's flying along between two revolutions: they're laying the foundation of the house I was . . . had been born in . . . where the author will be born (1937). But the author's head is aching now, mixing up the sixties with with eighties (yes, yes! of the twentieth . . .), while Odoevtsev is already in the other century (no, no, not the twenty-first, the nine-teenth!) mixing up the eighties with the sixties, flying over the village of Goluzino, and didn't send me his chrononaut's greeting. Why did you fly by so fast, my friend, without noticing me below you? He is I. . . . He is you sitting there, my dear author. How did you manage to get stranded in the dense spiderweb of TODAY (1985)?

But I can tell you precisely about something the numbed gaze of the hero didn't have time to take in but that he definitely saw: YOU AND ME. And you won't be able not to believe me. Here is the proof that everything I've told you and am telling you is TRUE. This is what I'm looking at: a three-day-old kitten in a box twitching in its sleep as if it were running, though it can't walk yet; the kitten dreams about run-ning and manages his paws better than when awake. Is he dreaming of a race or a hunt, is he running away or pursuing? That I don't know, but I know now that he doesn't see his experience, which he hasn't got, but his future in the form of the ancient past that existed before he did. . . . The kitten runs in his sleep . . . am I myself, sitting at my point in time and space, any more able to speed up or reverse what I see than the kitten? How can I reproach my own hero with inatten-tiveness when he crosses a century in the course of my page? Well, I'll stop watching the kitten, I'll fly along over this line from left to right, I won't try to understand anything that I'm writing at this second, I'll look to the left, out my attic window, which I was looking out of a minute ago trying to catch the moment when my hero would flash by above me: There stood a cow, chewing in the rain, moving her jaw horizontally; raindrops were dripping down her horns and falling on the grass like gems. . . . Now the cow's gone and the rain's stopped.

That's what I see. The rest I *know*: That below me my son was born eight years after I thought up and was about to begin this very story and now my son himself is eight . . . and all I have to do is write down this slander about him for him to make his way up to me by the ladder and here he is. "Who's this?" I say. "The distracter," he says, and laughs. What happiness! Here I am sitting in my own time and space and am unlikely to leave it MYSELF. God forbid . . .

"Do you have a color copier?" he asks right at the second that I'm typing this. "No," I say, and I can't synchronize events any more than this.

Igor doesn't have children yet, so he's the one who's flying. He'll return a hero, will get permission, perhaps, for the right to continue the race. Maybe the council will meet him halfway and whether there will be another Odoevtsev or not will no longer depend on me.

Thinking about his bride, Igor got distracted and missed the Crimean campaign (1854), and he had wanted to see the brave young Lev (Tolstoy) in the haze of battle. But in the haze of daydreaming about his Natasha he didn't notice him. . . . "Simple human happiness," he mumbled, grinning stupidly, and, letting another epoch go by below, entered the period of Nicholas I, the solid layers of Pushkin's time. Now he has to be particularly attentive in order not to miss it. . . . He presses the button with all his strength (it reminds me a lot of Mama's doorbell; I can even see the door in place of his fancy dashboard)—he hits the back of his head on the previous decade (the forties of the nineteenth) from the stress of braking and doesn't see Gogol either (the way he sits, frozen and unblinking before the camera in Rome—1842), and while he is slowing down . . .

It's completely dark out my window, and furthermore the typewriter ribbon is not only not in color but very pale. I can't see in the present, no less into the past from the future (a tense even English hasn't thought up), I have to go not into the visible but into the knowable—downstairs where my son is, where the light switch for the attic is. I went downstairs. Let the hero spend some time without me, and he will land in time. . . .

So if he slowed down to our time speed, if a minute became a minute and an hour an hour, and the sun rose again from the east, that means he is already living in *that* time, parallel to me, separated by the same one and a half centuries, but from the other side: I have a tomorrow and he has a tomorrow, I have a today and he has a today . . . but that means that it is already the second day since he landed in the desired epoch, because after I went downstairs I didn't go back up, and overslept.

It mustn't be thought, however, that his landing took place so smoothly and effortlessly, with the ease of an author's device. The author is not about to hide behind the monogram of a prosaic figure and thereby conceal the action.

There were complications. But they are as hard for me to explain to the reader as to myself. We are as naive in imagining the technological future in our times as Prince Odoevsky was in Pushkin's, imagining the distant future all hung about with air balloons. And time travel at the time of our hero had only taken its first steps, and they themselves didn't know what they would encounter. In short, our hero was the first to come up against a certain effect that, as a result of his humanistic background, he was unable to figure out, and we are even less able to explain the physical sense of the phenomenon—we can only compare it with our own experience, say, with interference in radio or television transmission. Historical time at such speed of intersection was arranged as if in stripes, sometimes stopping in a fixed, clear picture, sometimes beginning to tear and flash and swim, flare up and die out. The regularity of the sequence was extremely subjective: the interference arose right in the most interesting places for the observer. Considering the style of thought and perception of our Igor, not only humanistic but also, even unconsciously, poetic, one should note that the events that were grandiose or significant in the generally accepted sense interested him less than that which he called "alive." The grandiose would be depicted as immobile and dead, like a drawing on a slide, while that which was alive would immediately begin to tear and flash, evading the eye. It was as if you heard only the brass or the percussion in the orchestra but never the violin, the solo—the accompaniment drowned out the melody. However, musical comparisons are inappropriate, since the whole record was turning in the reverse direction, unpleasant to the ear, parodic to the eye.

He saw flags and crowds, shots and battles, leaders and tyrants; time broke against these cliffs, and chips flew in all directions like ocean spray, but to make out in this mighty array the sole thing that subsequently remained from it all, that which interested Igor not only professionally but as the living secret of his soul, to discern even a flash of the "modernist" epoch—Vrubel' at his easel, Blok at his desk—was impossible. All that remained of that grandiose history, that which was later cherished and preserved by his colleagues in time, including himself, that which constituted the treasures of national and world culture, was completely invisible in that boiling pot below Igor, in that historical brew. And after all, Igor Odoevtsev, in contrast to everyone stewing below him in that pot, swimming to the surface or going under for good, in contrast to them he ALREADY KNEW what was REALLY happening, while they didn't, but they, not knowing, were the ones who were able to see (if not to recognize) the "alive" that he so much wanted to see from the point of view of an eyewitness: It was given to them, but not to him. They were able to live, he was able to know. The barrier was insuperable: He saw only that which HIS time knew about. He wanted to have a look at what his time didn't know—but just at that moment he'd get the ripples, the interference, we don't know what to call it, maybe the "Odoevtsev effect."

Not only was it all invisible, but it all mocked him there below. . . .

Why, in the one hundred and fourteenth year of the flight, had he been drawn down so close to time that he could make out in detail a broken-down northern Russian village, wrapped at that instant in some amazing heavy rain, with drops like hail falling in dots the way children draw it, to make out an animal, large, horned, stubbornly standing in the rain chewing in syllables ("A cow! It's a cow!" he realized): That means someone, some last remaining person, was still living there; from the attic of a crooked little house, mixing with the harmonious noise of the rain, came the arrhythmic pre-heart-attack hammering of some decrepit ancient mechanism. . . . "It's me, it's me"—the tapping suddenly coincided with his heartbeat; confused and hurt, he glanced in the attic window: It was dark, no one was there, just a butterfly batting against the glass . . . why did this place matter? Why had they stopped just there out of three centuries? It was long gone, this abandoned village: Solid peasant houses grew up, a lot of people rushed in, they were all in red blouses going to the church that had risen up out of dust to the ringing of the church bells.

The *Caesarevich* went to the bottom, only the captain remained on his bridge. . . . Oh yes, the Russo-Japanese war . . . the *Caesarevich* surfaced before his eyes, the crew began dashing about like ants, the captain put a megaphone to his mouth. . . . Igor rushed across the whole empire to the other shore, the Finnish one, to find . . . the gray tonalities, the evening flowers. . . . His heart was leaping out of his chest when he finally arrived ON TIME. A skiff with a wonderful oarsman . . . white shirt, collar open, curls, a haughty gaze . . . at the stern a woman in a wide-brimmed hat with a parasol . . . sitting sideways, like a horsewoman, impossible to see her face under the brim . . . the boat, rustling, struck into the sand from its momentum, the youth leaped out and dragged it to shore . . . how slender! He offered his arm, and the lady raised her face . . . tearstained! There they parted, under the pines, on the sandy path. . . . Igor arrested the moment to the best of his ability: Alexander Alexandrovich!* To look at his face . . . but this was someone entirely different, although also in a white shirt, but with a racket under his arm: he was standing closer to the bushes and looking around left and right. . . .

Igor soared over time. It reared up and seemed stopped because of the speed, like the sun in a permanent sunset. Strange were its rays! He saw them, but they shone for others. A kind of silvery fine weave shredded all around in filaments. Time? thought Igor, in order to catch a glimpse of the unfinished Eiffel Tower below. For some reason he suddenly wanted to spit on it, but he wasn't *above* it, that was the paradox. His place in space was even more puzzling than his place in time. He wasn't in it at all.

He was no longer eager to see the pince-nez in Yalta. . . . The lady wouldn't have a Chekhovian little dog (1899). He passed through the decades sequentially and smoothly. And even so he almost missed his moment when he started daydreaming (he had secretly brought a package of penicillin for stomach inflammations)†—he had to stop exactly. No earlier and no later. That is, no later and no earlier.

At this point the "mockery effect" appeared with particular force. The author had assigned Igor an awfully precise point: May 23, 1836, Alexander Sergeyevich is returning to Petersburg from Moscow. . . .

And suddenly here's Gogol, sitting like a cuckoo in a fir tree and carrying on unprintably. From under the tree emerges a countess, giggling horribly, with a pot in her hands. "Merci," she says, "Merci buckets." So he's in Italy! Igor realized, tugged the pendulum toward him; with a crack the copper gear with its added weight slid down— and suddenly he saw what he wanted: Pushkin! He was lying on a window ledge in the Hotel Galiani in Tver eating peaches. (It isn't the season! thought Igor.) Igor stared at him wide-eyed and went mute, and he had spent so long preparing his opening phrase! Alexander Ser-

---

*Perhaps Blok (1880–1921), the last great Russian poet. —Andrei Bitov (hereafter A.B.).

†Pushkin died of an infection of the stomach as a result of the wound received in his duel with Dantès over the honor of Pushkin's wife, Natalya. —Trans.

geyevich looked at him and spat out a pit. And hit the target. And laughed with satisfaction. Here Zhukovsky, as luck would have it, brings in his own watch (a more expensive one than he can afford): "Pushkin! Pushkin!" He puts Zhukovsky's watch, as everyone knows, on the stool and says, "It's busted!" That's about US, Igor thinks, pulling the pendulum all the way down and this time, apparently, more accurately—he flew right to the house on the Moika Canal and glanced in the window: A lamp was burning, his children, little, littler, littlest, are sitting in a row drinking tea, every last one of them cross-eyed like their mother, and falling off their chairs by turns—first one, then another. . . .

Here the "Distracter" descends on me and I start telling him some nonsense about the insects clustered about my light, that they're punctuation marks, there's the semicolon, and the moth that's batting against the light bulb and the white sheet of paper is my Muse. "Who's Muse?" the Distracter puts me in my place reasonably. "Some butterflies," he says, "also gather nectar. If there are beekeepers, why aren't there butterfly keepers?" (He was stung by a bee today.) "Except then butterflies would bite, too." I finally got mad at the Distracter. . . .

When Igor came to on a couch, propped up on all sides with little cushions, a gentleman with Pushkinian sideburns was holding his head and waving ammonia spirits under his nose. The lady of the house, in a cap, was holding up a candle and adjusting a moistened towel on his head.

"He's opened one eye . . ." said the lady in terror.

"Very good. Well, thank God. I see that he is a fine gentleman, but altogether down and out. What hotel are you staying at, if you will permit me to ask, my dear sir?"

Igor sat up and rubbed his forehead under the compress.

"I realized at once that you were a foreigner," the sideburns said with pride. There was something parodically Pushkinian about his face: everything was exactly the same except the button nose. "Allow me to introduce myself. I am Nikander Savelevich Apushkin. . . . With whom do I have the honor . . . ?"

"What? Who?" Igor shook himself. "Opushkin?"

"Pray, do you speak Russian? Not O-pushkin, but A-pushkin," the man said, taking offense. "Like our famous writer, sir."

Igor jumped up. The delirium hadn't stopped! He was still in the zone of anecdotal overload associated with the landing . . . he was still flying!

"Thank you, sir, please don't trouble, sir," he babbled, freeing himself from his time loop, inappropriately inserting this ridiculous "sir" everywhere to be on the safe side. "But could you kindly tell me just what year it is now, sir?"

"What, sir?" The candle fell, the hostess fell, the host held the ammonia spirits to her nose, and Igor rushed to the door.

"Here is your trunk, sir, and your cane, sir," Apushkin said coldly, handing Igor his apparatus.

Igor grabbed it rudely and pelted down the stairs. . . .

And only when he had rushed out of the courtyard to the embankment—the Fontanka? the Moika?—did he realize that he had already LANDED. In St. Petersburg. But when?

The proof that he had arrived, in addition to the view before him, was this cane. It was *folded up!* It was that kind of old-fashioned shooting stick for elderly or tubercular people with a folding cane seat. That was his time machine. He had flown in astride the stick. And now it was folded, and he stood leaning on it to keep from falling. In the trunk, sir, were his equipment, hard currency, a change of underwear, and a forged passport in his own name.

"I write, I read, without my candle . . ."* he mumbled, thoroughly shaken.

And he strode into the white night.

But his next address also turned out to be wrong. And the folded condition of his little chair did not seem so significant. Conversing with Collegiate Assessor Notpushkin (who, as in Fedotov's future painting A *Major's Morning*, was in his dressing gown and night cap with a pipe . . .), Igor stopped believing in himself even more than in Gogol in the fir tree.

"Yes, yes," the major said proudly. "Not Pushkin. I, to my credit, have no relation whatsoever to writers. And not only not Pushkin, but Notpushkin, quite the opposite surname. And kindly get out of here, sir."

But one thing the major did reveal to Igor before he caught on, and that was that they had come nose to nose exactly on May 23, 1836.

Igor could not be offended at his behavior, even though he had been shown the stairs.

He went out into the white night. And it was THE SAME white

---

*Thus Pushkin extolls the white nights of Petersburg in *The Bronze Horseman*. —Trans.

night. At the end of Nevsky Prospect "there gleamed the Admiralty spire." And again, the SAME ONE.

Who knew at this moment that there would be Lermontov, Tolstoy, Dostoevsky? Little Lyova was eight. Fyodor was fifteen. Mikhail Yurievich was twenty-two. Igor was older than they were. And Pushkin was still alive! And no one knew. He, he alone knew!

He felt he was on the summit of time.

And he joyfully strode down from it, feeling himself Onegin, Bashmachkin, and Makar Devushkin simultaneously.*

On the other hand, Alexander Sergeyevich himself had already kicked him downstairs for the third time.

"Nikifor! Why are you making so much noise? You'll wake up Natalya Nikolayevna!" He stared at Igor with merry eyes after his affected anger. The mother was asleep and the newborn daughter was asleep. He had just left them and was creeping into his study, peaceful! With what precision Igor had picked just the wrong moment to land. . . .

"Do me a favor, Alexander Sergeyevich, I beg you," wrote Igor in his Khlestakovian† attic hotel room exactly two months later, "at least honor me with a reply. I do not even know how to ask you. Why are you not a general, a count, a prince? Indeed, I cannot say—Your Excellency! Your Most Excellent Excellency! Your Holiness! Most Illustrious Prince! and higher . . . so my request sounds weak, worthless and utterly weak. . . ."

He was now pretending to be a graphomaniac‡ (appending nothing less than Blok's poems . . .), trying (for the umpteenth time!) to get to Alexander Sergeyevich. Like an unlucky lover, he kept track of Pushkin's hours and routes, he would steal after him—just to catch a glimpse of him . . . mentally help him into his carriage, hand him his cane, and sit down next to him . . . and thus he would remain, gazing after the carriage, spattered with mud from the wheels. Pushkin would turn around and laugh. But then, too, how many times had Igor overtaken him on the Nevsky, pushing his way through to him among the book stalls. Trying to be inconspicuous, he acquired a multitude of habits

---

*The heroes of Pushkin's *Eugene Onegin* (1823–31), Gogol's "Overcoat" (1842), and Dostoevsky's *Poor Folk* (1845), respectively. —Trans.

†The impostor government inspector of Gogol's play *The Inspector General* (1836). —Trans.

‡A Russian concept; the word denotes a person who expresses his delusions of grandeur by obsessive writing. —Trans.

he was unaware of, which finally convinced the poet that he was a spy.
And, in fact, he became an expert on Pushkin's back and bald spot.
The poet's frock coat was worn out, and the button on his coat strap
was dangling, was just about to fall off. Driven to despair, Igor managed to press against him at a book stall and tear off the button—the
poet didn't even notice. It was his one and only trophy. Igor sewed the
button on the inside of his breast pocket, and his heart beat against
Pushkin's button at their every meeting. And Pushkin kept going around
with only one button. "There's no one to sew it on . . ." Igor thought
and almost cried. (He had seen Natalya Nikolayevna four times by
now: twice she had not seemed such a beauty at all to him, once she
had dazzled him, and the fourth time—the least attractive time—he
fell madly in love with her, but still, less than with *him*. . . .)

He sent the letter but got no answer (and admittedly, he hadn't expected one).

He learned a lot during those two months, experienced a great deal!

First of all, whatever he thought about his own time (secretly from
others and secretly from himself), however much he admired particular periods of the past, he automatically considered his own time to
have *outstripped* previous ones. He had descended from *above*, with a
head start of three centuries. He was three hundred years older; he
knew, living among these blind kittens, what would happen to them.
The superior rank of observer prompted conscious feelings in him—of
strength and condescension.

Some observer! He wasn't doing the looking at all, he was being
looked at. At first he kept catching himself making mistakes, his own
and his teachers'. They were legion. He would resort to comforting
himself by ridiculing the experts from the "Preparatory Seminars on
Social Adjustment." How approximate everything they taught turned
out to be! Especially the per diem he had been given in the hard currency of the thirties of the nineteenth century (literally hard; they were
weighty gold ten-ruble coins)—by what conception of current prices
had they been allocated to him with such strict accountability and
documentation of receipts? What did the experts know about the cor-
relation with dinner, hotel, and carriage? What a porridge! Porridge
was just what he ate, mostly in taverns that in no way corresponded to
his clothing and claims to acquaintance with Alexander Sergeyevich.
For porridge he had enough for ten years, but to try just once to be
treated as a human being, he didn't have enough for even a week. He

understood Pushkin's difficulties! But no one would trust him with a loan, that was the problem.

And so he took the cheapest room, ate porridge, ate cabbage soup like Khlestakov, and went on foot, not because he didn't have money, but because he might really need it, and then where would he get it? He seethed at the lecturer on finances who had discussed the inexpensiveness of THAT life. And the coins—there weren't any that new here . . . everyone looked at them strangely, just as they looked at him, but they passed the tooth test: gold! And that professorial conviction about the precise details of dress, pronunciation, manners! The more exactly they had reconstructed a detail from the past, the more suspicious it was. His seams were different! People stared at Igor so often that at first he was constantly checking himself: Was he buttoned up? Had he got dirt on his clothes? . . . But that puzzled glance expressed nothing more than puzzlement: everything is as it should be, but what is wrong? Had he gone out in his twenty-first-century body suit or naked, he would have attracted less attention. His voice sounded wrong, his words . . . the phonetics professor had taught him pronunciation from the church services, and he was trying to pass himself off as a gentleman! In short, there were countless gaps, but what betrayed him, as he later realized with surprise, were not the gaps but the coincidences, the accuracy. The accuracy stuck out. Only *everything* can be exactly right, not just *some* things. Oh, if only everything were equally approximate! He would have had no trouble. He would have appeared to be an eccentric, a foreigner, a madman . . . a provincial. A provincial! That was a discovery, and it rescued him. He was a provincial in epoch rather than in space, and finally, once he broke himself in, he learned to wear this very mask. They put it on him and stopped looking at him.

No, he did not observe, he was shown, the nineteenth century.

It is a strange feeling (even a law!)—he expected a visual, auditory shock from meeting the past, and there was nothing of the kind. He saw only quotations from what he knew; the rest (everything!) merged in a continuous and dangerous delirium of a completely different and inaccessible reality, as if he were visiting not the past but another planet. Another civilization . . . "Of course, that's just what it is . . ." he realized. Reality, complete, is like a fence with palings that have fallen out here and there. You imagine it—and there's a picture, you've seen it in your school textbook, you knew it already. But can you say you've seen it with your own eyes? What relation does it have to the Kremlin or the Leaning Tower of Pisa? The past he'd come to was as continuous and unknown as the present he'd come from is for the past. It turned out to be even more unknown for him. The past was the PRESENT with all its phenomena. The newcomer did not pre-determine it.

And he began to *live* in that time, worse than others, all alone, awk-wardly and uncomfortably, but—to live. And from that moment he came into the possession of priceless and unique experience that was equally pointless here and there. There they wanted slides and tapes from him but not this experience—here the tapes were useless. Here they needed NOTHING from him. He realized that he was absent in this century just as he had been absent from it before his arrival. This surprising feeling of absolute loneliness and abandonment granted him (although not now—will yet grant him someday . . .) a surprising happiness, too, equal to his despair: a feeling of TOTAL freedom un-known to anyone on earth at any time. He, Igor, dissolved in it.

Pushkin and Petersburg filled him, and that was enough. He lay for whole days on his sad bed and in his thoughts lived Pushkin's days pre-cisely as Pushkin did (he remembered that in some late memoirs he had read Pushkin's confession that when in love he never parts with the object of his love for a moment: getting into the carriage, he mentally seats his lady and sits down next to her; strolling, he picks her a flower, picks up her dropped handkerchief . . .); he rode with him to the pal-ace, forgot his three-cornered hat, came back for it . . . returning after midnight, having lost or won, he would kiss Natalya Nikolayevna on the forehead, she was falling off her feet . . . he would go into his study, call Nikifor, who already knew and would bring him a full de-canter of lemonade. . . . Pushkin would begin almost unwillingly to dig among his manuscripts: he wouldn't take up this one, he wouldn't take up that one. . . . Igor, after all, KNEW all this, he had learned all this and loved it, and now—what meaning all this took on, so sepa-rate, in parallel (half an hour on foot) with Pushkin's live existence! On the other side of the wall of his hotel room he heard Pushkin's sighs and steps.

Or he would wander for whole days around Petersburg, searching out NON-Pushkin places, where he HADN'T walked, HADN'T spent time, where they would build something else AFTER his death, and then, getting bored, he would return to PUSHKIN's Petersburg as if he had just flown in. His timelessness, by the way, like that of Petersburg itself (there's a newcomer of a city!), seemed to emerge in Igor's features; again they started staring at him, but differently: Had somebody been here just now? No. He became a shadow of Petersburg, merged with it. Here he succeeded, just where he hadn't expected or hoped to. After all, success also wants to get its chance. . . .

He really made an impression on one imagination. Pavel Petrovich Vyazemsky . . . yes, yes, *the* Vyazemsky . . . the son of the friend . . .* "Pavel, my soul . . ." Igor knew so much about him, while Pavel knew nothing about Igor. The one Pushkin taught to play cards, the one he ran around with . . .

Igor's scalp crawled with excitement when that nice young man, apologizing profusely, introduced HIMSELF. My page crawls from the profusion of moths that have flown into my light. When I finish a page and I turn it over, text downward, with satisfaction so that, God forbid, I won't be horrified by what I have written and will be able to continue, I put it on top of the previous one already occupied by a half-dozen moths—they are asleep, but when covered with the new page they begin to crawl around, and my manuscript starts to move, to my horror and delight. Three emerald mosquitoes of some kind crawl about, bugging out their microscopic but nonetheless extraordinarily precise little eyes at my rough draft. A tiny beetle with poisonous spots like a death cup mushroom falls on my page with a terrifying crack . . . who can say what time they're from? You will find nothing in a past epoch that the epoch did not leave you *itself*. And even of that you will not find everything. Humanity also lives its *private* life, hidden from the eyes of outsiders—that is what history is. It is inaccessible. You take a look at an epoch—and you're too late, sir. But why bother to write diaries and letters so carefully and secretly and leave dusty little packets of them in attics and pantries if you're not counting on Igor? Pavel Vyazemsky will also write his diaries, and there won't be a word about Igor in them.

He really pursued Igor in a manner considered indecent in society; he had a youthful crush on the older man, on his embodiment, on his Petersburg shadow. He took him everywhere, introduced him to everyone. To Mukhanov, the one Pushkin would read his "Monument" to

---

*Prince Peter Andreyevich Vyazemsky (1792–1878), a poet and critic, was Pushkin's friend and collaborator on the *Literary Gazette* and *The Contemporary*. —Trans.

first. . . . And Mukhanov didn't get suspicious, liked him. . . . And Igor became a regular *connoisseur*. Precisely by hiding his knowledge of the future, he somehow was particularly good at feeling out the present. He became what used to be called a *poet*, as was said about a man who did not necessarily write poetry. After all, poets also see the future. But looking forward, not backward. Igor was a poet who didn't write. And in that capacity he was important, he inspired great respect. . . . Pavlusha willingly told his secrets to Igor: How good Igor was at listening, his ear lying in wait as if in ambush for something about Pushkin, but never asking questions anymore. . . . Pavlusha confided his secrets of the heart, told him about his family, the university, his research . . . but not a word about Pushkin!

And then it happened! He was sitting in Mukhanov's apartment waiting for Pavlusha; the footman announced Pushkin.

"Again!" said Mukhanov with slight irritation.

Alexander Sergeyevich had not expected an outsider. His glance passed over Igor obliquely. Igor was introduced and, because of the quantity of what he wanted to put into his first phrase, he babbled something almost monosyllabic.

Alexander Sergeyevich fixed his gaze on him a little more steadily, pinned him like a butterfly. However, he appeared not to recognize Igor (who had long since stopped following his footsteps and had changed, as we were saying). He promptly sat down next to a bowl of grapes and began picking at them quickly, grape after grape, plucking them off with his enormous fingernails that looked more like claws. Igor was watching him eat for the second time, and for the second time he was eating fruit. "No, he doesn't look like a monkey . . ." Igor thought stupidly, and for some reason his heart ached from a sense of irreparableness.

Between grapes the poet asked what they'd been talking about. When he found out that they'd been discussing the recent discovery that the moon was inhabited, he became very merry.

"And do you believe it?" he asked Igor, emphasizing "you" and looking into his eyes with strange fixity.

"Do I? No," Igor answered with constraint.

"Of course!" Alexander Sergeyevich said incomprehensibly, and began proving in his own way why the moon could not be inhabited. It was particularly delightful for a person from the twenty-first century to hear.

"A daring canard," * the poet concluded. "A bold invention. Maybe we should play a game of cards? There are three of us."

Igor muttered something about being a poor player, but he could not resist the persuasion of his idol. Mukhanov went out to arrange things: candles, cards, coffee. . . .

There was an awkward silence.

"So it's uninhabited?" asked Alexander Sergeyevich.

"In about two hundred years it will probably be settled . . ." Igor answered as evasively as he could.

"You mean there's not enough room left on Earth?"

"There won't be," said Igor, and got scared.

"Then you already have a balm for any wound?" he asked suddenly as a shot.

"Balm? What balm?" Igor babbled, realizing at once that in his first letter he had written about the penicillin that could cure stomach inflammations.

"But you were the one who wrote me that you are from the future?"

Here's my moment. A genius . . . Igor thought with fatigue.

"No," said Igor, "I didn't write that."

"Oh, yes, excuse me . . ." Alexander Sergeyevich suddenly got bored and again began working on the grapes. The grapes resembled his nails, his nails the grapes. . . .

"But you wrote me about your poems? Isn't that right?"

There was no going back.

"Yes, I wrote that," Igor agreed. He had some hopes for Blok. HE could not fail to appreciate . . .

"Very interesting grammatical mistakes," the poet said approvingly.

"And the poems?"

"Were there poems?" Alexander Sergeyevich said with genuine surprise. "A pity. Who includes poems in a letter?"

Everything again struck Igor as being extremely reduced and distanced. In the infinite distance of centuries the genius swallowed his grapes. . . . And Igor again started rolling the shiny sphere in his palm, as if it were his own head. . . .

"And what do they think about horns in your century?"

Alexander Sergeyevich again seemed not to be eating grapes at all, but kept looking fixedly at Igor, and it was as if he were wearing a white

*Pushkin's own words. —Trans.

robe, so silvery did everything grow before Igor's gaze, in the haze, except for his eyes. . . .

My God! He knows EVERYTHING! He ALREADY knows. About me, about himself . . . Horns!

It turns out he said the last word out loud:

"Horns . . ." And knowing in advance the whole of this story,* and trying somehow to evade the issue, get around it, he started talking, and each time heard what he had said exactly one sentence after saying it; as with a loudspeaker, he was distanced from himself by the length of a stadium: "How to put it . . . In any case, biology is unable to explain them merely in terms of natural expediency, merely as a means of defense and attack. They are superfluous and clumsy. They are too varied and ornate, lacking in any particular purpose, to be anything but decoration. . . ."

Alexander Sergeyevich attentively inspected his endless fingernail. Igor got still more confused.

"Just like your famous fingernail, and rings . . ." he babbled, closing his eyes and jumping in, "this, too, can be in part related. . . . The nail and the horn have a common construction. They are male secondary sexual characteristics. . . . The tail of the peacock and the pheasant . . ."

He stopped.

"Amusing. Continue."

Igor opened his eyes and saw Alexander Sergeyevich unexpectedly close—face-to-face. A Negro was looking at him.†

"However, I am a humanist. I'm not very well informed." Shrinking into his chair, Igor moved away. "I am more comfortable with a not completely scientific approach. . . ." And he went on, swallowing, engulfed by the quicksand of his own speech. "That this superfluity—of horns—in its variety is yet another refutation of the theory of natural selection supports the idea of the createdness of the world, of the Creator. It's because he, like an artist admiring his creation, rejected boring purposefulness and decorated it . . . with magnificent horns. . . ."

He was expecting a slap in the face, but there was none.

---

*Of Pushkin's betrayal by his wife that led to his fatal duel. —Trans.

†Pushkin's maternal great-grandfather, Hannibal, was an Ethiopian who was brought to Russia for Peter the Great. Pushkin had somewhat Negroid features. —Trans.

Mukhanov was standing over him with a candle and a pack of cards. . . .

"Did you say something?"

Alexander Sergeyevich wasn't there.

"He left," said Mukhanov. "A good fellow. But often really." *

And Pavlusha stopped appearing, as if he'd been cut off. Igor several times failed to find him in, although up to then Pavlusha had always been the one to find Igor. When they would meet on the street, Mukhanov barely exchanged greetings with him and clearly avoided conversation. Igor understood. He could not be angry at Alexander Sergeyevich for what he had told Pavlusha, protecting the younger man. . . . But what was Mukhanov? Good Lord, dust from his boot . . . to breathe the same air . . . to see him from a distance . . . A spy, a madman, a graphomaniac . . . what's so terrible?

Igor lived with him until the end. There was not that much time left. He still tried to intervene; he blocked Natalya Nikolayevna's way, trying to prevent the fateful meeting at Idaliya Poletika's. . . .† And only succeeded in scaring the poor woman—she didn't understand his delirious speech: A trim, athletic colonel surfaced as if out of the ground and arrogantly gave the shivering and worn Igor one in the jaw. And when Igor came to, he recognized in the colonel, who was walking up and down guarding the entrance, her future husband. . . . How he hated Lanskoy! To keep watch during her rendezvous with Dantès, his subordinate, in order to ask for Natalya Nikolayevna's hand twelve years later . . .

Wasn't Mukhanov himself an agent from a still more distant epoch? Igor was already delirious. And Lanskoy—wasn't he an agent? This one from the twenty-second century.

Igor came to two weeks later, after lying unconscious in his attic

---

*From Mukhanov's writings. —Trans.

†The story of the duel with Dantès, which led to Pushkin's death, is so widely known in Russia that it requires no commentary. But the fateful meeting that Dantès asked of Pushkin's wife for their "final" explanation to this day inspires too many rumors unjustly disturbing the shades of the poet and his wife, who, in our view, was not guilty of anything. The meeting at the house of Idaliya Poletika, a lady of the court, who despised Pushkin for some reason, was too secret not to become instantly known. Colonel Lanskoy, whom Natalya Nikolayevna married twelve years after Pushkin's death, was Dantès's superior, benefactor, and patron. According to several accounts—

with a high fever. He survived. Everything was over. He had not thrown himself under the runners of the sleigh rushing to the duel, he had not knocked the pistol out of Dantès's hand, he had not been in the crowd of people at the apartment or the Stable Church, not he. . . . The troika with A. I. Turgenev and the coffin raced past him . . . only the snow whirled. Igor was about to give chase . . . but—apparently, still delirious—for some reason hung around the lycée and almost fell under the first steam engine, heading toward him straight from Pushkin's death.*

He couldn't manage without him. Without Pushkin he himself was gone. And being endlessly in debt to the landlord and the doctors, he unfolded his little seat, that is, he mounted his stick. . . .

He sensibly reasoned that Pushkin *then* still didn't know him.

And *there* he was still alive!

And he set off backwards, to *there* and *then*.

Armed with the experience of the year thirty-six, he now stole up with certainty, aiming his lens and microphone at what he estimated to be the high point . . . and then—what will be, will be! He broke his way through the autumn grove like a moose. It was baring itself with a sad sound. . . . A mist was settling on the fields . . . everything was right. He walked straight on, rustling along the lines as among the leaves. He saw nothing. His tall figure would surface out of the mist between hayricks and disappear back into it. He identified with these wisps, leaves, hummocks. . . . Before him a window glimmered weakly. There, inside, *The Bronze Horseman* was being written!

Having grown unused to himself, to his body, which he hadn't felt for a long time, he was not afraid of being noticed. Out of impatience he pressed himself to the window: There it was!

Yes, the candle was burning . . . yes, a man lay on a tiny little cot and was writing something so fast that it was as if he were just pretending to write line after wavy line like a child. . . . How strangely he was dressed! In a woman's bed jacket, a nightcap, wrapped in a scarf . . . but this was not Pushkin! The child was bearded and from time to time

---

granted, disputed—he "preserved" the secrecy of this meeting that led, ultimately, to the duel. If this is a fact, it is surprising. —A.B.

*The first steam engine in Russia set out three days after Pushkin's death from Tsarskoe Selo, where Pushkin had gone to school. —Trans.

he would stroke and twirl his little beard,* and then again trace his wavy line across the paper.

Losing his reason, Igor knocked on the window before he realized what he was doing.

In his underwear, throwing on his sheepskin, the bearded man came out on the porch, protecting the candle with his palm. There was a portrait for you! It was a bearded Pushkin! Shadows from the candle wavered strangely over his face from below.

"Who's there?"

"It's me," Igor said like a child.

The candle described a semicircle, Pushkin disappeared in the night, Igor squinted from the light.

They were both silent.

"Poor thing . . ." said the bearded man out of the darkness with inexpressible pain and compassion. "Poor thing . . . May God grant that I . . ." And suddenly something strong and light touched Igor's head and hand simultaneously. A palm slid over his face. How hot and dry it was! And wet . . . Pushkin wiped away tears that Igor had not felt, quickly turned away, so that the candle went out, and slammed the door. Igor unclenched his fist—in it lay a gold coin.

In the morning Igor woke up in a haystack. He went out to the lake, washed. He didn't like touching his stubble, and he took his *nécessaire* out of his little trunk. He attentively inspected his face that Pushkin had stroked in the night. . . . Only three years, and how he had aged! Those gray locks . . . And that insane pallor, and the eyes . . . "This is the precise dating of 'May God grant that I not go mad. . . .'" Igor grinned.†

And so he was drawn into the chase. He had the incomparable opportunity of correcting previous mistakes. He pursued Pushkin into the

---

*There exists no representation of Pushkin with a beard. However, there is an account that, returning home from Boldino in 1833, Pushkin rode through Moscow incognito so that his wife could be the first to see him in a beard. It is touching . . . and provides the possibility of the only precise answer to the question of how such a brilliant work as *The Bronze Horseman* was written . . . tugging and nibbling his beard. This happens to everyone who decides to grow a beard, even to a genius, even to Pushkin. —A.B.
†The exact dating of the famous poem "May God grant that I not go mad . . ." is still disputed by critics. Our hero's proposal does not contradict the latest hypotheses. —A.B.

depths of his life, where the poet had not met him. A strange business! The greater his experience, the younger Pushkin became and the older he was himself (a year later, that is, a year before *The Bronze Horseman*, they were already the same age!), the more quickly and easily (as if he, too, were getting more experienced) Alexander Sergeyevich got away from him.

The last meeting Igor managed was in 1829 at the future Pushkin Pass. He wanted to catch the moment when Pushkin would meet the bullock cart carrying Griboedov's body.* He had sometimes doubted that it had really happened like that: it was just too historical a confluence. Igor now knew a lot about history, what it was like—not like that.

He took a long time deciding when would be the best time to try talking with Alexander Sergeyevich—before the cart or after? He decided—before. Because if the poet really had met the cart, then he would most likely not be able to "make contact" after such a shock. And if he hadn't, then wasn't it all the same? By now experienced, Igor synchronized everything precisely and folded his little seat exactly on the right day and hour and on the right road. . . .

Pushkin was riding on a small shaggy horse accompanied by a Cossack with a rifle. Igor again did not recognize him right away—in a cape and a broad-brimmed hat. Igor, this time carefully shaven and combed, in renovated coat, with his stick and little trunk—a strange wanderer!—set out in Pushkin's direction from the turn, descending from the pass at the same time as Alexander Sergeyevich was riding up toward it, that is, slowly. It's easier to get into conversation on the road; his strange and European appearance predisposed Alexander Sergeyevich in his favor; Igor passed himself off as a traveling botanist from Vienna. . . . Everything went smooth as silk. Alexander Sergeyevich wanted to know where to spend the night on the way to Erevan; Hans Ebel (as Igor called himself) wanted to know what the weather was like in Tiflis. . . . Igor-Hans began telling him about the age of the moun-

---

*A. S. Griboedov (1795–1829) was a poet and a diplomat, author of the great dramatic epic *Woe from Wit*, and the namesake of Pushkin. His death initiates a series of premature deaths among Russian poets, followed directly by Pushkin's. Griboedov was savagely killed in Teheran by Mussulmans under mysterious and, to this day, unexplained circumstances. That Pushkin managed to meet his body is too symbolic a historical coincidence. That our hero doubted the event despite its having been described by Pushkin himself in his *Journey to Arzrum* is partially understandable. —A.B.

tains, a way he'd contrived to talk to Alexander Sergeyevich convincingly about the possibility of dislocations in time (faults, rock strata). . . . He appeared not in any way to have betrayed his knowledge that he was talking to a poet, that he was talking to Pushkin, but the gaze from under the hat suddenly lengthened, as if it were rushing upward and into the distance; the accustomed fear of previous failures ran along Igor's spine like ice, and the same coin that the poet had given him in October of '33 provoked a convulsive thought. He took the coin minted in '33 out of his pocket and held it out to Alexander Sergeyevich.

"What is it?" the poet asked absently, gazing upward into the distance as before.

"Look at the year!"

Pushkin looked at the coin with irritation.

"But it's twenty-nine now!" Igor exclaimed in despair.

"Of course. Wait a minute . . ." And he galloped off. Toward the cart.

He had met the cart.

And it was Igor who scared up the rabbit out of hibernation so that it ran across the poet's path in December 1825. . . .*

A strange thought suddenly stole into our time traveler's head. . . . What if . . . No, it can't be! However . . .

This chase has been going on for almost twelve years. And I've already given up trying to put an end to it. . . . Then, it means, then, perhaps . . . So he has seen me ALREADY! That's why he keeps recognizing me more easily. . . . Back then, in '36, I had a better chance . . . I was younger, more unrecognizable. . . . And here on a snowdrift, at the sight of a trail of triangular paw prints at the end of which, in the expression of a twentieth-century poet, "there will certainly be a rabbit,"[†] Igor broke into sobs.

---

*The role of this rabbit in the history of Russian culture is still insufficiently appreciated. Pushkin himself often stressed that had that rabbit not run across the road in front of him (a bad omen that caused him to turn back), he would have been on Senate Square on December 14. What would the Decembrist Pushkin have written for us in Siberia? I fear it would not have been the *Little Tragedies*. . . . It is unthinkable that this could have happened in any other way, and Pushkin's famous superstitiousness does not explain it all. —A.B.

[†]Bella Akhmadulina. —A.B.

And here in the snowdrift, having sobbed out his despair, he made the calm and final decision not to return to his century. "Well, so what. I'll give him time, let him forget," he reasoned, boldly mixing up the times. "I won't bother him in exile, he'll be back soon. I'll go backwards, to Petersburg, I'll live there for three years and wait for his return. . . ."

And we, sympathizing with the hero with all our heart, will not make him not recognize the poet again in his cap—young, handsome, in a red blouse. . . . He is striding along the village path and throwing his famous iron cane in front of him: * he throws it, catches up to it, picks it up. He's in training to keep his arm from trembling when he has to shoot. . . . Damn it, it's gone off into the bushes. . . . The poet is crawling in the grass. Igor is holding his breath in the bushes, holding his notorious stick—he almost hit me right on the head . . . Where is it? Lord, forgive me! He's crawling in the grass like a beetle, unobserved by anyone but Igor, that is, by now observed by *no one*. . . . Like a beetle in the grass crawls the genius who has just written *The Gypsies*.

So Igor turned up in Petersburg in 1824. On the way—that is, while he was sitting on his stick—he had another extratemporal experience: His clothes fell to pieces and his money disappeared—it was minted after 1824. Thus time robbed him like a highwayman, and he ended up naked with a trunk and cane. What was he to do?

There was nothing for him to do but to keep to this version of robbery. At the precinct they will discover many inconsistencies in the testimonies, send the case higher, right up to the Secret Police. There they will ignore the inconsistencies but propose collaboration, that is, friendship.

"How logical they are, at least!" thought Igor. "To find myself working right in the Third Section! A provincial, getting on, without means, without regular domicile . . ." He suddenly grew bored; he reacted to the proposal with limp indifference, agreeing to it as if to a sentence.

And suddenly it was as if there were a breeze, a flash, a swallow, the

---

*By our standards, Pushkin was a sportsman. He liked to ride, he took ice baths. . . . To the question of why he dragged this heavy toy around with him, Pushkin once replied, laughing, "So that my hand won't shake when I shoot." This is one more small proof that the poet foresaw his future. In the duel with Dantès his hand did not

coattail of a familiar frock coat. . . . "A genius!" Igor exclaimed in delight. "How right he was from the very beginning! He recognized instantly that I was a spy. . . ." He remembered his first steps in 1836, and suddenly from there, from that failure, Pushkin had at last extended a hand to him.

Igor seized that hand, pulled himself up, and got out of the hole. . . . But Pushkin's traces had cooled. "How wonderful!" Igor joyfully strode about in freedom. "How could I have looked him in the eye when he returns in 1826!" He marveled that he had gotten out of it. And we, too, it must be confessed, are amazed.

Imagine not just an intellectual of the end of the twenty-first century . . . but the contemporary intellectual. . . . How helpless he is! What can he do, what know-how does he have, what does he even know outside of the circle of those who know as much as he does about the same thing? Take him out of that circle of his honored career and support and what will be left? Neither a trade nor a means of existence.

And he is already an old man for those days, about forty, almost gray. Twelve years! And what years! One way or another shared with Pushkin. At home in the twenty-first, they would have given him medical retirement or some kind of a pension, like a ballerina, a miner, or a submariner, but here . . .

He did acquire a history of employment on the scale of one of our beginning writers.

A hawker, a clerk, a reporter, an interpreter at the port . . . Here he was, with all his education, finally having to learn how to do something almost three centuries earlier. How proud he was when he mastered the abacus! And long division and multiplication . . . He had to calculate not for himself, after all, but for his employer. "Where'd you get the figure?" the boss would ask. How can you tell him that a computer doesn't make mistakes? The boss wants to see it for himself. As if it were music, Igor listened to his own clacking on the abacus, becoming more artistic all the time, and contentedly forgot about the computer. And his Russian wasn't the best, but here, too, he was successful: to speak in a more and more Russian language was a slow and

---

shake even when he was lying fatally wounded on the snow. His answering shot was precise. But Fate had already decided things: Pushkin was to die, Dantès to survive. — A.B.

painful pleasure. And by now he wrote almost without mistakes, feeling particularly pleased when he remembered the "yat" in time.*

Following Pushkin's tracks, he moved to Kolomna, nearer to his past, to his first apartments, to his future poem.† He found himself the same kind of little house—"light, three windows, porch and door"—although it was a long way to work, but on the other hand, it was closer to the landlady's daughter, Natasha, whom he seemed not to think about but who nonetheless made it nicer to come home. She was angular and sweet—she blushed, he laughed, and she would always stumble and, having done so, would invariably run off somewhere behind the stove, behind the curtain, to the kitchen, and Igor would grin contentedly for a long time. He once blurted out the compliment that she was like her namesake Natasha Rostova, and could not forgive himself the anachronism for a long time. Natasha became painfully jealous of her predecessor. Her strict mama was more realistic about her daughter's virtues and above all about her dowry, and therefore, despite all her doubts, or perhaps because of them, was rather quickly inclined to think that a better match for her daughter could not be found. What of it that he was not young and had his peculiarities. . . . He was peculiar—he took long walks around the city and he muttered; he wasn't exactly singing and he wasn't exactly talking to himself—too little for a song, a lot for speech. The mother, however, was not about to entrust the happiness of her daughter to a stranger so easily—she followed him to see where he went, whom he saw. She followed him and was reassured: nowhere and no one. He doesn't drink, he doesn't smoke, doesn't visit anyone. . . . What more could one want? And he would wander about, muttering *future* verses, for example, the same "Simple human happiness. . . ."

And he kept grinning contentedly.

And so he acquired his modest émigré happiness.

And something else too: He began to write.

No, not poetry . . . You don't fool with poetry around Pushkin. He wrote prose. A record of his expedition, memoirs of the twenty-first century, he even tried memoirs of contemporary life in the twenties of the nineteenth century. Worse things had been written: All Russian prose was still in the future.

---

*A Cyrillic letter that was dropped from the Russian alphabet after 1917.
†*The Little House in Kolomna.* —Trans.

Two of his pieces were even published in the newspaper. They might be seen by Pushkin!

But here, too, there was an irritating anachronism: discussing contemporary city architecture, he called the Mikhailov riding school the Winter Stadium, and Peter's Square not even Senate Square but Decembrist Square. . . .*

And so he lived and waited. So far there had been neither the flood nor the uprising.

"Petersburg is strange without Pushkin! It is as if it had been built in his time. As if a hundred years were needed to resume its construction, one hundred years from Peter to Pushkin—and again the hammers started banging, saws whining, winches squeaking. Building started all at once on everything that later seemed to us to have been built in series: the Stock Exchange with its dock and embankment, and the barracks, and the horse-guard riding school, and the reconstruction of the Admiralty, and the boulevards, the bridges, the Kazan Cathedral, St. Isaac's, Trinity—whole groves of columns grew up, but far faster than groves, and three- and four-story houses simply grew like mushrooms.

"Remembering the Petersburg of 1837 from which Pushkin departed forever, you would be extremely surprised by the Petersburg of 1824, some twelve years younger: There were neither the buildings of the Senate and the Synod nor the sphinxes, the Alexander column nor either of the triumphal gates; the famous lions were two times smaller . . . almost nothing existed of that which will someday bear his name—neither the Alexander Theater nor Pushkin House. As if everything were rushing to get into Pushkin's verse, hurrying to shine in his eyes.

"No! He could have *not* died! I see him, see him alive, getting into a train in that same 1837, I see him sitting upright on a seat looking out the window, and a boyish laughter beams from his eyes. 'He feels the pain and yet he laughs. . . .' Damned Mr. Oblachkin!† That was January 7. I slipped Nikifor a ruble, he didn't resist, said he would take care of everything. I stood at the entrance, squeezing the package of penicillin; my heart was leaping out of my chest, and circles swam be-

---

*That is, the square where the Decembrists assembled in December 1825 that was subsequently renamed for them. —Trans.

†In Russian, *oblako* means "cloud," "cloudy." Pushkin was rarely as indulgent as he was to Mr. Oblachkin. —A.B.

fore my eyes, but an inexplicable certainty that this time he would hear
me out was stronger than fear. Then that boy-peddler, some fourteen
years old, rushes by me with his ratty notebook right up to the door. . . .
Vasily the cook opens it and he thrusts in the notebook. And I can hear
Pushkin coming down the stairs, his voice—Nikifor didn't betray
me. . . . But the cook shoves the boy out: Pushkin's busy, he says. And
he closes the door. Damn it, I think, the devil brought you—you've
messed it all up. But I felt sorry for the boy: He strode off hanging his
head, and his little face was like his name. Well, it serves you right, I
think, he didn't even read Blok's (my) poems, what does he need
Oblachkin's for! Then the door was flung open and I was exultant: It
was Nikifor, for me! But it was that same Vasily. . . . He pushes me
away, and runs off yelling, 'Mr. Oblachkin! Mr. Oblachkin! Come
back!' Oblachkin flew up the stairs, and Vasily again closed the door
on my nose. I had grown completely numb with cold by now, and no
sign of Pushkin, or Nikifor, or even Oblachkin. Finally the door opened
with a happy Oblachkin standing in the doorway; from behind him
Nikifor is looking at me in embarrassment. He shrugs his shoulders,
spreads out his hands. . . . 'Next time, sir,' he says. What can you do?
I run after Oblachkin. I'm ready to strangle him. This and that, I tell
him, I'm so-and-so, also a poet, I also brought poems to Alexander
Sergeyevich, and you were the lucky one, not me. . . . 'What's he
like,' I ask, 'very stern?' 'What do you mean?' answers Oblachkin. 'He's
a dear! No one I've brought my poems to ever talks with me, but he
read my notebook right away and praised it, and told me to come back
if I write any more.' I couldn't stand it. 'Show me!' I say. He's so elated,
he willingly hands me his notebook. I look: Well, what do you know
about that! There was simply nothing, not the least little thing, in his
verses! And that Pushkin himself would . . . 'What else did he say to
you?' I importune him, 'He asked me how old I was, whether my father's rich, and if I have my own name.' 'What do you mean, your
own?' 'Well, whether I'd taken it as a pseudonym. . . .' 'And?' 'And so
I tell him it's mine, all mine. And he was just so happy that he began
squeezing and tickling me, praising me. A fine fellow!' he says. What
can you do, a genius! What does he care about my penicillin when
boy-poets can run around the world with such names. . . .

    "I like waiting for him here. Everything is so slow—but so fast! And
all the time there's something. Whereas back home everything is fast—
and there's nothing. In the twelve years I haven't been in Petersburg,
how much is left to be built in Pushkin's time! And all this *will be*

built. It will be possible to look at it all for centuries and murmur his lines! While at home . . . There's nothing to describe: not a single detail, although there is nothing but detail. There goes the Okhta girl with her milk can, and she's wearing a Dutch cap,* while we get powdered milk from a special faucet with a meter—and the faucet is not made of metal, and the meter is electronic. There goes a sleigh, and its runners squeak, and from under the horse's tail fall smoking droppings, and the driver has a sash and a face as red as can be, while we crawl into our transparent shells, fold ourselves in three like a fetus, dial a telephone number, press a button, no one even says hello to you but that very second you're sitting opposite your interlocutor four hundred thousand kilometers away and he offers you an artificial aperitif that you imbibe through something clipped to your nose, and get high if you can. . . . In Petersburg they go to a tavern—like me now, out of annoyance at Oblachkin. A 'man' will serve me. 'Man' sounds almost scornful to them because he's not a gentleman, only a man, but to me the fact that it is not a mechanical hand serving me, that a cockroach and a fly, which had been alive just a moment ago, can swim in my soup, that the man is alive and his napkin is dirtier than the street—all this is pure happiness and very touching. And meters here don't come in squares but in bedrooms, living rooms, and dining rooms.† And there aren't all those hoses, pipes, and wires that maintain our life-support system: water, air, heat, light, communication, information . . . like a dying man being kept alive—disconnect the wires and where is the man? But here: Hey, my good man, what have you got? Well, even if it's only lemonade . . .

"How slowly everything was built in those days, how quickly! And all of it has remained right up to our time, none of it disappeared. The primitive tools and the almost slavelike labor. Engineering principles seem to be meager, technical means hopeless. . . . How did it all turn out so well? Better than it did later, with all of our devices? The hand was clever, and the mind used its hands. There wasn't a thoughtless motion, and there wasn't a careless thought. No, I still haven't understood. . . .

"But if there's one man I still can't forgive, it's Bryullov!‡ What

---

*From Pushkin's description of a Petersburg morning in *Eugene Onegin*, I, xxxv. —Trans.

†In the U.S.S.R. living space is allotted in square meters per person. —Trans.

‡Karl Pavlovich Bryullov (1799–1852) painted large historical canvases (*The Last Days of Pompeii*) and society portraits. —Trans.

would it have cost him to give Alexander Sergeyevich that painting?
He thinks he's a Rubens, the inflated European! Alexander Sergeyevich even got down on his knees; even if he was joking, he meant it,
and he got down on his knees . . . but Bryullov: 'Later,' he says, 'I'll
give it to you later.' And the poet only had three days left to live. The
main thing is that later he came to see him at his house. Alexander
Sergeyevich brings out his sleepy children to show off to him, and
Bryullov says, 'Well, why did you go and get married?' Suddenly, Alexander Sergeyevich got sad, bored. 'Well,' he says, 'they wouldn't let
me out of the country, so I got married.' But Bryullov had lived abroad
all his life, and he wasn't married, and he had no children—so he
didn't understand either Pushkin's joke or his sadness.

But he was right not to give him the painting! Because how was he
to know that Pushkin might die soon? And a live Alexander Sergeyevich would have ridden off in that first train from Petersburg to Moscow taking with him the painting Bryullov had given him. . . ."

"Thus he wrote verses, murky, limp . . ."* This is where the tale of
our poor Igor should have begun, since he's decided to live here. . . . I
should begin here, but there's no time. The author's time in the country is quickly coming to an end, and am I really not going to finish
anything again? What's more, I don't have any source material at
hand—not only on Petersburg during the Pushkin period, but I don't
even have a volume of Pushkin's own work. There aren't any such
sources at hand in the village, and there aren't any of the usual sources
in the village either. No lakes, no streams, no wells, although it pours
out of the sky without stopping: The hay won't get dry after all. There
are no sources—we're digging little ponds. The water stays in the clay,
doesn't disappear—we scoop it out of the ponds with buckets, carry it
into the house. It's warm in the house. If you heat the stove. But if you
don't, it's cold. And if you don't bring in the water, there isn't any. And
to go for it means going out in the rain and the mud. A ton of mud on
each boot, and it's slippery. And the electricity has been cut off, and
the transformer shed is on the other side of the field. It's a long way,
and in this rain. Everyone in our three houses is looking out the window to see who's going, and so far no one's going. They lit candles in
the windows and so did I. The thoughts of the author and the hero are

*Thus Pushkin describes the poetry of Onegin's neighbor, Lensky, in *Eugene Onegin*.
—Trans.

beginning to intersect: He's right about being kept alive. . . . Maybe our technology is not quite perfect in comparison with his future technology, but even I back there in the capital am connected by hoses—admittedly twisted, rusty, and ill-made—to the communal life without which I cannot survive a day—to the radiator, the toilet, the television. . . . I trip on the wires. And if, God forbid, there were what Chistyakov was just threatening? The news commentator threatens on television—he threatens once, he threatens twice, we get used to it. . . . It's not terrifying. It's not a threat, it's "the international situation," like furniture: England stands there, Zimbabwe is seething here, and a bomb is suspended over there. . . . But disconnect me. . . . But what am I saying, once it wasn't that they cut off the hot water temporarily, they had boiling water coming out of both faucets . . . three days you couldn't wash your hands, no less splash your face. In the city it's terrifying if you have no television and think Chistyakovian thoughts. But here in the village it's not so terrifying. Because there's nothing to be cut off from. Because here it's as if there had already been a war. The other day in the next village, Turlykovo, the last inhabitant died. He was riding in the back of a truck, the truck overturned, and a crate of nails fell on him. . . . I have been in that village. It's pretty, much prettier than ours, as is its name. The village itself is on a hill; there are meadows all around, around the meadows is a forest—the little village rises above ours like a church. It lived better than ours did, too, apparently. Because there are wells, and the windows are decorated with carved frames. That means that there was time not only for sustenance but also for comfort, for beauty—a sign of peasant civilization! The houses are still almost in one piece, just move in and start living, well, fix it up a little and start living—it's just that there's no one to do the living. I went into one of the houses: In the sideboard there were glasses and spoons, not valuable but usable, and in the wardrobe there were even dresses hanging on hangers. You could stock up on equipment: a good hacksaw, or a hammer, or a scythe. . . . As if they had run away in a hurry, from leprosy or a neutron bomb test. Of course this is a harsh region: neither the climate nor the soil is good—the north, clay. Water from the sky all the time, water and more water. Of course there are no roads. But they used to live here! Not just one generation, if they were already carving window frames . . . Into what time did they all run off? Into tomorrow.

They ran off, but what am I doing here? I'm trying to make something here, anything, as long as it's something, because where I come from you can't make anything because of *connections to the world*, not to work, but to the whole world, to the tele-world: -phone, -vision. A living detail can't be found.

The cow is mooing now, the grass is growing now, the rain is pouring now, and something has to be done right now. Not yesterday and not tomorrow. If you put a dam on time in an effort to store the past or accumulate the future, you will be flooded through the tiny little hole called "now," and you will choke in the flood of the present.

Igor, of course, knew about the flood. But they had not especially prepared him for this historical segment, since they had planned that he would arrive only in 1836. He knew that it would be in the fall, that it would be that year (1824), and that the harbor, Vasilievsky Island, and the Petrograd side would suffer most. . . . But then they were living in Kolomna, which hadn't suffered that much, as he remembered. And he worked at the harbor, therefore he would be the first to meet the flood and would have time to take measures to protect his future family. Besides, he had gotten going on his writing: his story about contemporary Petersburg life breathed the freshness of a newcomer and the knowledge of a habitué. Sometimes he felt that he wouldn't even be ashamed to show it to Pushkin. True, only sometimes . . . Remembering about the impending flood, he would mutter the immortal lines of the future *Bronze Horseman*,* as if considering it some kind of a guide to the approaching ordeal.

The day of November 6 was wretched, the rain whipped down, a piercing wind blew, the water in the Neva rose significantly. In the evening the signal lights on the Admiralty tower were lit, warning the population about the flood. Everyone slept peacefully, however, and Igor fell asleep with his troubled head on his manuscript. At dawn he rushed off to work—an hour and a half's brisk walk is no joke. The elements were acting up more than yesterday, the waves breaking against the granite embankments, and the spray rising up in a wall; water from underground pipes spurted out of the gratings in fountains, gathering the curious around them. Igor went to meet the elements and was not afraid because everything dear to him was in the rear: both Natasha and his manuscript. He made his way across the Neva via the

---

*Pushkin's poem (1833) about a poor man named Eugene who loses his beloved and his mind in the Petersburg flood of 1824. Eugene imagines himself pursued by the bronze equestrian statue of Peter the Great that was erected by Catherine the Great on the bank of the Neva River. —Trans.

Isaac Bridge; it kept getting harder to walk, bursts of wind knocked him off his feet, but Igor kept on persistently, as if by this he was protecting everything he had left at his back, and suddenly realized with this same back that this wasn't the threat of the flood or even the day before the flood, but it was the flood itself. Suddenly the boundless space before him turned into a boiling abyss. Above it flew a fog of shredded spray, the waves broke into sharp, whirling pieces like knives and flew in sharp, triangular fragments, as if losing the characteristics of liquid. Carriages and droshkies floated on the water, taking refuge on the high wooden piers as if they were islands. Suddenly he saw an enormous barge rushing right at him; it passed him by, however, and slammed into a brick house, which crumbled from the collision.

They picked up Igor, half drowned in the waves. The boat belonged to an English trade vessel that Igor had boarded the day before on business. He recognized the skipper. "It's hell over there," the skipper said to him in English, poking his thumb behind him. "Large boats are carried along between the houses, they crush them and crumble into splinters themselves." "Yes, I saw one," Igor agreed. He was seized by a kind of numbness. Now he wanted to rush back the same way he had rushed forward in the morning. Pieces of the broken-up Isaac Bridge rushed toward them, and one fragment almost overturned the boat. The infuriated waves raged on Palace Square as well, and Nevsky Prospect had turned into a broad river, but the disaster on the Admiralty side was not as terrible, and this slightly calmed Igor. In the middle of the day the water began to recede; toward evening the first carriages already appeared on the streets, and by midnight Igor had made his way to his house on foot. . . .

In place of his house he found a steamship of enormous size. A sheet of paper had stuck to its side like an announcement. Mechanically he pulled it off. . . . All the lines were washed away, but what author doesn't recognize a page of his own manuscript when he sees one! The waves, the wind, the fragments, the Idol with the raised victorious hoof . . . "He's in Mikhailovskoe now!* How did he know all this?" Igor muttered in horror, and again inside him a breeze seemed to turn up the tail of some frock coat, and a lightninglike flash flared up before his eyes, illuminating the black bulk of the steamship and the washed-away lines of his manuscript for the last time. Igor burst out laughing and started to run, gone mad like Eugene, muttering

---

*Pushkin's father's estate in Pskov province between Petersburg and Moscow, where Pushkin spent the last years of his exile. —Trans.

lines of Pushkin's future poem like an incantation. After him chased
the author of the poem, the wind ruffling his bronze cape. . . . But the
living Pushkin could not be here, the bronze one even less so—neither
Opekushin's nor Anikushin's. . . .* "And 'The Monument'† hasn't
even been written yet!" History had overflowed its banks like the Neva
and swept over Igor's head. . . . He hid from Pushkin behind the
church of the Protector, crossing himself timidly and awkwardly.

Here they found him, having spent an extra billion billions on a rescue
mission. Here, in the center of Kolomna, but—in our time, yours and
mine: Wet through and through, beneath a clear sky, he was loitering
around an architectural structure with the letters "M" and "W" on the
place where the church had been, clutching the fragments of his stick
in despair. . . .
    And there he sits, living out the twenty-first century. . . .
    Out the window, in the black cosmos, rustles the great three hun-
dredth anniversary: the sputniks are draped about like garlands on a
New Year's tree; holiday firecrackers fly from sputnik to sputnik, trailing sparks into the abyss of the rest of the universe.
    His ward is quiet and separate, but he doesn't hear anything anyway:
The times have mingled in his head; in his poor head the chase of the
future after the past never ends—he chases Eugene, Eugene chases
Pushkin, Pushkin chases Peter. Then they reverse directions and they
all chase him, and then he is terrified. Outside the window cosmic
gymnasts in individual diving suits with searchlights on their foreheads
form a flaming figure 300 in acrobatic flight. Igor is muttering like
Hermann—three, seven, ace,‡ repeating these by now ancient lines:

> A vain gift, a chance gift . . .
> Life, why have you been given to me?§

He clenches and unclenches his fist in which he holds—a button.
He cries piteously, thrashes, and wails if they try to take it away. They

---

*The sculptors of the most famous statues of Pushkin in Moscow (1880) and Lenin-
grad (1949). —A.B.
†"The Monument" (1836), Pushkin's famous poem, is considered by his descendants
to be his testament. —A.B.
‡Hermann, the hero of Pushkin's story "The Queen of Spades," goes mad when he
loses at cards and is last seen in the madhouse repeating this, his losing formula.
—Trans.
§From Pushkin's "May God grant that I not go mad." —Trans.

let him keep it, and he calms down. He is lucky—they don't realize that it's the real thing!

The author in his attic is overcome by increasing impotence. If the author could only see how similar his dwelling is to his own attempt to describe the future world! The rain has stopped, and the sky has cleared. The night is mute, and there is no traveler to see how the author's attic hangs in the night, mounted on little nails of light emanating from the cracks and holes, like the sky on the stars. There seems to be a fire in there. Or one is just going out.

They developed Igor's slides, listened to his tapes. . . . They confirmed the diagnosis. No, there was nothing to reproach Igor for; he had not exposed or erased anything. But only a shadow, like the wing of a bird flying up before the lens, came out. One was struck, however, by the unusual, senseless beauty of individual shots, especially in relation to the notes of the insane time traveler: The storm that preceded the cloud that had inspired the poet to write the line "The last cloud dispersed by the storm . . ."; the portrait of the cook Vasily slamming the door; the remarkable portrait of the rabbit in the snow—in a drift, ears erect, front paws folded under; the cart harnessed to the bullocks covered with the tarpaulin with Abreks prancing all around it; the hand with the candle and a piece of someone's beard; the waves carrying coffins . . . and all the rest of the shots were of water and waves.

And the tapes: rustling, crackling, the entreaties of the time traveler himself, someone's mumbling, as if the voice were at another speed or the recorder was on the wrong speed, and suddenly, distinctly, shrill and high: Nikifor! How many times have I told you not to let THAT ONE in!"

And here we place our final period, like a monument, a monument to an utterly selfless and unreciprocated love.

And we find ourselves, thank the Lord, in our own personal time. OUR time (mine and yours): dawn, August 25, 1985.

1985

Translated from the Russian by Priscilla Meyer.

AUTO ACCIDENT IN PARIS

Elchin

Shahrabanu-hanum: Did Hatamhan-aga and
Shahrabanu-hanum really die so that some Frenchman
would deceive Shahbaz and take him to Paris! . . .
Monsieur Jordan: Dommage Paris! Quel malheur!
Mon dieu! Mon dieu! Mon dieu!

M. F. Akhundov,
Monsieur Jordan, the Bota-
nist, and Dervish Mas-
talishah, the Famous
Sorcerer

1

Kerim-muallim had a confused dream about people long dead—not
his father or mother or relatives, but old neighbors, the director of the
school who had been in charge twenty-five years ago, his wife's distant
relatives, one of Nurida's former husbands. They had gathered together and were all eating a watermelon, a watermelon so enormous
that each slice was the size of a boat, and the long-dead people climbed
up on these chunks and sat on them, and broke off huge pieces of
watermelon with their hands. They ate, drenching their hands and feet
in watermelon juice. The watermelon was as red as could be, and
Kerim-muallim, while looking at its scarlet pulp in his sleep, seemed
to hear a shot, then another one. He opened his eyes, realized that
he had been dreaming, but again heard a shot, propped himself up

slightly, sat up in bed, and distinctly hearing the sound of yet another shot, jumped up and went to the window.

In front of the old two-story home where Kerim-muallim's family lived there was a little square and early in the morning pensioners would buy newspapers at the kiosk near the entrance and sit on the benches and read. Then the mothers, grandmothers, and nannies would bring little children to this square and the children's carriages would be lined up in a row, like piano keys; after midday the pensioners would gather here again and play backgammon and dominoes. Then night would fall and the little square would also empty out, silence would reign—and then morning would come and everything would be repeated with unvarying exactness.

Kerim-muallim looked out the window that faced the square and saw a man standing with a gun and aiming. Next to him was another person—wearing large mittens, and, to tell the truth, Kerim-muallim was afraid at first, because for the first time in his life a man with a gun stood in front of him and this man, although it was not yet fully light, was taking aim and shooting. Then it seemed to Kerim-muallim that they were making a film, because once, about ten years ago, a movie had been made here, but now there was no one else besides these two men in the entire square and surrounding streets. There was only a van parked at the far end, at a slight distance. Who in the world could they be, thieves?

The man who was aiming fired again and this time Kerim-muallim heard a dog howl at the same instant as the shot. He watched as the man with big mittens ran in the direction of the olive trees and grabbed the ears of the yelping dog, who was sprawled under the trees. With both hands he lifted the mongrel off the ground, carried it to the van, and threw it inside.

Kerim-muallim realized that these people were shooting diseased stray dogs; most likely they were from the Baku sanitation department. Nevertheless, the shooting of these unfortunate animals so early in the morning weighed heavily on Kerim-muallim; he even wanted to scream something out of the window to these people, but then he thought that each person in this world goes about his business and shooting dogs was their profession. He also thought that in all likelihood the man with the gun was not firing lead bullets but, rather, a sleep-inducing substance, and having sedated the dogs, they would take them away.

The two glanced attentively and tenaciously around the square a little while longer, so that even from afar Kerim-muallim could detect a certain avidity in the eyes of both the one with the gun and the one with mittens, and it occurred to him that the two of them probably got paid by the number of dogs they brought in. Then the one removed his mittens and the other put the gun in the cab of the van and both got into the van and drove away.

Kerim-muallim remained standing at the window for a little while, looking at the square, at the two- and three-story houses on the other side; everyone was sleeping, the August morning had just begun and no one had awakened yet. The fruit and vegetable kiosk at the intersection was empty; watermelons were gathered in a large metal cage near the kiosk and a large metal lock hung on the door of the cage.

Suddenly it seemed to Kerim-muallim as if the watermelons had been arrested, put in prison, and Kerim-muallim felt uncomfortable both at the idea itself and at his having thought of it, for Kerim-muallim did not like to speak idly or to think idly.

Yawning, Kerim-muallim scratched his hairy chest and wondered why no one else had been awakened by the sound of the shots.

He knew everyone in the neighboring houses. When he ran into one or another he sometimes stopped and asked how things were going, sometimes simply greeted them and walked by. Although there were some, particularly new residents, whom he knew only by sight, he remembered all of them, because Kerim-muallim had been born in the same apartment in which he now lived. He had never in his life lived anywhere else, although once—seventeen years ago—he had taken the family to Nalchik for a month and another time—nine years ago—he had gone to the sanatarium at Shusha for twelve days.

Looking away from the square, Kerim-muallim glanced at the wall clock—the clock that had been presented to Kerim-muallim in school in connection with the thirtieth anniversary of his pedagogical career; this gift was, in fact, the sole reward of his entire life. It showed twenty to six, there was no sense in lying down again, and Kerim-muallim quietly headed for the kitchen.

The apartment had two rooms, a glassed-in veranda, and a kitchen. When Kerim-muallim passed by one of the rooms, he froze for a moment: The infant lying in his little wooden crib next to Shargiya's bed was not sleeping and with his eyes wide open he was silently watching Kerim-muallim.

It was the first time that Kerim-muallim had seen the infant so silent and so serious.

Shargiya was Kerim-muallim's older daughter and the little fellow was her son, that is, Kerim-muallim's grandson, and he was a terrible crybaby. It was six months since the baby had made his appearance in the world and during those six months there had not been a day that he wasn't crying, if, of course, he wasn't sleeping. And now, seeing the baby neither sleeping nor crying, and moreover, so serious, down deep Kerim-muallim was even a bit alarmed: What kind of a morning was this?

Kerim-muallim, naturally, was not superstitious and did not believe in either fate or signs, but all the same the shooting incident before the light of dawn on this August morning, the strange thought about the watermelons, and now the fact that the baby wasn't sleeping and was looking at him so attentively evoked some kind of vague anxiety in Kerim-muallim.

He lit the gas in the kitchen, filled the tea kettle, and put it on the fire. Then he washed and, returning to his room just as quietly, began to get dressed. Kerim-muallim's wife, Zahra, his second daughter, Zuleiha, and son, Hamlet, were still sleeping. Kerim-muallim had gotten up unusually early this morning, but even so, no one in the house ever got up earlier than Kerim-muallim. At a quarter to seven without fail he would be on his feet, brushing his suit and polishing his shoes. While the household was still asleep he would go out and buy the day's bread, kefir, sour cream, and newspapers; he would return, have breakfast, and go to school. On the whole, for the longest time Kerim-muallim had been in charge of stocking the house with provisions.

Kerim-muallim taught geography in high school, but now it was vacation, so there was no need to go to school. Nonetheless, following his thirty-year habit, he took his blue bag and, moving quietly all the time, the baby still following him with the same serious gaze, he left the house.

The city was completely deserted; only the yard keeper was sweeping the street and, catching sight of Kerim-muallin, respectfully greeted him. The latter returned the greeting and continued on his way.

Of course the stores and newspaper kiosks were still closed, and Kerim-muallim, swinging his empty bag, headed for Seaside Boulevard, and while he was walking along the completely deserted streets it seemed to him as if he were in an unfamiliar, unrecognizable city. Indeed, Kerim-muallim remembered the names of at least 90 percent of the cities of the world, and besides that he was very familiar with all the streets, alleys, dead ends, and even individual buildings of Baku (with the exception of the new suburbs); but, be that as it may, on this August day—it was a Saturday—as Kerim-muallim was striding early in the morning along the absolutely deserted streets of Baku, it seemed to him as if he were in an unfamiliar, unrecognizable city, and the inhabitants of this city consisted only of yard keepers sweeping the streets.

In school the children had given Kerim-muallim the nickname "The Bag," because whenever the kids accidentally met the teacher in town, he always had a bag in his hands: either he would be standing in line or he would be buying something. As they progressed from class to class, as some graduated from school and others entered it, the kids noticed that the bag was always blue, and they added another word to the nickname, "blue"—that is, Kerim-muallim Blue Bag; then another word, "old," was added to the nickname—that is, Kerim-muallim Old Blue Bag. News of this nickname had even reached Kerim-muallim himself, whom the children were rather afraid of, but Kerim-muallim was not in the least upset or angry about the nickname because he thought, Never mind, they'll grow up, they'll take bags in their own hands and they'll understand everything. However, there was another fact that Kerim-muallim was unaware of: among themselves the teachers also called him Old Blue Bag.

Seaside Boulevard was also absolutely deserted; aside from Kerim-muallim there was nothing but a lot of sea gulls. The birds were flying along the shore, swooping down now and then and plunging their beaks into the water. In the complete absence of people, the birds' shrill hubbub could be heard so clearly, so distinctly, it was as if it were not ordinary hubbub and twitter, but as if the birds were talking about something, discussing something. Kerim-muallim, however, was not disposed toward figurative thinking, and at that moment he was more concerned about whether there would be sour cream in the store. Then Kerim-muallim got angry at the birds, or, rather, at the city's sanitation workers, because they did not pay attention to cleaning the shoreline and therefore the sea gulls came there in search of food.

Swinging his empty bag and striding along the shore, Kerim-muallim decided that either today or at the very latest tomorrow he would write a letter to the Baku city council about the sanitary condition of the city and he began to compose the first sentences of the letter in his mind, but once again he remembered the two men he had so recently seen shooting stray dogs and then the baby, silently looking at him with wide-open eyes.

Shargiya's husband, Salman, was a physicist; they said he was a talented scientist, but talent isn't an apartment or money or a car. Salman also lived with Kerim-muallim's family, and if there really is such a thing as bad luck, then Shargiya had been unlucky. True, Salman didn't drink or go on sprees, didn't grumble. He would leave for work in the morning and return in the evening and on Saturdays and Sundays he would take Shargiya to the movies or to the boulevard. Once he even took her to the floricultural *sovkhoz* in Shuvelyany. But Salman had nothing except for some rural relatives in Karabakh; it was from there that he had come to Baku after graduating from high school. Two years ago Shargiya—who knows how they found each other and where they met!—had married Salman because (at this point Kerim-muallim even coughed twice) . . . because no one else had married Shargiya.

Salman was not in Baku now—he was in Paris.

The institute in which Salman worked was connected with French scientists, and Salman had been sent to work in Paris for half a year. In exchange, one young French scientist was supposed to come to Baku from Paris for six months. Kerim-muallim realized that if his son-in-law were not an able specialist, he would not have been sent to Paris, but Salman was such a reserved, taciturn person that even a trip such as this had not become an event in Kerim-muallim's family. On this August morning, however, when Kerim-muallim was walking along the shore, swinging his empty blue bag, somehow it suddenly seemed strange to him that Salman was in Paris, living in a distant, huge, foreign city. Under the influence of this unexpected feeling, he lingered for a moment and glanced at the brightly glowing horizon: The crimson of the horizon, the purity and blueness of the sky, the tranquillity and boundlessness of the sea, even the flight of the sea gulls along the shore and their cackle pleased Kerim-muallim—Kerim-muallim approved of this picture of nature.

Since he had lingered on the boulevard, he had to stand in line in the stores. While passing the fruit and vegetable stall he decided to buy a watermelon, and after rummaging thoroughly through the pile, he bought a good Zyryanovsk watermelon. Then he stood in line at the newspaper kiosk, bought the radio-and-television schedule, the day's newspapers, and finally arrived home somewhat later than usual.

Nurida-hanum opened the door, and when Kerim-muallim saw Nurida-hanum at his place at such an early hour with a serious expression on her face, he realized that something had happened.

Nurida-hanum, Kerim-muallim's older sister, was one of the first female physical education teachers in Azerbaijan. She lived nearby in a house across the courtyard from Kerim-muallim's.

With the large Zyryanovsk watermelon in one hand and the blue bag in the other, Kerim-muallim, without taking his eyes off his sister's powdered, made-up, as-always-well-cared-for face, asked, "What happened?"

In a deep masculine voice Nurida-hanum said, "Nothing. Don't get scared, come in."

Kerim-muallim entered and saw Zahra, Zuleiha, and Hamlet on their feet. Shargiya was sitting by her baby's crib with her head down and it seemed that she was crying quietly. But, in any case, seeing the whole household alive and well, Kerim-muallim calmed down somewhat. It occurred to him that perhaps Abdulla had died. But Nurida-hanum's usual self-confident look said otherwise; Nurida-hanum did not look like a wife whose husband had just died.

"Salman was in an auto accident!" said Nurida-hanum, and Shargiya began crying out loud.

"Has Salman come back from Paris?" asked Kerim-muallim.

Nurida-hanum looked straight into her brother's eyes.

"What do you think, that there aren't any cars in Paris?"

Nurida-hanum had always been proud of her brother, although he was two years younger than she, and she always made an example of Kerim-muallim to her husband, Abdulla, but at times her sharp, unflinching gaze would go right through her brother, too, and then Kerim-muallim would become as flustered as a schoolboy. Nurida-hanum gave her brother the telegram that she was holding in her hand, and Kerim-muallim took it, went to the window where the light was better, and began to read. The telegram did in fact say that Salman had been in an auto accident in Paris and was now in the hospital, but that the condition of the victim was not life-threatening.

"Well, so what?" said Kerim-muallim. "After all, it says that his life is not in danger. For Parisian doctors, curing a person is like taking a drink of water."

Strangely enough, just a short time before, Nurida-hanum had said the same thing to Zahra. When Zahra received the telegram, Kerim-muallim had been strolling along the boulevard, composing a letter to the Baku city council in his mind. And whenever the routine Zahra had become used to over the years was in the least disturbed—whenever something unforeseen happened—she would become flustered and wouldn't know what to do. So, since her husband was not home, she had picked up the receiver and called Nurida-hanum to read her the telegram over the phone, but Nurida-hanum, annoyed that she had been interrupted in the middle of her daily morning exercises, had declared, "Well, so what? After all, it says that he's in no danger. Don't worry about Parisian doctors; Salman never had it so good; they'll fix

him—he'll be better than before." Nurida-hanum had no sooner re-
sumed her morning exercises than she broke off this sacred rite and
called Zahra back. "Read me that telegram again," she had said, and
then, dressing hastily, she had gone to her brother's. And now Kerim-
muallim repeated her very words.

Nurida-hanum sat in the sole easy chair in the room and said,
"Read on."

Kerim-muallim continued reading. It said that one of Salman's relatives could come to Paris and the company that owned the car that
was responsible for Salman's accident would pay for all the expenses.
Having read these words, Kerim-muallim looked at his sister once
again; at first he didn't know how to relate to this information, then he
grew angry.

"Have they no shame! First, for no reason at all they put a man in
the hospital, and then they offer money."

Indeed, when Kerim-muallim said this, he immediately sensed that
neither his words nor his anger had made an impression on anyone.
Then Kerim-muallim's gaze fell on the infant in the little wooden crib.
The baby's eyes were open, but he wasn't crying, and Kerim-muallim
very nearly asked what was the matter with him, why wasn't he bawling. But he didn't say anything and he looked at Shargiya. Shargiya
was crying, sobbing, and sniffling without uttering a word, and Kerim-
muallim thought, It's true when they say that husband and wife are cut
of the same cloth, because Shargiya, just like her husband, is a bungler.

Nurida-hanum saw that Kerim-muallim was looking at Shargiya.
"No, Shargiya can't go," she said. "She has a nursing baby on her
hands."

Zuleiha hastily joined in: "That's right. Shargiya can't go. It's better
if I go and do whatever has to be done!"

Shargiya began crying louder—not because she couldn't go to Paris
or because she had a nursing infant who was a terrible crybaby, but
because everyone, including Shargiya herself, knew very well that
Zuleiha couldn't stand Salman and was embarrassed in front of her
friends that her sister had married as clumsy, graceless, and meek a
fellow as Salman.

Zuleiha's words angered Hamlet, who, turning his back on the
household, went over to the open window. Hamlet was older than
both Shargiya and Zuleiha, but at home no one acknowledged his se-
niority, and Hamlet protested this attitude by getting insulted and
huffy.

Nurida-hanum said, "Where there are elders, the juniors are silent.

We"—Nurida-hanum pointed to Kerim-muallim—"never uttered a sound in our family."

Nurida-hanum was referring to their long-deceased parents, and, to tell the truth, she had cited so many different examples, related so many incidents to illustrate this, that Kerim-muallim no longer imagined his father and mother as they really had been but as they were in Nurida-hanum's examples and memories.

Zuleiha looked angrily at her aunt; Zuleiha considered herself the most intelligent and clever person in the family and she understood very well that Nurida-hanum herself wanted to take advantage of the opportunity to go to Paris.

Hamlet moved away from the window, walked to the middle of the room, looked at his aunt, at his father and mother, at Zuleiha, Shargiya, and even at the infant lying in his little wooden crib turning his little hands around and around and staring attentively at them without uttering a sound, and pronounced mournfully, "I'm respected everywhere except in this house!" He sniveled a bit, walked quickly to the door, opened it, and slammed it behind him.

Kerim-muallim had been going to the theater since his youth; he had seen *Hamlet*, and under the impression of the unforgettable play, had named his only son Hamlet. Now Nurida-hanum watched her nephew with open irony because Hamlet was already over thirty and to this day he had no profession; to this day, like a little boy, he would construct plans for the future: Now he would write a screenplay and be consumed with it day and night; now he would get himself a job at the airport and begin to live for the idea of becoming a famous customs officer; or else, sitting in the library from morning to evening, he would read the philosophers, particularly Kant and Hegel, and, filling up extra-thick composition books with notes, he would prove the superiority of Hegel over Kant and dream of becoming a philosopher.

"Let's sit down and talk it over," said Nurida-hanum. "If you have good instructions when you sew, the dress won't come out too tight."

2

Kerim-muallim was one of those newspaper readers who studies all the articles and notices from the first page to the last, and now he was sitting on the veranda reading the papers.

Nurida-hanum was still there, in the kitchen, flushed both from the

August heat and from the gas stove—she was helping Zahra prepare dolma (meatballs wrapped in grape leaves in a sour-milk sauce).

Zuleiha was lying on the sofa in the large room reading a diary. It had been given to her by a girlfriend who worked with her at the street-car depot. The diary was filled with pretty handwriting; its pages were decorated with flowers, nightingales, and hearts pierced by arrows from one side to the other. (Zuleiha's friend had drawn all of this with colored pencils.) The diary was about unrequited love, about male treachery, but Zuleiha couldn't concentrate, couldn't immerse herself completely in it because, making up some excuse or other, she kept popping into the kitchen to find out what Nurida-hanum was saying. Meanwhile, Nurida-hanum was saying nothing in confidence because she had complete faith in Kerim-muallim. She had faith in him even now, although she wasn't about to go home for fear that Zuleiha would put up a fuss and the Paris problem would be resolved without her. As always, however, Nurida-hanum trusted her brother and knew that in the end she would be the one to go to Paris.

Abdulla sat, dozing, in the adjoining room. From time to time he would look at the telegram lying on the table, grin, shake his head, and then, yawning, doze off again. Abdulla, a hairdresser, was Nurida-hanum's fourth husband, but unlike his predecessors, he turned out to be monogamous, he hadn't run away, and they had been living together for exactly sixteen years. Nurida-hanum had phoned home and summoned Abdulla, and now he was sleepily waiting for lunch while considering various excuses to leave immediately afterward, because he had hidden a five-ruble note in his eyeglasses case. If he could only manage to slip away, life today would be marvelous. Every time she passed by Abdulla, Zuleiha tried not to breathe because, as usual, Abdulla reeked of cheap men's eau de cologne, and after the heightened feelings and emotions aroused by the diary, after the charming pictures sketched in it, Zuleiha was repelled by the smell.

Abdulla was cunning in his own way and only Nurida-hanum could see through his ruses. He reeked of cologne not because he worked as a hairdresser and was steeped in beauty-parlor scent—that went without saying—but because he bathed his face in eau de cologne to drown out another smell.

Shargiya, sitting at the end of the veranda, was nursing the baby, and the baby, as before, wore a serious expression. He wasn't crying, which hadn't happened since the day he was born, and each time Kerim-muallim's gaze fell on the baby, he was astonished.

The August day gradually became hotter and hotter; by noon it was so hot in Baku that it was impossible to breathe, and suddenly Kerim-muallim remembered beautiful Shusha, high atop the mountains. In Kerim-muallim's imagination lightning flashed, thunder rolled, and such a cloudburst began that his hands, which were holding the newspaper, dropped, his eyes stared off into the distance, and Kerim-muallim suddenly thought, It would be interesting to know whether there are thunderstorms in Paris too.

Of course Kerim-muallim was very familiar with the climactic conditions of Western Europe, including France, but now, for some reason, Paris had suddenly turned into a mysterious city, filling a man's heart with strange feelings.

Kerim-muallim knew that it rained often in Paris, but were there heavy thunderstorms there?

Nurida-hanum announced that everything was ready and Zahra began to set down the dishes and silverware. Kerim-muallim was starving, but down deep he did not want to sit down to lunch. He didn't want them to sit down at the table because he didn't want to part with his daydream about the thunderstorm and the cloudburst. Kerim-muallim understood that the tranquillity in the house was temporary; he knew that everyone was thinking of the same thing and now a serious conversation would begin.

At that moment the doorbell rang. Hamlet entered hastily, looked at each member of the household in turn, then went up to Abdulla and asked him something in a whisper. Abdulla shook his head as if to say no, and Hamlet sat down at the table.

They all sat at the table eating the dolma; the baby, lying in his little wooden crib, was twirling his tiny hands and looking at them wondrously, as if in looking at them, he was beginning to recognize the world.

All were silent; the tinkling of forks on the plates was audible. Abdulla coughed quietly a couple of times. Zuleiha twice turned her face away from Abdulla; she ate the dolma and regretted that she was unable to immerse herself in the world of stormy amorous feelings so brilliantly described in the diary, and she looked like a mother hen.

Nurida-hanum was always Nurida-hanum, and it was she who broke the silence: "It's too bad that Shargiya has the baby on her hands. A nursing mother has so many things to take care of."

Zuleiha looked at her aunt with a concealed smirk because Nurida-hanum had a daughter from one or another of her previous marriages. The girl, apparently, now lived in Kazan, but neither Nurida-hanum nor Kerim-muallim ever spoke about her. This daughter never wrote letters, she never visited Baku, and in general Nurida-hanum herself and all the members of Kerim-muallim's household acted as if this daughter didn't even exist. Everything concerning her remained a sacred mystery, but Zuleiha suspected that she had run away from home with someone.

Nurida-hanum continued, "Shargiya can't travel to Paris. . . ."

"I am going to Paris!" said Zuleiha.

Shargiya's eyes filled with tears but, as usual, she said nothing.

Nurida-hanum looked angrily at Zuleiha, and then at Kerim-muallim, as if to say, well, why don't you have your say? Of course Kerim-muallim had the last word, and everyone sitting at the table knew it. They also knew that Kerim-muallim's last word, as always, would be in favor of Nurida-hanum.

Indeed, Kerim-muallim had put the newspapers aside, come to the table, sat down, and started on the dolma. But while chewing on the grape leaves, he was still standing under the cloudburst, under the sudden Shusha cloudburst, and the strangest thing was (Kerim-muallim himself sensed this) that secretly he did not want to get away from this downpour. Such a thing had never happened to Kerim-muallim before. Kerim-muallim always perceived warmth as warmth and cold as cold and never had he felt the need for an imaginary rain; he had never given himself over to idle daydreams. Yet now the lightning suddenly flashed, the thunder rolled, the rain poured down, and the coolness of the rain filled his heart with new sensations. Kerim-muallim could only wonder about what kind of feelings these were, what they meant, but he felt a kind of freshness, a kind of novelty, and this freshness, this novelty, simultaneously concealed a kind of sadness, reminiscent of life's passing and the monotony of being.

Kerim-muallim turned to his wife: "And what do you have to say?"

Kerim-muallim's question was extremely unexpected because for many years everyone in the house had become used to the fact that Zahra was on her feet from morning to evening preparing dinner, washing the dishes, doing the laundry, in summer making jam, marinating eggplant, putting clothes in mothballs, and in winter preparing starchy dishes, so naturally Zahra did not have the opportunity to take part in serious matters. Indeed, Zahra did not even have the desire to take part in serious matters; in this Shargiya resembled her mother. Zahra's answer, however, was even more unexpected than Kerim-muallim's question.

"Really and truly, Kerim, perhaps I should be the one to go."

Kerim-muallim's eyes popped.

"What?"

"Well, yes! I'll go and buy all of you a lot of nice things!"

Zuleiha couldn't contain herself. "But do you really know anything about fashions?"

"Why not?"

Kerim-muallim asked in amazement, "You'd go to Paris all alone, all by yourself?"

"Really, Kerim, for once in my life I'll get to go someplace. . . ."

Nurida-hanum only now came to her senses and said angrily, "What do you mean, for once in your life? You've been to Nalchik, haven't you?"

Kerim-muallim looked away. "Come to think of it, it would be interesting to know whether there are thunderstorms in Paris."

Hamlet began speaking for the first time since he had come home. Trying to hide his agitation, he asked loudly, "Do you have any idea what you're saying? You think Paris is like traveling to Mashtagi! Paris is Paris. Hey! Paris! A person who goes to Paris ought to have experience. He ought to have been abroad!"

Abdulla had been paying no attention to the conversation and had been thinking only about how he could contrive to slip away, open the eyeglasses case, find himself at liberty, wet his throat a little, and then go and play backgammon with Martiros, with whom he had been working in the hairdressing salon for forty years. But, having heard what Hamlet said, he couldn't believe his ears. Then he saw that after Hamlet had finished speaking, everyone, including Nurida-hanum, looked at him in amazement, and puffing out his chest, he straightened up; suddenly a wave of emotion seized him, sending a tremor through his entire being. The fact was that not one of the people sitting around the table in Kerim-muallim's home on that hot August day had ever traveled to another country and not one had any experience in these things except Abdulla, who had reached Vienna during the war, where he had remained for several months. He almost never thought about it, but Nurida-hanum did and quite often.

Of course Abdulla had not expected them to take him into consideration or value his experience. He had been absolutely certain that Nurida-hanum would be going to Paris, and all the remaining talk was just so much noise. As a matter of fact, deep down in his heart Abdulla was glad that Nurida-hanum would be going to Paris because then—at least for ten or fifteen days—he would be on his own; for ten or fifteen days he would breathe freely in this transitory world and he would live untrammeled—if not in Paris, then in Baku. It hadn't even entered

Abdulla's head that he himself would go to Paris, but now suddenly the pretexts for flight that he had been deliberating so carefully since the morning were forgotten, as were the fiver in the eyeglasses case and the desire to beat Mr. Martiros at backgammon. Suddenly Abdulla's chest filled with pride and he rose in his own estimation.

After his wife's unexpected words Kerim-muallim was now astonished by what his son had said; he looked at his son, then at that tippler Abdulla, but he didn't lose control and he asked his son calmly, "What are you trying to say?"

"I'm trying to say . . ." Hamlet began to blush. "It would be good . . . It would be good . . . It would be good if Farida went!"

"Who?"

"Farida! She has experience in these things! Last year . . . Last year she went to Bulgaria!"

Kerim-muallim didn't understand a thing. "Who is this Farida?"

Hamlet blushed even more, and Zuleiha said, "For five years he's been in love with Farida, he pines away for her day and night, but Farida won't have anything to do with him. Now, most likely, she has set her terms—a trip to Paris! He even wants to change his name for Farida."

Kerim-muallim was sincerely amazed. "What for?"

"Farida doesn't like his name!"

Kerim-muallim looked askance at his son and said only, "Terrific!"

Abdulla was covered in a cold sweat, a noiseless groan escaped from Abdulla's chest: Oh, you fool, you've lived so long in this world, and your head is still missing the stuff called brains. Like a cock you fanned your tail and puffed out your chest! Didn't you know that the world is rotten, that life is deceptive?

An annoyed Kerim-muallim was sitting in his own home at the table that still remained from his father's time. He was eating dolma made out of meat and grape leaves and leading the conversation. Although he marveled at the words he heard, at the same time Kerim-muallim couldn't get away from the cloudburst in Shusha and, indeed, he didn't want to get away because the coolness of that rain had an incomparable freshness and that freshness beckoned to him—it wouldn't let him go—and there was a special kind of sweetness in it.

It would be interesting to know whether there are thunderstorms in Paris.

Children finish school, go their own ways, new pupils appear, and they also call Kerim-muallim Old Blue Bag.

Kerim-muallim glanced at Zahra, Zuleiha, Hamlet, Shargiya,

Nurida-hanum, and Abdulla in turn and suddenly it occurred to him that not one of these people ever thought of saying "You go to Paris yourself." And this unexpected thought, to tell the truth, almost upset Kerim-muallim, but the hell with them, Kerim-muallim didn't need their advice. Then Kerim-muallim's gaze fell on the baby lying in the little wooden crib, twirling his little hands and examining them attentively, and again he was surprised: My God, why hadn't this baby cried once since morning?

It would be interesting to know whether there are thunderstorms in Paris.

But here Kerim-muallim got angry at himself: What a stupid question! With a shudder, Kerim-muallim tore himself away from the cloudburst, returned to the stifling heat of the August Baku day, and again became the usual Kerim-muallim.

Shargiya opened her mouth for the first time that day and started to say, "It would be interesting to know whether poor Salman—"

Kerim-muallim angrily cut off his daughter: "Why do you keep repeating, 'Salman, Salman'? What does Salman have to do with it?" And Kerim-muallim declared resolutely, "I shall go to Paris!"

Hamlet jumped up. "But you see, I . . . But you see, I . . . But you see, I gave my word to Farida!"

Kerim-muallim looked his son over from top to bottom and merely waved his hand in the air and uttered, "Ah, ah!"

None of Nurida-hanum's former husbands, none of the members of Kerim-muallim's family, none of her acquaintances, in short, no one had ever seen Nurida-hanum cry, but now her eyes suddenly filled with tears and, twisting her mouth, she declared, "But, as it is, you know the whole world. . . ."

Kerim-muallim, trying not to look at his sister, responded, "It's one thing to know but another to see with your own eyes."

Nurida-hanum said nothing more. Two teardrops rolled down her cheeks (it seems that she had finally begun to age), and she stood up and left Kerim-muallim's apartment. Abdulla also got up, looked at Kerim-muallim, shrugged his shoulders, and followed Nurida-hanum.

Kerim-muallim realized that Nurida-hanum would never enter his home again.

Once again Hamlet looked at his father, mother, and sisters in turn and asked sadly, "But what . . . But what . . . But what will I tell Farida?"

"Tell her that you're a fool!" Zuleiha cut him off and went into the large room.

3

It was the evening of the same August day.

Kerim-muallim was sitting on the veranda, drinking tea and think-ing that tomorrow he would have to get up a little earlier and, instead of going to the market or the store, he would go to the appropriate in-stitutions in order to arrange the details of his trip to Paris; one by one the faces of his fellow schoolteachers passed before Kerim-muallim's eyes and, to tell the truth, the frank amazement on their faces pleased Kerim-muallim.

Zahra was washing the dishes in the kitchen and thinking that she had to get up early and make halvah for her husband to take on his trip, because halvah is the kind of thing that never spoils and besides that it's filling, and after all, it's a foreign country—who knows what they'll have to eat there; they say that in France people eat snails, and even, they say, frogs.

Hamlet had left angry as Satan and said that he would come back in the evening, pack a suitcase, and leave the house for good, but every-body knew very well that Hamlet would soon return, sit in the kitchen, and have supper. He had taken offense and stormed off like that many times—and always, as soon as he got hungry, he would return.

Zuleiha was again lying on the sofa in the large room, reading the diary, and now she was completely immersed in the world of exalted feelings, and when she came to the place where two movie tickets were neatly affixed to the page, she couldn't hold back and began to sob and weep bitterly, because Zuleiha's girlfriend and her beloved—a shifty fellow—had gone to the movies for the last time with these tickets and they were a reminder of her unhappy love.

Shargiya had spread an old shawl on the table where they had re-cently eaten the dolma, and she was ironing baby diapers.

The baby was lying in his little wooden crib and as before he was twirling his little hands in front of his eyes.

Suddenly the doorbell rang.

Kerim-muallim opened the door.

It was the postman. He handed Kerim-muallim a telegram, and after getting Kerim-muallim's signature on the receipt and a little some-thing for the delivery, he left.

Kerim-muallim ran his eyes over the telegram, which he was hold-ing in his hand, then read it again.

The telegram was from Salman. It said, "Don't worry, I am leaving the hospital and there's no need for anyone to come to Paris."

Zuleiha, tearing herself away from the diary, got up and went to the door. Without asking Kerim-muallim anything, she took the telegram, read it herself, and said, "The fool Salman! If I were in his place . . ."

Kerim-muallim, heading for the bedroom, thought that at the family council he should have suggested that Nurida-hanum go to Paris, but who could have known that it would turn out this way; then Kerim-muallim stopped by his grandson's crib.

The baby was looking at his little hands, which he was twirling in front of his eyes, then he looked at Kerim-muallim, then again at his little hands, and suddenly he began crying loudly.

Kerim-muallim couldn't hold back: "Well, what do you know, he's howling again."

"He's voicing his protest!" Zuleiha smiled.

"What kind of protest, against whom?" Kerim-muallim frowned.

"Against us. All of us!" said Zuleiha, and she began to laugh. Then she went into the living room to contemplate the tickets again—the last relic of an unhappy love.

Not having understood a word his daughter had said, Kerim-muallim went to the window and gazed out at the little square. The pensioners were sitting there, playing dominoes and backgammon, and they didn't know that this morning, before dawn, sanitation workers had taken away several stray dogs from this very square. Then Kerim-muallim remembered that he was going to write a letter to the city council and one shouldn't put off today's work until tomorrow. He took pen and paper and sat down at the table, but the baby was crying so loudly that Kerim-muallim couldn't concentrate.

They didn't manage to pacify the baby; he cried until the middle of the night, when he got tired and fell asleep.

1985

Translated from the Russian by Stefani Hoffman.

NO SMILES

I. Grekova

The meeting ended. I had told them everything.

Perhaps I was too sharp. My friends advised me to be careful. Me—careful! That's not me, not my talent. Slick, now he's careful. He probably even came into this world carefully: poked his head out and looked around.

"Fallacious orientation in research"—that's what I was being accused of. What idiots! Anyway, I wasn't careful, I even offended a couple of the important ones. I'll have to take the consequences. That's all right, I'll take them.

After the stuffy, hypocrisy-filled hall, the street enveloped me with its coolness and simplicity. Evening—no longer spring, but not yet summer either—didn't fall, as evenings should, but, rather, soared. Swallows etched the rosy sky. I was struck by the pale emerald daylight streetlamps, prematurely and extravagantly lit by someone in this sky. How beautiful life could be. . . .

I looked at the people in the metro. They rode with concentration, swaying gently, the direct and harsh illumination from above causing the bones on each of their faces to stand out. A strict reserve separated them from one another and from me. Some were reading, many seemed tired. Next to them, softened and beautified by the depth of the dark windows, rode their reflections, which seemed kinder and simpler than the people themselves.

From the last metro stop to my house one can take a bus or walk. I walked. My legs felt heavy, but the air was cool and light. Other people's windows shone brightly to the right and to the left. Behind each of them something was going on, someone's life, which from here, from the darkness, seemed like a miracle of stability and happiness. A deep rose sky still shone in the west. Across from it dark storm clouds gathered in clumps and a wind was blowing from that direction—there could be rain tonight. A June bug hit me on the cheek and thumped onto the asphalt.

I couldn't get Slick's face out of my mind. He seemed to have spoken in support of me, but in such a way as to be able to do an about-face at any time. Two-faced virtuoso!

At home, in my empty apartment, which I am always surprised to find empty even though I have been living alone for two years, the refrigerator was singing, a window was rattling, night sounds—substitutes for crickets in new houses—were carousing: the wood floors were cracking, the wallpaper was sighing.

Whatever happens, there it is—my room, my bed, and above the bed, like a low star, the soft lamp I read by at night; for many years now I can't fall asleep without it.

Whatever happens, the day passes, night comes, the low lamp-star lights up, and I read, reveling. Daytime anxiety, my own, departs, and a foreign, nighttime one arrives and harasses me for a long time, sometimes until dawn, but more often after an hour or two my thoughts mercifully congeal and I can turn off the light, stretch my legs, and sleep.

Over the years I have gradually lost interest in everything invented, but my interest in that which is genuine has grown. Memoirs, diaries, letters, and stenographic reports rather than novels see me off to sleep. This might be a malady of advancing age; I have noticed it in many elderly, very busy readers. I use the word *readers* here as I would *smokers*.

I once asked my friend Slim about this: "Listen, don't you find that you are less and less drawn to fiction and more and more to nonfiction?" "Oh, and how!" Slim answered, and his tautly drawn face smiled. "And why is that?" Slim thought for a minute and said very seriously, "The percentage of truth is higher."

The percentage of truth. That's just it. Thank you, Slim.

I read books by the cubic meter, like a whale sucks in seawater and then lets most of it back out, leaving inside, on its baleen, only a fraction of what it ingested—the percentage of truth.

Earlier, in my youth, I was interested in the invented work. Now I am more interested in the inventor of the work. What made him, the writer, invent this and not something else? And in general, how did he live? How did he get up in the morning, was it difficult for him to get out of bed and put his perhaps swollen feet on the rug? How did he get dressed, sit down at the table, break off a piece of bread? Who brushed the crumbs off the table?

Or let's take not a writer but an actor. And not some world-renowned one, God forbid, but an ordinary, provincial actor who was known only for one talented shriek in one part of one role. This shriek has been preserved in one line of one book, *Pages of the Past,* say—reminiscences often have such titles—and the line shrieks with the voice of the long-dead actor and amazes me, and I am ready to kiss the book.

Perhaps it's not only a matter of the percentage of truth but of something else as well: the game. With age one loses the need and the ability to play the game. A kitten plays all the time. An old cat, his paws tucked under, merely squints at a paper bow.

Some people retain the ability to play longer than others; Slim and I lost this ability relatively early.

As a rule I am not very skilled at games. Chess, for example. I tried, but I just can't. And not because I am particularly stupid, I simply cannot take the rules of the game, or, as we say, the RG, seriously. In anything. In literature, say. Many people like detective stories, science fiction, but I don't. I don't accept the RG.

And I am persecuted by the RG everywhere, and everywhere I fail to understand them. There are special RG for scientific articles, for marriage, for funerals, for anniversaries. I could never master them. Perhaps I have impoverished myself as a result. If RG exist, then for that reason alone they deserve attention, which means they deserve to be studied. My purely negative, nihilistic position toward them is too emotional and unworthy of a scientist.

"Don't laugh, don't cry, just understand," Spinoza said. That's true, but for me, alas, impossible.

In many respects, I simply don't have the right kind of mind.

No, not that elementary, mercantile mind that Slick is endowed with to excess. Lord save me from such a mind. I am much more attracted to Slim's mournful, ironic mind. But I wouldn't change places with him either, no. His type of mind is, I would say, too distilled. It lacks a dash of vitality. In every wise person, it seems to me, there should be a touch of the fool. I have known Slim for many years now, but I have never been able to detect the fool in him. Either it is not there at all or it is very deeply hidden. In me, on the other hand, there is more than enough of the fool. Out of the two of us—Slim and myself—one could probably concoct one wise person.

But Slick . . .

Ugh, what a specter. He has once again appeared before me, very real, cut off at the chest by the podium: a smooth, pleasant face, a soft strand of hair combed to the side, almost free of gray. Aging bags in the corners of the cheeks are at variance with this face and almost indecent on it. Such a face should be eternally, carefully, invulnerably young. The fact that it had slightly given in to time, as if it had been dented, jarred with its decorous completeness.

Slick is the head of our Segment. Up to now he had been a rather convenient head; he didn't interfere in our work. He supported me, even promoted me, but at this meeting he realized that he had blundered. He hadn't retreated yet, but he had cleared the way for retreat. His face expressed regret—for me, but mostly for himself, for his blunder.

But these thoughts were inappropriate now, they wouldn't put you to sleep. I willed myself to banish Slick from my mind and started to read.

That night I was lucky: I happened to have a volume of *The Russian Past* for the year 1875. I get such rarities in the Book Center from our redheaded Informania, a kind soul, may God grant her a good son. The volume, as it turned out, contained Wilhelm Küchelbecker's diary, which he wrote while imprisoned in the fortress of Sveaborg in 1831–32.

The diary was prefaced by a brief history. After the event that *The Russian Past* evasively terms "fateful December 14," or "the December 14 disturbances," Küchelbecker managed to go into hiding. He was arrested in Warsaw in January of 1826 and incarcerated in one of the cells of the Peter and Paul Fortress. From there he was soon transferred to Schlüsselburg, and then to Dinaburg. "During the first period of his incarceration," writes *The Russian Past*, "when he had not yet been given either pen or ink, Küchelbecker composed poems in his head and memorized them, walking from one corner of his cell to the other."

One fortress after another. In Dinaburg—five years. Then the Revel Citadel and, finally, Sveaborg. Here Küchelbecker was held until the end of 1835, having thus served ten years in solitary confinement out of the fifteen to which he was sentenced. "Grand Duke Mikhail Pavlovich," *The Russian Past* reports, "petitioned to shorten Küchelbecker's term of incarceration by five years. . . . At the end of December 1835, he was exiled to eastern Siberia, to the city of Barguzin. . . . Grand Duke Mikhail Pavlovich sent the prisoner a beautiful bear coat, in which he traveled the many thousands of versts from Sveaborg to Barguzin."

Küchelbecker's diary begins in December 1831, that is, after six years of imprisonment. The beautiful bear fur was not yet even in the offing. The prisoner fully expected nine more years of incarceration.

I see the Sveaborg diary as a singing bird perched somewhere on the boundary between the past and the future—six years already past and nine years of the grave yet to come—and singing, singing, no matter what.

What does the prisoner write about? About the epic poem. About Schiller, Byron, Goethe, Homer. About Pushkin's poem *Eugene Onegin*; he doesn't consider it a lasting work. About humor. About the meaning of the word *tsevnitsa*.

> January 29. There are certain words on whose behalf I would like to take issue with the Academic Dictionary, such as *tsevnitsa*. For a long time I used this word in the meaning of a string instrument; Pushkin, on the other hand, attributes to it the meaning of a *wind* instrument, a flute, a reed pipe. I don't remember where, but in the work of a writer of Catherine's reign, on whom one would think one could rely, I found this word in the latter meaning and began to think that Pushkin was right. Now I revert to my previous opinion, basing it on the Slavic text of the prophet Jeremiah: "Therefore the heart of Moab shall thrum like a tsevnitsa." . . . Neither a reed pipe nor a flute ever thrums; moreover, the very meaning of the usage confirms my original opinion. *

I read the diary greedily, as children drink water after running in from outside, gurgling with every swallow. Slick, with his pleasant appearance, disappeared, vanished into nonexistence: rubbish, recycled garbage.

I read half the night, then I slept and dreamed of a garden.

---

*In the King James version this line actually reads, "Therefore mine heart shall sound for Moab like pipes . . ." (Jeremiah 48:36). —Trans.

I didn't start thinking over my situation until morning. My alarm clock, with the gentle voice of its new, merciful construction (before it starts clanging it tinkles melodiously for a while), led me out of sleep and out of the garden in such a way that the first tinklings were still in the garden and only the last ones here, in harsh reality. By the time the alarm clock finished its prelude and began roaring with all its might, I was fully awake and it had all come back to me. Well, then, we will do battle. Slick irritated me like a callus. I didn't want to go to the Institute but I had to, so I went, but only after taking my own sweet time to wash, dress, drink tea, and even sit with my hands between my knees.

No sooner had I stepped across the threshold of the Institute than I realized that everything had changed. Before, without my even being aware of it, I had lived in a world of smiles. And now, in the course of one night, they had disappeared. Almost completely. I met with only two or three smiles in the corridor. With revulsion I noticed that I was counting them.

In the Special Division I was told that a commission had been appointed to my Case, which would be discussed in a week. The girls were distressed and full of sympathy, in spite of the inevitable element of joy with which every one of us delivers a piece of news, however unpleasant. The pure joy of possessing Information.

Fine, if there's to be a commission, so be it. Outwardly, I didn't blink an eye, though my toes curled as if a snake had slithered by.

I wished I knew what was behind all this. What and who.

The worst of it was that I had to wait a whole week. Waiting is difficult in any case, waiting for something bad—loathsome. Would that it were worse, if it were only quicker. The week didn't go by, it stuck, bogged down, clung with all its minutiae. And, as bad luck would have it, my work didn't go well.

"Don't be nervous, just work calmly," Grayhair told me, stroking his vest. I looked at him with hatred. Somehow everything about him became repugnant to me, his large, clean ears, his turned-up beard, his unhurried speech full of subordinate clauses. An old intellectual with the soul of a young coward.

All that week I went to the Institute with the persistence of a pendulum, although I could have not gone. I could have said that I would go to the Cryostatic Center or somewhere else. I simply could have failed to show up; nobody would have penalized me for it. But I went and, as before, counted smiles; there were fewer and fewer of them every day. Or did it just seem that way to me? I looked very attentively at the people I ran into—they weren't smiling. Some pretended that they were going in the wrong direction. Others averted their eyes to avoid greeting me. Still others greeted me but didn't smile. The very few who did smiled forcibly, with only one side of their mouth.

But how I needed them, the smiles! I hadn't noticed them before, I had lived in them like a fish in water. I was still a fish, but on sand, moving my dried-up gills. With my gills I begged for smiles, implored, extorted. So that no one would notice this, I affected a haughty air. I answered nods with something like a reverse nod: instead of dropping my chin, I jerked it up.

Sometimes I thought I saw sympathy on the faces of people I met, a desire to come up to me. I walked past even these with the same stiffness, afraid to destroy it: it was my crutch and it was fragile. Who knows how many possible friends I walked past with my reverse nod?

It was particularly unpleasant to run into Slick. All these days he seemed not to leave the corridor and I encountered him at every turn. Each time he bowed with exaggerated politeness, with that heartfelt sorrow with which the faithful kiss the shroud of Christ.

Still, I was not lonely. I had three friends: Slim, Dark, and Bald. I have already spoken about Slim, but Dark and Bald were also my friends. We once worked together, now we're in different departments, but the friendship has lasted. All three came to see me right after the incident and they were all prepared to support me if necessary. I was unpleasantly struck by their concern. No, I was not yet drowning, thank God. I told them, "I know of no blame on my part; but I am afraid for those who were compassionate toward me—it is horrifying to think that they might suffer unpleasant consequences for their philanthropy."

Dark and Bald looked at me as though I were crazy. Slim asked:

"Where is that from?"

"Küchelbecker's diary," I answered.

"Let me read it," he said avidly.

"And so you shall when I finish it." Here I burst out laughing: They had such funereal faces. "My friends, you look as if you're at a wake. Strictly speaking, nothing is going on. A commission, a discussion, so what? I know that there will be a lot of stench, but no one dies of stench."

"They choke," said Slim.

"Don't exaggerate," Bald scolded him.

"In any case, you can count on us," said Dark.

"We'll just see what happens."

Loving them as I did, I was cold: all three of them stood there for a while, sympathizing, then left.

I read Küchelbecker's diary every night before bed and I still couldn't part with it: I finished it and started reading it again.

The prisoner lived. He discussed art, science, religion; he observed scenes in the prison courtyard. He studied Greek. He wrote poetry.

Küchelbecker was unlucky as a poet; his poems were amicably ridiculed by literary tradition, starting with Pushkin: "Wilhelm, read us your rhymes, / So that we may fall asleep betimes." For me, on the contrary, these poems thwarted sleep, resonating in me with a hazy, terrible, dim harmony. Certain verses were positively beautiful:

> But throngs of suns that roll above,
> Can never by a living soul
> Be weighed on scales of holy love:
> Not ours the scales of the Perpetual.

And hardly a word about his own fate. About his suffering. About his hopes—he had none. Only in one or two places does a kind of wail break through: "My God! When will it end? When will my ordeal end?" And then, again tranquillity, reflection, poems, dreams.

> January 12. For about a week now I have been having extremely lively dreams: last night I flew, or, rather, strode through the air—this dream, in various forms, comes to me quite often; but tonight I saw unimaginably lifelike horrors. It is most pleasant when I dream of children: then I am supremely happy and become a child along with them.

How true it is that bright dreams help us live! I, for example, would dream of the garden: green, lush, varied, with coarse gravel on moist paths that bore the imprint of someone's footsteps—nobody was walking on the paths; the footsteps appeared all by themselves. The dream would stay with me all morning and fully disappear only at the Institute. My days were filled with fruitless thoughts. I would spend them not in the Apparatus Division, which was my post, but in the Winding Division. There were fewer people there, only two were doing the winding and paid no attention to me; perhaps they hadn't even heard about my Case. I would take a pile of journals with me and look through them—an almost mechanical function, like knitting. Or I would draw labyrinths of pathways, branching patterns, with a question mark at each dead end. I would think. I would survey the troops. Quite honestly, there were not many of them. Slick would sell out; he already had. Fussy was on maternity leave—her usual bad timing. Then there were two students—First and Second. First was more knowledgeable and talented. Second was young and uninformed, easy to divert. I decided not to involve my friends. If they came of their own accord, that was their business.

I imagined how the Discussion would turn out—what they would say, what answers I would give them. If they said this, I'd counter with that. "Facts," I would say, "cannot be fallacious, and here are my facts." No, that wouldn't be right. I would simply ridicule them, that's what I would do. And I imagined myself ridiculing them. I made speeches without restricting myself to the time limit. Fortunately, I made these speeches only during the day. At night I slept, and every night I dreamed of the garden.

The appointed day came at last, ushered in by rain and cold. The Discussion was to take place at four o'clock—at 16:00, as it said in the notification. I spent the morning at home, reading the Sveaborg diary again.

> August 15. Today I witnessed a scene similar to the one that amused me on July 23, that is: I laughed aloud watching a kitten making advances toward an old hen: the kitten fawned on her—it would run toward her from one side, then from the other, it would crawl up to her, hide, jump out, hide again, and several times even patted her with its paw with the utmost care and courtesy; but the philosopher-hen pecked one grain after another with stoical firmness and paid no attention whatsoever to the rascal. For this indifference she was rewarded with absolute victory: every time the wind ruffled her very inelegant feathers, Mr. Kitten, probably thinking that she was about to punish him for his impudence, beat a shameful retreat; but the magnanimous hen was just as mindless of her victories as she was scornful of her cowardly and yet audacious enemy; she did not even glance at him, did not turn her head toward him, she was occupied with something much more important: Kernels of grain were to her

what mathematical computations were to Archimedes, for which
he was killed by a Roman soldier.

I should be such a hen, huh?

It was already time to get ready, however. I dressed with the greatest
care, as for a holiday. Oh, how good it would be if I were pretty today;
unfortunately, that is no longer possible. There was no point in being
nervous, so I took two tranquilizers just in case, and two more—jolly
and green—with me. Purse, pencil, pad of paper, cigarettes.

After two, Dark called and said that he and the other two (Bald and
Slim) were denied permission to attend.

"Why?" I asked with a dry mouth.

"They say we're not specialists."

"Nonsense! As if only specialists are going to be there."

"Call the chairman so that they'll let us in." He gave me the number.

"I'm not going to call."

"Why? Don't you want us to come?"

"No, I don't."

It came out rudely. Dark took offense and hung up.

Well, that was unnecessary. I should have explained to him. . . . But
first I should explain to myself: Why don't I want them to come?

Why?

I thought about it all the way to the Institute. The bus was crowded.
My bag was squeezed between two backs, I was angry and ready to bite.
Other people's mouths breathing at close range made me think of con-
tagion. *That's it*, I thought, *It's all a matter of contagiousness. I am like
a contagious patient, I don't want to infect others. I will try to sneeze
past them. . . .*

There was more room in the metro and my thoughts changed. Now
it seemed to me that the reason was that all three of them were not my
coworkers but friends. They would stand up for me because it was me,
and for my Case because it was *my* Case. Neither I nor my Case
needed such standing-up-for. That is to say, it was all for the best. It
came out reasonably and even nobly.

Only when I approached the Institute did I realize that this was all
nonsense, that it was not at all for the best and, in fact, I wanted them
to come.

Oh, human stupidity!

In the large auditorium of the Council, with its creamy-white molded
ceilings, it was cool, and I immediately froze. Why the devil had I put

on summer clothing? The tall, graceful windows were open, letting in a breeze that shook the leathery leaves of the rubber plants. These rubber plants—the pride of the Institute—have been growing here since time immemorial. They were huge, treelike, beautifully taken care of, each leaf like a boat. It was as if the meetings of the Council took place in a garden. I used to like it, but now I didn't. I didn't want to be worked over in a garden. I would have preferred an ordinary room with standard furniture and inventory numbers on the tables and chairs. But when I looked more closely I saw that even here there were inventory numbers: on every rubber-plant tub shone a little oval plate. This somehow consoled me. The wind, however, was blowing too hard; the hairs on my bare arms stood on end, each on its own goose bump, and I was afraid someone would notice. It would be better to close the windows. I walked up to the nearest one and entered into battle with the latches. The massive bronze latches with roosters' heads—antiquity incarnate!—turned with difficulty. Slick ran over when I was at the third latch:

"Why are you doing this yourself, M.M., you should be ashamed. With so many men around . . ."

And, indeed, there were a lot of men. I stepped back. With a knightly air, Slick clambered onto a chair and busied himself with the latches.

The members of the Commission assembled slowly. The musical palace clock (it played something that sounded like "How Glorious") had long since struck four and the members were still arriving. They greeted each other with a quiet solemnity appropriate to the occasion and took their seats. Before sitting down each one made a low bow in my direction. At four fifteen the clock played its tune again, yet the members kept filing in. In such a garden filled with chimes, fountains should have been gushing. The men kept increasing in number; there were now about forty—or maybe less, because I was seeing some of them double.

The last to come in was the chairman of the Commission—a gnome with the little yellow face of an embryo, a lost and very likely pained face under a round, swollen, and utterly barren skull.

"Comrades," said Gnome, "insofar as we have, so to speak, a quorum of Commission members and invited guests, allow me to open the meeting. On today's agenda . . ."

I barely listened to the opening speech. I knew it ahead of time. I could have delivered every phrase of it for him. These were the RG (rules of the game) in their purest form, without subtleties. My mouth was dry and I was gradually overcome by a heavy feeling of flight. It carried me over the rubber plants, over the lowered, permed heads of the two stenographers. As if from above, I saw the foreshortened faces of the Commission and invited guests. They were very serious, I would say impassive, faces. Only one face was animated—Blowhard's. He was sitting very actively; in fact, he wasn't so much sitting as prancing on his chair, jumping, itching for a fight. Everything in him spoke: his fat hands, sagging face, energetic belly, fingers drumming on the side of the chair.

"Of course, we all respect M.M. as an old and honored member of our collective . . ." said Gnome.

"No point in sweetening the pill," shouted Blowhard, jumping up about ten centimeters. "Respect has nothing to do with it!"

"We have great respect for M.M., but . . ." Gnome continued imperturbably.

"Speak for yourself!" shouted Blowhard. "Personally, I don't respect her. She has placed herself outside respect!"

"You will have your turn to speak," Gnome said calmly.

Blowhard stopped talking, but his body continued to speak.

After about ten minutes Gnome finished his introduction and proclaimed:

"Comrades, who would like to speak?"

Several hands went up. Among them, naturally, was Blowhard's fat, zealous hand. It even quivered with fervor. However, not he but Slick was given the floor first.

Slick didn't speak, he enumerated. This was not the primitive standard on which, say, Gnome operated: this was a standard of a higher order, grade A. To the inexperienced mind he may even have sounded sincere, with a tear in his voice. An artist, no doubt about it. His artistry was also displayed in his ability to support each sentence with stipulations, just in case. . . . His general tone was extremely soft. In music this would probably be marked *dolce, con pietà* (tenderly, compassionately).

"Don't beat around the bush!" shouted Blowhard from his chair, which was about to explode under him. "Say it straight, without all this intellectual mumbo-jumbo, do you or do you not condemn this outrageous, this unpre . . . unprede . . ."

He got stuck, of course, on the word *unprecedented. Oh, my friend,* I thought, *you've been going through life in sheep's clothing. . . .*

"Unprend . . ." persisted Blowhard. I noticed several timid smiles. "Go ahead and laugh, comrades," howled Blowhard. "We'll see who laughs last!"

The smiles faded.

"Of course," Gnome said with dignity and sadness, "we all regret—"

"We do not regret, we are indignant," Satanic said distinctly.

Only then did I notice him. He was sitting quietly, symmetrically, like a statue of a pharaoh, holding his briefcase upright on his lap. His dyed hair grew low on his forehead, almost from his menacingly shaggy, slightly beetling eyebrows.

Slick was confused, thrown off balance, and, crumbling, feebly finished his speech. Under Satanic's iron gaze there was no salvation even in duplicity.

Then Blowhard finally got the floor. He stood up, surrounded by his sagging belly like an air balloon by its casing, and pointed his fat finger at me. That finger, aimed directly at my face, seemed thicker at the tip than at the base, just as in photographs taken at close range.

"She . . ." shouted Blowhard.

He was already fired up and now he was turning white-hot. He shouted tensely, floridly, in his own way eloquently and in his own way with talent. He suffered. He sweated. He was bathed in sweat. His outrage poured out of him at a pressure of several hundred atmospheres.

The finger mesmerized me; it seemed directed straight at my brain, where, who knows, perhaps a lethal tumor nestled. I listened, and the heavy feeling of flight grew. Some sort of drills were boring in my ears. Outwardly I remained calm, shuddering only occasionally.

"She . . ." shouted Blowhard, and I flinched as if lashed by a whip at this third-person-singular feminine pronoun.

What's the matter? I thought during the intervals. *It must be my sensitivity. Until now no one has said "she." They've said "M.M.," or more often "respected M.M.," or even more often "our respected M.M."*

"She . . ." Blowhard shouted again, and my whole body quivered like a horse.

Why doesn't the chairman stop him? I thought in dumb amazement. *But then, maybe neither he nor Blowhard understands that it is insulting. How are they supposed to know what a woman feels like when they call her, when they shout at her, "she" as though they had brought her out onto a square in front of a tavern for corporal punishment. . . . Maybe none of them understands?*

I looked around, seeking some kind of response in the faces. No, there was no response. Save perhaps one man, sitting in a chair to the side—he looked completely satisfied. Red, sturdy, he sat casually, his legs spread apart, his hands resting on his knees, his elbows bent like some kind of pretzel. He was enjoying himself. He was basking in the proceedings. He was nodding in approbation. I didn't know him; he must have been sent by some outside party.

And Blowhard was shouting, vibrating from the effort. Now I understood why he was shouting. By shouting he was driving himself toward sincerity. The louder he shouted, the more he believed in his own words. He had already switched from "I" to "we." This expanding "we" poked its finger at me, as though there were many of him, and many fingers, millions and millions, and all were united.

The drills bored cruelly in my ears. I might as well have bent down and sought refuge under the table. *If I can only hang on*, I thought. Surreptitiously, I got out one of the extra tablets and swallowed it, awkwardly, maneuvering my tongue. It didn't help, my mouth only became drier and the heavy feeling of flight grew until in some sense I felt as if I were walking on the ceiling. I closed my eyes so as not to collapse. Someone touched my shoulder from behind. I turned around and saw a friendly, openly sympathetic pair of eyes. I knew Touched only slightly: he worked somewhere in a distant Transistor Division. I smiled at him as at a friend. He leaned over and whispered something in my ear. At first I didn't understand.

"Louder," I said. "My ears are ringing."

"He's ruining himself," Touched whispered louder. "And he's a fine one himself. A moral degenerate–recidivist. You know, I was told . . ."

I waved Touched away like a fly. I turned back to the Finger and staunchly looked at him to the end. And the end came suddenly. Blowhard fell silent and sat down abruptly, as if he had been punctured and the air had gone out of him. Breathing heavily and wiping the sweat off his face with two handkerchiefs, he drooped over both sides of his chair. He had already sat down and was mopping his brow when he remembered something, jumped up again, and shouted in a fantastic falsetto:

"I advise her—renounce your work in writing! That would be a noble deed!"

And then he sat down for good. He earned his bread by the sweat of his brow.

What followed became all muddled in my mind. I no longer remember who spoke and how. I remember that they railed at me with a fierceness that amazed me, those same people who used to smile at me every day. Naturally, otherwise they wouldn't have been assigned to the Commission. . . . But I was no longer listening. I was busy with my ears. Something was wrong with them: I would either go completely deaf or I would suddenly begin to hear with an extreme acuteness, so that my little wristwatch ticked like a tower clock, playing "How Glorious." When I went deaf, people acted like characters in a silent movie: they moved their mouths as if they were chewing and made incongruous gestures. The absence of subtitles was painful. Then I realized that I could imagine the subtitles myself, and the fun began. They talked and I provided the subtitles. I was guided by the face of the red one, who sat like a pretzel. He sat in his chair as on a platter, on his own silver platter, and nodded good-naturedly, from which it was clear: All was well, they were blasting me.

It was during one of my attacks of deafness that Blond began to speak. He was unknown to me: Tall, erect, thin-nosed, his fine hair neatly combed. He got up, knee deep in people. My deafness was not total: through it I could hear that Blond's voice was high and irritating. In the subtitles I read how he vilified me, what civil, well-oiled words he used. By then the drills in my ears had turned to cymbals: bam!— and shhh . . . bam!—and shhh—there was a whistling rattle at the end of each strike that resembled the sound "sh" stretched out like a vowel. The abusive subtitles ran on. Just in case, I again checked with Pretzel. Amazing—he didn't seem all that pleased! He changed his pose, took his hands off his knees, no longer looked like a pretzel. Suddenly a wrinkle of skin rolled up his red face and I realized that Blond was not vilifying me at all, that he was speaking—for me!

"Oh, let me hear, let me hear!" I prayed, looking at Blond's face. And lo—a miracle!—the cymbals fell silent, the deafness vanished, and the high voice speaking "for me" broke through clearly. It wasn't irritating; on the contrary, it was calm and precise, with that gentlemanly restraint toward the opponent that only truth possesses.

But who is he, where did he come from? In Blond's words I recognized my very own thoughts, only better, more perfect, free of that female emotionality of which I, alas, cannot rid myself. I looked straight at his mouth.

The Chairman raised the hand on which he wore his watch and said, "Time limit."

"I am almost finished," answered Blond, "but it seems to me that the others spoke longer."

"Call him off the floor!" shouted Blowhard.

"Time limit, time limit!" many shouted.

Blond shrugged his shoulders, smiled, and fell silent.

Oh, it was intolerable to me that they hadn't let him finish! Not because of me, Lord, no! What were all these squabbles compared to scientific truth? No, it was just that I desperately had to know what he, that is, what I myself, thought about one issue on which I had not yet formed an opinion. . . . Oh, my God . . .

"And who invited this comrade? We didn't ask for him," said Satanic in a funereal voice.

"Don't worry, I'm leaving." Blond turned his tall back to the hall, gathered some things from his chair, and moved toward the exit.

. . . Now he'll leave, and I'll never find out what I think about that issue. I jumped up and mumbled something, stretching my arms, yes, stretching them toward the door. Satanic's reptilian gaze was fixed on me—I felt it as two hot points on my back. Someone was running toward me with a glass of water.

"It's nothing, I don't need anything," I said, and sat down. The glass stood on the green cloth, and the water rocked in it.

"We will resume the discussion," said Gnome, "the floor is now given to . . ."

From that moment on I heard everything. I wasn't interested, but I heard everything. There was a pad of paper in front of me, a pencil in my hand. I wrote down some expressions that seemed particularly characteristic. The RG, taken to their grotesque extreme.

"The author allows herself to make mocking remarks about certain comrades . . ." (Oh, that word, *certain!*)

"For a long time now one cannot help but notice a tendency toward regression and decline . . ."

"That may be what it says overtly, but isn't the implication clear to us?" I wrote. The orators were upset by this. I saw them mentally stand on tiptoe and glance at my pad over the shoulders and heads of the audience. One of the speakers said, "Idealithm." I wrote down the word with a huge "th" and showed it to him from a distance. He probably couldn't make out a thing.

Two or three of the speeches were in support of me. One quite old Speaker (a friend in the past) defended me with flowing ambiguities. He emphasized my sterling personal qualities. It turned out that, in spite of my errors—and who does not make them?—I was all in all not a bad person.

"And, moreover, a woman," said Speaker sweetly, "and where is our chivalry, comrades?"

At this point I purposely blew my nose—very loud, very unfeminine.

My Second student spoke "for." He was young, a fumbler, with feathery hair. He, thank God, defended, or tried to defend, not me but the Case. Blowhard once again started to prance in his chair. Second spoke, convulsed with nervousness; he squeezed a manuscript in his hands, inserted "you know?" into very sentence, scared himself by doing this, poor thing, unaccustomed as he was to speaking at such an Areopagus, not knowing any of the RG, nothing.

"Demagogy!" shouted Blowhard. "Everyone knows she wrote his dissertation for him. She scratches his back, he scratches hers!"

Second moaned softly. Blowhard jumped up and knocked over a rubber plant. Soil poured out of the numbered tub. The rubber plant lay there like a person with outstretched arms. They ran to it, lifted it up, calmed it down.

After the fall of the rubber plant Second wasn't given the floor again. He didn't even request it. He sat there hanging his head, and a premature bald spot showed pink among the feathers. He was marked, in some sense condemned.

Unexpectedly, my First student, my greatest hope, my ace of trump, deceived me. I realized immediately that this ace was beat. Or the other way around—now, how was it in the "Queen of Spades"?

The ace won.

"Your queen has lost," said Chekalinsky sweetly.*

And so the ace won. At first he hedged, not wanting to speak for or against. Listening to him was like drinking from a clyster: it was water, but it was disgusting. Blowhard jumped up and pointed his index finger at First. "Get him, get him!" I said, completely on Blowhard's side. First couldn't take it. He began to babble, turning for some reason to me:

"You see, I had to admit my mistakes to defend you."

I laughed.

"Will you allow me?" an agitated voice was heard. "I haven't signed up, but . . ."

"Why not, we are fully democratic here," Gnome answered with dignity.

From the back rows Slantbelly squeezed forward with some diffi-

---

*Germann, the ill-fated hero of Pushkin's story, had inadvertently caused the death of an old countess, from whom he had been trying to elicit the identity of three winning cards. Her ghost then appeared to him and told him that the three cards would be a three, a seven, and an ace. Playing against Chekalinsky, Germann won the first two cards, but in the third game he drew the queen of spades (the old countess) instead of an ace. He subsequently went mad, mumbling, "Three, seven, ace! Three, seven, queen!" —Trans.

culty. His bald head, high and egg-shaped, shone above the chairs. Along the way he was busy opening his briefcase and taking papers out of it. Under his arm a roll of paper hung obliquely. This turned out to be a graph. He hung it on the blackboard and directed the dark gaze of a maniac at the auditorium.

"Comrades," he began, "comrades!"

Something decisive was bound to follow.

"I am in full agreement with all who have spoken here. . . ."

A murmur passed along the chairs.

"But that is not the point. I consider it essential, precisely in connection with the serious discussion at hand, to raise once again an urgent matter. This is the matter of payment for scientific publications. . . ."

"Please, more to the point," said Gnome.

"The point should be examined in its totality. And what is our situation? The fee for scientific publications is paid out only if those publications are not part of the plan! Notice the *not!* And this in our planned economy, where, as they say—the plan is law!"

The murmur grew.

"What is the result, comrades?" exclaimed Slantbelly. "In order to receive a well-deserved fee, a hard-earned kopeck, I have to present to the publisher a disgraceful certificate, I repeat, disgraceful, that my work was done not as part of the plan but outside it!"

"He's right!" shouted Blowhard.

"It turns out," Slantbelly continued, becoming inspired, "that if I scribbled some nonsense with my left foot in my spare time it will be paid for! But if, working honestly, I wrote a book as part of the plan—zip!"

With his thumb planted squarely between his first two fingers, he raised a maliciously flashing fist. Many laughed.

"Order, comrades," Gnome said paternally. "And I would ask you once again—more to the point."

"How much closer could it be!" Slantbelly gave a laugh. "The facts are before you! On file and numbered! I was not supported last time, but I have not been napping since then, I've covered all the bases. Here on the graph you can see the print runs of all publications, including scientific ones, including the library of military expeditions, including so-called artistic prose. Ha-ha! I personally read it and found nothing artistic about it. Colorless, petty, as our critics correctly describe it. And the fees? Well, here I have . . ."

He began to read aloud from one of the files, which listed print runs and fees for all writers from A to Z.

"But this is still not quite to the point," noted Gnome patiently.

"Why not, it's interesting!" several voices rang out.

Slantbelly continued to read, breaking into a sardonic laugh from time to time. Large print runs, and fees in particular, elicited a cackle.

. . . They seemed to have forgotten about me. Everyone was listening.

"We believe you, we believe you," said Gnome. "You can show these materials to those who are interested in the lobby."

"Very well." Slantbelly threw down the file. "Let's speak in general terms. From the cited facts it is evident that we scientists have fallen tragically behind in terms of both fees and print runs. And why? Because there is no paper? Nonsense! There are more than enough notebooks. Toilet paper is produced by the bolt. It's true that there is never enough of it, but that is just self-indulgence. Produce is packed in paper wrapping. And desk calendars? I was just recently telling M.M. . . ."

He looked in my direction and faltered. Everyone looked at me. They remembered me.

"Everything that you have reported is very interesting," said Gnome, collecting himself, "but with regard to our topic for today—"

"I haven't used up my time yet," objected Slantbelly.

"Your time is up," said Gnome gently. "And so, let us return to today's agenda. Who would like to speak on the subject?"

And then Satanic stood up.

He put his briefcase on the chair, raised his hand like a semaphore, and began to roar. His belligerent voice immediately cast aside all thoughts of fees and print runs. He roared to the point—that is, against me. His dyed hair from his eyebrows up stood on end. There was something shamanistic in his bearing. He posed rhetorical questions and then immediately answered them himself, as if in the name of some subservient spirit.

His belligerent voice made one's flesh crawl. But in a certain sense Satanic was better than the others. He believed, they didn't. No, they believed, but only in themselves, in their vulnerable well-being, in its very vulnerability. Now it was less dangerous to condemn—so they condemned. Well, Blowhard—he simply begged forgiveness for moral recidivism. In general, not one of them would risk anything for my sake—not a square centimeter of their living space, not a kopeck of their pay.

Satanic was different. He would probably even agree to a 10 percent pay cut just to destroy me. I watched him with interest verging on compassion. I wondered what he was like inside. What did he think about when he was alone at night, alone with his dreams? And what were they like, those dreams? I imagined that belligerent void and I felt sorry for him, I honestly did.

"Comrades, we have been working for over three hours," said Gnome, "there are no more registered speakers. A motion has been made to adjourn the discussion."

"Adjourn, adjourn," the rows responded.

"Then allow me, as chairman, to summarize."

The results were summarized in the usual manner. Gnome spoke about the healthy comradely criticism, about the fruitful discussion, in the course of which it was disclosed that . . .

"I hope that respected M.M. will draw the proper conclusions from our discussion, will admit her errors, and will restructure herself. . . ."

He turned that sad face of an embryo toward me.

"Would you like to have the floor?"

Yes, I did.

Strangely enough, although I knew I would have to speak, I was completely unprepared. However, it wasn't important. No matter what I said, it could not influence the Summary. Everyone present looked at me attentively, with rounded lips; on these lips I saw, already prepared, the smiles with which they would reward me if I accepted the RG. But what can you do? I had no choice.

"No," I said, "I refuse to admit my mistakes, because there were none. I am right. Burn me if you will, but I can't do anything else."

"No one plans to burn you," Gnome interrupted me seriously.

"Well, okay. I used the wrong term. Do with me as you will. . . ."

I couldn't speak anymore and sat down. Something was going on with my heart. It was expanding like Blowhard. It sagged over the chair. Some kind of auricles or ventricles . . . A *heart attack factory*, I thought. *No, not on your life, I'm not going to allow them to drive me to a heart attack. Hey, you there,* I said to my heart, *hush, keep in line.*

Then the noise started. It rained down like a massive thunderstorm. Individual streams of water pounded. And then, as it intensified, everything was drowned out by Satanic's wolfish howl. This was more than I could take. That howl was killing me—in the most literal, physical way. Tripping over chairs, stumbling on the wood floor, knocking against the rubber plants, I made my way to the door and left.

As soon as I closed the door behind me, I was set free. Blocked by the door, the howl was not as deafening. The door created the illusion of safety. My eyes burned. That's all I needed—tears! I hated that despicable feminine weakness. I hated all fluids on earth, all the tears and snivel and saliva in the world. My hatred bucked me up. By the time I reached the front door, I was already calm, thank God. On the street stood my three friends: Dark, Slim, and Bald. They had come after all.

"Well, how did it go?" they asked in unison.

"Not bad," I answered.

"Was it awful?" asked Bald compassionately.

"Moderately awful."

"As the saying goes—all against one, one for all," said Slim.

Dark laughed. Bald dismissed him with a wave of his hand and continued to question me:

"Most important, what position did the chairman take?"

I told him:

"The standard one. And he looked like an embryo in alcohol."

And so my new life began. The arms of Failure embraced me. I got used to them remarkably quickly. As though it had always been this way.

And yet it had always been different. As long as I could remember I had always been accompanied by Success. It elected me to every presidium, spoke about me every March 8.* And how: A woman scientist, author of serious works, translated into other languages, and so on and so forth. I became used to Success, as though it were something to be taken for granted. It turns out that it was not to be so taken.

Perhaps the thoughtlessness with which I accepted Success turned into my submissive acceptance of Failure. Some writer, Dostoevsky, I think it was, said that man is a creature who can get used to anything, and that is his best definition. That's how one grows accustomed to illness, grief, slavery.

My name became a common noun, then a swear word. It was declined, mentioned, knocked about, malevolently criticized at dozens of meetings.

I was caught up in the iron stream of the work-over. It seemed as if everything had been foreseen, spelled out in stock phrases like notes in a musical score. Very specific, particular RG ruled here, with the clear features not simply of custom but of ritual.

Before, this ritual was foreign to me: basking in Success, I observed

* International Women's Day. —Trans.

it from the outside, with no great interest in what it was about and who was right; I had enough concerns of my own. Now I had the opportunity to observe this process from the inside. I was given the opportunity to study the phenomenon of the work-over from the most advantageous position—from the point of view of the worked-over person. Well, what of it? I can't say that it was pleasant, but still, it did give me some intellectual satisfaction. The ineradicable habit of the scientist: to look for regularity and repetitive features in everything. I will probably die that way.

By observing, recalling, comparing, I was able to outline the following general rules:

Every work-over (of whatever scale or significance) has at its foundation someone's personal interest. Let's say someone wants to free up a position and install his own candidate; another is desperate to become a member of the Academy; a third wants to boost his flagging authority; and so forth. At the foundation of a work-over one might also find a group's rather than an individual's interest. The connections of the various interests to the course and direction of the work-over often may be unclear, clandestine, and not subject to ordinary logic.

Once started, a work-over develops in a branching process. First of all a certain deed (an article, a book, a personal statement) is condemned and introduced into a resolution (of what kind is unimportant). Thus is born the basic trunk (or riverbed) of the work-over process. Then it begins to branch out, like a tree or a river delta. Both analogies are imprecise because the branching of a tree or a river takes place in space; that of a work-over, in time. With a correction for this one imprecision, the analogies apply.

And so the work-over branches out. The process of the multiplication of resolutions goes on. In every small, secondary subresolution the condemnation formula is adopted from the basic parent one, literally where possible, after which variations become possible but within narrow limits. In general the precision of the RG decreases in proportion to the distance from the basic riverbed. On distant branches one not infrequently notices deviations. Sometimes totally wild branches appear, of the type, "Wonders abound there, / And goblins ramble."*

Having flowed out along a multitude of tiny tributaries, after a time the work-over displays a kind of tendency to peter out. Sometimes, as an exception, it happens like this: A work-over may, for example, wither away in the shadow of a new and younger one (an intraspecies

---

*From Alexander Pushkin's *Ruslan and Lyudmila*. —Trans.

battle is possible among various specimens). It is more often the case, however, that the weakened work-over mechanism gets a certain invigorating impulse and starts to function with new strength. A second wave appears; often it rises higher than the first. New victims (objects) are dragged into the process, particularly those who opposed the first wave or promoted it with insufficient zeal. In rare cases a distinctive pulsating process develops that periodically produces waves of nearly uniform force.

Every wave is usually accompanied by someone's heart attack, sometimes two or more. By the number of heart attacks one can indirectly judge the intensity of the process. It must be noted that not only the victims (the objects) of a work-over suffer heart attacks, but the performers (subjects) as well.

The performers can rarely be equated with the interested parties. The truly interested parties prefer to remain out of the spotlight. This allows them, if necessary, to renounce everything. The performers talk about the true initiators enigmatically: "we were told," "it has been recommended to us," "it is believed."

The life span of a work-over varies—from several months to two, three, or, in rare instances, more years. There are specimens that, after a period of aggressive and prolific functioning, seem to fall into a state of anabiosis. The objects of work-overs in such cases are considered neither directly guilty nor directly vindicated (an analogy: souls in purgatory for Catholics). Mentioning them either in a positive or in a negative way is not recommended.

There are instances, and not all that rare, when a work-over that has not run its full cycle of development dies a sudden death. There may be various causes: a phone call from a powerful person, a successfully directed complaint, an article in an influential periodical.

I was now observing the conception and development of my own personal specimen of a work-over and, naturally, it interested me more than others (just as, say, your own tapeworm is of more interest than one preserved in alcohol).

So far, events were developing as expected. A month or six weeks after the Discussion, an apparent period of calm set in, but I did not delude myself: Ahead, by all indications, one could expect the second wave, which promised to be higher than the first. Petty repressions began: They took away my second laboratory room, my winder's salary, my transformer cross. First one person, then another was called in, including both of my students. Contrary to logic, First got hit harder, even though he had renounced me. Such violations of logic are not infrequent, particularly on outlying branches; I relegate them to the category of deviations.

One at a time my three friends, Dark, Bald, and Slim, were called in. The word *faction* was used. From another source I found out that Blond—he, it turned out, worked in the Radial Division—had also been called in somewhere. Slantbelly dissociated himself from me in a penitential letter addressed to the proper authorities. The letter was received with bewilderment; all in all, he did not raise the value of his political stock.

In the meantime I did not take a leave of absence: there is nothing worse than being absent during a wave. I did, after all, get something accomplished. I managed to get an appointment at the Measuring Equipment Department, KIP, where I was favorably received and promised that my request would be looked into. The person who had promised immediately went on vacation, and his substitute, who knew nothing about my request, was cold on the phone.

I wrote a letter to Blond at the Radial Division and asked him about the issue that was unclear to me. It turned out that it was also unclear to Blond, but he wrote nicely and intelligently. In the meantime my experiment was showing some promise—at my station it was sometimes possible to forget about everything.

The deviations continued; my article was unexpectedly published. It had been lying around for over a year in the Periodical Section in limbo for being too debatable. . . . Now they went and published it. Obviously, it had slipped by the editor. I only hoped no one would suffer. The growing awareness of my own contagiousness was torturous: the very air around me was becoming plague-infected. I reread my article: It seemed boring and arrogant. . . .

The transformation of my surroundings into a world with no smiles was reaching completion. Slick and a few others stopped greeting me just in case.

I couldn't have cared less about that, but quite independent of them a dull dread settled in me. Even at home, under the low lamp, it did not leave me. In despair I clung to Küchelbecker's diary, reading and rereading it, squeezing every last drop out of it.

May 5. An amusing and bloodless way to wage war: On the Danish shore the Icelanders lost a ship, which was looted by the Danes. This enraged the Icelanders so much that a directive was given to everyone in Iceland to turn in, as a kind of tax, one abusive song apiece about the Danish king. . . .

All in all my life went on and time passed. At the Institute it dragged on—petty, disturbing, anxious. But close by and on a totally different scale, summer was progressing. Even profaned by the city, it was festive; it unfolded, ripened, prepared to subside, and tugged at my heart with all its evenings, rains, smells, reminding me of everything that was unrealized and squandered. . . . I went to visit Fussy—while we were wrapped up in work-overs she had managed to give birth to a son. Tiny as he was, with the face of a peach, he lived on that same grand scale as the summer, thunderstorms, doves. And his eyes were a stormy dove color.

About two months after the first, the second Discussion took place. Unlike the first one, it was unanimous. Blond, from the Radial Division, didn't come; he had obviously not been admitted. My Second student kept silent; I myself had asked him to for the sake of his wife and child. Some young graduate students from the Biophonic Division tenuously spoke against me. Hiding his eyes, Grayhair read the indictment. Slick admitted my errors and his own. One abusive song apiece.

Blowhard once again pranced in his chair, Satanic once again played the shaman, but it was all smaller, more boring than the first time. I no longer walked on the ceiling. I was once again given the opportunity to admit my mistakes, and once again I didn't do so. I was calm, presented the facts, but they fell into a vacuum—nobody listened to me. Worst of all, I didn't even listen to myself. My inner consciousness was no longer solid, as though my innocence had cracked.

Yes, it's a terrible thing, public opinion. Even though it might be imposed, prescribed, when it turns all against one it is difficult for that one to feel she is right.

Totally crushed after the second Discussion, I came to the Institute the next morning and sat down at the phone. I had to call KIP. I picked up the receiver—and intercepted someone's conversation. This repulsive Institute phone system—something was always getting tangled in something else. Sometimes I hate the telephone as if it were a living person. I wanted to hang up, but I recognized the voices and listened in. Slick and Slim were talking. May my ancestors forgive me—I eavesdropped.

SLICK: But yesterday's discussion was unanimous.
SLIM: When a soul is borrowed, it is not hard for it to be united.
SLICK: It wouldn't hurt for you to have at least some respect for public opinion.
SLIM: Have you ever seen how a school of fish, obeying some

mysterious signal, instantly makes a turn? There's a model of public opinion for you.

SLICK: Such an ability must be useful to fish.

SLIM: No doubt. However, not everything useful to fish is also useful to people.

I hung up. What conversations. A school of fish. Slim was right, but that didn't make me feel any better.

I reached KIP after a few minutes—Promiser's substitute had also gone on vacation, and no one knew anything about my request. Oh, well, life goes on.

Judging by a series of signs, one more wave was yet to come—the third and decisive one. The quiet before this wave wore me out; at times it was simply difficult to breathe. If I only knew what to expect. But that was the problem—I didn't. One could assume just about anything.

Lack of information creates cowards. Man in general is not all that cowardly; he boldly faces danger if he knows what it is. But he freezes before the abyss of the unknown. Torture by the unknown is an old, tried-and-true device. It leaves the body untouched but shatters the spirit, which has already grown weak in its spiritual gums and is ready to fall out. . . .

Besides, I had nothing to read. I had given the diary to Slim, who latched on to it with the avidity of a small dog, no new sustenance happened along, and my dreams let loose. Most often I dreamed of carrion crows. They shouted "wrk, wrk," flapped their wings, and crowded around a corpse. One of them stood out in particular; it was bigger than the others, its left side was always turned toward me, and it had a partly dragging, deeply gashed wing, a fixedly aimed round orange eye, and a fixedly aimed beak. In its beak hung scraps of the corpse, and the corpse was me. "Wrk"—this obviously meant "work-over." The shallow symbolism of these dreams, like that of some turn-of-the-century writer, enraged me, but still oppressed me all day.

Yet the worst evil was not outside but within, inside me. In a position such as mine, the most difficult thing is to hold on within yourself to your own truth. Whatever happens—hold on to your own truth. No matter how you're forced—hold on to your own truth. But what can you do when the truth itself is persecuted and dying, when even for its own adherent it is almost no longer truth, and more and more often the question arises: And what if . . .

No, I had not admitted my mistakes, that was simply out of the question, but the truth within me lay on its deathbed.

I don't know what I would have done during this dreadful time if it hadn't been for my three friends. Meeting with them was like drinking the water of life.

Dark in particular was remarkably sweet: his childish forty-year-old face was such a joy. One often thinks: Where does the charm of a child go when it grows up? Looking at Dark, I could see: It doesn't go anywhere, here it is. Dark was one of those people—there may be one in ten thousand or even less—who grow up and even grow old without losing their gentle, childlike charm.

The oblong shape and milky swarthiness of Dark's face, his slender hands, even the gold crown in his pink mouth expressed something totally naive, childishly cunning. How I loved to look at that face! Dark's sympathy was as pleasant as a warm bath. When he spoke he would touch his interlocutor's hand from time to time with his slender, warm fingers.

"You know what, M. M.," Dark once said to me with a childishly mischievous smile, "maybe, it does make sense after all . . . well, to repent, that is . . ."

"What are you saying!" I said, indignant. "Well, I never . . ."

"Take it easy," said Dark, and touched me with his fingers.

"You are trying to persuade me to repent? You, a friend?"

"Only minimally, within the bounds of propriety. Figure out an acceptable formula, so that they'll leave you alone. And then go on working, of course, in your own way, without abandoning your basic principles. Perhaps you could call it something different somehow. . . . A way to save people, your work. To wait for more favorable times. Well?" Dark once again touched my hand with his thin warm one.

"No, just drop it," I said, resisting his warmth. "That course is possible, perhaps it might even be reasonable, but not for me. To each his own."

"I only say this because you . . . you are dear to me."

"I know, thank you. You want what is good for me. The only question lies in how one understands 'good.' You understand it as well-being."

"And you?"

"More as overcoming."

"Well, but if you have a strong force against you? You can't overcome it directly. That means you have to prepare a devious maneuver. And in the meantime—"

"I'd rather let them rip my head off."

"Always 'I,' 'I'! But have you thought about others? There will be people who will come after you, you know."

"A dishonest move. I've thought about everything, maybe even before I was born. You know, I'm now going to speak carelessly, and therefore histrionically. In general there are two courses of action— Galileo's and Giordano Bruno's. The former recanted and continued working, while the latter stupidly burned at the stake. The first course is clearly the more sensible, but . . ."

"Galileo, Giordano Bruno!" said Dark ironically. "Well, now—"

"Hush up!" I shouted. "You're not fool enough to think that I'm comparing myself to them! We're all dwarfs next to them. But every dwarf is tied to his own little stake—"

"How much romanticism you have in you, after all," Dark interrupted me. "A regular Red Sail.* Forgive me, I am younger than you are, but I often feel older and see you as some kind of child. . . ."

And he smiled his childlike smile.

I thought a lot about this conversation later. Undoubtedly, Dark was right in some sense. But my whole being rejected his rightness. Was that stupidity?

I met with Slim more often than the others. He depressed me by the very fact of his being so smart. He radiated intelligence and melancholy.

"Don't rush," he told me. "Just sit it out in your Winding Division. You have to let the campaign die a natural death."

"It's not certain which one of us will die first," I answered peevishly.

"In all probability, the campaign will. It wouldn't be like you. And remember that times are different. In our time driving a person to his death does the driver no credit. Those who conduct work-overs have learned to fear heart attacks, suicides, even ordinary complaints. They understand that at any moment the wheel might turn. And then what? The ones on top would find themselves at the bottom. And have you noticed how they avoid putting their signatures on documents? Directives are given orally. They don't even like making public speeches, they try to put forward front men. Blowhard, for example. If the wheel turns, they'll pick him as the scapegoat for sure. . . ."

*A symbol of realized hopes, from the novella "Red Sails," by Alexander Grin. — Trans.

"And Satanic? Is he also a front man?"

"No. He's a more complex figure. He's his own man. He hates you all on his own and with complete sincerity."

"For what? We work in totally different areas, after all."

"And how. He works in the area of platitudes. Not their use, but their production. That's his profession, the only one he has. In an ideally structured society, such a specialist would be able to survive no longer than a person who doesn't eat. . . ."

Slim was intelligent but difficult. With him you had to be on your toes constantly, so as not to make a fool of yourself. Sometimes after a conversation with him, such a depression would come over me, I'd want to hang myself. Fortunately, he could also make you laugh. He could do everything.

It was easiest with Bald. He offered no advice, didn't try to explain anything, he simply felt sorry for me and talked to me like a nanny:

"Now, now, that's enough. Don't torment yourself so. Everything will work out."

Now with him I neither had to be on guard nor had to argue. Once I simply put my head on his shoulder and burst into tears. He embraced me lightly and held me, patting me on the back while I wept.

"Now, now, M.M., don't."

"I know," I snapped. "Do you think I'm doing it on purpose? I simply can't help it."

"Well, then, have a cry if you can't help it."

His shoulder smelled of wet cloth, and I had a sweet cry on that shoulder. The important thing was that one didn't feel embarrassed in front of Bald. . . .

My life went on and time passed, and summer ended, and the nights turned black. The process of adjusting to my new condition also ended. A world with no smiles became habitual, like an old chronic illness or street noise. Arriving at the Institute, I tried to scurry down the corridor quickly and hide. A new idea was developing in my work, but slowly, lazily, like a potato sprout in the cellar. Often I sat all day with an empty head. What a weak person I am, after all!

At the same time my new life had its own joys. I began to take pleasure in getting up early and walking all the way across town to the Institute. The early-morning city—businesslike and unassuming—got up, hung laundry on balconies, rattled garbage cans, saw off a multitude of people, each on his own way, with his own burden. Each one went and endured, and bore what was required of him without a sound.

Looking at the morning city, I began to understand something that before, when I was accompanied by Success, had been inaccessible to me.

An insidious thing, Success. It gives, but it also robs. Before you know it, you're impoverished. Did I want it back? No. I wouldn't accept it in its former guise.

And I understood one more important thing: What was happening to me was not a misfortune. People helped me understand this.

Once, as I was approaching the cloak room, I heard a conversation between two attendants: "I prefer to hang them up," one of them said. "And I'd rather hand them out," answered the other. "Handing them out is more interesting." And I thought, *Indeed, which is more interesting? I guess, in fact, handing out. I would also prefer to hand out.* A kind of joy touched me: What was I afraid of, after all? There are a lot of interesting things in the world besides science.

I walked up to the counter and handed my coat to the one who preferred to hang up.

"You seems to have gone thin in the face, gone gray," she said. "You got some problems, maybe?"

"Yes, some unpleasantness," I answered.

"Well, don't you give in," said the other, the spunky one. "I never does. Some problem come my way, I just sock it in the jaw."

"What sort of problem do you have?"

"They arrested my son. He was a driver, ran someone down. A guy was walkin' along, drunk as a skunk, right under the wheels—and that was that. And they tell my son that he's guilty. Found booze in him. Been drinkin' beer since mornin'. Now that's a problem."

Indeed it was. And I . . .

"Now, now," I told her, as Bald had told me, "don't worry, maybe it will work out."

"God willin'. I'm tired of bein' brave, tired out."

That night I once again dreamed of carrion crows. They were crowding around the corpse as usual. One of them, the chief one, standing on pink legs, somehow stayed on for a very long time and looked at me with his attentive, sad eye, as if he were pitying me in his own way. As before, I was the corpse, but the carrion crow was also pitiful, and his deeply gashed wing dragging on the ground seemed moth-eaten. We parted unwillingly, but what could I do, I was being called to the phone, and I woke up.

And in fact the phone was ringing, for a long time apparently. I answered it, but it was too late—a dial tone. Who could have been calling so early?

I looked at the alarm clock. The damn thing had overslept! Quarter to nine. That's those new models for you. In a rush I got dressed and ran down the stairs—the elevator wasn't working, the devil take both it and the alarm clock. It was raining. The street was full of umbrellas. Bubbles appeared and burst in the puddles. One huge, royal bubble held out for a long, long time, but even it burst. The bus smelled of flowers. Someone's large wet bouquet was pressed right up against my cheek. The people were jolly and jostled each other in a friendly way.

The ancient entrance of the Institute met me with its wet lanterns. Around each of them was a halo of skipping raindrops.

Slick was walking toward me down the corridor, and—oh, what a miracle!—there was a smile on his face. He stopped when he came up to me.

"Congratulations! You have probably already read about it?"

"Not yet," I answered.

"Truth always wins out in the end," he said, beaming moistly, as if he had been washed by the rain.

"In spite of all your efforts."

He saddened.

"You are mistaken, M.M., I assure you, you are mistaken! I personally have always defended you. Just ask anyone."

Now I exploded:

"I don't have to ask anyone. I myself understand everything about you. You are as plain to me as the palm of my hand. See?" I held out my palm. He politely looked at it, not understanding a thing. "Ha!" I said throatily. "Pathetic coward! Do you think you can spend your whole life sitting between two chairs? Well, you can't! Mark my words, it will get you yet. And when it happens you won't even have the consolation that you behaved honorably."

He went pale.

"You don't understand, M.M.," he began to mumble, "there's still a lot you don't know. . . . It's not all that simple! Unfortunately, I can't tell you everything. . . . Oh, by the way, have you heard about . . ."

He named Satanic.

"What about him?" I asked rudely.

"His wife just called. A stroke . . ."

I didn't answer right away. This was tough for me.

"Eh, the wrong one . . ." I said, and walked away.

Slick stood there totally confounded, shaking his head, and, with his head still shaking, he disappeared from view.

People were coming toward me and smiling.

One person—one smile.
One person—one smile.

It's not all that simple.

1970; first published 1986.

Translated from the Russian by Dobrochna Dyrcz-Freeman.

THE SLEEPER

Valentin Kataev

He dreamed about the yacht. It was moored at the wharf of the yacht club, its furled sails dark from the predawn dew. Its graceful mast swayed like a metronome.

The sleeper saw our whole gang making their way single file, one after the other, trying to keep their balance along the unreliable plank onto the damp deck.

In the darkness before dawn the lights of the port were still burning here and there, and lights could be seen atop the masts of steamships.

He saw all of this so clearly, so tangibly, that the dream tormented him. The sleeper knew he was asleep, but he didn't have the strength to break off the dream and force himself to wake up—to surface from the fathomless depths of the dream. He made a desperate effort to stop the dream, and he even thought that he had woken up. But it was only a dream within a dream. He saw himself on the curb of a familiar street near the station square, which was filled with Austrian soldiers who had just disembarked from a military transport.

The city had surrendered without a fight, in accordance with the terms of some peace treaty or truce.

The inhabitants of the town were looking with curiosity at their conquerors, in grayish-green uniforms and steel helmets. Right there on the station square field kitchens were steaming. Alongside them cooks in white hats were unhurriedly wielding ladles.

The people of the town were fascinated most of all by the spectacle of the foreign soldiers preparing bean soup with margarine and stewed pork. The conquerors paid absolutely no attention to the townspeople, who were examining the soldiers with curiosity, as if they were exotic animals.

On the whole, the scene was absolutely peaceful.

Soon the conquerors finished eating, formed columns, and were marched away from the square. The townspeople dispersed and the square was left empty.

Thus began a strange new life in the town.

The empty station square was somehow transformed into a gambling house, into which a robber suddenly burst, revolver in hand. It was Lenny the Greek. There was something unquestionably Greek in his childlike face with its short black brows, in his Mediterranean smile. In the port they called him "the Greek Pindus on a pair of wheels."

Short, slightly bowed legs in tattered trousers, pancake cap, jacket of indeterminate color, faded striped vest.

His theatrical appearance at the door—which, with its red plush drapes trimmed in tasseled gold braid, gave the room a hint of if not a cabaret, then at least a run-of-the-mill brothel—paralyzed all those present. For some reason Lenny the Greek thought that most of the gamblers were foreigners, primarily Frenchmen. He had therefore prepared in advance a French phrase, which a certain Manfred, an educated young man, had taught him on the yacht. This phrase was supposed to represent something on the order of the Russian "Remain calm." When pronounced by Lenny the Greek, presumably in French but with an abominable Black Sea accent, the phrase stunned not only all those present but even the robber himself, who was struck by his own impudence, as with effort he forced himself to say in a hoarse voice, "*Soyez tranquils.*" At first they all stood petrified. But then the unexpected happened. One of the gamblers burst out laughing, and the raid didn't come off.

Lenny the Greek didn't have time to get to the green table and grab the pile of tsarist ten-ruble gold pieces before someone tore the revolver out of his hand and gave him a sound punch in the neck.

It was only natural: Everyone realized that the robber was acting alone, that he was working without comrades, and that it wouldn't be hard to deal with him.

"What are you doing?" whining, with resentment in his voice, whimpered Lenny the Greek, and, breaking out of the arms of someone in starched cuffs with gold cuff links, he threw himself forward, turned over the table, and, beating them off with his arms and legs, rushed out of the room. And just in time: The whistles of the Imperial Guard could already be heard.

Badly shaken, he leapt into the street, plunged into an alley, made his way through several courtyards to the town square—deserted at that hour of the night—and, like a lizard, hid in a chink between the wall of the opera theater and a café-pastry shop famous for its whipped-cream meringues and punch glacé made with real Negro's Head Jamaica rum.

Meanwhile, on the premises of the gambling house, two lackeys in livery rented from the costume department of the operetta theater were crawling along the carpet, gathering up gold coins and foreign currency as well as paper rubles, which pictured a handsome youth, his hair in a pudding-bowl cut.

And suddenly this was all put in order, covered by a long sea wave and the obliquely flying, swelled sail of the yacht, on the deck of which was seated the whole group of young people, including, strange as it may seem, Lenny the Greek—they took him on fairly often as a sailor.

The yacht abruptly rounded the lighthouse, which was shaped like an elongated bell and on which a small but real signal bell hung from a bracket. A row of portholes stretched from top to bottom along the white body of the lighthouse, so that the lighthouse looked in the dream like a gentleman in a single-breasted overcoat with all its buttons done. Sea gulls were flying around its crystal hat.

The farther they got from the shore, the more the sea turned the color of malachite, the more it resembled an Aivazovsky painting.*

My God, what bliss that was!

"How desolate is our sea," Manfred's powerful voice rang out, drown-

*Ivan Konstantinovich Aivazovsky (1819–1900), Russian marine painter. —Trans.

ing out the whistling of the wind in the shrouds. The wind was particularly noticeable at moments when we were listing, when the mast tilted
and the long bowsprit with the swollen triangle of the jib rose over the
crests of the waves, from which the wind tore the foam, dashing spray
into the face of the singer as he continued his duel with the breeze,
"Day and night it roars, many misfortunes are buried in its fateful
expanse!"

The sleeper knew that not only many misfortunes but many secrets as
well were buried in its fateful expanse. Moreover, the sea was not desolate. Two passenger ships could be seen moving away on the open sea:
one sending up smoke on the horizon and the other sailing just beyond
the foamy line of the breakwater.

The steamships were carrying people out of the doomed city just in
the nick of time.

So the sea was not really all that desolate if it were taken into account that, in addition to the yacht, even farther out, beyond the horizon, the shadow of the French battleship *Ernest Renan* and maybe
even of the English dreadnought *Caradog* could be discerned.

Moreover, the sea didn't roar day and night. Sometimes it rested.
Then its expanse did not seem fateful. But all the same the sleeper was
disturbed by the thought that somewhere in its depths "many misfortunes are buried." Many misfortunes and many secrets.

The rays of the sun were disappearing into the deep, illuminating with
gradually diminishing light the bottle-green water and the keel of the
yacht, from which schools of little fish dashed away.

The underwater current slowly carried a broken-off clump of seaweed, an even darker green than the water. A spherical clump of
seaweed.

Misfortunes and secrets could be sensed in the dark depths of the
sea, into which the light of the sun barely penetrated. There in the
murky darkness glimmered the granite pavement of the station square,
long empty since the boots of the conquerors had marched across it,
since the wheels of field kitchens had rolled through, and since the
tobacco smoke of porcelain chibouks with cherry-colored bowls and
tassels had dissipated.

We shall never know who that young man with the dark face was, the
one who appeared in the sleeper's dream as Manfred. Perhaps he was a

demobilized warrant officer of a guards unit who had escaped from the Kronstadt sailors in civilian clothes and had somehow turned up in the South, in the city of the three lighthouses, in the group on the yacht.

He always appeared unexpectedly and just as unexpectedly disappeared. No one knew where he lived. Probably in some hostel for former officers.

He didn't wear a tie. There was something Byronic in the turn of his head, in his girlishly white, aristocratic neck.

There were a few girls, all wearing colorful silk scarves around their heads. Among others he dreamed of two sisters and their girlfriend, who had landed in the group by chance. Then again, all of them had landed in the group by chance. The girlfriend spent the whole time sitting in the little cabin on a narrow leather couch giving herself a manicure: she rubbed her nails with a pink stone and then polished them to a mirrorlike shine with a little suede cushion. All the while she kept saying that if the yacht were wrecked and they all drowned, people would be able to tell by her nails that before them lay the corpse of an elegant lady from good society.

Vasya, the decent fellow who was sitting at the helm, turned the yacht even more sharply into the open sea, and the second lighthouse appeared on the distant shore. It was old, no longer in operation—the remains of a stone tower. And a little later the third lighthouse appeared, new, white as snow, metallic, as if clad in a knight's helmet with its visor lowered, made of beveled crystal lenses, out of which at night in times past two sharp rays of electric heliotropic light would shoot—one strictly horizontal and the other strictly vertical, staring into the starry sky of peacetime.

The boom of the mainsail swung from right to left in the wind, and the sail swelled even more. A small skiff, a so-called dinghy, tied to the stern, skipped along the waves like a nutshell.

Vasya was the son of a millionaire—a former millionaire, but then again—who knows?—perhaps a future one as well. Not long before the war he had ordered a small yacht from England, from Greenwich, and had given it to his son. Now this yacht was essentially all that remained of his former millions. So Vasya's fiancée, Nelly, the elder of the two sisters, daughters of the former public prosecutor for the

Chamber of Civil Affairs, stood to gain nothing from the courtship, although she continued to hope for better times and the return of Vasya's millions.

As far as the public prosecutor himself was concerned, he had almost nothing to do anymore. All of the inhabitants of the city of the three lighthouses had nothing to do anymore.

A divine idleness reigned in the city, *dolce fare niente,* as they say in Italian.

So how did they live?

They lived perfectly well, selling family jewels and domestic objects, for which the local peasants willingly exchanged flour, oil, and pork fat. Every morning the local peasants would come to the market or simply drive their carts and traps right into courtyards, where the bartering would be conducted. The jewels—articles by Fabergé, diamonds, sapphires, high-standard gold—were bought up cheaply by shady jewelers. From time to time countless riches were sent abroad.

No one thought about what would happen tomorrow. They hoped it would go on like this forever. Of course that was a pleasant delusion. Even the public prosecutor, who, in essence, had nothing to do—no one to try—surrendered to that pleasant delusion. And for days on end he wandered in his dressing gown and worn-out slippers from room to room through the apartment.

Bushy, graying whiskers, just as traditionally bushy public-prosecutor brows, olive face wasted away by idleness and on his nose a pince-nez, which, like faith and truth, had served him in the examination of judicial cases. Now the pince-nez served him in examining stereoscopic pictures of scenes of the Castle of Chillon and twin sails over Lake Geneva through a bioscope. Through this same pince-nez the public prosecutor liked to examine the journal *The Cornfield* for the year 1897 with its portraits of admirals, generals, senators, and bishops. . . .

As for the public prosecutor's wife, she was a sweet, completely gray, silver, small, thin old woman who maintained prerevolutionary order in the house: breakfast, dinner, five o'clock tea, and in the evening a hot supper of ground cutlets.

The cook and the maid had long since vanished, enticed away by sailors from the messenger vessel *The Diamond,* so the public prosecutor's wife had to do everything herself, including going to the bazaar to exchange things for food. Ever fewer articles remained for exchange, although there were still more than enough. Everything was all right in that regard, discounting the distress caused her by the out-of-town peasants' utter incomprehension of the true value of the articles exchanged.

The peasants, especially the women, sitting on their carts and covering with their skirts the produce they had brought, would examine a diaphanous batiste chemisette dating back to the end of the nineteenth century and pay absolutely no attention either to the style or the quality; they would only examine the fabric critically in the light, judging that the more solid the material, the better, and say scornfully, "Too thin!"

But what could you expect from them! Simplicity! The people!

Sheets went better than anything else, and enough of them had been accumulated for a lifetime—heaps, so there were always cutlets for supper.

The sleeper saw with particular clarity a dish of hot cutlets sprinkled with dill—so lacy, so green, the kind that can be seen only in a color dream—floating past.

The evening cutlets held a special attraction for the group of young people after a lengthy excursion on the yacht. Not only cutlets, however, but strongly brewed, almost red tea with sugar. The cutlets rivaled Nelly, the beauty, and her younger sister, Masha, for attention.

Nelly sang romances, and Masha accompanied her. Mainly Rachmaninoff, Grechaninov, and that other one, what's his name—I forgot his name again. Oh yes, Cherepnin.

"I'd kiss you, but I'm afraid the moon will see. . . . A little star fell in the sky. . . ."

Or something like that.

He could hear it even now in his dream.

Nelly sang in a strong, although still untrained, homespun mezzo-soprano. Her charming voice seemed to dash against the raised black-lacquer cover of the as yet unsold piano, filling the room with wonderful sounds, which flew through the open windows, first into the small inner courtyard, then into the street, to the crossroads, to the boulevard, and died out somewhere on a country highway leading out of the city, at the spot where a long-immobilized green steam rammer with a smokestack like a steamship's and an asphalt gray forward-ramming wheel stood.

And her voice just kept on ringing and ringing: ". . . in the garden the robins sing, and for you the roses have bloomed . . ."

In his dream the sleeper wept from happiness and saw the country highway with the green rammer, heaps of road metal, and the two girls—Nelly, the beauty, and her sister, Masha, who were walking to a tennis court, holding rackets in their hands. They were dressed identically in summer sports outfits—terry-cloth jackets and English skirts, also terry cloth, a nubby white. The elder—a beauty with shiny black hair smoothly combed into a straight line, a Spanish tortoise-shell comb at the back of her head, which lent something regal to her appearance, an elongated face the color of ivory, as they say, and brows that left no doubt that she was the public prosecutor's daughter. And the younger, who was considered a plain girl, small, still not fully grown, nearly a kid, took completely after the public prosecutor's wife: the same affectionate, calflike eyes, blond hair, goodness, which spilled out over her whole gentle face, with a birthmark on her neck, below her ear, all aglow with milky whiteness, with eyelashes that threw a shadow on the wings of an unattractive but endearing, sympathetic little nose, and something unfinished in all her movements.

The elder strode confidently, fiddling with her Davis racket, which shone like glass in the sun, and half a step behind her walked her fiancé, Vasya, the owner of the yacht, a stocky youth who had just graduated from the gymnasium, still in his school blazer, although without the belt, and there was something innately Russian, perhaps even something of the peasant, if not of the merchant, in his gait, in his light brown, neatly trimmed hair. At one time Russian millionaires were born of such boys. He worshiped his fiancée and had named the yacht after her: *Nelly*.

Like a happy slave, he followed his lady, carrying a little mesh bag of fuzzy tennis balls.

And at that very moment, out of nowhere, appeared yet another young man—this one with a suntanned gypsy face and wiry dark hair—Vasya's friend from the gymnasium. It was me.

Somehow the beauty of the elder sister passed me by without notice, but at first sight the charm of the younger reached right to my heart. I didn't yet realize that I was in love, but I already wanted to walk next to the younger, to babble all sorts of nonsense and recite Fet's poetry.*

The sleeper saw two couples on the highway walking toward the tennis courts.

But when was all this happening? In the spring? In the summer? In the fall? In any case, it wasn't winter.

In the dream all the seasons occurred simultaneously.

A miracle of concurrence.

It seems that the sky was slate dark, almost black, promising a May thunderstorm, agonizingly imminent, like first love. The large buds of horse chestnuts were distinctly etched against the background of the threatening sky, as if smeared with joiner's glue, just at the point of bursting—now they've already burst—and set free newborn five-fingered hairy leaves, still hanging helplessly like rags, with tiny waxy herringbones of still-unborn racemes.

The chestnuts had already bloomed and were even casting shadows.

At the same time a watercolor autumn sky with a wedge of cranes shone over bonfires of fallen leaves, and at night the starry sky glowed silver, reflected in the surface of the gulf, and, strange as it may seem, the sunset on the steppe died away over the white stone wall of a monastery and over the crumbling tower of the old lighthouse, and in the monastery they rang the summons to vespers—the evening chime, the evening chime—and over the precipice in the monastery garden the May lilacs bloomed wildly. We picked some and then returned with huge dark-violet-light-dark-blue bouquets on the tram to town, only to set off at the crack of dawn through the streets, as deserted as if it were still night, to the port, where the yacht was swaying at its moorings. And in the evening the public prosecutor's wife again came into the dining room from the kitchen, and the whole group fell greedily upon the cutlets.

The sleeper saw the group as a kind of whole, poorly distinguishable except for a few familiar faces. The rest were simply an assemblage of young people who had been brought together by chance and didn't know one another all that well.

*Afanasy Afanasievich Fet (real name Shenshin; 1820–1892), Russian romantic poet. —Trans.

Some of them would crop up unexpectedly and were faceless. Others would not appear at all, and then would suddenly start appearing again, one after the other, and all this was in the spirit of that strange time of unconcern and freedom.

After the cutlets, Nelly, the beauty, sang once again. She had cold eyes. And Vasya stood next to the open piano and watched his betrothed with adoration.

Then the younger sister walked out of the stuffy room onto the balcony and placed her hands, which were tired from the keyboard, on the iron railing. As if drawn by a magnet, I, too, walked out onto the balcony after her. Masha and I stood next to each other, hanging over the well of the courtyard, our hands on the railing, and silently looked into the green evening, nearly night, sky as the first stars appeared over the tiled roofs.

Overcoming an uncharacteristic timidity, I moved my hand very slowly, almost imperceptibly, along the iron railing toward Masha's hand. I thought that she would move her hand away, but she didn't. Her little finger flinched but didn't move away. Perhaps it even moved a bit closer. Then, as if by chance, unconsciously, I placed my palm on Masha's hand, which was clasped to the railing. Masha didn't move, as if nothing special had happened, but I felt her heart beating, and her hand, covered by my palm, grew still, like a little bird, like a dove, and we remained that way for a rather long time in the silent swoon of a dream. We could have gone on forever if the time to part had not come: after all, you can't spend a whole night standing on a balcony in someone else's house.

The next day, still not saying a word to each other about love, the two of us sat alone in her little room, where last year's gymnasium textbooks were neatly laid out on the desk, and two small mirrors, facing each other, suddenly appeared out of nowhere, and a stearin candle burned between them.

What was this? A physical experience or a dream within a dream?

Between the two mirrors the tongue of the candle is sharper than a dagger. Its rays run down in little streams into the mirrors. The eyes of the mirrors gaze at each other like two faces. A single candle above the milky abyss, paler than white. And, aglow, infinite, it has no number.

Enchanted, we would gaze into this mirror corridor, this corridor of reciprocal reflections stretching into infinity.

The sleeper lingered in the vista of this endless mirror corridor, and his sleep became even deeper than before, but not for long.

Something had changed in nature. Perhaps the night thunderstorm had passed and he hadn't heard it.

The malachite-green waves grew black. The foam on them grew even whiter. Manfred's shadow fell on a distant coast, where a squall was about to break.

The yacht had already sailed far into the open sea, and Vasya turned the helm hard over right, wanting to change tack quickly, before it was too late. But he came about too slowly. For a time the mainsail and the jib stopped catching the wind, began to quiver, and hung lifelessly, but at almost the very same moment the boom of the mainsail swung slowly and heavily from right to left, nearly hitting Lenny the Greek— who was securing the sheet of the jib, which had been torn from his hands—on the head. By now the sails were catching the wind, which apparently had begun to blow from the other direction.

The yacht moved away from the squall, which had already covered the sea with the black shot of its gusts. The black shot of the squall was overtaking the yacht, which had begun diving deep into the angry waves. The nutshell of the small dinghy careened like mad behind the stern, trying to break loose from its tether.

"Clouds race over the sea, stronger grows the wind, blacker the swell, a storm there will be. With it we shall spar and show our bravery," Manfred sang in his powerful voice, trying to drown out the noise of the squall.

Of course he wasn't really Manfred. That was only his nickname. What his real name was, no one knew. And this disturbed the sleeper.

Manfred stood tall, his legs spread apart on the swaying deck, and never took his eyes, too bright and amorous, off Nelly. She was sitting on the deck near the descent to the cabin, her arms clasped around her knees and her chin lowered onto them.

Something was happening between Nelly and Manfred. Some kind of silent argument in which Nelly was already prepared to yield.

The wind of the squall, gusting, set the yacht on its side. If it hadn't been for the keel, with the lead cigar at the end, which served as a counterweight to the whole magical apparatus of the yacht, the yacht would of course have been laid flat with all of its sails on the waves— like a butterfly that had carelessly fallen into a swimming pool.

The yacht twanged to the wind like a mandolin.

The sky had grown completely black. They were all seized with fear. The girls shrieked like sea gulls. Sea gulls scudded about above the yacht—white against the black background. Someone dashed into the cabin. Someone lay flat on the deck, clasping the bronze cleats around which were wound the ends of the sheets. Someone pressed up against the mast.

I put my arms around Masha's shoulders, and her bright silk scarf suddenly came untied and flew away into the sea, uncovering her disheveled, wispy, flaxen hair. Drops of seawater, which even looked bitter-salty, glistened like tears on her cheeks.

The bright scarf flew above the waves for a while longer, as if wanting to be carried off beyond the black horizon, until it disappeared from sight, swallowed up by a storm cloud.

Only Manfred and Nelly remained calm, immobile, and there was something ominous in their immobility. They were like Lermontov's Demon and Tamara. Anyone who had paid any attention to them would have realized that at that moment their fate was being decided.

Good, kind Vasya worked the tiller with his whole strong body, trying with all his strength to force the yacht toward shore, which was quite a ways off.

Dolphins, fellow travelers of the storm, accompanied the yacht. Their black humped backs kept emerging from the waves and plunging back into the bowels of the angry sea. Their triangular fins darted out of the foam and vanished again before they could catch the reflection of the distant lightning.

The yacht, it seemed, was threatened with inevitable doom.

But Vasya, one arm leaning on the tiller, the other straining with all its might to keep the sheet of the jib from tearing away, his face covered

with sweat and sea spray, nevertheless managed to bring the yacht to shore and heave to in a small cove, where a calm prevailed.

Lenny the Greek hurled the anchor into the water. The yacht stopped, circling around the anchor chain, which disappeared vertically into the depths.

Together, Vasya and Lenny the Greek, both wet from head to toe, took down the mainsail and the jib, then began to ferry the whole group—two and three at a time—in the dinghy to the rocky shore, which was covered with slime and mollusks.

A charming picture opened up beyond the ridge of rocks: the shore and a fisherman's reed hut, buried in clumps of wild grass, the heady scent of which carried as far as the white stripe of surf . . . and nets hung out to dry on crossed oars dug into the clay.

A fishing scow that had been dragged onto the shore lay with its flat tar-coated bottom up. Fishermen were sitting on it, watching the dinghy ferrying our group from the yacht to the shore.

Beneath the high reddish-clay cliff, covered with bright moist patches, a divine silence reigned.

The smell of wild herbs filled the air.

The barefoot fishermen in their rolled-up trousers turned out to be hospitable people, and soon a fire, built out of wood chips and reeds cast ashore by the surf and dried in the sun, began to crackle.

The water boiled in the teakettle, and tea makings were thrown into it right away: a handful of herbs and wildflowers that had been gathered back in May. The smell of mint and something like chamomile spread through the air, mixing with the iodine smell of seaweed.

The wonderful brew was in no way worse, perhaps even better, and in any case healthier, than the Chinese tea of Vysotsky and Company.

The group, drying off by the fire, drank the medicinal drink with pleasure, burning their lips and fingers on tin cups made out of cans. Of course there wasn't any sugar. But it wasn't necessary. The tea, with its wild herbs, possessed the capacity to arouse the imagination: The small piece of coastal land, cut off from the rest of the world by the high cliff on one side and the subsiding squall on the other, seemed somehow like that blissful country where "the heavens don't grow dark, the silence never passes."

The reed hut, the fire, the smell of fragrant tea, the smoke from the *makhorka** the fishermen were smoking, good friends—what else did a person need to be happy?

A heavenly little place, something like a model of that strange world in which we lived—cut off from the entire rest of the world conflagration that was raging somewhere around us. A funnel of unmoving air, caressing sun, clear sky, love, friendship, idleness, and complete freedom, miraculously formed in the center of a typhoon or cyclone. But nearby is the agitated sea, out of which dolphins with human eyes leap, and above them stormy petrels and sea gulls swoop, and in the dark depths of the sea octopuses, also with human eyes, coil, and the shadows of submarines float past, and near the rocks mines torn away from their anchors explode like geysers—remnants of the bygone war.

But all of that seemed to bear no relation to the quiet world in which the inhabitants of our city of the three lighthouses, its neighboring villages and hamlets did not live but only temporarily existed.

Soon we bade farewell to the hospitable fishermen and our yacht set off on the return trip. The waves had grown calm; the swell, smooth. The evening breeze gently inflated the mainsail and the jib. All dangers were left behind. The dolphins no longer accompanied us. It seemed that nothing dangerous could happen anymore.

But the sleeper felt alarmed, as if in the depths of his dream he had fathomed some dangerous alien secret that threatened inevitable disaster.

And so he had.

He had unconsciously fathomed the secret of Manfred and Nelly, their emotional bond, their silent dialogue, which had begun long ago.

It was impossible to predict when the cyclone would pass. And would it have to pass at all?

It was difficult to imagine a different life. However, no one was thinking about the future. Only Manfred, with his lips pressed together, passionately dreamed of something different, of some truly blissful

*Cheap tobacco. —Trans.

country to which "the waves carry only the strong in spirit." He considered himself strong in spirit. For a long time he had secretly been beckoning Nelly to that country. He would take her there, and they would both be rich and happy. He was sure that beyond the sea was "that other, that different" blissful country, to which steamships from the city of the three lighthouses sometimes sailed, carrying away rich people escaping the imminent storm from the north. They carried away to that place their treasures, their lives, their dreams.

Manfred was himself from a rich family—heir to an enormous estate in the Smolensk district, an aristocrat, a naval officer, or perhaps only a naval cadet from a guards unit. But all that was left behind in the irretrievable past. He had to begin all over again from the beginning.

He stood, his arms crossed on his chest, leaning against the mast, the top of which glided through pink evening clouds that appeared as though painted by an Italian landscape artist. It was easy to imagine Manfred dressed not in a shabby civilian suit but in a naval uniform, a dirk peering out from under a full-dress coat with gold epaulets.

That's how Nelly imagined him.

Manfred had fallen in love with her at first sight, but he was cautious. She realized this at once and suddenly looked at her fiancé, Vasya, with completely different eyes. When did she manage to come to an arrangement with Manfred? No one knew or even suspected. Women have a knack for that sort of thing.

He promised her a heavenly life in Italy. Singing lessons. They would train her voice. A debut at La Scala. Worldwide fame. Love until death. Wealth. Happiness. But to begin with they needed a lot of money. He swore to get hold of it at any cost. He said it wasn't all that hard in a city where diamond buyers operate. All you had to do was to come to terms with someone or other and do something or other.

The yacht was approaching the port lighthouse. The sun had set, had sunk into the pink dust of the Novorossisk steppe, had disappeared behind the Scythian burial mounds. The light of the sunset faded. A starry night rose from the east. The red eye of the lighthouse was rotating up ahead. It died out and flared up at equal intervals. When it flared up, in the smooth folds of the swell at its base a shining red snake wriggled—the reflection of the ruby eye of Mr. Lighthouse.

The yacht entered the port. The trip was over. The sails were taken down. The naked mast swayed at the moorings, its tip almost brushing against the W of Cassiopeia.

This time, however, Lenny the Greek and Manfred did not join the group gaily going off to eat cutlets and drink strong tea with sugar. Without leaving the port, their shadows dissolved in the evening darkness, in the uncertain light of the port lanterns. And then someone else joined them, a third shadow. And they vanished. But no one paid any attention. Everyone acted as he pleased, gave no account of his actions—complete freedom!

However, perhaps this illusory freedom was only the fruit of an imagination incapable of seeing the truth.

Imagination seemed more powerful than reality. And perhaps reality subordinated itself to the imagination of the sleeper, who in those deep hours of the night was at one and the same time himself and all of us and the yacht and the blinking lighthouse and the constellation Cassiopeia and me.

I was lying in striped bathing trunks on the hot pebbles of what was called the Austrian beach. Masha was lying next to me. Everything had been said between us. Words no longer had any meaning.

An adolescent girl in a wet bathing suit that was drying out in the blistering midday sun lay faceup on a terry-cloth sheet, her eyes half closed, a half-smile on her soft lips, giving herself up to the rays of the sun. Coarse sand resembling pearl barley was drying on her bare feet and short little toes. We lay at some distance from each other, the length of our outstretched arms, our hands barely touching. These light, impalpable touches seemed to instill the heat of youthful blood in us. This was already intimacy, making us lie stock-still in confusion.

I looked sideways at her nearly transparent, translucent in the sun, crimson earlobes under the blond locks of hair peeking out of her bathing cap. On her creamy-white arm, which was unamenable to a tan, glittered a small gold bracelet in the form of a chain—her last remaining piece of jewelry. She took it off her wrist and placed it in my outstretched hand, as if giving up her whole self to me.

I dandled the little golden heap on my palm and returned it to her outstretched hand, as if giving up my whole self to her in turn.

She again tossed the bracelet to me, and I again dandled it in my palm and again returned it to her.

It was like some kind of children's game.

The little gold heap transferred from her to me and from me to her the heat of silent, chaste, but burning love.

We smiled at each other.

And the life of the beach seethed all around. The somewhat muddy coastal waves rocked unhurriedly, lazily lying down on the edge of the beach, where a line of ooze cast ashore by the surf was drying in the sun. The farther out toward the horizon, the bluer the sea, but along the shore the water was muddy from the agitated clay and looked like soup laced with sour cream. Flat-bottomed barges painted different colors rocked on the waves. They traveled back and forth along the shore, which was dappled with bathing caps, towels, water bottles dug into the sand. Naked boys from the surrounding area, their bellies tightly wrapped in rags, threw themselves into the water at a run. Women, with shirts blown up like water wings, dog-paddled, dangling their arms and legs. Gurgling laughter and exclamations rang out, sounding particularly sharp in the heated air, almost like the predatory squawks of sea gulls.

Someone came to swim, bringing along two inflated ox bladders tied together with a string.

The cloudy, semitransparent bladders took the place of expensive cork life jackets. Usually old women and small children used such bladders when they swam, spitting salt water out of their mouths.

Someone grabbed on to the stern of a passing barge with sunburned hands. A merry fellow, his hairy chest bare to the waist, was rowing it standing up. He had a colored rag tied around his head like a pirate.

Little naked children crawled on the wet sand along the edge of the water line, building cities and canals in which tiny sea fleas flitted about in the water.

A few Austrian soldiers came to the beach to bathe. They threw their grayish-green full-dress coats—the underarms soaked with sweat—and their sturdy short boots, with two thick seams around the top, on the pebbles. They neatly placed their web belts with zinc buckles on top of the discarded clothing.

They behaved modestly and rather politely for conquerors. They didn't bother the female bathers and, after wading carefully into the water up to their waists, lathered their armpits with government-issue soap. They also found themselves in a state of bliss, little suspecting that soon their heavenly life as conquerors would come to an end and they, together with the German soldiers, would have to run like mad out of the occupied territory where they had lived so well under the rule of some strange Ukrainian hetman, placed on the throne by the German general staff, who had been driven out by the revolution.

The sleeper saw their flight across the steppe in the cold autumn rain. They ran, discarding caissons, cannons, and camp kitchens along the way, and at railroad stations they stormed trains leaving for the West, "*nach Vaterland.*"

The shadow of a sea gull swept along the beach.

"But what will happen to us, after all?" she said, without opening her eyelids, which were framed by light lashes and behind which a milky, calflike blue could be divined.

"Nothing will happen to us," I said with a reckless smile.
"Why?"
"Because we are the poor in spirit. We are the blessed."
"Yes, we are the blessed," she said, sighing.
"We are only in someone else's dream," I said.
"Yes, we are only in a dream," she said.
"In fact, we don't exist," I said.
"In fact," she said.

We were lying under the burning rays of the sun, listening to the cries of the men and the squeals of the women, and the splashing of oars in the water and the bass horns of the steamships carrying people away with their treasures, people for whom no homeland, no past or future existed, only the present, lingering on like an endless dream.

And at the same time as the shadows of sea gulls were flying across the beach and the Austrians were lathering their hair with government-issue soap, filling the water around them with gray foam, at the same time, or perhaps earlier or later, in the center of the familiar and unfamiliar city something horrible was happening, and the sleeper moaned heavily, bathed in sweat, and his heart contracted and palpitated.

. . . Three men were standing on the landing of a small marble staircase that led from the sidewalk to the corner entrance door of a rubber-manufactory store over which hung a large red galosh—the company's trademark. All three were pressed by a crowd against the store's heavy entrance door, but they couldn't get in because it was securely locked from the inside. Luck wasn't with them. The accidentally locked door ruined them. If the door hadn't been locked, they still could have escaped by passing through the store and running out the back door into the courtyard, and from there they could have stolen away from the crowd through the second gate, which opened into the alley. But the door against which they were pressed was deadlocked. Perhaps it was lunch break.

They had nowhere to go.

All three were surrounded by the thick black crowd, which grew larger with every passing minute and by now inspired terror.

"What's going on? What happened?" asked passersby, joining the crowd near the corner building of the rubber manufactory at the crossroads of two familiar and unfamiliar streets.

"They caught some robbers who broke into the apartment of a jewelry store owner and made off with a strongbox containing a million in diamonds."

A strongbox of the type that is painted oak-brown on top and red inside stood at the robbers' feet and seemed to be radiating shafts of diamond light from within.

Members of the hetman's Imperial Guard and agents of the Criminal Investigation Department were already running from two directions, pushing aside the crowd.

The robbers towered over the roaring crowd, brandishing their weapons.

The sleeper recognized two of the robbers. The third was unfamiliar. He was appearing in the dream for the first time.

Lenny the Greek was holding a standard-issue rifle with half the barrel sawed off, similar to a sawed-off shotgun, and directing it at the crowd. Manfred, his head uncovered and hair streaming, tall and graceful as a granite statue, was holding in his raised hand a heavy American semi-automatic pistol of the kind that came from abroad at the end of the war to arm the officers of the army and navy—a Colt ten-shot, to the handle of which was affixed a cartridge clip containing fat cartridges. The third robber, a complete stranger, wearing a soldier's washed-out summer field shirt, minus belt and epaulets—a deserter from a former reserve battalion—was waving a hand grenade like a little lemon, and this held the crowd at some distance.

The standoff between the three robbers and the infuriated crowd lasted an improbably long time—perhaps an hour, perhaps two or three, if not a whole day, and this unnaturally motionless standoff between death and death, characteristic of an endlessly protracted dream, wore out the sleeper with the impossibility of waking up.

. . . The soldier-deserter swung his arm and tossed the little lemon into the crowd. The lemon did not go off. At that very moment the members of the Imperial Guard and the agents of the Criminal Investigation Department opened fire on the robbers from different directions and killed all three on the spot. No documents were found on the robbers, and they were taken, unidentified, to the morgue by truck. They were covered with a tarpaulin and their bodies bounced up and down on the turns. Manfred's head stuck out from under the tarpaulin—hair disheveled, eyes open and glazed, full of hatred and passion.

The crossroads of the strange city emptied, and the flower girls at the crossroads of the two most fashionable streets again set up their green stools with buckets and blue-enameled basins in which roses were floating, tormenting the sleeper with their incredible beauty and brightness, which might have killed him in his sleep had not a long sea wave, smooth and cool, calmed him.

. . . He again caught sight of the yacht, which was rounding the lime-white tower of the port lighthouse.

The yacht sailed out into the open sea. The weather was wonderful. The fact that Lenny the Greek and Manfred hadn't shown up for today's excursion surprised no one. Everyone was used to unbounded freedom of action: they didn't come because they didn't want to. Only Nelly was unpleasantly surprised by Manfred's absence. She hadn't expected anything else from him, however: he was a common fop, a phrasemonger, and a braggart, unaccustomed to keeping his word. As for Italy and La Scala, wealth and worldwide fame—that was all so much empty talk. He had simply deceived her and disappeared. All the better. Her Vasya was by far more reliable. She almost loved him.

She sat next to him at the stern. With one arm he protectively embraced her shoulders, and with the other he held the tiller, taking the yacht farther and farther out into the open sea, where departing steamships chugged on the horizon.

The rest of the group behaved as usual, enjoying the breathing of the light breeze and the divine freedom. Drops of seawater glistened on all their faces as always, and it was pleasant. Especially for Masha and me.

And, as always, one of the girls, whose name the sleeper did not know, was sitting in the cabin on the narrow leather divan polishing her nails.

1985

Translated from the Russian by Catharine Theimer Nepomnyashchy.

CAT-STRANGLER SILVER

Viktor Konetsky

There are several chapters in my travel journals that came to me in manuscript form from a chance reader, an engineer named Matyukhin, who had become mentally ill after a car accident. His illness was strange: He imagined that he lived in the belly of a whale. From time to time I sift through his stories, sketches, and diary entries and type them up.

Here and there the trace of my own pen can, of course, be detected. But I wouldn't want the reader to confuse Gennady Petrovich Matyukhin, their real author, who died quite some time ago, with V. Konetsky, as I am somewhat afraid of maritime medical commissions and landlubber critics.

I am retaining the author's title for this story, "Cat-Strangler Silver."

> "And the mighty expanse envelops me menacingly, reflected in my inner self with a terrible strength. . . ."
>
> (Matyukhin did not indicate the name of the author of the epigraph. It's N. V. Gogol. —V.K.)

By the end of that little-known war with Finland, I had just turned seven. But I had already read *Treasure Island* on my own, and I dreamt of Silver and Jim Hawkins, the cabin boy. I dedicate these reminiscences, written under difficult circumstances, in the belly of a whale, not to Robert Louis Stevenson, however, but to Dr. Jekyll.

And so, I'm seven years old, it's a very cold winter, and I'm living with my mother in a five-story brick building. It's a solitary building. Around it there are only some woodsheds and, beyond them, abandoned lots and dumping grounds. The building is somewhere between the Seraph and Theological cemeteries. The building's gone now. It disappeared. Sometimes it seems to me that that huge solitary building never even existed.

A five-story building that wound up, for some inexplicable reason, between two remote rural cemeteries. In the basement, in the attic, and in the woodsheds—a horde of cats. Dozens, hundreds, thousands of stray cats, hungry, wretched, emaciated cats.

Dusk. Blue lights burn in the doorways, and all of the cats are blue. . . .

At first they laughed at the young Renoir. I saw a caricature of one of his paintings in a magazine once, a wonderful painting—*Girl Sleeping*. Under the caricature there was a vicious caption: "Girl dyeing a cat in a pail of water blue with indigo." What malicious nonsense! All my life I've felt sorry for Renoir.

During the war Mama worked in a hospital, where she wore a uniform as white as the stars; the young soldiers chased after Mama; she was often cheerful and would bring me big shiny oranges. It was so cold outside that as soon as she brought the oranges into the house they would frost over and I would lick the transparent drops off them. And I read *Treasure Island* again and again. And when Mama left for the hospital she never locked me in the apartment.

Where could that huge five-story building have gone? Even the foundation is gone—I looked for it later, when I was an adult, when I was already sick and would take lots of walks on the outskirts of town, especially in the spring, and gather bouquets of Chinese lilacs. The doctors tell me that white spring nights are bad for me; I'm even lonelier then.

Yes, freezing cold, blue lights in the doorways of our building, shiny oranges and dozens, hundreds, thousands of cats. Both Mama and I were afraid of cats. I'm still afraid of them. They're exquisite, of course, but they have round eyes with narrow slits in them, and they torture mice for a long time. The tenants in our building held a meeting in the bomb shelter and decided to call an exterminator. I know now that killing cats used to be known as *bulgaking*, which also means to swindle people and pass cat skins off as valuable furs. . . .

The exterminator came and said that he would catch and kill all of the stray cats in one night.

He was a frightening man. He had no ears, no left eye, and his left leg was missing below the knee. In place of his leg there was a wooden peg with a rubber tip—like Silver's. And he wore only a light cap on his head, even though the ice was crackling in the cold. He told all of the tenants to go away and leave him alone. And he sat down on the steps right next to our apartment.

It was late in the evening, but Mama had not returned from the hospital yet. There was a snowstorm outside, but once in a while the storm would let up, and then the moon would shine brightly through breaks in the snow clouds—such weather is rare in Leningrad. The storm lapped at our ridiculous solitary building from all sides and howled in the attic.

The exterminator sat on the step in the blue light smoking a gnarled pipe and muttering:

> "Rat-tat-tat, rat-tat-tat,
> Little pussy wed the cat . . ."

I looked at him through the drafty keyhole.

I had already thought up a name for him—Cat Strangler or Cat Killer.

Even then I wanted to be a smart kid.

Suddenly this scary man turned toward me and beckoned with his finger. And I realized that he could see me, too, through the keyhole. And I obediently went out to him. He wasn't really very old. He smelled of horses or, rather, like a stable. Two empty bast bags lay beside him on the step. He asked whether we had another bag in the house. I told him we didn't have any bags, but we did have a knapsack. He told me to dress warm, get the knapsack, and come back, because he needed a brave kid to help him.

I asked this strange and frightening man if it would take him a long time to kill the cats, because I had to get back before Mama got home from the hospital.

He straightened out the peg on his leg and told me not to ask childish questions. It seemed to me that he was Flint, the pirate captain.

Through a broken window in the stairway I could see the woodsheds way down below. Above them the snow swirled in the flashes of moonlight. The wind blew from the Neva, from the bay. Hordes of cats were slinking through the moonlit snow across the tops of the woodsheds toward our building.

By the time I put on my warm clothes, took the knapsack that we use when we go to our dacha, and went out to the exterminator, the cats had already climbed up the stairs to the door of our apartment. They walked confidently, as if they knew what they were in for and why. The exterminator took them, one by one, and put them in the bast bags. And all the time he kept muttering:

> "Rat-tat-tat, rat-tat-tat,
> Little pussy wed the cat . . ."

The cats plopped into his bags silently, without hissing or meowing. For some reason I ceased to be afraid and was no longer surprised at what was going on. But I asked something like:

"How're you going to kill them, mister?"

"None of your business," he said.

When both of the exterminator's bags were filled to the top with cats, he tied them with harness reins.

There were about five cats that didn't fit into his bags; they sat on the steps looking inquiringly at the Cat Killer with gleaming eyes. He took my knapsack, opened it, and, one after another, the cats jumped into it.

"And that's that," said the exterminator. "Let's go. Now you'll see how I throttle 'em." And he put the knapsack on my shoulder. Right away the cats started to squirm and meow as if they were killing each other. . . .

I write about cats so persistently because here, inside the whale, it smells strongly of fish, and everybody knows that cats like fish. . . .

Roerich brought a lot of lilacs to Vrubel's coffin. Although Blok didn't know Vrubel, he made a speech at his grave in Novodevichy cemetery. They were all crazy, those people. . . .

But about the exterminator.

He threw the bags over his right shoulder, put on his mittens, turned up the collar of his sheepskin jacket, and we started off.

We went down the stairs and out into the black snowstorm.

Not one light shone from the windows of our strange building.

"Have you killed many of them before, mister?" I asked.

"Shut up, kid, or you'll get a sore throat," said the exterminator.

"What happened to your eye and your ears and your leg?" I asked. "Did you lose them in the war?"

He didn't answer. With the two bags full of cats slung over his shoulder it was hard for him to walk on his peg leg, with its rubber tip, over the icy cobblestones of our courtyard.

"Where are we going to kill them?" I asked.

"Patience, kid. You'll find out when we get to the place where the highway turns. And that's that."

It was about half a mile to the place where the highway turns. We covered the distance without saying a word.

When we got there the exterminator said, "Sit down in that snow-bank by the side of the road."

I squatted down.

The exterminator threw the bags of cats off his shoulder and took the knapsack from me. Then, leaning heavily on my head, he sat down next to me in the snowbank, caught his breath, took out a bottle of vodka, and took a swig from it.

"We have to wait for the truckers," said the exterminator. "Two bags and your knapsack. Who knows, maybe one truck will be enough. And that's that."

"You throw them under the cars?" I asked.

"You'll see."

Darkness, snow, a deserted rural highway. Even in the pockets of my overcoat my hands were freezing—I had forgotten my mittens. I probably muttered something about wanting to go back home to Mama.

The exterminator did not answer; he untied the knapsack, took out the cat at the top, and, holding it by its skin, shook it in front of him, admiring the hearty black creature. The cat started to howl and twist every which way.

"Here, take him," said the exterminator. "Warm your hands on him. That cat has a wife that must be the size of a Grenadier guard. And that's that."

"He'll run away," I whimpered.

"No," said the exterminator. "We're not going to kill them. And they know it. We'll send them to the Chukhs. They live high. And that's that. You just be quiet. The old women get wind of this and they won't give me so much as a quarter liter in the morning."

"Who are these Chukhs?"

"The Finns. No cars for some reason. Just my luck lightning will strike me again here."

"There is no lightning in winter," I said, warming my hands on the cat, which wasn't trying to get away.

"It finds me everywhere and punishes me. And for what? The first time I was a youngster, like you. I was driving the cows out into the field, lightning strikes and—one ear gone. . . . Look sharp, your eyes are young, what's that, headlights? A car? Stand on the road and spread your arms out. The driver won't hit a kid, he'll stop. Tell him you got lost, okay? Understand? And that's that."

"I'm scared. The car will skid when the driver steps on the brakes."

"You got it, kid. That's why I took you, so they'd slow down. How am I going to throw these bags in the back of a truck on one leg? Have to do it carefully, so the driver doesn't see."

"It's scary, mister," I whimpered.

"It's scary for everybody," said the exterminator.

I went out on the highway and spread my arms like a cross.

The black cat hung on to my coat, clawing and howling. As the truck got closer the cat shone in its headlights like a huge blue diamond.

The truckdriver stepped on the brakes and the exterminator threw the two sacks into the back of the truck and shook the other four cats out of my knapsack into it as well.

He gave the knapsack back to me.

And when the truckdriver had driven off, he said:

"Wait, kid. Many years will pass, and when you're grown-up, and sad, and sick, my son will come to you. He's your age. His name is Lekha. Then many more years will pass, and you'll be completely alone. And then my granddaughter, Lekha's daughter, will come to you. She will be called Sonya. She will help you, but then she'll die. A meteorite will kill her. Don't be afraid, kid. Go home and wait for them. And that's that. You'll recognize them, the same way I recognized you through the keyhole."

Today I realize that I am in a hospital. And I understand that thoughts of cats torment me only because it smells of raw fish in the whale and cats, as is widely known, love raw fish. . . . And today I can fit beginnings and endings together with my knowledge of such unpleasant concepts as death, for example.

But how can I learn not to explain things to people? People, surprisingly, don't understand anything! Even something like why dogs don't like cats has to be explained to humanity in detail! And it's so simple. Dogs are usually just jealous that people like cats. It's so ordinary, but for some reason all the people around me are surprised by it.

Having weighed everything carefully, I have decided that if I live and get out of here I'm going to spend the rest of my life blowing the money I earn on dressing well, chic.

When you eat hospital food and nobody brings you anything from the outside to add to it, it's like being an orphan, and I remember Mama again and again.

A dream last night: I enter an imaginary apartment that is mine and somehow not mine at the same time. There's a strange woman there, and I start throwing whatever comes to hand at her, including paper arrows that I make by tearing the old, peeling wallpaper off the walls. The woman hides someplace. I go outside—a policeman. I complain that there's a stranger in my apartment. The policeman pricks up his ears in alarm and doesn't want to go with me to chase the woman away. I go back alone. Nobody's there, the apartment is empty. I sit down to eat in the kitchen. And suddenly I realize that I didn't check the bedroom. I go there. In the bed where my Mary-Masha once lay there's a fairly young thin woman with a dark complexion whom I, overcoming my fear, poke with a little scissors. But the woman won't be driven out. And now, after breakfast, I think that this could be a symbol of death.

I really like my neighbor, who talks about going hunting.

Where can I find out what "rig-friggin'" means? He often says, "I'll fix your rig-friggin' wagon!" And this expression of his reminds me of Cat-Killer Silver's "And that's that."

Masha looked beautiful and alarmingly young in her coffin. The makeup artists from the theater probably tried hard; they always liked her—professionally, for her beauty: it's always easier to make up a beautiful woman as a monster or a young woman as an old lady than the other way around. In general, everybody liked her. That was clear from the number of people at the funeral and from the number of flowers. Again, lilacs, lilacs, lilacs . . . Paying my last respects, I touched my lips to her cold forehead and dropped a small icon—inconspicuously—into her coffin. Masha always claimed to be religious, but in practice, as a woman, it seems to me, she wasn't completely able to follow the dictates of even our church, which is far from the strictest on earth. . . . Just take the way she came to me for the first time. . . . No, I'm not ready to think about that yet. . . . Better if we recall the time she and I took a drive out to the monastery not far from Mikhailovskoye, a working monastery; she met an old man in the courtyard of the monastery, the gatekeeper or something, he introduced her to the abbot and it was impossible for me to tear them apart. And again, lilacs, lilacs, lilacs . . . Then we drove over to the Pushkin Hills, I was tired, it was hot, I steered into the bushes and went to sleep, laying my head on the wheel: we had left Gatchina very early in the morning. It seems that she, too, fell asleep to the rustle of the treetops in the grove; there was a gentle June breeze, and suddenly bits of shrapnel drummed the roof of the car. I woke up, jumped out; I thought some kids were goofing around—there was nobody there, it was just that the wind had picked up, boding a storm, and with every gust it tore acorns from the oak under which I had parked the car; the acorns drummed the thin body of the car deafeningly. Masha started to laugh as only a happy child can laugh; it was then for the first time that she stopped being afraid of thunderstorms, and I didn't have to convince her that I had grounded everything well. At night we walked up to Pushkin's grave; a new friend of hers, whom she had met in the cafeteria, a poetess, put a candle in a niche in the headstone, and we stood there in silence until the candle burned out. . . . It was somewhat theatrical and pompous, but it's good that we did it. . . .

I was reading Amosov today: "There's no need to be afraid of the last moment of life. Nature, wisely, has taken care of us: consciousness shuts down before death. . . . An unjustified exaggeration of the fear of death. . . ." He very interestingly gauges the character of man by his ability to endure stress—by its magnitude and duration. Man improves himself by constantly developing his ability to endure intense and protracted stress. . . . My God, my God! What a shame that I am so seriously ill and will never be strong again. For the future of the planet is in the hands of the strong and only the strong will be able to take full advantage of the blessings of the future that they create.

She never had a lot of luck with roles, of course. But then she probably didn't have a lot of talent. And the leading role she got was the most unlucky one—to this day no one believes that the fire in the theater started because a meteorite landed right on the stage. Not too many actors die onstage. Fate chose her. And thereby ennobled her—and deservedly so, because Masha truly loved the stage. And besides, since her early childhood, that eternal sense of fate, fear of lightning. . . . And those lilacs, lilacs, lilacs . . . Where did I stash her mother's diaries, frightening in their feminine candor, precious for me, I who suffer eternally from ignorance of women, from imagining them. . . . In her mother's diary there is a passage addressed, most likely, to her beloved, who abandoned her: "I always remember how you played with my breast, the way a child plays with a favorite toy. . . ." What's going to become of those diaries if I never get out of here?

Last night I dreamt of a horse that some artist by the name of Vovikov left me. That's what he was called by the invalids at the market, who explained to me that he had asked them for three rubles for a bottle, but they didn't give it to him. And so this artist Vovikov left me a horse and a complete harness and saddle and coupons for feed and hay; the coupons are the same kind that they give out for gasoline. The horse is in a barn. It's summer. I had nearly forgotten about her when I suddenly thought, She's hungry! And I started stealing sweet-smelling hay. Then I saddle her. And then old Lekha comes but can't, of course, help at all in the complicated business of saddling the horse. I ask him, "Should I feed her first or give her water first?" She's a good horse, smart. I saddle her, climb up on her, and she obeys me, like in my childhood, when we drove the horses out into the field for the night and I had a mare, Matilda, and her bridle came unfastened. . . . And so I'm riding this kid's horse that the artist Vovikov gave me to the bazaar to buy food for her, but at the bazaar they sell his paintings. And again, lilacs, lilacs, lilacs . . . But that's neither here nor there, I just happened to remember it; in the dream there were forests, fields, a slope covered with grass, and I let the horse gallop and I understand that I keep the saddle well, and think about how Tolstoy was right. . . . But then the saddle slips down under the horse's belly, I fall, and I note that it's not at all frightening to fall from a horse! Maybe I'll get better? And I climb up on the horse again, and seat old Lekha behind me. And the horse puts up with it all, remarkably patient, a good animal. . . . At this point the nurse came in to give my neighbor, Yury Nikolayevich, a shot, he lies there with a hot-water bottle, he has a lump, and he yells when they give him the shot. . . .

Grasping the essence of another person's work is as slow a business as understanding one's own talent and predisposition. And vice versa.

I, a radio engineer, am not superstitious and do not believe in ghosts. Unfortunately, sometimes many of my educated colleagues do not think very hard about the arguments they use to try to convince the general public that there really are no such things as ghosts.

Certain of my colleagues claim there are no bio-fields either. What do they mean? My body temperature is 98.6, and the room temperature is 68. That means that around me a thermal field of biological origin forms. It's another matter that, in my opinion, the bio-field is an ordinary physical field. But we don't yet know its properties as it is, most likely, a combination of fields—thermal, electrostatic, etc., possibly modular, that is, capable of carrying sufficiently detailed biological information. Rejecting this bio-field is the same as denying the existence of brass only because it's an alloy and not in Mendeleyev's table of the elements. Or, say, somebody claims that science is concerned only with reproducible phenomena. Then what about ball lightning, which, so far, cannot be reproduced? What do you want— to exclude it from physics?

Many years after the war I was working as a lab director in an institute for scientific research on Vasiliev Island. And a bushy, red-haired man of about fifty with scars all over his face came to see me there, right in the lab.

It was lunchtime and I was sitting alone in the laboratory, drinking tea that was boiling in a flask. The tea leaves were floating up and down beautifully in it.

The man walked in without knocking and said, "Rat-tat-tat, rat-tat-tat, little pussy wed the cat! . . . I'm Lekha, and you're Geshka?"*

He introduced himself so strangely.

Then he explained that he was the son of the same good man who had long ago rid our house of stray cats.

I offered him some tea; he sat down and said:

"My thoughts will hardly be of interest to you, Gesha. You should read this instead."

He took a bulging packet of newspaper clippings out from under his shirt. The clippings, in various languages, were yellow and decayed. He put a picture of a mutilated tree on top of them. Printed under it was: "This poplar is a mute but eloquent witness that ball lightning is 400 times stronger than TNT. Pieces of the tree up to 200 kilograms in weight were strewn over an area about 30 meters in circumference. Surprisingly, A. M. Sidorov, a ranger, who had been fishing under the tree, came away unharmed. The ranger claims that this is far from the first time such things have happened in his life. . . ."

I read this interesting item, and Lekha watched me over my shoulder, breathing hotly in my ear.

*Geshka, Gesha, and Gena are all nicknames for Gennady. —Trans.

"It started," he said, "after they took out my appendix. And right off, ball lightning. It shot into the operating room, injuring the surgeon after he had already finished cutting me and had begun to wash his hands. And after the incident you're reading about now, they fired me from the rangers. And that's that," he explained to me, calling me Gesha all the while, even though we weren't even well acquainted enough to tip our hats to each other.

"And have you met the snowman?" I inquired.

"I drank vodka with him. And that's that."

"And how are you with aliens?" I asked.

"I drank vodka with them. And that's that," he explained casually, taking another newspaper clipping out and laying it in front of me:

"LIGHTNING KNOCKOUT. A rare event occurred in the Swedish city of Malmö. Lightning, striking a soccer field during a match, knocked the players of both teams and the referee from their feet. But, fortunately, the Swedish soccer players and the Arabian referee came away with only a little fright. . . ."

"One word—Swedes," Lekha noted with disdainful contempt, still breathing in my ear. "'They came away with only a little fright!' I was twenty years old. I was playing for our republic's team, Sledgehammer, against the Armenian team, Pink Tufa. Right end. I remember it as if it were yesterday. Pour me some more tea. From the very beginning we showed those Armenians in no uncertain terms that we were playing to win. In the first two minutes they assailed our Sledgehammer goal from the side three times. Thereafter the Armenians attacked more aggressively. At halftime, when it seemed there was no way we could stop the Armenians, there was a clap of thunder. I realized right away what it meant. But it was too late to do anything—my fear turned to terror, and it's impossible to ground yourself when you're running. Five bolts of lightning all together! The first one hit me, of course, and my shoes flew off, burned rubber all over the field, and I flew right into the Armenian goalie. Knocked him right through the net with the ball. In short, such a brawl started that all three of the referees, Georgians, ended up in the hospital. And there was a crater left on the spot where I was hit. And that's that. Those were no Swedes, Gesha. Since then, they won't even let me play on the city team. 'He's nuts,' they say. The idiots."

"Did you have to pay for the net?" I inquired.

"You laugh? Well, laugh, laugh. But listen further. Fate played a trick on me here. After the fight an Armenian girl with a mustache, about fifteen years older than me, comes up to me and inquires how I feel and all that. I was still excited and, well, I sort of ran off at the mouth about how both my father and I attract lightning, usually ball, but sometimes, like today, the ordinary kind too. In a month she had me at the altar. And that's that. Turns out she was writing a dissertation on physics and her father is a professor, an Egyptologist. And, well, I got married. There was only one condition—that I not wear galoshes or ground myself in any other way. Our life-style was remarkable—an apartment in Moscow on Vernadsky Prospect, a dacha in Red Plowman, and if we got tired of the dacha, off we'd go to the Slender spa by chauffeured car. My wife didn't take her eyes off me. A movie camera, a tape recorder, a loupe, a notebook always at hand. Whether in bed or outdoors. The first month—a honeymoon. Praise God! I wasn't zapped once, either by ordinary or by ball lightning. Half a year we lived together and not a single clap of thunder, no less lightning. But storm clouds gathered on the domestic horizon. The deadline for her dissertation was nearly up, but her research had come to a standstill and she was pregnant to boot. And that's that. I began to feel uncomfortable myself.

"I hobnobbed with academicians. They're a dense bunch, Gesha, I'll tell you that straight out. You ask one, "Your profession, Mr. Scholar?' He: 'I'm a corresponding member of the Academy of Sciences of the U.S.S.R.' You: 'Very nice. And what is your specialization?' He: 'Last year I received the RSFSR state prize.' You: 'Very nice. But what do you study and where?' He: 'I'm a professor, the head of a department at Ural University.' You: 'Very nice. And your speciali—' He: 'There are a hundred seventy people in my department, but I ended up at Ural totally by accident, actually I'm a real Muscovite, you see, used to live on Kutuzovsky Prospect, between the Minister of Foreign Affairs and the Vice-General Director of the State Planning Commission of the U.S.S.R.' You: 'Very nice. And your specialization? I'm interested. . . .' He, finally: 'Political economics of socialism.' You: "Thank you. Good-bye. It was nice to meet you.' And that's that. He thinks you're unsophisticated. You think he's a complete idiot. And then my little Armenian gave me a daughter. We named her Sonya. And right after that she took up with just such a Ural professor, and I went back to Sakhalin. Now I'm superintendent of a dorm at the curriers' vocational school."

Lekha related all of this with the mild-mannered circumstantiality of a skilled master. And then went on about how he can see flying bul-

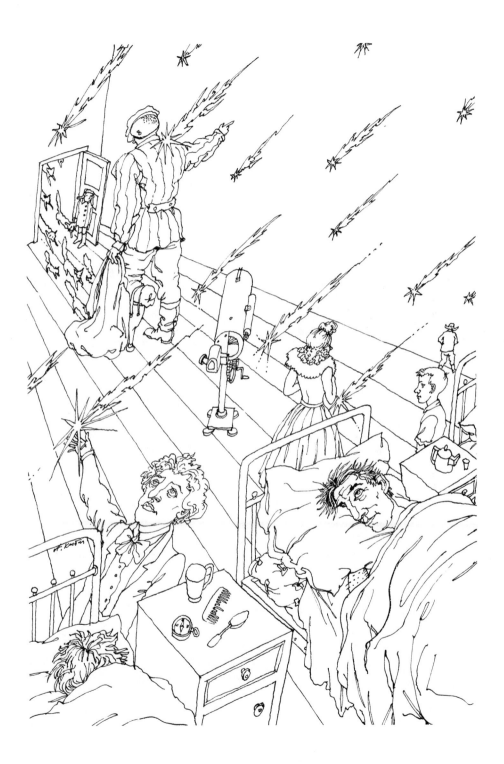

lets, sense drops in the intensity of geological radioactivity, and see stars during the day, and how ball lightning struck Lermontov at the same moment as Martynov's bullet.

Then Lekha gave a wonderful rendition of "Were Only the Night Darker Tonight" and "There's Smoke in the Chimneys of Russia's Manchester."

It was winter, but it seemed to me that something menacing was rumbling outside the storm windows.

"Do you ever get hit in winter?" I inquired.

Lekha grinned ruefully:

"It happens, Gesha, anything can happen. After all, how did I end up on Sakhalin? Thunderstorms on that island, with its cold climate, even in summer, are an extremely rare phenomenon. I joined the volcanologists there. A coefficient of 1.8 percent. And that's that. The nature's remarkable—bears, lava . . ."

"You probably mean Kamchatka," I said. "There are no volcanoes on Sakhalin."

"You know best," said Lekha. "On exactly the thirteenth of December the entire population of our region was surprised to witness one of nature's rarest phenomena. The residents of Sakhalin saw bright flashes of lightning during a blizzard. It's not easy to surprise those descendants of convicts, but they were shaken! I was released from the hospital with second-degree burns—and headed straight for the department of hydrometeorology, where I insisted that I was at the bottom of it all. But the meteorologists had their own explanation: "A current of warm air, carried north by a cyclone, on contact with a mass of cold air prevailing over the island. . . .' Ha! Inertia of the brain."

Another peal of thunder outside the window.

"Listen, Lekha," I ventured to say, "it's not going to hit us here today, is it? I haven't gotten around to writing my will, you know: it's a tough job coming up with heirs. Whom to leave all my Saxon porcelain to, and the crystal?"

"You're making fun of me," said Lekha.

"And what about your father's power, have you got it too?" I asked. "I mean his power over cats."

"Of course."

Outside the laboratory window I could see the roof of an apartment building, bristling with television antennas. Snow swirled along the roof and through the snow cats trudged, one after the other, toward the attic window and gathered around it.

"They're the most obstinate—they're going to deliberate and vote," explained Lekha.

"Will it take long?"

"It takes thirteen for a quorum, no less. And that's that."

All of this seemed a little strange to me and all of a sudden I had a great longing for spring, sun, gentle warmth, and lilacs.

"Open the door to the stairway, Gesha," said Lekha.

No sooner had I opened the laboratory door than a huge black cat entered and came to a stop on the threshold. Having come to a standstill, he proceeded to exude a hidden energy by wagging his tail ferociously and decisively. The cat didn't look at us. It turned away in disdain.

"He's a direct descendant of the great martyr. The one whose wife was the size of a Grenadier guard. Remember?" Lekha introduced the cat.

"I remember the snowstorm. I remember the blue light. And the way he shone like a diamond."

"When you see such a brigand you understand right away how many bastards there are walking around on two legs," said Lekha.

"They're beautiful creatures, it's just that they torture mice and I can't forgive that," I said.

"They suffer a lot for that themselves," said Lekha, stroking the cat. "I was kicked out of the curriers' vocational school too. Now the cats are my only livelihood."

He undid the bags that he'd brought with him. And the cats competed with each other to get into them.

"But that's terrible," I said.

"What can you do? Have you ever seen ball?" Lekha asked.

"What?"

"Have you seen ball lightning?"

"No."

"You will," he assured me vaguely, and left, the bags filled to the top, describing to the cats in gruesome detail the execution awaiting them.

Yes, it's my misfortune that I can't get by without human companionship, yet social isolation is obligatory for the author of an immortal book. But, in the many years I've spent inside this whale, I've grown used to loneliness.

I'm not sick at all, but on that January evening I really wanted somebody to stop by. I was at home on vacation, it was late, I didn't feel like sleeping, I was lolling on the couch watching television. I always have it on. On television I get a good look at what men and women, children and soldiers are like today. Out on the street they all sort of flash by quickly. Or else I just don't feel like observing them in real life. But on television I examine them, like under a microscope. It's no picnic either, it's the hard work of an artist.

And so I was lolling about on the couch, smoking, looking at the men and women on television, and praying that somebody would suddenly ring the doorbell.

January is the most difficult month for me. The cold, the dark, the snowstorms. The Voice that I almost always hear when my nerves act up I hear even more often in January: ". . . Professor Zimmerman died; Professor Renz died with the word 'meat' on his lips; senior astronomer Berg died; senior astronomer Elistratov and his wife; Messer, the manager of the machine shop; Sapozhnikov, the head librarian's assistant; Dombik, an astronomer; Voitkevich, a computer programmer; Professor Kostinsky's widow; and almost all of the junior technical staff. Two things I forbade myself, son—to think about food and to indulge in reminiscing, since neither the one nor the other helped in the fight against death—or, rather, in the fight for life. But it was so hard on the night of the eighteenth to the nineteenth that I couldn't resist the temptation and gave myself over entirely to reminiscences. Scenes of the recent past rose up before me, one after another, with staggering clarity. . . . Dear Pulkovo, the garden bathed in sunlight, the scarlet peonies, the jasmine bushes, the fiery lilies by the veranda. The house, filled with music, joy, and love. Dear faces. Comfort, contentment. God, what a contrast! I fell asleep late. I woke up from a strange sensation—the pillow was wet and sticky. There was a faint glimmer of light through the frost-covered windows. There were dark spots on the sheet, on my robe, on the pillow—blood. My nose bled for two days, day and night. Nothing could stop it. I lay motionless on my back, on the pillow, but it bled anyway. You put bowls on my chest, under my neck, and the blood ran down my lips and my chin in a steady stream. There was a deep silence in the empty, icy ten-room apartment, where some of the people had been evacuated and the rest had died. Frightened, the children clung to me. There was nothing to eat. I divided my bread between you—more for you, less for Nadia. The next day brought no changes. A treacherous apathy crept in that resigned me to everything. . . ."

The enthusiastic idiot on the color television is yelling for the hundred and fiftieth time: "A paper airplane . . . Who could have known that it would turn out like this? Who could have known that it would turn out like this, a paper airplane?" There's something ominous in the inanity of the popular singers of today, something heralding the inevitable end of the universe. I don't even want to discuss the idiocy of these songsters. . . . Fifteen billion years ago there was no universe! There was no airplane—or any of this. And that's a scientific fact, not propaganda.

". . . And suddenly the thought struck me—I'm dying, but what about them? That's when my heart started beating wildly, my mind started racing. Have to do something, have to eat something to give my body strength to fight this new incomprehensible disease, hunger. What if I tear the wallpaper off? The paste on the back is made from flour. No, it'll take a lot of energy and won't make much. My eyes fell on the two bowls filled to the brim with partially congealed blood. That's the answer—cook it and eat it. I could already see it in a hot frying pan, turning into flat gray chunks that could be chewed. How to go about it? First of all get rid of you for a while; the soul of a child should have no part in such things. Then light the wood-burning stove. Weakness overwhelmed me; I fell asleep and woke up again right away. I told you that you should go out and play, which came as a great surprise to you since, in light of the incidents of cannibalism that had sprung up recently, I hadn't been letting you go out alone. You puttered around for a long while and I hurried you along, worrying the whole time. Finally you left. I stopped up my nose with a terry-cloth towel to keep the blood from flowing and, holding on to the wall, made my way to the next room, where the wood-burning stove stood. I bent over to pick up a log—and blacked out. I came to at the sound of your footsteps. You had come back. The freezing cold had scared you and you had come back. My plan was shattered and I threw the bowls of blood out the kitchen window. . . ."

Basically I understand why the Voice has been so insistent today. I found a scrap of paper in the morning—an old list of hers from about ten years ago that had gotten caught in a book: "Repair the kerosene stove—7 rbls.; half a cord of firewood—30 rbls.; two pairs of socks—20 rbls. 60 kpks.; Olga for January—200 rbls.; five rubles for a comb; meat—14 rbls. 60 kpks. Debts: 50 rbls. to Anna Vladimirovna by the 10th of January; 36 rbls. to Maria Ageyevna by the 1st of February . . ."

The Voice kept coming and coming until, finally, somebody rang the doorbell.

I would have been glad no matter who it was, so I opened the door without asking anything and saw a huge German shepherd on the staircase landing. And then, behind the shepherd, I saw a beautiful young girl in a hooded fur parka.

She said:

"Don't be afraid, Uncle Gena, Dick doesn't bite. And that's that."

Behind the shepherd and the girl I saw six cats on the stairway leading to the attic. Each one sat on its own step and looked at me with green eyes. Only one turned away.

"Who are you and what do you want?" I asked, secretly delighted.

"I'm Lekha's daughter," she said. "Remember? I wrote you a silly letter last spring because I had a dream about you."

"Of course. Delighted!"

Of course I was delighted. I had wished so for someone to come and drown out the Voice that I hear when my nerves act up. And here a charming young woman had come with a huge German shepherd.

There was a transistor radio on Dick's collar. "The Aria of the Varangian Guest" blared from the radio. He had a purse in his mouth.

Dick's face expressed a submissive disgust for the transistor radio, for "The Aria of the Varangian Guest," and for the purse, which probably smelled of perfume, although my guest was completely devoid of worldly luster.

"Please, don't shut the door," she said. "A few more animals should still be coming. There's a terrible snowstorm and they're freezing."

"Ah, yes, of course, it runs in your family, I understand everything. But forgive me—I'm not shaved and basically . . . I'm not quite presentable."

"I'll only be about half an hour," she said, and threw off her fur.

"Very nice. I thought it was the half-witted kid who had come. He delivers telegrams at night," I said, and hung her fur on the coat rack. "And I never have small change for the kid, and I hate to give him more than that. Says he needs it to buy macaroni for his sick grandmother. He's probably lying."

"My name is Sonya," she said, calmly walking into the room. "Do you like my name?"

"I love that name. Ever since I read *War and Peace.*"

"Very good. Dick, put the purse down on the couch and take off that transistor radio! I'm tired of classical music, Uncle Gena."

Dick did everything she commanded.

The cats crept delicately into the room after us. They weren't afraid of the dog at all. But a funny expression of complete despair appeared on Dick's face, as though he were standing at the edge of a whirlpool, ready to throw himself into it and drown.

"Sonya," I said. "There's not a bit of sausage or meat or fish or even a drop of milk in the house. What are we going to do with this horde? They'll eat us up, the way the second lieutenant was eaten up in Schweik."

"That's out of the question. And that's that. They're not at all as hungry as it seems. They're all a bunch of fakers and beggars. Scat! In the corner!"

The cats went off into the nooks and corners and hid.

I am indebted for the disarray in my life to my predilection for literary endeavor. What else, if not that, sits inside me and dictates my absurd actions? What else, for example, had suddenly commanded me not to leave the house, to disconnect the telephone, and, what's more, to stop seeing people. I was tired of my dreary engineer colleagues, who tell the same old jokes and forever blame all of their failures on their wives or their bosses. So I took my vacation in the middle of the winter and spent two weeks like a hermit in the center of the huge wintry city, drawing the curtains so my friends couldn't see a light in my apartment from the street. I didn't give a damn whether anybody was worried about me or thought that I was already lying dead in some gutter under a snowbank. I hadn't shaved all this time, there were bags under my eyes, and my teeth had turned black from nicotine. And even while reading I kept hearing my mother's voice: ". . . astronomer Zimmerman died; astrophysicist Renz died with the word 'meat' on his lips . . ." She herself died of cancer.

People have been dying of cancer for a long time. And none of them can understand that it's heaven giving them a sign. After all, cancer is uncontrolled cell division, their chain multiplication, it's the standard model of an atom bomb! Just as the horrible cells multiply, so the planet will swell and die, if . . . The ability to radiate light is a universal property of life: rabbit and cat livers give off light, as do plant shoots; our brain is surrounded by a nimbus. When life goes out luminescence disappears. I have to shine for people even from the bottom of the grave. Whence my solitude, my alienation.

And this is my reward—a charming girl with a big, kind dog. I wanted to touch Sonya with my finger to convince myself that she wasn't a dream. Serov once took Grabar to see his *Girl in the Sun* in the Tretyakov Gallery and said, "I painted this work and then, for the rest of my life, no matter how I strained, nothing came of it—I burned out entirely on this one. And I even find it strange myself that this is my work, it is so unlike me. At that time I sort of went crazy. You have to sometimes—once in a while you go a little crazy. Otherwise nothing comes of it." Thus I, too, decided to go a little crazy and locked myself in the house. Even though I basically don't agree with Serov. Material cannot be overworked and depleted if that material is your life, singular and inimitable.

"What were you thinking about when I rang the doorbell?" Sonya asked.

"I have to paint a portrait of a white night in words, but it slips away. I guess it's impossible to paint something that doesn't cast a shadow."

"You mean you haven't noticed that I don't cast a shadow either?"

"You can't tell right away when light is coming from various directions."

"Do you believe in premonitions, Uncle Gena? Ay, look at all the butts! Smoking is bad for you, but if you like, smoke in good health. Did I write you that I often go to the movies in the afternoon? Fortunately, the Biryusinka Theater is right nearby. I love children's films. It's all because I'm actually a witch. I even learned how to fly in a mortar like Baba-Yaga." She got up, walked around the room, and stole a glance at the alarm clock that stood on the dresser. "But my superstitions are not dangerous for society. Both Grandpa and Papa told me a lot about you. And I started to dream about you. That's why I flew here."

"What are you looking at the clock for?"

"But I'm not looking at it," she said with needless and fleeting insincerity. "If you want, I'll stop all the clocks. How many clocks do you have?"

"The alarm clock on the dresser and my wristwatch. I'm not wearing my wristwatch, and anyway it stops by itself."

"Hey, clock on the dresser!" she said in an authoritative and capricious tone. "Stop at zero!"

The minute hand of the alarm clock, the bell of which had been broken for a long time, spun around like the propeller of an airplane. Then, all of a sudden, the lights in the apartment went out and in the dark a shimmering blue flame floated slowly toward us from the foyer.

In its light I saw Sonya sit down on the floor, cover her face with her hands, and start crying bitterly.

"I'm afraid, I'm afraid," said Sonya through her tears and through her palms that were covering her face. "What if it suddenly strikes me in the eye? I'm not a witch at all. Having to expect every minute that it will come and strike me—that's the worst! Having to think all the time—what else will happen? And how will it happen? And waiting for it—where, when? I have to wear galoshes, and nobody wears them anymore!"

The blue flame made a circle around the room and disappeared in the doorway, and the lights came back on immediately.

"Oh, well, there's nothing I can do about it. What a fool I am, ruining all the clocks in the house. What time is it now?" Sonya asked, wiping the tears away with her fist.

"I don't know. The television's already off the air."

"It just burned out. . . . Well, and that's that. Time to go."

"Oh, don't go!" I begged. "Mama will start talking again right away. How long can she go on with the same thing over and over—'. . . senior astronomer Berg died; senior astronomer Elistratov and his wife; Dombik, the astronomer . . .' I don't remember any of them, but she just keeps repeating it and repeating it!"

"Do you know how Papa got killed?" Sonya asked, wiping away her tears.

"I thought that he just died by himself."

"A meteorite hit him right in the heart. And that's that. Dick, give me my purse! I had the bittersweet pleasure of paying my last respects to Papa in a crematorium—as my scholarly Mama says."

Dick took the purse from the chair and brought it to her. She took out a perfume sample box in which there was a small meteorite.

I took it from her. It was very heavy, with sharp edges like a fragment of an antiaircraft missile. And it smelled wonderfully of perfume.

"Right in the heart," she said, and pulled her skirt down over her knees. "It's cold in here, Uncle Gena. There's a draft on the floor. The windows probably aren't sealed. It's dangerous. And I don't like it when people look at my knees."

"A wonderful death—he was buried in the Milky Way," I said comfortingly, and held out my hand to her. "Come on, get up now! To tell you the truth, I wouldn't mind getting a piece of the universe right in the heart and having a night star put at the head of my bed. May I stroke your hair?"

"Don't touch me!" she screamed, recoiling. "I'm charged with a strong electromagnetic field, Uncle Gena."

"What the hell! Is there really no remedy?"

"There's only one other person in the whole world charged with electricity. Mr. Roy Sullivan. We have different charge signs, and we could make a beautiful couple, but he lives in America and he's already over seventy, Uncle Gena."

"Poor thing! What misfortune hounds your family!"

"So far nobody's been able to explain this rare phenomenon," said the girl. "Turn on the hot water in the kitchen. I like to wash dishes and hang curtains, because I'm half Armenian."

"Ay, Sonechka, you'll be stuck there till morning. I haven't washed a thing in two weeks. You won't be able to get near the sink."

"That's all right. The animals will help us. Dick, stop pulling at my purse! Mr. Roy was hit for the first time on the seventh of August 1963. He was driving his car. Lightning from a low, absolutely tiny cloud. It struck him in the head and burned right through his hat. It burned off all of his hair! It's nothing for men, there are good-looking bald men too. But what about me? Okay, I'm going to wash the dishes, the sink, and the stove. Is the stove dirty too?"

"Most likely."

"I don't like cleaning stoves. But I won't calm down otherwise. Don't hiss like that," she shrieked at a black cat. "A regular rattlesnake, not a cat. Let's go, everybody! Is there an apron in there?"

It occurred to me that she, of course, was bored with me, so I couldn't bring myself to ask her to get rid of Dick and the cats and stay with me. Even if she agreed to stay, it would be out of fear of lightning, of the night, of the freezing cold, and of snowstorms. A snowstorm rages and the whole earth shivers. And I have no right to take advantage of a charming young girl's fear. And there's not one clean sheet. It's shameful. This is what I've come to. I don't need anything from her. Just as long as she doesn't leave. Let them all spend the night— her and Dick and the cats. And then we'll all wake up together—her and Dick and the cats. And I'll go out for milk, and we'll drink coffee together.

"I know what you're thinking about, Uncle Gena," said Sonya.

"If you know, then climb up next to me on the couch."

"You really want me to?"

"Absolutely."

"And if I don't?"

"I'll drink up what's left. There's enough till morning. And I'll think about how to paint a portrait of a white night. I need a prototype. For summer, for the night, and for death—have you ever seen death depicted as a man with a sickle? Models for wisdom and love could always be found among existing women. It's only for a white night that none can be found."

"I would climb up on the couch with you," said Sonya after giving my immodest proposition brief but serious thought, "if you were about ten centimeters taller, about five years younger, a little richer, and if your eyes were dark."

"There's no figuring you out," I said, feeling a little hurt, although I value frankness and trustworthiness in people. "You were just complaining that you can't touch anybody!"

"Do you have any paper clips, Uncle Gena?"

"What the hell!" I said. "Over there, on the table. As many as you like."

"Here's what I do before I kiss anybody," Sonya said, and started to rub her palms together. "Toss me the box of paper clips. Never mind! Dick, bring me the paper clips!"

Dick went up to the table, stood on his hind paws, took the box in his front paws, and brought it to her. The paper clips flew out of the box and hung in a long chain from each of Sonya's palms. She started laughing and ran up to the mirror. . . .

I'm not really sick at all. It's just that sometimes everything seems so clear to me that, later, you can't tell what was a dream and what was real. But they're treating me with electric shock therapy. I control time with ease, because ever since I was a child I've loved making things up. Robert Louis Stevenson, Dr. Jekyll, and Mama, who loved flowers too much, are to blame for this. The first thing that I remember is a huge painting in a heavy gold frame—lilacs in clay pitchers, lilacs, lilacs, lilacs. . . . Where on earth did our five-story building go? Even the foundation is gone. We burned the painting of the lilacs; first we chopped up the frame with an ax, then we cut the flower-covered canvas into pieces with papa's razor and age-old dust flew out of the canvas. Or was it Vrubel's *Lilacs?*

Last night my neighbor in the ward read what I've been writing, I don't hide it—let them all read it! After he read it he told a story about a family whose cat would howl terribly every Saturday. He asked them,

"Why does your cat howl? It keeps me awake." They told him that they gave the cat a bath every Saturday. He said that he gave his cat a bath every Saturday, too, but it didn't howl. Then they asked him, "Do you wring your cat out after the bath?" He said he didn't. It turned out that they wrung theirs out.

It's funny, of course, but it's also kind of sad.

. . . Sonya ran up to the mirror and stuck her tongue out at me in the mirror.

"Last year, on the twenty-fifth of June," she said, "When that capitalist, Mr. Roy, was out fishing, he got zapped for the seventh time. Now he's in the hospital, in a special armored room, with burns on his chest and stomach. What a shame that I'll never be young again! Even if I live to old age and lapse into a second childhood. Just think! Seven times some Ku Klux Klanner was struck by lightning, the ordinary kind—not ball lightning! He was thrown all of three meters, you see, from his car. And they write about him in all of the papers! Am I a beautiful woman, Uncle Gena?"

"Very. But you're not a woman yet. When you learn to love about yourself not your beauty, but your soul, only then will you become one."

"My God! Not you too! I'm sick of hearing about it. Oh, by the way, Uncle Gena, I saw a mermaid once. And you know what was coming out of her eyes? There was a black light coming out of her eyes! You know, I've decided to wash the dishes tomorrow. And stop drinking that junk! Dick, chase all the cats into the kitchen and lock the door, and stand guard in front of the door and make sure they don't get out! What are you looking at me like that for, Uncle Gena? Turn around. You can see that I'm getting undressed! You're completely shameless. . . . Hey, what's the matter? Are you crying? Would you like me to peel an apple for you? Do you often confuse dreams with life? Oh, your hands are so cold! First I'll warm them up for you. Don't be afraid, why are you shaking so? Thanks to the paper clips, I've become perfectly normal. And we'll sleep peacefully till morning. You don't snore, do you, dear?"

No, only women, after all, are capable of existing in Lobachevsky's geometry, that is, of gliding through time on two parallel yet intersecting planes. We men stand with our heads planted firmly in Euclid. Better to stare at a mirror than at a blank wall.

Let's take a well-known instance. Overcoming your shyness and shame, you make an immodest proposal to a woman, as I did. Or, for example, you tell a most fascinating political story. Or—sweating and agonizing—you formulate a hidden, highly complex truth of your own discovery. And you're completely absorbed in your immodest proposal, as was the case with me and wonderful, gentle Sonya. Or you're completely absorbed in your explanation, in syllogisms and images. And you believe with every cell of your body that the whole of the civilized world is obliged to listen to you with bated breath, but she says, "Shall we make some cabbage broth, dear?" And this at the very peak of your discourse, at its very culmination. And—that's it. The Tower of Babel crumbles, a piece of brick flies right into your mouth, and you, of course, bite your tongue—just like in the Bible.

I made it up of course. Nothing of the sort happened between Sonya and me.

After washing the dishes, she left.

I sat in the kitchen and watched her washing the dishes.

"That window with the light on across the way, is it always lit up at night? Yes? And do you look at it? I thought so. My God, where can I put these bottles? Don't you have a garbage chute? My hair always gets in my eyes—it's a constant nuisance. . . . Have you read about the Pied Piper? No? Oh, he played the flute in such a way that he could lead away whoever he wanted. It's a legend from the Middle Ages. And he led out of town all of the rats that had flooded Hamelin, but then, offended by the ingratitude of the townspeople, he lured away all their children. . . ."

I phoned for a taxi and walked her to the car.

A snowstorm swirled in the nocturnal darkness above the city, and the wind blew from all sides—no matter which corner you hid behind. And we turned numb waiting for the taxi. Lightning pierced through the snowy twister in all directions. Buildings were wrapped in the twister, and tram tracks, along which the wind swept the snow, flashed in the lightning. The frozen branches of the old poplars on the boulevard, surrounded by the snowstorm's whirlwinds, made a racket. Scared, Dick huddled close to my legs, St. Elmo's fire shining on his ears. And thunder amid the snowy, sleeping city; thunder, exalting man suddenly and exposing the whole of his pitiful genius.

The taxi drove away in a canyon between two snowbanks, spraying me from under its rear wheels with prickly bits of ice—they were frozen lilac petals.

In memory of Sonya, that strange and charming girl, there remains a postcard with a reproduction of *Procession of Cats* by the Japanese artist Tomoo Inagaki. That postcard is here, with me, in the hospital.

At night, when my neighbors are asleep, I take the postcard out and read it: "I'm not at all what you think, Uncle Gena. On the other side of life I'll be a bright, gentle angel. And even if you go to hell, and I don't believe you will, I'll fly to you, a bright angel, and recognize you in the burning pitch, and hold out my hand to you. I'll ask permission of Jesus Christ himself. I never ask God for anything for myself, I just thank heaven for everything and for your being on earth. And I really was at your place and I did take 20 rubles from you for a ticket to Moscow. Sonya. And a black light really does shine from mermaids' eyes."

There are six cats painted on the picture by Inagaki.

Four are going to the left.

Two to the right.

All of them are in profile, that is, their bodies are in profile. And there are five feline faces turned toward the viewer. And ten feline eyes follow you—no matter which way you turn.

Three of the cats have whiskers.

Three do not.

One cat is entirely in profile, not looking at you.

There's some profound Japanese meaning in the picture.

I feel it.

I wonder whether a man sentenced to death would be happier if they showed him the galaxies and the Milky Way through a telescope and played Beethoven?

1987

Translated from the Russian by Steven W. Nielsen.

ANTILEADER

Vladimir Makanin

1

When Kurenkov got mad at someone his face darkened, his complexion deepened, and a sort of weathered country tan settled on his forehead and cheeks. He lost weight. And it could be said that he grew small. His looks gave him away.

"So what is it now?" Shurochka asked threateningly.

Inspecting his tan, she added:

"You mind me now, Kurenkov!"

He shrugged his shoulders guiltily and mumbled something. He was eating, chewing. Shurochka inspected him again. (When her suspicions were unjust—and that happened occasionally as well—it was Tolik's response, affectionate and somewhat embarrassed, that calmed her down. Shurochka would say:

"You mind me now, Kurenkov!"

To which he, really embarrassed, would answer:

"Don't you worry, Kurenkova. . . ."

It was all rather sweet.)

But this time he didn't answer. And when he had finished dinner, he went to bathe, and asked to have his back rubbed, which was also a symptom and a sign for Shurochka. To others these signs might seem trifling, but a wife knows her husband. He ran the shower in the tiny apartment bathroom, so thoroughly steaming up the place that he felt warm and good, as if he were in a steam room, but then it started dripping here and there, everywhere (Shurochka had yelled at him more

than once, because it made the walls damp: "Lazybones! You could at
least go to the bathhouse!"). When he had worked up a good sweat he
peeked out the door, and sticking his head through the doorway, he
asked Shurochka: Rub my back, would you? It was as if he didn't have
the strength: he stood naked and thin, diminished, and he whined,
plaintively begging to have his back rubbed, like a little boy who's sick
and asks you to bathe him, poor weakling, if only out of pity. Shurochka busied herself with the dishes. Seeing his outthrust pate, she
grumbled, but of course she rubbed his back, noting once again that
not only his face but his body had darkened. He had suddenly grown
swarthy.

At this point Shurochka had little doubt that Kurenkov had taken a
dislike to someone. Thinking about it, she figured out who it was:
Tyurin; Vasily Tyurin had joined their crowd quite recently, about a
year ago, and he already stood out. And it was true, they had taken
quite a shine to him: he was cheerful, talkative, physically strong, and,
moreover, he had a car. He could pick you up or drop you off.

While the technician tinkered with the television it was Shurochka's
responsibility to write down what he said and list the repairs. But catching the dark flap of carbon paper and placing it under another sheet yet
again, Shurochka suddenly stood up. She went to phone; she was worried about her husband, after all, and a pretty, not to mention shapely,
woman can get away with a lot, Shurochka knew this. Even the nervous customers (it was the busy time of day—close to lunch) kept
quiet. It suddenly seemed to her that all these crude people were deliberately silent. She got through to him quickly. Kurenkov worked for
ZhEK, the housing maintenance office, and at lunchtime was usually
lounging about at home.

"Kurenkov!" Shurochka shouted into the mouthpiece. "The parents' meeting at school—you haven't forgotten? And pay the rent. And
the telephone bill! The telephone bill!"

When Shurochka was especially worried about her husband, she
loaded him down with all sorts of errands or simply scolded him at
will. On those days when his face darkened it was useful to give him a
lot to do.

That evening Shurochka called the Zimins; she spoke with Anya
Zimin and with Alik. "It seems my Tolya's off again," said Shurochka.
But they only laughed. They didn't attach the least importance to
her signs, and they loved Tolik. How could they not love him—they

were childhood friends, after all! The Zimins, and also Olya Zlotova, Marinka, and Gena Skobelev now lived in the large, multistory building complexes that had replaced the old Moscow yards and courtyards in which they used to live and of which nothing remained any longer, if you discounted the friends themselves, but then, of course, they had grown up. The onetime boys and girls of those yards and courtyards— that's who they were.

Of course Shurochka felt that there was a lot lacking in the company of her old friends. They didn't know how to converse intelligently and interestingly, they didn't know how to dress with taste—even Alik Zimin, a jazz musician, looked a little like a parrot when he dressed up. But you can't expect everything in the world from people. Shurochka found subtlety, taste, and the ability to reason in others, but then, it was really friendship that she valued in her old friends, the memory of childhood, and the fact that you could drop in to see them anytime. Hanging up the phone, Shurochka thought about them and her heart warmed: everything will work out all right.

"How I love you, Tolik," she exclaimed to the empty room, alone with herself. ("How I love you when you're quiet, when you're calm. How I love you when you're good!" is what she meant.) Shurochka could be sentimental, sometimes positively gushing.

To keep an eye on him, Shurochka also went with Kurenkov to purchase a present for their daughter. Heading for the department store, they walked hand in hand, but just as they started to cross the street a passenger car, braking on the snow, forced them to the sidewalk. At first they slowed down, then they stepped back, and then, a bit angry, they looked over at the driver and . . . burst out laughing: Vasily! As always, the friendly, charming Vasily Tyurin immediately pulled the car over to the side of the road; he even drove right up onto the snow-covered curb, threw open the door, and climbed out. He extended his hand to Kurenkov right away, with a smile that said: Hi there, Tolya, let's take a break and have a smoke together. They were planning to celebrate New Year's at the Zimins', and that's what they talked about. They stood by the car. Being a favorite is no easy matter, and Vasily Tyurin may have sensed that someone was secretly storing up hostility toward him, only he didn't know who.

Taking a drag on his cigarette, Vasily Tyurin said, with some concern in his voice:

"We'll have a good time. . . . I just hope there are no fights. No one'll get too drunk, will they? What do you think?" And after the foretaste of shared festivities, this was rather surprising—it was as if he were saying that you couldn't even drink on New Year's.

Kurenkov answered him quietly and simply and spoke only for himself: I won't get drunk. To which Vasily Tyurin responded with a grin:

"You, of course not, it goes without saying. I'm not worried as far as you're concerned, Tolik." And he smiled again and asked something or other about how things were going, but then, suddenly pensive, he said: "Maybe I won't even go to the Zimins' after all—I don't know."

Once again Kurenkov answered quietly and simply:

"Maybe I won't go either. We'll see what happens."

Shurochka held him by the arm; as she listened to their conversation she felt a slight shiver down her back and across her shoulders.

"No, Tolik, you have to come. What, am I going to be the only serious guy there?" And here Vasily Tyurin tried to smooth Kurenkov's feathers; if they weren't friends, weren't especially serious people— they could easily do without each other, particularly at a New Year's party. Listening to them, Shurochka even felt kind of sorry for Vasily, he was trying so hard.

"Tolik, you've gotta come," repeated Vasily Tyurin. "We'll drink. We'll talk. I love to listen to you talk about life, Anatoly!"

Now he was really laying it on thick; You and I, the two of us, pal, we're in it together. But maybe he always worried before a get-together and talked to everyone that way—maybe he always stopped his car and acted all buddy-buddy. Shurochka also noticed that he said Anatoly, not Tolik. Exactly why Vasily Tyurin didn't want to turn down a gathering wasn't clear (if he really had such a strong premonition!). Vasily lived with Marinka Knyazeva; they had hooked up not long ago and, obviously, he could spend New Year's at her place. The two of them could celebrate together, without any fuss at all. In fact, it was through Marinka that he'd ended up as part of their crowd.

"Well, I'm off to the store," Shurochka said to them. Moving away, she glanced back: they were also saying their good-byes, shaking hands, and of course it was Vasily Tyurin who wanted to shake hands, he just couldn't lay off. Vasily got into the car and sped away, waving at Shurochka as he passed. He was a powerful man; when he sat behind the wheel his chest bulged against it. Her Kurenkov, looking like a runt next to Vasily, also went on his way. Shurochka followed him with her eyes—he didn't head directly toward ZhEK, where he worked as a plumber, but first turned toward the beer stand. It was a cold winter day, but their beer stand was marvelous: the beer was served heated up and there were pretzels and crackers. At the entrance to the store Shurochka glanced back again: Kurenkov was already at the stand sipping his beer.

Kurenkov felt more or less the way people feel when they're coming down with something. He was agitated, even anguished. He would have blown Tyurin off, to hell with him, but that was the problem, the feeling of irritation grew by itself now, ungovernable. He stood and sipped his beer and in his chest he felt a burning. Outwardly calm and controlled, however, he drank three mugs. He usually drank two. The beer didn't relieve the feeling, and, unsatisfied, he dragged himself to ZhEK, where he sat through a lengthy dressing-down from his boss— Kurenkov didn't snap at him, he was a peaceful, patient person.

So they not only bawled him out but also forced him to work over-time—after dark he was still going from apartment to apartment on calls: it wasn't the first time they'd loaded him down with other people's work. At ZhEK he was thought of as a good-natured guy who had never quite learned to stand up for his rights.

But work didn't alleviate the feeling either. Back home, the plumber, grown thin and dark-complexioned, roamed about his own apartment and mechanically touched the faucets. Tormented, he fretted in the kitchen for a while, then in the other room. His daughter and wife soon fell asleep, so he stuck to the kitchen, pacing it off softly and un-hurriedly in his wool socks. Now and then he held his hand near his stomach: he felt the burning there. It grew stronger at night, rising al-most to his heart.

Unable to fall asleep even in the middle of the night, he went to his wife; he felt chilled from all the walking, and his wife was warm, heated by sleep and the blanket. He caressed her, but when he touched her breast again a half hour later, Shurochka blew up: "Stop it, for heaven's sake—just like a seventeen-year-old boy!" "All right, all right!" And now he spoke coarsely and roughly: Give a husband what's his, some people do. But later, still tossing and turning, he couldn't sleep and he went back to the kitchen again. He paced, smoked, and the burning in his chest bothered him even more. He heard his wife's snores; by now Shurochka had been hurled into sleep as though from a cannon, while he kept feeling under his ribs, as if determining the exact location of the burning and trying to stop it. He smoked and looked out the window, where a fine snow was falling.

The party wasn't yet in full swing when Vasily Tyurin began to get nervous: he joked awkwardly, nervously, in fact, and they started needling him and egging him on. Suddenly he began boasting about his car and his artful way with dough, and Alik Zimin, the host of the party, shouted at him (joking, of course):

"Hey, windbag, what are you bragging for?"

"I feel like it!" Vasily Tyurin instantly retorted, and started to make fun of Alik. But Shurochka and Kurenkov were at the other end of the table—next to Alik Zimin's wife—so they were sitting at some distance, as it were. Shurochka was no longer worried. She was even thinking: Why not call, say, the film critic Panov (now *there* was someone who knew how to speak tastefully and dress tastefully; suede sports jacket, corduroy trousers) and wish him a Happy New Year? It might be awkward, but then again it might be just the thing.

Then Shurochka noticed that Kurenkov, who kept filling and refilling her glass, had somehow quickly and suddenly gotten drunk himself and was barely following what was going on—and thank God, thought Shurochka, because a drunken Tolik was usually well behaved and calm. He sat, quiet and a bit pale from drink. True, he did try to sing a song softly, but they booed and hissed him left and right, because singing songs at a New Year's party was, well, not exactly called for, and anyway it was too early—and then he quieted down altogether.

Shurochka herself (she had decided not to phone and wish Panov a Happy New Year) said to him: Don't sing, Tolik, shut up, would you, and go call our daughter. And Kurenkov obediently traipsed off into the bedroom, where the Zimins' phone was; there he settled down, hunched over, and Shurochka could hear him dialing the numbers with an unsteady finger. He finally got through. "Gone to bed?" he asked his daughter. "Not yet." "How's your homework, did you do it?" "What homework, it's vacation!" "Mmm. S-sorry, sweetie. I've had a bit to drink and I'm already talking n-n-nonsense." And with that he hung up the receiver, and Shurochka was pleased that her husband was acting like a husband and that he was so obedient and that he called home at a word from her.

Kurenkov was also pleased: although he'd had a lot to drink, he'd still talked to his daughter. He was pleased he'd managed. And the thought occurred to him, why not just leave and go home to his daughter, let them go on drinking without him, but then he felt the burning in his chest again, and hesitating, he returned to the other room, where there was a ruckus going on and where the party was still gathering force. The color television no one was watching was broadcasting the holiday variety show "Little Flame"; everyone was clinking glasses and, on seeing Kurenkov approach, they cried out:

"Come over here, Tolik! . . . Let's have a toast, eh, Tolik!" Full of cheer, they would have cried out to an elephant: Hey there, elephant, let's drink to each other. Kurenkov still wanted to leave, but they called to him and extended their glasses toward him and made a racket. Their tipsy all-round favorite, Vasily Tyurin, shouted out of the blue, as though asking for it:

"And if anyone has a bone to pick with me—come clean with it. Let's go out in the street and talk man to man!"

Everyone burst out laughing, and Vasily, grinning and laughing, stood and straightened his tie over his slightly protuberant, premature stomach. Vasily's strong, bull-like face burned and glowed from drink.

"Let's go out, then! Let's go right this minute!" Kurenkov said to him, and the inequality of the combatants caused everyone to burst out laughing with renewed force. They begged Kurenkov, who was pale and had already managed to go and get himself drunk, to sit down, to drink a cup of strong tea, and better yet—to eat a little something with fat in it. The two of them, however, Vasily Tyurin and Kurenkov, were already heading for the door, and at that moment in the "Little Flame" show Alla Pugacheva appeared on the screen in a light kerchief, smiling with her bewitching, widely spaced teeth, and began to sing. Everyone watched; everyone seemed spellbound. Only Shurochka was worried. Knowing her husband, she wanted to get up and follow him, but getting up was a problem: the champagne had sort of weighed her down to the chair, and her legs were gone. Shurochka thought about Kurenkov; he'd gotten her drunk, the snake, he'd out-witted her. She started waving her arms about, she even yelled: Forget about Pugacheva, run downstairs right away! But no one listened to Shurochka. She cried out to them once more. Legless, she couldn't stand. She could only squirm, seated, from chair to chair, closer to the window, to look out; the air was thick and they were smoking and the window was open a crack.

Kurenkov hit Vasily as soon as they were out the door and on the street; they had gone out in suit jackets and it was freezing, and the New Year's snow crunched underfoot; there was not a soul on the street. Vasily Tyurin slipped but stayed on his feet.

"What's got into you, Tolik?" he said, dumbfounded and still un-able to take Kurenkov seriously. He thought that Tolik Kurenkov had simply had too much to drink; moreover, he was much stronger than Kurenkov. But Kurenkov was already hissing, overflowing with bile:

You, everyone's fed up with you, you worm, why don't you split and go back to your own part of town, your Southwest. You can party and flash your money around there.

"What? Is that you talking—are you completely drunk, Tolik?" Vasily took a step, he even opened his arms wide, wanting in his intoxication to embrace Kurenkov and maybe exchange kisses out there in the cold, but as he stepped closer Kurenkov punched him in the face.

After that the fight started in earnest. Tyurin was stronger but Kurenkov more frenzied, and he fell twice but got up. Both their faces were battered, both of them breathed heavily. In his heart Tyurin still thought that of course someone or other had put Tolik up to it and fueled his irritability, and that sweet, stupid, drunken Tolik was, more likely than not, a stand-in. Tyurin had no malice. And the instant Kurenkov collapsed in the snow, Vasily Tyurin, spitting blood, said: "Next time you'll know better!" and turned away, heading for the door. At that moment Marinka Knyazeva and Gena Skobelev rushed out to reconcile them. Alik Zimin, the host of the party, was also with them, of course. Arriving too late, they were driven on by Shurochka's cries. "They're fighting! For heaven's sake, go down—they're fighting!" she yelled, sticking her head out the window.

Tyurin began to explain, though incoherently, that he was only defending himself, that Tolik was a bastard and that they couldn't be reconciled on equal terms. Right then and there Kurenkov jumped up and in a flash flew at him through everyone standing around, and punched him in the face, punched him forcefully and insultingly, in fact. Vasily Tyurin raced to his car. He managed to jump in, slamming the door right in the face of the frenzied, indefatigable Kurenkov, who had torn after him once again. Swerving sharply and spraying snow, the car sped across the road; fortunately, Vasily's sheepskin coat and his hat were in the car, so now he drove to the sixteen-story high rise on the other side of the road, where Marinka Knyazeva lived. He had nowhere else to go in that neighborhood. Marinka, realizing that he'd gone to her place (We'll have to finish celebrating, just the two of us), dashed after the car, wrapping a scarf around her as she ran.

So it was that Vasily Tyurin, a friendly, cheerful man, disappeared from their crowd. Everyone thought he'd taken it too hard: all kinds of things happen among close friends. Marinka Knyazeva cried a bit, but she knew that Tyurin had intended to return to his family, who lived somewhere in the southwestern part of town, in two or three weeks anyway—Marinka alone knew about this. She cried because she wanted to have him back if only for two or three weeks. But everything was settled when Vasily came by again one time for something he'd forgotten at Marinka's; they spent the night together, talked for a long time—and he left for good. Someone, Alik Zimin, it seems, phoned and invited him over, but Vasily never showed up.

2

Later it came out that when Vasily Tyurin sped off in his car and Marinka ran after him, when everyone, discussing the fight, started back upstairs to the Zimins' in order to continue the party somehow, Kurenkov didn't go with them. Actually, he did wave as if to say: I'll be there in a minute. "Let me cool off a bit," he shouted, grabbing some snow with a trembling hand and applying it to his battered lips. Even after cooling off, however, he didn't come.

He crossed the street almost at a run. A completely empty New Year's trolley bus rolled along the street and two taxis zipped by jauntily as Kurenkov crossed the wide thoroughfare, which was dusted with snow. He ran, shivering, in a jacket and a white shirt, the collar of which was slightly soiled with blood. On the other side of the street, he came upon the intermittent trail of Marinka Knyazeva's footsteps in the snow. He followed mechanically step for step until he arrived at her doorway.

When Marinka opened the door he pushed right in, not giving her the opportunity to shut him out, after which he rushed into the kitchen, where Tyurin was. They started throwing punches again on the spot; then they grabbed hold of each other, twisting each other's arms. The tablecloth flew to the floor, dishes fell, and Marinka Knyazeva screamed at Kurenkov, lashing out at his face: I'm going to call the police!

"Call them!" snapped Kurenkov, and then attacked; he was still worked up, while Vasily was now fighting without fervor, exhausted by the noise and the shouting. For a moment they separated and stood clenching their fists, out of breath. "Throwing your money around, huh, g-get out of here!" Kurenkov spat out darkly. He seethed with such fury that Marinka was suddenly afraid; she moved aside, grew quiet, and didn't rush to the telephone.

Tyurin finally flagged—he stepped from the kitchen into the other room, opened his suitcase, and, throwing his clothes in, snapped the lock shut. He was ready. He put on his sheepskin coat, his hat, and didn't say a word to Marinka. But he stopped at the door and, smiling crookedly, said to Kurenkov:

"You don't know what throwing money around is, Tolik. And I wasn't rude to anyone—someone's filled your head with a lot of . . ." And he left, while Marinka Knyazeva sobbed.

"Stop sniveling," said Kurenkov. "If I hadn't kicked him out, someone else would've."

Having banished the favorite, Kurenkov returned; he crossed the wide road, this time stopping to let the empty trolley bus pass on its way back. His battered face ached. He could already see the cheery windows where the party continued. Leaning out the open window, Shurochka threatened him with her fist.

For some time Kurenkov walked around guiltily—there was nothing more shameful, of course, than getting drunk and fighting on New Year's. A man of thirty isn't a boy, after all. He felt particularly guilty around Shurochka. Submissive and repentant, he only occasionally tried to say something in his own defense.

"But, Shura," he would say softly, "how come some people get away with everything—money . . . and bragging. And everybody loves them . . . and grovels."

That was his way of explaining and justifying himself, but Shurochka quickly cornered him: And just who was groveling in front of Tyurin? What kind of nonsense are you inventing? Vasily Tyurin was loved, yes, but no one groveled. Then Kurenkov would begin to hedge: I just drank too much and I don't know how it happened. But, as usual, his prevarications drove Shurochka to even greater rage. She even hit him on the neck with her strong hand. She lashed out; he, as usual, took it and said nothing.

"What are you, some kind of pervert?" Shurochka would say in anger, while he sat quietly opposite her.

The discussion was lengthy.

"I'd believe it if I didn't know you! After all, it's not the first time! Don't forget, I know you!" Shurochka screamed, while he held his tongue and kept on nodding his head: Yes, it's my fault.

When Shurochka said: "Straighten him out," her friends didn't understand. Shurochka even had a fit and reminded them of certain incidents in which Kurenkov had been involved, but for them these incidents didn't add up to anything. "Things happen to everyone sometimes." "Get outta here, you're nuts—what are you tyrannizing Tolik for?" Their childhood friends accorded no significance to his outbursts, which, moreover, were very rare. "A guy can't even have a drink anymore." They really thought he'd simply had a bit too much to drink; it happens, after all.

And what's more, Alik Zimin's wife called Shurochka a pain in the neck. From time to time they all complained to one another about their husbands—wives will be wives, but enough's enough. As Alik Zimin's wife saw it, Shurochka exaggerated.

"Just calm down, won't you!" she said.

But Shurochka couldn't calm down, knowing from Tolik's stories how a burning dislike for someone would well up in him and how he couldn't help himself. When was it—last year or the year before—he had felt such hatred for some successful guy that he himself was frightened by his own hostility. At night in bed, he suddenly sat up and said to Shurochka:

"Don't let me go there tomorrow, Shura. Don't let me!" And she didn't let him.

Shurochka phoned her mother-in-law.

"Mama"—that was what Shurochka called her mother-in-law—"Tolik's had another fight."

"Oh Lord!"

"Mama, he's gotten away with it once, twice—but eventually he'll wind up in jail!"

Her mother-in-law lived outside of town. She promised to come and talk to him, but didn't. Judging by her sighs, even she, his mother, thought that what had happened was the usual drunken fight; she advised Shurochka not to let him drink, especially when he had a hangover, but to herself she figured that by about age forty her son would grow out of it. No one understood Shurochka. In the television shop Shurochka sat at the reception desk, her job was considered smart and fashionable, but, well, you couldn't exactly talk to a customer. Finally the crowd dwindled. The technicians, moving off to the staff room, clacked their dominoes from the depths of the shop. Shurochka relaxed. To the left of the long reception desk three televisions stood on display (a color one in the middle—as if to say, look what good work we do!). Yesterday's hockey game was showing on all three, and the whistling was enough to make you plug your ears.

You weren't allowed to turn them off, but it was all right to turn down the volume for a while.

When Shurochka told him about her husband, the old technician shook his head:

"Mmm, yes. You've got yourself a touchy one there."

"No he isn't! No!" And for the nth time Shurochka explained that Kurenkov was not proud at all, and not touchy either.

It goes without saying that as soon as it was possible Shurochka rushed off to her lover, the film critic Panov, a cultured man about forty-five years old who once, long ago, had brought a television into the shop and immediately struck up an acquaintance. The film critic had married late and, as he himself put it, had not yet completely dissolved into his family. He frequently sent his wife and their small children off on holiday to the seashore or to his mother-in-law's in the country, and he, too, as he put it, felt as if he were on holiday whenever Shurochka came to see him. And of course Shurochka talked to him about her Kurenkov more often and in greater detail than she did to others.

This and that happened, he had another fight, Shurochka announced, hardly saying hello, whereupon she burst into tears, to which film critic Panov responded with silence. Then he stroked his handsome, graying mustache and said:

"But he's a maniac. Put him in an insane asylum."

"So that's how it is!" said Shurochka, flaring up. "Straight into the insane asylum, is it?"

The film critic sighed and said hurriedly:

"Sorry."

Their conversations didn't always get off the ground right away. They sat quietly for a bit, then Panov had a smoke and touched Shurochka affectionately; all in all he was an affectionate, kind man. But at the moment it wasn't affection Shurochka wanted, she wanted to talk, and Shurochka spoke to him firmly about the coffee—Some coffee, I want some coffee—and when he went to the kitchen to make it, she got into bed, as she loved to do. They'd taken to drinking coffee in bed some time ago. He brought two cups on a beautiful tray decorated with a drawing of the city of Riga, and sipping the sweet, burning-hot drink, Shura reminded him:

"He's not some kind of nut, I mean, I wouldn't live with an idiot, you know." (She reminded him that her Tolik had a very unusual personality.)

Film critic Panov cleared his throat ironically; however, he was unable to say or suggest anything serious this time—he only muttered commonplaces: With age, you know, everything passes. Shurochka knew this herself. She demanded that he delve into the problem and not brush it aside. Then Panov said something else to her—maybe she shouldn't carry the cross all the way to the mountain. Maybe, if Shurochka was really so afraid, she should get a divorce and marry someone else, someone her age. While she was still young, he added affectionately, and at that Shurochka got angry again and reminded him, since he was so slow to grasp it, that she didn't fear for herself but for Kurenkov; she loved Kurenkov and would hardly go and trade him in for someone else:

"I mean, by himself he's a peaceful person. And he loves our daughter. And by the way, he loves music just like you."

"Music?"

"Yes." And for what must have been the tenth time, Shurochka told him that her Kurenkov would drink, well, for a month or two at a stretch, but that he was a good plumber, not a drunk, and not one of those profiteers who soaked the tenants for rubles.

As usual, film critic Panov escorted Shurochka to the trolley bus; he stood and watched her leave. From the trolley bus she waved, even though people were pushing her. Panov thought about her and Tolik Kurenkov, whom he'd never seen. He thought: How wonderful dramas are in the movies and how awful in life, when they're right next door.

At home Kurenkov had just given their daughter dinner, and now the two of them were washing the dishes together. Kurenkov was so obliging, so peaceful, that Shurochka's heart melted. The darkness had faded from his face, and he didn't seem thin—he seemed normal. Shurochka was about to say something sweet to him but changed her mind. The New Year's fight was still too fresh in her memory, strictness had to be maintained, so Shurochka said:

"Kurenkov, you mind me now!"

He nodded. He washed the dishes and nodded to her, as if to say: Don't you worry about me now, Kurenkova. And he smiled calmly.

About three months passed, however, well, maybe four, and on a clear spring day Shurochka phoned film critic Panov from work and said that it seemed to be starting all over again: her Kurenkov was building up hostility.

"Your life certainly isn't boring," answered Panov, already sighing in his usual manner. It was as though he, too, carried a bit of her cross. Talking with her on the telephone, he didn't forget that Shurochka sometimes sat in his bed and held a cup of coffee in her naked hands.

Panov conjectured: You know, it's quite possible that your Tolik is jealous of the newcomers in your crowd. It's possible (even subconsciously) that he's protecting his childhood friends and the memory of childhood itself—it happens sometimes, there's even a special type of psychological displacement (he didn't say illness). But Shurochka objected. Shurochka said: No. It's true they'd been friends, you could say, since childhood, but their crowd had grown every year and Kurenkov wasn't jealous of everyone.

Shurochka remembered the time in their youth when they went mushroom picking. Shurochka had had a fight with Anya, Alik Zimin's future wife—and Alik and Gena Skobelev reconciled the girls. Suddenly everyone gasped: Tolik had ripped open his foot on a rusty tin can in the bushes. Tolik wanted to suck out the blood but couldn't get his heel into his mouth no matter how hard he tried. Everyone was convulsed with laughter. They carefully washed his heel, after which Alik Zimin and Shurochka took turns sucking out the blood. The others didn't want to.

The wound looked like dark, protruding lips. Tolik kept yelling that they were tickling him. He sat near a tree stump, his head slumped to one side—it lay on his right shoulder, and his long fair hair tumbled down. In those days he rarely cut his hair.

3

"Is that Syropevtsev really so much better than everybody else?" Kurenkov asked, and blew the foam off his mug. He wanted to speak his mind.

They were drinking beer at the stand that over the years had become their favorite place, in their opinion the best in the area and in fact the best in the entire, huge city. It was on a natural rise partially covered with decorative trees and bushes, and the stand itself was clean and tidy. There was a view to boot: down below stretched a wide, grand square where trolley buses turned around and where people, clearly visible with their string bags and briefcases, hurried back and forth. All those people, if you were to stop them for a second, would have looked like figures in a painting.

"So is that Syropevtsev really better than everybody else? Syropevtsev here. Syropevtsev there. Butts in everywhere, when nobody asks him."

Alik Zimin grinned.

"So the guy likes to show off, so what?"

Polishing off his mug, Gena Skobelev also smiled.

"What's eating you? You're not jealous, are you?"

Alik added:

"As soon as a guy with a Zhiguli turns up, he sticks in your throat!"

Faced with a remark like that, Kurenkov was at a loss: he could swear that the Zhiguli had nothing to do with it. Occasionally Kurenkov didn't like someone, true, but he was never jealous of anyone. Whatever his problems, there was none of that crap in him.

"I'm not jealous, it's just disgusting to watch you all licking his rear end."

They weren't offended, they laughed, and Alik Zimin thumped Kurenkov on the shoulder. Shurochka walked up from behind, approaching slowly in order to hear their conversation, if only fragments of it. Apparently, she did hear it. Shurochka told him to go on home, although she knew that he liked to stand around like this with his friends. She raised her voice: Go home! And Kurenkov went, of course, but first Shurochka made him go with her to the store—let him lug the shopping bags.

At home he was silent, and then Shurochka asked him straight out:

"So now you're after Syropevtsev, huh?"

He didn't answer; Shurochka rattled the dishes around, then she sat and stared at the television. Shurochka liked to watch a movie before going to sleep. She had her favorite position: she heaved her huge breasts onto the table and propped her head up with her arm. She was a large woman, and as soon as she settled into her favorite position their small kitchen became crowded. The film was about the war.

"Let me get by," said Kurenkov angrily, standing up and squeezing behind Shurochka to get a cup of tea.

"And he doesn't go out with just anyone, no, he starts up with Olka Zlotova. . . ."

This erupted from him suddenly (about Syropevtsev), and Shurochka bristled immediately:

"What are you picking on him for, you blockhead? He's a handsome guy, if he feels like it, he has a good time! She's divorced, after all!"

Kurenkov didn't reply, he bit his tongue. When the film was over, his wife went to bed. So did his daughter. But he kept thinking about the same thing, cultivating his spite, until he stopped himself: What misfortune! He lay down but didn't sleep. He tossed and turned and kept touching his fragile rib cage; the burning began in the area of the stomach, but Kurenkov knew that it would rise, day after day getting closer and closer to his heart. He moaned suddenly, as if from a toothache.

When they were leaving the house in the morning, their neighbor Tukovsky, a wise, elderly man, seemed to want to stop them near the mailboxes. His name was Viktor Viktorovich. At one time, owing to his youthfulness, Tukovsky had served two terms in prison. Everyone knew that he had seen a lot there and that he had a sharp eye. No, at first he simply took his newspapers out of his mailbox. Greeting them in a neighborly fashion and chatting a bit with Shurochka, all of a sudden and completely out of the blue he addressed himself to Kurenkov: You're a good guy, Tolik, but I can see from your behavior (forgive me, an old man) and even in your face—you're headed for time in prison.

"Why is that?" asked Kurenkov. Tukovsky grew embarrassed, and then (he had to answer something), grimly and somehow unwillingly, he added that you can't get around fate, even if you double your precautions.

"Neither my mother nor my father did time—and neither will I," Kurenkov retorted, partly hurt and partly defiant, but Tukovsky only shook his head.

And to Shurochka he commented:

"Keep an eye on him, Shura."

"It's none of your business! An old man, saying such things!" Shurochka herself snapped, though the conversation had been going along in a perfectly peaceable, neighborly tone.

Viktor Viktorovich was certainly not about to insist. He nodded right away, as if to say: Of course it isn't any of my business, and please, excuse me. Tukovsky hurriedly collected his newspapers and left. He went up to his fifth-floor apartment and by then may have already forgotten what he had said; after all, early morning conversations are often only a matter of passing mood. But right after the worldly-wise neighbor had jinxed them so unpleasantly, Shurochka became uneasy. She called her lover Panov and told him that she was worried and that Kurenkov was apparently building up hostility once again; then the film critic, sighing, replied:

"Oh, Shurochka, your life certainly isn't boring."

They arranged to meet and she went to the film critic's house. They drank very little and made love even less, after which Shurochka immediately started talking about her own, pressingly painful problem: I'm scared that my Tolik will end up in prison. What am I to do, what can be done, if ex-prisoners already take him for one of their own? I'm scared he'll end up in prison, she repeated. Her voice trembled, but Panov asked indelicately:

"What? You mean he's never done time?"

"Never!"

"Really?" the film critic asked again, and then he and Shurochka argued. She was even hurt. If she'd told him practically her whole life story once, she'd told him a hundred times, yet he forgot her words and stories, or didn't recall them, or simply got them mixed up: apparently it wasn't conversation with Shurochka that he liked, but Shurochka herself. Shurochka accorded a lot of importance to conversation with intelligent, sensitive people and that, it could be said, was what she loved Panov for. True, he also dressed wonderfully, with taste. She couldn't resist that either.

Shurochka reminded him again: Kurenkov is a peaceful, calm person, but sometimes (once a year, once every two years) he gets sort of jealous and suddenly starts accumulating hostility toward someone who stands out from the crowd. If someone puts on airs—he doesn't like him. If Vasily Tyurin stood out, let's say, because of his fashionable chatter, carefreeness, and a certain surplus of money, which he threw around left and right, then the engineer Syropevtsev, who'd started hanging out with their crowd, stood out even more distinctly—he was handsome. Not only that, Syropevtsev also had a car.

"He doesn't like this one, doesn't like that one—tell me, who does he think he is?"

"Ask him."

Lighting a cigarette, the film critic said:

"I think he's pathologically envious."

"Ohhh, no."

"He just knows how to hide it."

"No, that's not true!" Shurochka got angry (at this point Panov sat down on the ottoman, smoking and dangling his legs, and Shurochka reclined on the bed). Shurochka jumped up in a rage and, gesticulating, told him about Kurenkov's lack of interest in money and clothes, about his indifference to cars. She also explained about the burning in his chest: the focal point of his accumulating hostility. And about how he lost weight and became ill.

"But he's an antileader!" exclaimed Panov this time.

"What's that? A psychopath?"

"Something like that." Panov nodded. And then Panov asked

whether, in childhood and in school, Kurenkov beat up the teachers'
pets and the good-looking boys who were popular with the girls. Was
he deliberately belligerent as a child? There is a notorious (even a bit
frightening) human type of this sort, which manifests itself in early
childhood. Shurochka could have said Yes! Yes! to avoid an argument—but Panov didn't have it right. Kurenkov and Shurochka grew
up together on the same block, Tolik was a peaceful boy, not a trouble-
maker, and what was certain was that he didn't bully pretty teachers' pets. She would have noticed. Even as a little girl she was very
observant.

"Still, it's connected with his childhood." Panov stood his ground.

Shurochka grew worried, she trembled; in the street she bumped
into old ladies. Returning home, she said:

"Kurenkov, you know what intelligent people say about you? You're
an antileader."

"Who says so?"

"Whoever says, knows."

Shurochka deliberately intimidated him with the unfamiliar word so
that he'd watch himself.

Before her meeting with Panov, Shurochka had gone to get pigs' feet
to make *kholodets** for Marinka Knyazeva's birthday. She bought the
feet unexpectedly quickly. She bought carrots as well. There was a lot
of time left, and that's when Shurochka set off to see Panov, whose
gentle conversations soothed her better than any valerian. She rushed
to him as if on wings, and by the time she reached the door, she was
already in tears.

"I'm heartsick."

She could feel something bad was going to happen, she complained
to him—and Panov, beating around the bush, eventually said that
her Tolik had probably been rotten and no good practically since
childhood.

"You're actually happy to write him off as a nut case."

"Whether I'm happy to or not has nothing to do with it now. When
is the birthday party?" (Shurochka was afraid that Kurenkov would
come undone at the party.)

"Day after tomorrow."

Panov had been drinking a bit of cognac. Finishing off another
glass, he grinned.

"You're being silly, Shurochka. If he's really like that, the sooner

*A meat or fish aspic. —Trans.

they lock him up, the better. It's better for you. How long can you live on top of a volcano!"

But at this Shurochka blew up.

"Lock him up?" she said. "You certainly are quick, mister! I love him, he's my husband—have you forgotten that? Family is family, we still have our daughter to raise!"

He softened, started calming her down:

"What grade is your daughter in?" He was forgetful; she had told him many times.

"What grade, what grade—sixth!"

Panov softened, sighed, sympathized with Shurochka, and then turned on the tape recorder; he wanted to enjoy himself and listen to a little music, but unexpectedly the tape contained the very song that her Tolik liked to sing with Alik Zimin—and Shurochka burst into tears. Shurochka sat down on the bed, burying her face in her hands. Panov decided that the song had moved her deeply, and started telling her how sensitive she was to music, how gentle and how feminine. His tenderness moved Shurochka even more and the tears kept flowing, but it was time to go, she'd already overstayed her visit. She dressed in haste, and while she was dressing he kissed her awkwardly. Really, he, too, had been deeply moved. After Shurochka left it turned out that she'd forgotten the pigs' feet in his refrigerator. She was already on the street when she turned back. She was out of breath.

When he saw her again Panov suggested, as though it had just dawned on him: Why don't you have a little talk with your Tolik, Shurochka, heart to heart. Panov reasoned this way: Maybe Kurenkov doesn't feel he's a part of things. He should open himself up to Shurochka, he should confide in her.

"What?" Shurochka asked. She didn't understand right away; she was stuffing the parcel in her bag and breathing heavily.

But the heart-to-heart talk had to be put off, since Alik Zimin and his wife came by; Anya Zimin smelled of expensive perfume. The four of them drank vodka and whiled away the evening together—two families, that was always wonderful. At first Alik played the saxophone for them, then the guitar. Kurenkov loved to sit and listen like that, Shurochka herself adored such moments. She and Alik's wife sat arm in arm and their intoxicated husbands sat nearby. Impending misfortune was forgotten. Shurochka felt good: tomorrow the morning would come, and the sky would be crystal clear and so blue it would hurt your eyes.

When they had seen the late-staying guests off, Shurochka, who was still in the mood, lay down and cuddled up to him. Tolik, Tolik, she said, but he turned away from her toward the wall. Nothing like this had ever happened, and Shurochka flew into a rage. You so-and-so, she shouted (in a whisper), you've had your fill on the side, have you, and now you don't have eyes for your wife? In a fit of pique, Shurochka pushed him out of bed. He went into the kitchen and smoked cigarettes till he was yellow. But Shurochka followed him: Admit it, why don't you? She shoved him in the back once more. He didn't say a word, just stood there smoking; then Shurochka started smashing dishes. She flung one teacup after another on the floor until her daughter, who had been up late memorizing a fable in her room, ran in shouting: "Mama! Mama!" "Go to bed!" And she went out, yelling something. Only then did Shurochka finally calm down, quiet down. Suppressing a sigh, she swept the broken dishes into a corner. Fortunately, her daughter fell asleep quickly. They also went to bed. They lay with their backs to each other.

They were silent for some time, then, turning around suddenly, Shurochka whispered straight in his ear: "You watch out, don't you dare lift so much as a finger against Syropevtsev! I don't want to be married to a convict!" And Kurenkov flinched because Shurochka had read his thoughts as surely as her own. He rolled up into a ball. He said nothing. Then he began to shiver slightly. He turned to Shurochka, became talkative and affectionate, but Shurochka was no longer in the mood—why all this affection when it's time to sleep? And then she remembered Panov's advice. She grew soft, gentle, and whispered to him:

"Tolik . . . tell me, tell me what you were thinking about . . . confide in me."

She kissed him on the neck, stroked him tenderly, and he opened up: Yes, his chest was burning again and he was afraid of exploding, especially at the birthday party. "Ah, Tolik," whispered Shurochka, struck by how accurate her premonition had been and how valuable her lover's advice was. Panov was so smart. But how secretive Tolik turned out to be (after all, she had asked him to get by without fights, she had begged).

"I was planning to have a steam bath tomorrow, and wanted you to rub my back."

"Tolik!"

"I won't touch him, I won't touch him! I promise. I'm just telling you, so you'll know."

They were both glad, she because of his trust, he because of her readiness to understand him. They whispered endearments to each other. They talked on and on incoherently and suddenly realized they were famished—they jumped out of bed half naked and at that late hour went into the kitchen, but even there, having put the kettle on and sliced the sausage, they kept talking in bursts, interrupting each other: "I won't go to the birthday party." "Say you're sick." "Yes, that's exactly what we'll do!" "How I love you when you're good, Tolik. How I love you!" Shurochka sobbed, happy to have had a weight lifted from her shoulders, and he, also happy, replied: "What about me? I love you too."

Marinka Knyazeva managed to send her daughter to her mother's, and without her daughter around they would be able to party freely, until all hours if they wanted to—as Marinka informed Shurochka by phone. Since Shurochka had purchased the pigs' feet, she'd take on the *kholodets*. She'd make the *kholodets*, but Marinka ought to make her wonderful cabbage pie, she was good at it. If Marinka did her best, the pie would be wonderful, and Alik Zimin's wife would come and help her set the table—as for the drinks, the men, of course, would take care of that. Their local store might not have any vodka, in which case Syropevtsev and Olka Zlotova could drive downtown and stock up, and we'd settle with them later. Syropevtsev had a car, so, logically, they'd be the ones to go for the vodka. That way, he and Olka could take part too. Shurochka bustled about and gave advice, but her heart sank—her heart ached.

Tolik announced he was ill first thing in the morning, despite his friends' persuasion, despite how offended Marinka was. Tolik held out well; the day, however, was long—the day was not over yet. Shurochka Kurenkova made the *kholodets*, distracting herself with activity, and took valerian, finishing off the whole bottle by lunchtime. By evening she was extremely edgy—Alik Zimin dropped by to plead with Tolik, but Tolik, good for him, held his ground! It helped, too, that Tolik had actually taken sick. His face darkened even more and he suddenly felt ill. He shivered. And his temperature, as if conspiring with him, jumped to 100 degrees.

He was pleased when he found out that he had a fever. He said, as usual:

"Don't you worry about me now, Kurenkova," and started undressing. He went to bed early.

He told their daughter to eat dinner but didn't eat anything himself.

He lay in bed, watched a soccer game on television, but not even to the end, he was shivering too much. By that time Marinka's birthday party was in full swing. Olya Zlotova and Syropevtsev were there, and Alik Zimin with his saxophone and guitar, and Gena Skobelev, who always showed up with his somewhat squint-eyed wife. Shurochka brought over the *kholodets*, sat there for an hour, downed a few glasses—and went home. No, first they all called from Marinka's: Tolik, old man, we're drinking to your health, get better soon. They heard his voice, and then there was silence on the line. Shurochka immediately rushed home—what a blessing that they all lived nearby, an old, undissolved group of Moscow friends. When Shurochka ran in, Kurenkov was in bed, delirious, muttering a bunch of nonsense. He talked about previous binges and flings, about some women. He was burning up.

The crisis came that night, his fever broke, and in the morning Kurenkov lay in bed, weak, but already smiling. Shurochka didn't go to the television shop, she sat close by, feeding Tolik tea and telling him how they all drank to his health last night at Marinka Knyazeva's. He was interested in how it went and who was there. Shurochka described everything thoroughly, tastefully.

"Yes," he sighed, "no luck for me."

But Shurochka thought: *You* might not have been lucky. But she, Shurochka, was lucky for sure. And so were Syropevtsev and Olya Zlotova—all of them were, in a manner of speaking, lucky.

But he exploded all the same, and for the first time Shurochka thought that just maybe it was true that you couldn't get around fate (it was all too sudden for her). The accumulated and, so to speak, unspent charge of anger in Kurenkov made itself known. Not a week had gone by when, still frail, he got mixed up in a fight that started on a bus, then rolled out onto the steps and turned into a street fight. Kurenkov didn't know any of them—and why he got involved wasn't clear. When he was knocked down he fell on the pavement and, while they were kicking him, grabbed some hard object that was at hand. It was just a coincidence.

Afterward, it came out that the leg of an elegant magazine table had been lying on the pavement, dropped there or lost by someone during the commotion. In the courtroom the elegant leg, when held up, looked like a cudgel. The trial was swift and fair. Along with the other brawlers, Kurenkov was given two years, but he was to serve his sentence on the "soft" system: one year in prison, one year in exile.

He looked lost in the courtroom: he had never fought in buses and didn't understand how this had happened to him. There weren't many people present, only friends came. Shurochka cried, almost wailed: she sat there till the end. Puffy and homely, when they were allowed to see each other, she kept on asking:

"Tolik! Tolik! How did this happen?"

He spread his hands in a gesture of uncertainty; his head had been shaved and he gaped at her as if to say: I don't know how it came about. He, too, sobbed for a moment when they spoke of their daughter.

Panov comforted Shurochka, he was very attentive to her, and in particular he explained that what had happened was for the best, however bitter a pill it was to swallow. Eventually it would have ended in prison anyway, so Shurochka should take into consideration the fact that a minor street fight could have been bloodier, the outcome worse. Let Kurenkov figure himself out and come to some understanding while in prison, before it was too late. He isn't stupid: he has a lot to think about. She should be glad it happened this way. He could have ended up by maiming some interesting, outstanding person—precisely the kind of people he didn't like and toward whom he accumulated hostility—would that have been better? "You mean—this was meant to be?" asked Shurochka. "I didn't put it that way." "This was meant to be," Shurochka repeated with bitterness and pain, utterly incapable of coming to terms with the idea that the best place for her Tolik was in prison.

She sent a letter to him in eastern Siberia, full of loving phrases, both the usual ones and new ones she composed, swallowing her tears. The letter ended with the most important thing, and now the most important thing was for him to return alive and well. This meant that now, *there*, he should finally behave cautiously. "You mind me now, Kurenkov!"

He answered that of course it wasn't easy for him to get used to things, but people were people here, too, after all, and he was getting used to it. And so she was losing sleep and worrying for nothing, in *that* sense everything was all right—and he also ended the letter with the usual: "Don't you worry about me, Kurenkova. . . ."

They were not allowed a visit, so Shurochka wrote him letters and sent parcels. And of course she sent him greetings from their friends; their neighbor Tukovsky, Viktor Viktorovich, on seeing Tolik's return address, told Shurochka not to worry, those were the regulations—they'd be allowed a visit next year.

When she and Tolik, who had been childhood sweethearts, got married, it was so simple, so natural, that it seemed to Shurochka that nothing had happened. They didn't even have a wedding party. After the registrar's office they had a drink at the Zimins', then at Gena Skobelev's. And then they went to the movies. They saw a fabulous French comedy, Shurochka laughed a lot and was happy. She loved the movies then, too. When the film was over, Shurochka said, "Well, so long," at their usual street corner.

"I think you've forgotten something," he said, laughing.

"Oy!" She suddenly remembered.

And they both laughed loudly.

4

Kurenkov was serving his second year more or less at liberty—about three hundred kilometers from the corrective labor colony in a small Siberian town. There, too, he was a hard, diligent worker. There, too, he was quiet. He worked in his own specialty, as a plumber, without any guard at all. He just didn't have the right to leave the town, where every week he had to check in with the police.

They could have seen each other. It was already clear that a visit would be permitted. Even Alik Zimin was asking, with a bit of impatience in his voice:

"Why don't you go to see him, Shura?"

The parcel that his friends put together was wonderful. Gena Skobelev, Marinka Knyazeva—all of them—said: Go on, give him our greetings, visit him, but Shurochka still didn't go. She waited. The thing was that Tukovsky, who understood more about Tolik, advised her not to use her right to visit now, but later—when the need arose.

"When will that be?" asked Shurochka.

"You'll feel it," answered her experienced neighbor. (Panov advised the same thing, repeating that a visit wasn't for seeing each other, but in order to help. It was as if he and Tukovsky had agreed on it, although they didn't even know each other.)

And sure enough, one time Kurenkov sent a letter that was suddenly dry and short, and Shurochka's heart began to ache in the old familiar way.

Requesting time off immediately, and leaving her daughter in the care of Olya Zlotova, Shurochka set off on the long journey. Her heart hadn't deceived her: Tolik had grown noticeably thin and his complexion was dark. When they met, Shurochka's temples throbbed and she cried.

Tolik lived in a barracks with a roommate, and for the three days that Shurochka was there the administration moved Teterin into someone else's room so that the Kurenkovs would feel better and more at ease—but Shurochka didn't feel better. It was true that people were people here like anywhere else, but her Tolik for some reason had ended up in horrid surroundings, where a certain Bolshakov ran the show and bullied everyone. (Having done time for robbery, Bolshakov was also waiting to be released soon.) He was the large man with great hairy hands and a fuzzy chest who met Shurochka in the barracks corridor and without a second thought said something flirtatious to her. Shurochka immediately called him a pig. She called him a pig and even shook her fist at him.

A burglar of average ability, Bolshakov wanted to come off as a real gangster before being released, so he bossed everyone around, frightened them, and took particular pleasure in meting out all sorts of minor punishments. He knew how to instill fear. He beat those who hadn't paid up, or were holding back the money they owed him, almost with a kind of ecstasy; he beat moochers and guys who simply wandered into the barracks to bum twenty kopecks for a beer—and in the last days before his release he really went to town. Once released (he willingly talked about this), Bolshakov intended to be a completely honest and reformed citizen. Moreover, he intended to forget the past forever. He had a good wife and intelligent, grown-up children. So these were his last days. In the Vostok, the only restaurant in town, Bolshakov acted as if he owned the place. The head waitress, Larisa, was his mistress.

The restaurant turned out to be a dump and the band awful, so when they got there Shurochka, wrinkling her nose, said that she didn't dance at all—she didn't know how. But the others were having a good time, they were keyed up. Freedom and reunion with their families awaited them in the near future, and toward evening this feeling was particularly strong in the lousy little dive. They ate well and a lot, even her Kurenkov ate as he never did at home. And Bolshakov, lounging about jauntily, was enjoying life: glancing over the bottles and appetizers, he commanded his toady, Rafik:

"Dance with Nadya, Rafik. Waitresses are people, too, and she wants to."

Then he said to Kurenkov:

"And you, Tolik, take care of mine—dance with her, she likes it. I feel sort of heavy on my feet today."

Rafik went off to dance. And Kurenkov danced with Larisa, with Bolshakov's mistress, though Shurochka sensed that Tolik didn't like it. He couldn't like it, and shouldn't Shurochka know? Teterin sat at the table next to Shurochka—a balding, strong man with a steep forehead, and here he was kowtowing to Bolshakov, like a kid or a lackey. Shurochka took stock of each of them. Kurenkov finished the dance and returned, but the band played on and on, and, probably to forestall Bolshakov from sending him again, Kurenkov said:

"I'm not going to dance anymore. . . . What are you playing the big gang leader for, Vyacheslav Petrovich?"

Bolshakov gave him a lazy, displeased look, as if to say: What's it to you? Bolshakov cleared his throat, and Kurenkov (his complexion suddenly darkened) had already opened his mouth to say something venomous, but Shurochka was on the alert—she kicked him and shot him such a look that Tolik instantly shut up. That was better. All right, then . . . Falling silent, he drank a glass and sat peacefully, but a moment later Shurochka noticed that he was holding his stomach, soothing the burning there.

After the restaurant, when they returned to the barracks (and as soon as they entered the room and were alone), Shurochka gave Kurenkov a talking-to: Be patient! When you get home, that's another thing, let it burn if you have to. But be patient here, because Bolshakov is no Syropevtsev and company. Shurochka didn't ask how and what. She already knew her husband well. Shurochka and Kurenkov lay on the hard camp bed, it was quiet and she admonished her husband, sparing neither words nor time:

"You mind me. I know your tricks, Tolik!" And, raising herself up on the pillow, she shook her strong fist at him.

The next day, when Bolshakov, swaggering and drinking hard, called

Kurenkov into his room to drink some wine, Shurochka was cautious: You've been invited, you have to go, no use making a face. Especially since it's close—five steps down the hall. Shurochka even insisted. Don't, she said, make him mad, Tolik—you'll stay awhile, drink a glass, and leave quietly. Shurochka put on her makeup and went with him: she wouldn't leave him alone, she hadn't come for that. They arrived. Bolshakov was already drinking and boasting, of course, and forcing Rafik to dance the lezginka, which he'd never danced in his life. Wine and vodka were almost never brought into their settlement. But here there were both. Shurochka didn't take her eyes off Kurenkov. It was as though she were coaching him: If you want to return alive, put up with it, you're not a baby, you didn't have to end up here. And, in fact, they drank a little, even sang a bit, passed the time of day.

They were ready to take their leave when Rafik, all worked up and soaking wet from another round of the lezginka, started complaining. Life here was confining and the police watched your every move, he whined, and not only that, the local barber was hitting on his, Rafik's, favorite woman. He seemed to be speaking about Nadya, the waitress. The complaint was registered. Bolshakov, self-satisfied and well fed, decided to set things straight; he rose from his seat. And all of them rose, also ready to take the local Figaro in hand. The barber lived close by.

Shurochka wouldn't have gone and wouldn't have let Kurenkov go—they'd been there two hours drinking wine, it was enough—but Bolshakov very peacefully, even suavely, said to all of them:

"Well, then, friends, let's get a breath of fresh air—and we'll have a talk with Figaro while we're at it."

They came to a neat, well-to-do little house. And, in fact, they took their time getting there; it was so lovely to breathe the astringent, pine-scented air. But as soon as they entered, Bolshakov began to beat the barber in his own home, right away for that matter, not wasting a minute—he only said hello. In shock, Shurochka grabbed Kurenkov's shoulder. They all watched the punishment in silence. They entered and stood right next to the door. That was what Bolshakov had brought them for—he liked people to see his strength. His fists were enormous.

The barber's wife ran into the other room so she wouldn't see; covering her face with her hands, she gasped at every audible blow. When the barber crawled under the ficus, Bolshakov dragged him out, hitting him so that he wouldn't crawl in that direction anymore. Bolshakov didn't strike with his feet. He probably knew that he could kill; even with his hands he used only half his strength. Finally even Rafik begged: "That's enough, Vyacheslav Petrovich." His handsome enemy and rival was sprawled on the floor in hideous shape. "That's enough, Vyacheslav Petrovich." "Wait, I'll just give him a little poke"—and Bolshakov lightly jabbed the prone figure in the buttocks with a knife, which he had quickly and deftly extracted from his pocket. The handsome barber lay on his stomach. He clasped his head in his hands. When jabbed in the rear the barber yelped, but he didn't turn over and didn't uncover his head—one doesn't expose a vulnerable spot. The knife jabbed him once more. Again he yelped and again held his head tight. And he waited for them to get their fill of violence and of his humiliation, and leave.

They left.

In the barracks they all gathered at Bolshakov's once more—to continue the evening, so to speak. Shurochka was still numb with shock— she went along mechanically and mechanically sat down at the table. They sat in a circle. They drank. Becoming sentimental, Bolshakov passed around photographs sent to him from home: his youngest son, who had just gotten married, was in all of them. A young man resembling Bolshakov, smartly dressed and bowing slightly, was placing a ring on his young wife's finger. There was one photograph with champagne. One with relatives. In another picture the young couple, finally leaving the registrar's office, were getting into a car with ribbons. Kurenkov genuinely liked this one, you could see a bit of a Moscow street—the houses looked very familiar and the stand in the distance seemed to be a beer stand. Examining the photographs, they admired the young man, admired the bride, and even approved of the relatives, when Kurenkov, feeling a sudden pang of homesickness, burst out:

"Enough, already, enough—why are you all kissing his rear end?"

"Whose?" asked Rafik.

"Whose, whose? . . . That ape's." Kurenkov spoke the words quietly but clearly, and in a moment of silence. Bolshakov heard, as did everyone else. Unable to restrain himself, Kurenkov left then and there, slamming the door in anger, either at himself or at the whole human race, and Shurochka, of course, rushed after him. She caught up with him in the barracks corridor: he was opening the door to his room.

Shurochka didn't sleep the whole night. She was shaking and thoroughly alarmed; she had to leave the next day. She kissed him, and her lips trembled. Lying next to him, Shurochka alternately gave him orders and pleaded tearfully:

"Tolik, control yourself . . . for our daughter's sake, do you hear, Tolik?"

He promised. He said: Okay, okay. Shurochka stroked him and whispered to him, then threatened. Suddenly, in the silence of the sleeping barracks, she cried out:

"You mind me now!"

In the morning, before her departure, Shurochka went to the authorities. She asked them to transfer Kurenkov to another barracks or another settlement, even one way out in the sticks. She wasn't foolish, she didn't snitch on anyone, she only explained that her Kurenkov was restless from being in one place, he's restless and getting nervous, a breakdown is possible. They were surprised: But what do you mean—he's so quiet, they don't come better than that. But Shurochka held her ground. Shurochka didn't know the rules here, but she knew that she was pretty and that men liked her, and that she was stylishly dressed, like a city girl. She smiled a little, even shed a tear. In short, they promised.

But when she returned, inspired, to talk with Kurenkov and give him his last orders, a fight had already taken place in the barracks: Her peaceful Tolik and Bolshakov had exchanged knife stabs. It had been a morning encounter that had flared up momentarily and then died down; they had been walking toward each other along the barracks corridor, and Tolik struck first. You could say that they struck simultaneously. They were pulled apart. It was immediately apparent that Kurenkov had gotten off easier—he was hit in the shoulder and could still move his arm more or less freely. Bolshakov was hit in the stomach, though not very deeply. They didn't really have to be dragged apart, they separated on their own, fearing noise and attention. Each was sitting in his room.

"How could you! How could you, Tolik!" Shurochka chided him, while he sat on the bed, guilty and silent. After the outburst he immediately weakened, both physically and morally. He dolefully confessed: Yes, it happened. He muttered something to the effect that if he hadn't hit first, it would have been worse.

Shurochka wept:

"You promised, Tolik."

They managed to conceal the fight. Kurenkov went off to work, and Bolshakov lay in his room, where the former medic Teterin washed the wound, bandaged it, and gave him injections of antibiotics for three or four days. Shurochka was nervous: she was leaving and wouldn't know how it all turned out. She didn't have the right to stay on, they'd already produced her exit permit for her.

After three days in bed, supposedly with a cold, Bolshakov changed. He softened, constantly asked others to tell Kurenkov that he held nothing against him, and, in fact, never had, didn't Tolik realize this. When they told him, Kurenkov, screwing on copper faucets and rattling wrenches, spat out: Tell him he can stop shaking, I won't touch him again, what do I need a piece of garbage like that for. The whole affair sorted itself out even further. Everyone behaved quietly and cautiously, everyone wanted to go home. It was obvious that for a knife fight everyone, without exception, would have been given extra time. A feverish Bolshakov went to check in with the police by himself, unaccompanied, displaying a good deal of willpower.

Some rumor of the fight leaked out all the same, or perhaps Shurochka's request worked; in any event, Kurenkov was soon transferred. He was sent to live in a completely impoverished little Siberian town. He was transferred without censure. It could have been a simple coincidence: a request for several qualified plumbers had come from the impoverished little town. Separated from Bolshakov and his gang, Kurenkov wrote a letter to Shurochka from the new place; he wrote that it was far better here. The place was to his liking. He wrote that the barracks were the same and the work was the same, but the place was beautiful, very tranquil. A photograph was included: Tolik had filled out, gained weight, which for Shurochka was the most important sign. The photograph confirmed it.

All the same she wrote: "You mind me now, Kurenkov!"

Shurochka also wrote him that Galya, their daughter, had grown up and that she'd have her first decision to make when she finished eighth grade—maybe she'd go through tenth grade, or maybe she'd go to vocational school in the evenings. And if she were going to work, why not in the same television shop as Shurochka; the work wasn't bad, it was clean. The letter became endless. Shurochka wrote about their friends as well, who sent their greetings and were waiting for him to come back, it wouldn't be long now. Of course she wrote about Alik Zimin, too, who'd just had his second son. She wrote about Gena Skobelev and even about Marinka Knyazeva, who had a new, well-heeled lover.

Shurochka didn't write about other things: about how ugly she'd become. A plump woman with a neat, clear face, Shurochka was not a beauty; she was one of those nice-looking women who suddenly grow old at thirty-four or thirty-five, sometimes for inexplicable reasons. Maybe her troubles were showing. Somehow losing her playful appearance all at once, Shurochka both lost her looks and gained too much weight. I've let myself slide, she thought, passing the mirror in the foyer. The affair with Panov was over too. It could be said that they'd parted company. Shurochka often cried.

Panov wanted to see her less and less, and lately he kept claiming that he was very busy, although Shurochka knew that his wife and children were away and that there wouldn't be a more convenient or better time to talk about Tolik's last letter. And wasn't it the intelligent human being in Panov that she valued above all? In the final analysis, she was used to talking things over with him—there was no one else. After several stubborn calls from her, the film critic agreed to talk, but only sitting on a bench somewhere in one of the little parks. And it was spring; the benches had only just dried off after the thaw and the rains. The benches still reminded one of snow. Panov listened to Shurochka unwillingly, he read the letter without interest, only skimming the lines. He said:

"He has his own destiny." And he added: "You're worrying and suffering over him in vain, Shura."

They didn't manage a heart-to-heart talk. Shurochka didn't get anything off her chest and she felt ill, but there was no one else to go to. With her friends, Alik Zimin and Marinka Knyazeva and the rest, communication was too routine and humdrum, and anyway they didn't know how to carry on an insightful conversation. They didn't know how to analyze the psychology of a given action. They would invite her over, tell her to "forget about it," and pull out a bottle of vodka. At best, Marinka would go to the movies with Shurochka. Shurochka could do that by herself. She didn't need Marinka for that. A lot of people weren't exactly averse to pursuing Shurochka and tried to pry their way into her friendship, but then she loved who she loved. She was used to his graying mustache, to his voice—however, things with Panov were at an end, that was the upshot, and in bitterness Shurochka thought: Why not get together with, say, the journalist Terekhov—he, too, is cultured and, it seems, intelligent. Lately, bringing his Elektronika television back and forth, Terekhov had smiled insinuatingly at Shurochka; in his eyes there was that perfectly clear, familiar . . . And he wasn't the only one, there were others, all different. Work in the shop not only gave her the opportunity to meet cultured people, but to choose among them. But would it be the same with Terekhov? The idea of change itself bothered Shurochka. It isn't easy to step off the beaten track. She was even more bothered by the change in herself: having lost her looks, she had lost her previous self-assurance. That intelligent Terekhov would see her once or twice and that would be the end of it.

"I'm going. It's too hot to sit," said Shurochka, offended, taking the letter from his hands and rising from the bench.

Panov agreed:

"Yes, it's sultry. It's a hot spring."

Without any reason and, as they say, out of the blue, Shurochka burst out sobbing at the birthday party of Gena Skobelev's wife. Her childhood friends jumped up and comforted her—one pressed valerian on her, another said: Swig half a glass of vodka. They didn't like it when one of their own cried. They would have scratched the festivities, but she said firmly: No, no, we'll continue. The party continued, but now they drank to Tolik, to his return, to Shurochka, as though the birthday were hers and not Gena Skobelev's wife's. The oranges, piled in a pyramid, lost their gloss. And the songs they sang, when Alik Zimin started playing his saxophone, were sad. They sang about how they pined, longed, and waited for their beloved, and so on.

It's possible that the tears at the birthday party were a kind of premonition, because—what was it—three days or so later she received a letter from Tolik and she didn't like the sound of it. The letter was very short and dry. Shurochka immediately sent a reply in which, after many affectionate words, she included their usual exchange in large letters: "You mind me now, Kurenkov!" It was a tearful shout across the distance, a plea.

5

The premonition continued to torment her: at night Shurochka would awake with a stitch in her heart or fling herself headlong from the bed for no apparent reason. There was no one to talk to. During the day in the shop she was so lonely she could have cried. She stood at the reception desk—after lunch the customers were a dull, uninteresting lot, or else troublemakers. On the three large television screens, the color set in the middle, they were showing a dolphin being trained and were explaining that this dolphin could already understand people. The dolphin jumped through a hoop. And since the three televisions were next to one another, it looked as if three dolphins (in the middle a whitish-blue one) were jumping through the hoops in perfect unison. It seemed that three dolphins at once could already understand people.

Shurochka wrote down the repairs from the technician's words. She wrote out receipt after receipt. People came. People brought TVs. Shurochka felt her gorge rising and realized that she couldn't stand it any longer. Finding a moment, she left, causing disgruntlement on the other side of the counter that would soon turn into shouts. Let them shout a bit, Shurochka decided.

Shurochka went to see the senior technician: she asked him to let her go. She burst into tears, told him about her premonition, and asked him to give her time off to visit her husband.

"But you just went there not long ago. Do you really want to spend all that money—there and back—it's so far."

The technician grumbled, but he agreed:

"Go on, then."

That evening Shurochka dropped in to see her experienced neighbor Tukovsky, Viktor Viktorovich, who had once done time himself. He lived two floors below. Shurochka simply dropped in, out of weakness, and it turned out to be a good thing, though she had expected nothing good at the end of such a miserable day. Gray-haired Tukovsky and his wife, also gray-haired, were warm and friendly toward Shurochka, and they turned out to be fairly cultured. They gave her tea and cookies and she sat with them the whole evening, sometimes crying, sometimes ardently talking about Tolik. For the first time in a very long while, she talked herself out.

She kept coming back to her premonition: her heart never deceived her—she was certain that Tolik was in trouble now, and that was why she wanted to go. She'd already gotten her things together.

"Have another cup of tea, Shura dear," said Tukovsky's wife, tenderly looking after her.

Having listened to the very end, Tukovsky became glum.

"It's doesn't matter so much that he's quarreling with someone again, what's important is *who* it is."

"Yes, yes," Shurochka agreed.

"It's important he doesn't get himself into really bad trouble."

Tukovsky explained: It's even surprising, you know, that with such a peculiar personality he's somehow managed to stay alive and unharmed there among all those gangsters, goons, and strongmen. After all, life there isn't like being free. It's simpler there. As soon as he crosses the real thing—it's curtains. He's just been lucky up to now. These Bolshakovs and Rafiks she'd talked about were just riffraff; they were, you see, just ordinary jerks—braggarts, not dangerous. Tukovsky lit a cigarette.

When his wife went out for a minute to make a fresh pot of tea, Tukovsky said quietly, as if to a daughter:

"You poor thing, Shurochka. I'm afraid he won't come back alive."

He spoke as if looking into a crystal ball. And he asked:

"How much longer has he got there?"

"Four months and ten days."

He whistled: Whew, that long, eh?

To her daughter, Shurochka said: I'm going to visit your father, is there anything you want me to tell him? And her daughter, just like the last time, blushed and didn't say anything. She had shot up this year and become gangly. She already understood everything. Still blushing, she quickly went to her room; the second year had almost gone by and she was still embarrassed about her father, the convict.

Shurochka managed to arrange the papers for the trip quickly, but since she'd used up her holiday, they gave her ten days with no pay. Eight days on the road—there and back. And two days there.

Tukovsky was not mistaken: during those two days Shurochka saw her Tolik for the last time.

The remote town would have been more aptly termed a settlement. The barracks, however, were like barracks anywhere, divided up into little rooms, and beyond the partition, just like the last time Shurochka visited, someone was making noise and swearing now and then. The beds were also arranged in exactly the same way, and even the gray blanket with two stripes running across it seemed to be a carbon copy of those other blankets—so that the only thing that could surprise her was Kurenkov's isolation. It did indeed surprise her. Her Tolik lived alone, while everyone else lived two, in some cases even three, to a room. When Shurochka, pointing to the second bed, asked where his roommate was, Kurenkov sat silently, then he grumbled, muttering something indistinct, and only when Shurochka pressed him did he admit:

"Yes, well, there you have it. He didn't want to live with me."

"Why not?"

"I don't know."

Kurenkov was depressed, and of course his face was thin and dark, and of course Shurochka knew everything in advance. Experience is like habit. Shurochka didn't waste any time. Telling Tolik that she was going to take a look at the store, she quickly went outside. There she looked around. She had to ask and, having found out, she had to walk up the street and ask again—and there she was. She was offered a seat. She was given a cup of good tea and asked how the weather was back in Moscow. Everything was quite pleasant, except the main thing: the local authorities hadn't had time to take a close look at Kurenkov, and they didn't understand Shurochka. That is, they didn't understand her at all.

"He's quiet," they said, "he's a quiet one, yours is. Why transfer him somewhere?"

The second administrator, who sat to the left, was very young, sensitive. He offered her tea and told her not to worry. There was nothing to fear. With a smile he added: If only all of them were like yours. Right, thought Shurochka, the quiet type. Right, she thought, if they were all like that . . . She returned to the barracks not the least bit reassured. Her heart ached because in the barracks something unseen was already moving in on her Tolik. Something was going on in the barracks. Shurochka could feel it through the walls.

Tolik himself kept silent. No, he said, nothing in particular. Yes, he'd argued with someone. Yes, the same old story, what difference does it make to you who it is?

During her last visit the confrontation also developed gradually, but at least outwardly the people around could be seen and understood. Here he was alone. Moreover, people in the barracks avoided him. It was as if he'd already been marked by something—or someone. It wasn't only that something was being planned or plotted against Kurenkov—it had already been decided, so that even walking up to him or having a smoke with him was taboo. He had been isolated—quarantined. And when Kurenkov walked along the corridor, with or without Shurochka, anyone coming toward him looked past him, as if Tolik didn't exist at all. Shurochka saw all this herself. No one said hello. No one even nodded.

So they quite literally spent the whole day together, just the two of them. They went out for a walk several times. Then they sat in his room again.

"Tolik," asked Shurochka, "I know you, I understand, tell me about it, what it is and how it happened."

She asked again:

"Tolik, it's not the first time, you know."

He only brushed her off, as if to say: It's a long story, and there's no point in telling it. Silent for a while, Shurochka herself started talking. She suddenly livened up. She told him about their friends, about how they had gotten together not long ago at the Skobelevs'. She told him about things she'd bought and the money she'd spent and told him about their daughter, who had a young man now, they go to the movies, the girl is growing up, next thing you know, you and I will be grandparents. "I've gotten so ugly this year, Tolik, that I look the part of a grandmother," and at that Shurochka, as women know how to do, suddenly asked him again tenderly:

"Tolik, tell me . . ."

But Kurenkov said nothing.

She tried tears, swearing, she tried pressure; he finally cried out:

"Lay off!"

"I'm leaving tomorrow," she said. (Both a reminder and a last bit of pressure.)

He didn't reply.

"Tomorrow, Tolik . . ."

But he said:

"Let's go to the movies."

The club was located in a small gray barracks. There weren't many people; the audience consisted mainly of boys who were kicking a soccer ball around at sunset. Sticking his head out, the projectionist yelled: "Hey, people, flock on in to see the show!" "Go flock yourself!" someone yelled back, but then the fifteen or twenty people who had lazily gathered wandered in to see the film, Kurenkov and Shurochka among them. The hall turned out to be dreadful (there was no comparison, of course, with their local theater, or even with the one in the Siberian town where Kurenkov had been before), and Shurochka suddenly felt very sad. Shurochka thought: How can Tolik live here?

Though she loved the movies, Shurochka was able to lose herself only toward the middle of the film. The father in it went sailing on a yacht, then set off to have a look at his plantation, where he unexpectedly recognized his own child, who had been born out of wedlock; at one time he hadn't loved the child, but now he fell in love with it— Shurochka even cried a bit. Shurochka couldn't tear her eyes away from the screen, and she would have been even more deeply moved if she hadn't been prevented. Some girl sitting behind them was munching on seeds, spitting out the shells deliberately, it seemed, down Shurochka's collar. The hall was almost empty. She could have sat somewhere else with her seeds. "You're not in a barn!" Shurochka remarked to the girl, but the girl, sitting with her young man, snapped back at her. The young man laughed. The spitting stopped, but a little later, in the midst of the music and during the most lyrical scene, oblivion apparently descended on the girl, and the shells started flying onto Shurochka's head and shoulders and down her collar once again. Shurochka got mad. Kurenkov got doubly mad; lurching back abruptly, he grabbed the young man by his collar: "Why don't you explain to your girlfriend there that I'm going to spit on her so hard it'll take her a year to dry out!" He half-hissed, half-wheezed the words, and Shurochka didn't recognize his voice. Shurochka grew quiet. Her Tolik, so well mannered, had become coarse. Meanwhile the usher, an old woman, blew some kind of whistle. The lights went on. A policeman appeared. The girl and the young man unwillingly moved to the almost empty left side of the hall. The lights were turned off and the projectionist ran the film from the beginning so that nobody would miss the plot; Shurochka glanced over at them once or twice—the girl was again spitting shells, but into the emptiness; there was no one in front of her, and in the beam of the projector sunflower-seed shells flew in an endless fountain. Nevertheless, Shurochka left the hall fairly satisfied and relaxed: she loved the movies.

"Tolik," she said, "it wasn't a bad picture. Why are you so quiet?"

He said: Yes, it wasn't bad. He agreed too quickly, somehow. They walked silently in step. In the past Tolik used to love to discuss films.

They returned to the barracks; the official, uncomfortable room could not cheer anyone up, but they drank a bottle of good wine that Shurochka had brought, turned out the light, and went to bed. They went to bed early. They wanted to be together; they lay next to each other a long, long time. But then suddenly Shurochka was seized by fear. "Tolik, is the door locked?" "It's locked." Beyond the partitions (on either side of the room) you could hear noise, voices. Someone was roaming down the barracks corridor, you could hear the squeak of boots, and Shurochka, stricken with fear, thought faintheartedly now and then that it must be that unknown person walking. The one who was so terrifying that people not only didn't want to help her Tolik but were even scared to come up to him, to say hello, for fear of angering *him*. She tried to imagine his face. She thought that this man must live at the end of the corridor opposite the sink, in the room with the unpainted door and the number seven on it; she wanted to know at least one thing. "Tolik, what does he look like?" she asked suddenly, but Kurenkov didn't answer. He softly touched her lips with his hand and said: "Ssshh, now." He lit a cigarette.

"Tolik, I'm chilly."

"There's some left here. Shall we finish it off?" Groping in the dark, he deftly poured out the wine. Carefully finding each other's hands, they clinked glasses. He smoked a little more. He stroked Shurochka's temples gently and she, silently, started recalling people—their faces. The ones she'd seen in passing when they were walking to the sink with towels slung around their necks. And in her memory they kept walking and walking, just like in the movies, while Shurochka watched: the faces weren't clear. Shurochka fell asleep to glimpses of these faces and the swaying of the towels as they walked.

She awoke for no reason. She opened her eyes—it was dark and gloomy (she didn't understand right away where she was), but Tolik was nearby, Tolik wasn't sleeping. Feeling faint, she whispered: "Let's take a walk Tolik, let's go out."

"What do you mean, take a walk?" he asked. "It's nighttime."

"So what?" she whispered tenderly. "When we were young we used to take walks at night."

They started to dress. It wasn't too cold. Actually, thought Shurochka, I have to leave tomorrow, we don't have much time, and taking a walk means being together. She wanted Tolik to feel good. The forest began almost immediately beyond the houses. There were no streetlights—the dark little street and rows of tiny houses with fences could barely be made out in the moonlight. Shurochka once again started talking about their friends, who remembered him and were waiting for him back home, but Kurenkov remained so quiet that Shurochka even got angry.

"Why are you so sluggish?" she said.

Her voice softened:

"Pull yourself together, Tolik. Only three or four months—and you'll be home. You'll have a beer with the guys at the stand!"

He nodded: Yes, of course, only four months.

They walked and walked, and Shurochka felt her legs getting tired.

At the edge of the forest they turned back, and once again, in a glade surrounded by dark bushes, they saw a little house. A window was brightly lit, and behind the curtain someone was playing the accordion. They went toward the house. Tolik warned her that the people here meant business, they were tough, they had no use for the cons settled here and kept Berdan rifles in their homes, supposedly for hunting. "Oh Lord!" Shurochka exclaimed. "You can't blame them," said Kurenkov. But the night was quiet, and he himself went up quite close to the house. He leaned on the fence, listening to the melancholy accordion. Shurochka pressed up against him. Kurenkov lit a cigarette. But at that moment the sky cleared, the moon hung like an orange, and suddenly, sensing them, a dog started barking. The moon had awakened it: it barked frantically and ferociously. The playing stopped, and then whoever had dropped the accordion came out and croaked in a rough voice, so unlike the sad melody: "Who's there?" A long silence hung in the air, and only the leaves rustled. It turned chilly. Kurenkov and Shurochka walked on without answering.

When they reached the barracks Shurochka felt her exhaustion retreat along with her sleepiness. She was glad. She started joking, and as soon as they lay down she was already snuggling up to him. "Tolik, I don't want to sleep a wink!" She decided: Let him have a good time, it wasn't every night she was here. Shurochka tried so hard and got so excited that they both went to sleep thoroughly exhausted.

When Kurenkov went out to buy bread Shurochka became pensive. She suddenly got up and swiftly searched his living quarters. The search was simple as pie and of course she soon found the knife, wrapped in a rag. She gasped. She looked at the gray rag and didn't know what to do. She wanted to throw it away immediately but thought: What if they come to get him, if there's no way out, and he starts searching the whole room, searching and rushing about. Don't make it worse. She was a woman, what did she know. . . . Wrapping the knife in the rag, she put it back in its place. She sat crying, and when Kurenkov returned with the bread he said:

"Now, now, stop it. What's gotten into you?"

Having cried, Shurochka once again grew pensive. She started begging him. She didn't once raise her voice:

"Tolik, I beg of you, don't get involved with him—get out of it, give in, you're not a little boy, Tolik. . . ."

"All right. I'll try," he promised.

And half an hour later he asked:

"I, well, I managed to get us a steam bath. Will you rub my back?"

Shurochka's heart skipped a beat—she burst into tears again. Of course, Tolik, she said, of course. There was just enough time. It was lunchtime, and in the evening Shurochka had to get on the bus that would bump her along endlessly toward the train.

Tolik had made arrangements for the steam bath in a private house; they paid one ruble for the whole thing. Shurochka praised it—whatever you said, it was a separate bath, and inexpensive. Shurochka also praised the old woman who heated up her own bath for them for her cleanliness. Instead of one ruble Shurochka gave her two, and then the old woman left. The bathhouse was indeed tidy and smelled of the forgotten aroma of conifer mingled with birch. Shurochka felt happy and a certain playfulness overtook her, the kind that comes after long, despondent thought. When they undressed she joked: You don't have tattoos, do you, Tolik? He hadn't gone and tattooed any gorgeous women on his buttocks, had he? I'm going to check and see right now. And Shurochka turned to look at him. Already undressed, he was sitting apathetically on the bench.

"Tolya."

He didn't budge, he seemed to continue thinking deeply.

"Tolya . . ."

Shurochka's heart sank. He was so very very thin, he'd never been that way. His face was dark. And his body was dark. Shurochka sensed that she wouldn't see him again. She sensed it even then.

"Oh, Tolya, my poor, poor Tolya!" she lamented, and burst out crying. Such was this moment in the bath: scrawny, all small and tiny, he sat on the bench, and not far off stood Shurochka, tears streaming, her body corpulent and white. She had always been large, now she was fat; in tears, she threw herself at him, trying, it seemed, to warm him, to enclose him and protect him with her large white body. The steam was thick. It grew hot. But Kurenkov just sat there as though frozen stiff. He sat there without stirring, and pressed his knees together, as if he were shy. He kept his thin hands on his lap.

Shurochka washed him; he was like a pensive child, and she helped him as she would a child, she rubbed his back and washed his hair twice. Then she washed herself. When they left, Shurochka took out her comb and combed his hair. The wind blew his hair, drying it. The wind wasn't very strong. His hair became silky, he walked next to her all clean and upright. He was smiling now.

He ran into the barracks alone, grabbed Shurochka's things, and went to see her off. They headed for the bus immediately because less than half an hour remained.

1983

Translated from the Russian by Jamey Gambrell.

A QUESTION MARK AND AN EXCLAMATION POINT

Revaz Mishveladze

Let no man claim, *batono*,* that he knows people. A person can sometimes pull such a stunt that afterward he himself won't be able to make head or tail of his actions—and somebody else, of course, will understand them all the less. For this reason, you know, nothing surprises me in this world. You can't guess ahead of time how your own friend will behave and what he'll do. Now, apropos of that, I was in court recently, heard the case of some people I know pretty well. Well, did they lay it on thick—not only did nobody expect it of them, but when the indictment was read we couldn't believe our ears. A lawyer, you'll say, a laywer can figure people out, surely he, a lawyer, knows what's what. No, *batono*, a thousand times no: a laywer is a person just like you and me. It's not granted to him to peer into the very depths of the human soul, its innermost recesses, and besides, he doesn't have the time for it. You must believe me—not a single clairvoyant can penetrate the thickets of the soul of Adam's son. An investigator is armed with the beacon of the law and supposedly with its help lights up the hidden passages in that very soul. The only thing is, he can't go a step further than the law stipulates, he's limited and bound by the law. And, after all, human deeds and actions cannot by any means always be reduced to law or lawlessness! Man, *batono*, is an unfathomable, confused, enigmatic creature. Yes, and then there are the psychologists, who pretend to a knowledge of the psyche, that is, the

---

*Georgian for "sir," "mister." —Trans.

soul; only it's empty talk, don't believe them, they don't understand a smidgen about it. Some of them claim that instinct rules man's actions, others shout—no, it isn't instinct, but reason, reason is the origin of everything, while still others declare it's both reason and besides that—genes. That's how it is. But there are actions, after all, that don't submit to any logic, and the motives for which are beyond understanding. If you take things on the whole, abstractly, then wherever they might lead you can still kind of define them and put them in their proper cubby-holes, but when it comes to something concrete you get tangled up and squirm like a mouse in a trap. But what am I doing talking about other people, trying to fathom others? Let me tell you about myself. And if I am lying even the slightest bit, may my enemy be struck dead.

At the time this incident took place I was just under thirty. It's a well-known fact that at that age a man is no longer a child. I lived upstairs, you know, on Uritsky Street—I was renting a room in the cobbler Dzhikia's house and was working in Mtsvanekvavila* at a brick factory. It was a tiny little room—I got married late, you know, I was still a bachelor at the time, and besides, I was short of funds and therefore tried to spend as little as I could. Well, even though the room was tiny, it had a window facing the street, it was sunny and dry. . . . And besides, I had no need for a big room. The little tin stove heated mine up right away even in the bitterest cold, and during the summer heat waves I spent almost all my evenings at Rioni; I swam, splashed about—in a word, kept cool. While in the wintertime I would run in from work, light the stove, and tumble into bed—I'd relish the warmth and rest.

One fine evening—I remember it as if it were yesterday, it was New Year's, old style†—I was sitting by my stove listening to the droning of the wind. It was cold outside, a north wind was kicking up its heels. Suddenly somebody knocked at my door. It wasn't very late yet, it had just recently gotten dark. In the winter, you know yourself, before you have time to turn around it's already dark. Who could it be? I thought. However, unlike others, who are forever asking "Who's there?" I never ask. God is my witness, for good or ill, whenever someone knocks at my door (it's true even now, at my considerable age) I go to the door

---

*A suburb of Kataisi, a Georgian town on the Black Sea. —Trans.
†It is common practice in the Soviet Union to celebrate the New Year twice, both on January 1, according to the current Gregorian calendar, and on January 13, the date on which it falls in the "old" Julian calendar, followed in Russia before the 1917 Bolshevik Revolution. —Trans.

and open it without thinking twice. And so I opened the door and on the threshold stood our police inspector, Morgoshia. A round-faced sort of fellow, thickset, always full of smiles. The two of us had chatted a couple of times. He had shown up for the first time when I had just settled into this room. He wrote down who I was, what I was, then we split a jug of *tsolikauri** and parted quite pleased with each other. Since then we exchanged a very friendly hello whenever we met, and that was all. What brought him, what kind of business does he have with me? I thought.

Morgoshia opened his folder, pulled out a paper, and silently held it out to me. "What's the matter?" I said. "A neighbor has a complaint." Which neighbor could it be, what neighbor, whom did I offend, and how? I live quietly, peaceably, like a bug in a rug. . . .

I began reading that complaint and just plain broke out in a sweat. But when I had read it to the end I just didn't know what to say. First laughter grabbed me, then, after I looked at Morgoshia and saw his unusually serious round face, I also tried to put on a serious expression, but there was no way I could gather my lips together—they kept spreading into a smile.

What do you think, what was I accused of?

Beyond the wall, in the other, neighboring half of the house, there lived a certain Ucha Chumburidze. A solitary man like me. At that time he must have been a little over fifty. I don't know if he's still alive. . . . He was a squat, stout man with a big head and an immense birthmark on his forehead. He was a hatter, it seems. He went out of the house extremely rarely. As long as I had lived there, I hadn't spoken to him once. I had nothing to do with him, nor he with me. Besides, the entrance to that half of the house was on another street. Our courtyard, I should mention, was partitioned in two: my landlord and this same Chumburidze had each built half the house, then a quarrel had broken out between them and they stopped talking to each other. And so it was none other than Chumburidze who was making a complaint against me: such-and-such, says he (it turned out that he knew both my first name and my last, and where I worked!), climbs up to the attic in the middle of the night, crawls across to my side, moves aside the attic trapdoor, and looks into my room from there. I ask you to ascertain, he addressed the police, what he wants from me.

---

*A Georgian wine. —Trans.

"What, are all his screws loose or something?" I asked Morgoshia. "All I've got to worry about is looking at his birthmark, for that I even climb up to the attic, right? Come on, what nonsense!"

Nevertheless, Morgoshia examined my room, then went out to the gallery, stared at the ceiling, and— "Where," he said, "is the exit to the attic?" "How should I know?" I said, frowning. "What would I be doing in the attic, am I a chimney sweep? That half-wit Chumburidze makes up heaven knows what, and you, Morgoshia, get it into your head to check me out for real, is that it?" "Why, no," he said, "I have no particular reason, I'm interested for myself. I have to look into this business, you know, so I can explain to the man that he was dreaming."

Well, all right, he and I went down to the courtyard. An iron staircase there ran along the blank brick wall of the house to the garret roof. To tell the truth, I hadn't even noticed it before, that staircase. So, it meant that in such freezing cold, at night, I was supposed to have gone out into the courtyard, climbed the iron staircase to the roof—in the dark, mind you—made my way along the tin gutter to Chumburidze's attic, crept in there, found the trapdoor, moved it aside, and—contemplated the hatter's blackhead-speckled, idiotic face! . . .

Morgoshia, like a tried-and-true detective, examined everything in detail and, with me at his side, clambered up to the attic, lighting the way with his flashlight. And, after convincing himself that not only in the past few days, but even in the past five years, no one had set foot there (the dust all around was a finger thick—if anyone had walked on it, he would have left footprints as deep as those Armstrong and his colleague had left on the moon), he and I silently climbed back down.

"The devil take that Chumburidze," he muttered when we were at last standing on the ground. "Making us swallow all that dust! All I needed were his fantasies! Well, all right, go ahead and get a good night's sleep. I'll unscramble his brains for him, I'll show him what it means to make up some cock-and-bull story about a person."

The inspector's visit to me, of course, didn't escape the notice of my landlord's family. As one they all spilled out onto the balcony and silently, raptly, observed our stroll to the roof. They also heard Morgoshia's concluding speech, but went into the house without saying a word, without asking me about anything. It was plain to see they knew what an oddball our precious neighbor was.

Meanwhile, Morgoshia came out on the street, rounded our courtyard, and went in Chumburidze's gate. I don't know what they talked about, only Morgoshia didn't leave there for a long time. I was about to go to bed when I suddenly heard loud voices. I opened the window, listened.

"You should see a doctor, a doctor!" Morgoshia said, exasperated.

"I don't need to see a doctor! You're barking up the wrong tree! You better quit making such statements, or else you'll be stripped of your rank!" Ucha said, not giving in.

Morgoshia stood in the middle of the courtyard.

"What can I answer? I don't have the right to get mixed up with you, I'm here on duty! The tongue is loose, it can say anything. But you leave him in peace, he has troubles enough of his own without having to deal with your fantasies. He doesn't have anything to do with your ceiling," Morgoshia answered him very reasonably. And on that it ended—the inspector left.

The next morning I went to work as usual and, to tell the truth, I forgot about the incident, not having attached much importance to it. Well, I thought, it happens, a person imagines some absurd thing; maybe he was in a bad mood, or what have you. The hell with him.

One day passed; the second day nothing happened either. On the third, as soon as it grew dark, Morgoshia appeared once again.

"We just barely calmed your neighbor down," Morgoshia said. "He came this afternoon and claimed you peeped in at him twice yesterday from the ceiling. I was about to pipe up about visions and dreams, but he flew into such a rage. 'You,' he said, 'think I'm crazy, a psycho, but he and I'—he meant you—'looked at each other yesterday just like we are doing right now. What,' he said, 'does he want from me, what's he staring at me for? If I'm a psycho,' he said, 'why don't I imagine other things, why don't I attack people on the street, huh? This is already the fourth night that he's been gawking into my room from the ceiling, he doesn't give me a moment's peace.' Then I said to him, 'Board up that damned door, and that'll be the end of it, you'll get some peace.' 'I already boarded it up,' he said, 'and he tore it off! How can I get rid of him—it's beyond me!' 'But he's not a bird, you know, he can't fly,' I said. 'So how come he doesn't leave footprints anywhere?' But there's no way of getting through to Chumburidze, he keeps repeating the same thing, until you could burst," Morgoshia related rapidly, almost gasping, with bulging eyes and puffed-out cheeks.

"What in the world should I do now?" I asked.

"Write that Chumburidze is slandering you, that the thought of climbing up to his attic never even crossed your mind, that your attitude toward him is good, neighborly. That you harbor no evil against him in either head or heart, and that for the entire time you've been living here you haven't said as much as a nasty word to each other," Morgoshia advised me.

I wrote down everything just as he said. Morgoshia took my statement and left. And I got into bed without even eating supper, thinking that if I didn't come up with something the next day, that raving Chumburidze would have me under his thumb once and for all.

And it was at that very moment that the inexplicable and improbable thing happened inside me, which is the reason I've been telling you this story in the first place.

I was lying down and sleep didn't come—what am I saying, sleep? I wasn't even getting drowsy. I was tossing and turning. And Chumburidze's sour puss with its swollen eyes and that birthmark on his forehead loomed before me.

What does he want from me? I thought. Why is he pestering me and spreading all that nonsense to boot? There's no doubt about it, he is imagining something, but what does it have to do with me! And what if I went to him right now and said, "Let's talk things over man to man, without any ifs, ands, or buts, what do you have against me, why have you blackened my name? . . ." But what if he decides that I've come to attack him and lets out a scream or, worse still, lands me one on the head with a stick? You can expect anything you like from his type. And what if I make a complaint against him? I'll say he's slandering me, I can't go on living like this. Well, who knows what would come of it. . . . My case has already begun, Morgoshia knows me, but a new investigator would start interrogating and pumping me, "Who are you, why have you come, how much do you pay for your room? . . ." All these questions wouldn't do either me or Dzhikia any good at all. . . . Still, I'd like to know what that screwball hatter does at night, why he's so afraid of somebody seeing him. No, there's definitely something shady going on, no two ways about it. As for me, for instance, I don't care, go ahead and peep in at me if you want. It doesn't worry me at all. I wonder if he's sleeping now or not? Most likely he's sitting and gaping at the ceiling. What if I really did peep in on him—what would his expression be then?

I don't remember how I jumped out of bed and got dressed, how I went out to the courtyard. I was driven by an irresistible urge to peep from the ceiling into Ucha Chumburidze's room, to see his bewildered face and find out what it was he did nights. With great difficulty I climbed up the iron staircase, crawled as stealthily as a cat across the garret to Chumburidze's half of the roof, made my way into the attic, gropingly found the trapdoor, and, the very instant I moved it aside, encountered the bulging eyes of the crazed hatter and heard an inhuman howl:

"Morgoshia, save me!"

"I'm here!" barked Morgoshia almost right above my ear, whereupon Ucha cried in a triumphant voice:

"What, am I imagining things now too? Are you going to say I'm dreaming again?"

Then steps began to stomp and rumble about the attic, a flashlight shone on my back, and I heard Morgoshia's voice:

"Don't move or I'll shoot!"

After a short pause the inspector declared peremptorily:

"Climb out on the roof and go down the staircase, I'll be waiting for you below."

Only when I was climbing down the staircase, ashamed and disheartened, did it occur to me what a mess I had made. Until then some mysterious, insuperable force had guided me.

I was greeted below by Morgoshia, my landlord's entire large family, Chumburidze with a cast-iron frying pan in his hands, and a police car.

My first testimony turned out to be so confused, tangled, and inconsistent that the Lord God Himself couldn't have made sense of what I had wanted in the attic. Then somebody took pity and prompted me: Say it was a joke, that you just wanted to give him a good scare. To make a long story short, my case was turned over to a comrades' court. I was fined fifty rubles and had to sign a statement that from then on I would never allow myself any "jokes" of that kind.

It was out of the question, of course, for me to go on living in that house. The very next day I gathered my belongings and settled my account with the landlord. And a couple of months later I also bade farewell to the brick factory and moved to Tkibuli.

1987

Translated from the Russian by Edythe C. Haber.

THE ART OF NEEDLES AND SINS

Bulat Okudzhava

Before the start of the school year in the village, all I had for the winter was my student jacket of threadbare worsted that looked as if it had been made under the old regime. In a jacket like that you could get through the winter in Tbilisi, although even there it wouldn't be easy— but the Kaluga winter, which was already making itself felt in October, would make short work of me—and I could feel it. What was a young teacher to do? It was fine for those who had parents and relatives, generous and warmhearted. But I had no one. So I scraped together, from wherever I could, six hundred rubles (sixty in today's currency) and set off for Peremyshl, our district center. I was in luck. The store had winter overcoats for sale, and they cost only four hundred fifty rubles. I took a coat one size too big, returned to the village the possessor of my very own winter coat, and gave the remaining one hundred fifty rubles back to my creditors.

What would you make of this coat, this winter coat, this lifesaving garment? Of course examples of finer apparel existed in nature. I have had occasion to brush against them in trams and cloakrooms. I have felt their soft, warm folds that had been cut to accentuate their charms and conceal their faults. Their noble and varied colors were a treat to the eye. They were light as a feather and warm as a glowing stove. My coat was completely different. Its fabric was also called worsted, but it was more like badly processed plywood: it was almost impossible to bend and could scrape off your skin. This worsted was woven together with straw, twigs, and chaff. Sometimes, as I sat in reception areas or in stations waiting for a train, I would kill time by plucking the building material out of the coat, gathering it by the handful. Handful upon handful. Besides all this, the coat was lined with quilting cotton like a mattress. It was impossible to throw it open elegantly. You could only pry it open—and with great difficulty at that, as if prying open a badly oiled double door—then enter it, stick your arms in the sleeves, and slam it shut with a crack. How did I feel about it? If you can imagine, I was happy, because the first cold weather testified to the excellent impenetrability of this worsted armor. I was also happy because it fit into my household budget, which in those days amounted to six hundred eighty rubles (sixty-eight by the new system), and because, no matter what it looked like, I had an overcoat instead of a threadbare jacket. And the overcoat, with felt boots and a fur hat with earflaps, conferred upon me an air of stability, solidity, and weight.

In photographs from those years we are standing in front of the half-ruined Shamordinsky Cathedral: my new friend, Semyon Alekseyevich Sysoev, his wife, Marya Petrovna, and me. They are sitting on the ruins of the cathedral, and I am standing in my new, unbending coat, in felt boots and a fur hat, an expression of reverence on my face. I look solid and very important.

Well, all right, dear heart, what are you going to do with such solidity dressed in an inferior coat, wounding your arms at the slightest brush against the worsted fabric, unable to bend, hardly able to move wooden legs that throb under the weight of cotton armor? Well, what should I do? I'm warm, impenetrable, secure. Of course, if only . . . but here we don't have time for refinements, and if some of us in the city, that is, some of you in the city, allow yourselves the luxury of not dressing like others and acquire imported clothes, then I, that is, we, here, all of us here, are busy with other things. Perhaps we here have the spirituality that you there only talk about while we cultivate it and live by it. . . .

Now about Semyon Alekseyevich.

He was still a rather young man of medium build, wiry, with ears that stuck out and a sudden, unexpected smile on his small, wide face. He was a team foreman and trained tractor drivers. He treated us high school teachers with great deference, probably because Marya Petrovna taught in our school, and he loved to say, "Here in our, well, educational system . . ." Apparently my involvement in the educational system explained his rapport with me. I felt it right away: how a person looks at you, how he talks with you—you always feel it. And I was drawn to him as well—maybe out of affection, maybe out of loneliness—but in any case I was drawn to him. He was very amused and touched by my dim acquaintance with everyday matters. It was sheer pleasure for him to take me under his wing. When I demonstrated my lack of practicality or put my foot in it, he would merrily gush and joyfully begin to teach me. He was a thrifty man, a villager from these parts. He loved durability and sturdiness, as he understood them, in everything. He'd never waste a ruble, but he constantly insisted on making loans: "However much. The main thing, Bulat Shalch"—as he called me, in rough abbreviation of my patronymic—"is not to be shy. You'll get used to the village. It's hard for you city folks at first, but then you feel at home and you get yourself a cow . . ."

"A cow?" I teased. "That'll be the day!" To be honest, I didn't intend to stay long in the village. But I liked to tease him, so I mischievously played the simpleton, a sort of city slicker, which really set him off.

"What about it?" he blustered. "You'll get a cow, mark my words. . . . How else? Where else will you get milk from, and sour cream? Masha, will you just look at this oddball! And how about cream?"

"Well, if you're talking about cream," I said. "Cream—that's a different story. . . . When I was little they made me drink cream with my almond cake." For some reason that made him angry.

"Almond cake," he said, offended.

Their home was welcoming to a lonely person like me. It was a hospitable place, and an invitation meant a chance to sit in contented warmth in a room that almost looked like a city apartment. It usually came about like this: Sysoev, dusted with snow, would burst in on me, glance with annoyance at my smoky little stove, the dim ceiling light bulb, and say, "Enough reading books—you'll never read them all." He'd chuckle at his own wit. "Come on over to our place—we'll have some tea." And we'd set off through the snowdrifts.

Vodka appeared right away in his home, along with homemade pickles marinated in currant leaves, and cabbage, and pickled tomatoes, and flaky boiled potatoes, and tender fatback, and hard-boiled eggs, and sometimes even jellied meat. We'd all sit down. Sysoev performed all the gestures appropriate to the occasion: He hiked up his shoulders and rubbed his hands together; he sighed and cooed and swore and gushed—he was happy.

I never could understand why he liked me. Besides the fact that I had graduated from a university and was a teacher like his wife, as I've already mentioned. Evidently my Georgian background, my exoticism, I guess you'd say, contributed, as well as my mustache and one other circumstance. It was 1950, and in those days wherever you looked you saw every conceivable depiction of my mustached clansman. I can't say that I was a particular admirer of him—in fact, my parents had been relocated far away—but Sysoev revered him, and perhaps somewhere in his murky consciousness he linked together my ethnic background and his idol. I don't know how precise my observations are, but more remains to be said about this.

And so we sat at the very peak of January, throwing back shots and munching on pickles to the accompaniment of a snowstorm. And Sysoev, as usual, was teaching me how to live, and I was thinking that if I had more money, I wouldn't have these dirty-gray, clumsy felt boots that I had had the good fortune to buy at a flea market in Kozelsk but white boots of brushed wool felt—light, warm, and springy. A soldier's fur cap with earflaps wouldn't adorn my head but a fleecy wonder made of the best sheepskin, or maybe even wolf. Anything's possible with money. . . . I don't need your cow and your cream, if only I could buy five cubic meters of dry birch instead of the damp aspen so generously distributed to the teachers.

"You just wait, Shalch," Sysoev said, "What an oddball . . . Masha, will you just look at him. . . . You're a real oddball, all right. You save up and I'll chip in."

"I don't need your cow," I said. "What am I, a shepherd? After all, at the university I—"

"Well, you know how it is here in our educational system? Uh-huh . . . You have to adapt."

"That's easy for you to say," I said. "Look at all your holdings—you've got cucumbers, and a fur coat, and a tractor—"

"Listen, you," he said, getting angry. "Listen, Shalch, there's no talking to you, nothing's right by you. I'd give you a tractor—what would you do with it?"

"That's enough, Semyon," Marya said. "Why are you bothering him? The man bought himself a coat that's made out of twigs and you go on about your cream."

There was a pause. Then he said, bursting into laughter, "What's the problem? We could make you a leather coat in two shakes. . . ."

"*What* kind of coat?"

"Listen to you, university," he snorted, "what kind . . . This is what kind, listen to what I tell you. . . ."

By the way, my new impenetrable coat could be stood in the middle of the room and it would remain standing that way without falling over or sliding down. It would continue to stand, like a strongbox. But a leather coat?

What was that village wizard up to? What did he have in mind, the skin of an old pig, crudely tanned like the stuff used to make those iron-stiff boots that, in the end, I never did get at the front? What kind of hide was he thinking of as he stared at me sadly?

"All right," I said, chuckling, "tell me, Semyon Alekseyevich, what kind of hide? Buffalo? Pig?"

"What do you mean, buffalo?" he said, offended. "When I say leather I mean leather. The kind they make coats out of."

"But what kind is that?" I asked. "Old boar?"

"Oh, you!" He wagged his finger at me. "Masha, hey, Masha, will you look at him. . . . Old boar . . ."

"Well, from what, then?" I wouldn't give up. "Box calf?"

"What do you mean, box calf?" he said acidly. "They make boots out of box calf. We can use calfskins."

"Calfskin?" I couldn't believe it.

"Calfskins," he confirmed.

It was beginning to sound like the truth. He was angry.

I decided to make him happy and tease him, may God forgive me. I stared at him naively and asked, "You mean you can really make a coat out of calfskin? They're so little, maybe you could get a pair of gloves out of one. . . ."

He gushed, delighted to have an idiot to so pleasantly enlighten. We drank another shot.

"It's like this," he said in his teacher voice. "You make coats out of calfskin. I had set my sights on one for myself, but now, maybe, we could both get them."

"I don't believe you!" I shouted, feeling a chill. "Do you mean you can do that here?"

"Sure you can!" he shouted, enjoying himself. "You get the hides and make them into a coat!"

"But where are you going to get the hides?" I shouted, beginning to see that this wasn't mere talk.

"You just listen to me, listen!" he shouted, and screwed up his eyes craftily. "Don't you believe me?"

"Now you listen to him, Bulat Shalvovich," Marya said sternly. "If Semyon Alekseyevich says something, that's the way it is."

"That's right," he blustered.

"So we get our hands on calfskin, and we sew . . ."

"Well?"

I was terribly excited, and I enjoyed driving him crazy, setting him off as I played the idiot. I saw what a joy it was for him to reveal to me something I didn't know, to lord it over me, to tease me about my ignorance and take care of me.

I was touched, and to make him laugh and comfort him, I said, "By the way, if you stand my new coat in the middle of the room . . ."

But he didn't get the joke, and he scolded me, "Why put it on the floor? A coat should be hung on a hanger and put in the closet."

He didn't get jokes. One time I met him on the street and said, as we did in the city, "Now here comes a young, promising foreman." He looked at me dourly and said, "We didn't promise you anything."

"Fine." I waved my hand. "But what's the story with the hides?"

And here he initiated me into his project, astonishing in its feasibility. Everything fit together: In March, for some reason, it seems they kill calves in the village, as if they were hurrying to sacrifice them to people like me who long to dress in a leather shroud. The hides, naturally, were fleeced and sold to the highest bidder. We buy them and take them to an acquaintance in Kaluga who's a furrier. In a month he gives us tanned calfskin, and all we have to do is find a seamstress. In a maximum of three months, maybe even less—we're wearing splendid new clothes.

That was the fantastic ending to our usual repast. All this had barely penetrated when a familiar buzz of impatience started up inside me. I was in a fever of excitement. I could already see those inconceivable hides in my hands. I even believed that I didn't have to wait for the ministrations of the furrier, which might happen and might not, but that by myself I could tan the Gift of the Calf with salt and . . . What else do you need? Grain alcohol? Vinegar? I would scrape away all the excess with a knife and pluck out every bristle in my spare time, after classes, at night—until dawn, for God's sake! And then I would finally hang the soft, glossy, flowing, aromatic, black-matte leather about the room as a prologue to needle and scissors.

Today, when a third of the population has a leather coat, or jacket, or pants, it's hard to imagine the enormity of the wealth that had fallen into my hands. In those days if you had a highly developed imagination, you could try to fantasize about leather clothes, but to own such a garment—there was no point even dreaming about it. I had the great fortune to see one on a lucky fellow. I even reached out to touch it.

The subtle aroma, a blend of perfume and a rosy future, reached my nose even before I saw it. Those mysterious, exciting waves heralded the appearance of something wonderful, and at last it materialized. It was like silk to the eye and to the touch. It flowed, it obeyed, it hugged the body, conferring refinement and elegance; it glowed in the crowd like a diamond amid cobblestones, and it carried the stamp of foreign prosperity and the mark of that special clan of individuals graced by good fortune. Besides all of these fine virtues of appearance, it had a great number of purely practical advantages that should not be ignored. It was sturdy. Rubbed with castor oil, it acquired great elasticity, and it was waterproof. Dirt disappeared from it instantly with the touch of a damp cloth, and if it got wrinkled, it soon regained its previous shape by itself and never needed ironing. What more could you want?

Everyone waited for March impatiently, but no one more so than I. By the time it arrived I was at fever pitch. I tortured Sysoev with questions and doubts. He patiently laughed them off.

One fine March day toward the end of the month, a day brilliant with sunshine, embellished by the sound of water dripping and brooks gurgling, there was a loud knock on the door of my solitary, damp cell. A villager I didn't know stood in the doorway.

"Did you order calfskins?" he asked.

"Oh, yes!" I cried. "I did! I did!"

"Well, looks like you got them. All six."

Six! Six skins for me! Not tanned yet, but already mine!

"Like we agreed," the man said, "seventy apiece."

I quickly multiplied: six times seven is forty-seven? But no, if six times six is thirty-six, then six times seven . . .

"Four hundred twenty," he said calmly. He took his money, threw a parcel from his sled, and drove off.

The parcel turned out to be heavy. I dragged it into the house and opened it with trembling hands. The repulsive stench of decaying meat filled the room. Six damp, slippery skins lay in front of me. The stench began to permeate my dream. But Sysoev fortuitously appeared and asked, smiling grandly, "So, they brought them? You see, Shalch? That idiot, I had to spend a half hour explaining where you live. Well, now we're off and rolling. They've got to be salted or they'll go bad." And he left.

I fooled with them all evening, hunting up salt, salting them over and over again. Then I packed them down tightly, and finally rolled them up and tied them with rags and string. I put them on the scale—

terribly heavy—and dragged them into the storeroom. Afterward I washed my hands for a long time and aired the room. My mood had fallen a bit, but hope still raged within me.

It all happened exactly as I've described. Do any of you doubt me? Sometimes it even sounds made up to me, I seem so vain and unsympathetic. What was the matter with me—didn't I know how to face deprivation staunchly and steadfastly? Didn't the expression on my rosy-cheeked face say that I was nobly and proudly above it all? Could I really have been so greedy and envious? Could something as superficial as attire have played such a role in my life? The last days before we set off for the mythical Kaluga furrier were especially hard. Now I think that the difference between the impoverished circumstances in which we all—and especially I—lived in that hard year of 1950 and the possibilities suddenly opening up—their head-spinning proximity— raised a frenzy in me that now seems shameful. But it's easy to condemn one's past self from the vantage of these prosperous times. I leave that nettlesome occupation to the reader, while I myself rush off to meet Sysoev, as we agreed, on a Saturday, after classes, at the very end of March.

He rode up on his tractor, fresh and smiling, while I was pale from not having slept all night. I had valiantly dragged out of my hiding place the precious, inordinately heavy bundle. The tractor was to take us a couple of kilometers through the horrendous spring mud to the main road. And it did. We unloaded and settled down to wait for any truck going our way, since there was no other means of transportation in those days. The road was hardly a main thoroughfare, so travelers could only hope for a miracle.

In about three hours dusk began to fall. The road was deserted. Thank God I was warm in my impenetrable coat, but Semyon Alekseyevich became uncomfortable in his durable one. He danced around while I stood leaning against a pole, and neither of us spoke. I don't know what he was thinking about, but I was savoring in my imagination a scene I already knew by heart: I'm dressed nonchalantly in my leather coat. I'm wearing a cap of light gray material. Can you imagine it? A black leather coat and a light gray cap! And of course I'm wearing some sort of scarf. . . . I'm slowly walking along a Moscow street, exuding an aroma that titillates the crowd. I keep on walking. Where am I going, you ask? Nowhere. I'm just walking.

Finally, as dusk began to thicken, a truck loaded with half-rotten potatoes was, incredibly, going our way and took us to Peremyshl. We sat on the potatoes, our backs to the sharp wind. It was more than thirty kilometers to the district center along a gouged and bumpy road, along the old Kozelsk Road, along my nerves and along my bones.

We crawled into Peremyshl about two hours later without incident. Dusk had fallen completely. There we were lucky: We made arrangements fairly quickly with the next truck going straight to Kaluga. We dragged our bundles over and set off. Another thirty kilometers along another dismal road. May the inhabitants of Kaluga forgive me: The road was probably splendid, and the forest along it splendid, and the meadows too. But that was the last thing on my mind as I sat in the dark on sacks in an open flatbed, in a jolting truck, under an icy wind.

It began to ice over. The tough peasant Sysoev was openly freezing, but the happy sybarite in his impenetrable coat thanked fate for his sound purchase. No matter how much you city folks complain, you can always dash into an entryway and warm up by a radiator, while we here, in an open truck with a biting wind . . . You laugh at us in your metros and your buses, making yourselves look good at our expense, while we here become numb with cold and don't rest for a second to produce the milk, cream, potatoes, and so forth so that you can fill your bellies. . . .

And then, when the lights of Kaluga appeared and the aroma of tanned leather again wafted through the air, Sysoev shouted through lips stiff with cold, "There's no bridge, Shalch! We'll have to swim across!"

"What do you mean, swim across?" I yelled from the depths of my coat.

"I mean, go into the water," he said with a shrill laugh, "holding the skins above our heads so they won't get wet!"

"But there's ice in the Oka!" I yelled as the burning wind burst in under my coat.

"That's good," he yelled. "We can cross the river on the ice floes!"

We stopped at the place where a pontoon bridge usually stood. The bridge had been taken down because of the ice run. In the darkness, illuminated by the dim light of the stars and the city streetlights on the other bank, ice floes rustled, gnashed, and scraped past us one after another. The truck turned around and left. A few pitiful shadows were still vaguely discernible on the edge of the water.

"We shouldn't have come," I said. "Where do we go from here?"

"Now, Shalch, if you don't want to go for a dip in the water," Sysoev blustered, "we're going to look for a boat. Maybe someone will take us across."

It was nearly midnight. We shivered. My head was spinning from hunger. Our ill-fated, icy bundles rested in the dark at our feet. But I was still alive, and I wouldn't have traded that precious, stinking load for a bowl of hot borscht and borrowed wings to take me home. Kaluga glimmered on the other bank, and its calloused hand held me by the throat. And although it had dimmed, the image of a prosperous young man in a black leather coat and light gray cap still shimmered in my consciousness. For the sake of that image I was prepared to take on even greater feats, and even the icy Oka River didn't seem impossible to breach. Little Sysoev wasn't about to succumb to gloomy thoughts. He picked his way along the sinister riverbank and disappeared into the darkness. He reappeared and finally called to me from a barely visible rowboat, "Load them on!" which sounded to me like "Lend a hand!" And I, like Hercules, managed, straining, to drag both stone-heavy bundles to the boat and crash along with them to its damp bottom. The old owner of the boat pushed off with an oar, and we spun among the ice floes in the dark.

"Hey, man," Sysoev shouted, "how much are you charging us to drown?"

"Not much," the boatman said. "Sit still and find out."

Out in the middle of the river I discovered that the boat was slowly but surely filling up with water. My felt boots were submerged up to my ankles. I picked up my soaking wet bundle and held it in my arms like a big icy infant. This is nothing, I thought; there was worse at the front. The bank was getting closer, but the water was rising faster, and dark blue chunks of ice were hitting the sides. I don't know how the boatman managed to slip through them. Now I recall that all three of us were screaming, drowning out the gnashing and scraping, shouting classic examples of Russian obscenity at the weather, the Oka, every approaching ice floe, and Kaluga, which wasn't getting to us fast enough, and the oar, and the water in the boat, and the hides, and this life, and our dreams. . . . But I held fast, and my silhouette, elegant and important, still loomed large above a Moscow sidewalk. Was there fear in my heart? There was insanity. I wanted victory. If only that energy and strength had been channeled into great deeds! How many great deeds would have ennobled mankind! But that was the joke—nothing was greater to me than what I was doing. And besides, who knows what a great deed is until it's done?

We managed to jump out of the almost submerged boat and stood on the Kaluga firmament.

"Hey," Sysoev said to the boatman, "you might patch up those holes. We could've drowned."

"Don't have time to," the boatman said. "Everyone wants to cross."

"And you're ready to drown for the money," Sysoev said.

"How can I say no?" The boatman laughed. "Spring only comes once a year."

It took us a long time to drag the bundles up the slope, pulling with all our might. Kaluga was already asleep. And the furrier was alseep. The Oka raged far below us. The hotel was called the Oka—old, gloomy, with peeling plaster, but when we finally crawled in, as goggle-eyed as fish, I choked on the thick warmth and peace and quiet.

Yes, it was quiet. And the elderly administrator seemed like an angel and savior behind her desk. Above her golden head Sysoev's idol, an unlit pipe in his hand, gazed down at us from his gilded frame.

I remember how I held out wooden hands to the administrator, unable to utter a word or hear what Sysoev, smiling pitifully, said to her. Perhaps he told her the story of his life, how it wasn't a very easy one and not the most successful, how he lived on this earth, what he had gone through—and now there wasn't a bed for him in all of this splendid, ramshackle old building. And she looked past him dismissively, with the air of a person who is used to having life and death depend on her.

What didn't he tell her! He pointed at me and then at the portrait of the Generalissimo, and suddenly she came to life and showed a reaction. Something human flashed across her otherworldly features, and finally we were allowed to sleep on the painted floor at the very end of a corridor until dawn—no later. I remember that I was struck by how discourteously kindhearted she was in permitting us to bed down next to a hot radiator. We spread out my wonderful coat, took off our felt boots, shoved them behind the radiator, and lay down next to it with our feet up against the hot pipes. We covered ourselves with Sysoev's coat and swiftly began to leave this world. . . . The bundles gave off a light steam, the stench seeping through the wrappings, but we were already far from these parts.

In the morning we were awakened by squeamish comments. We dressed in silence, sniffling, relishing the warmth of dried felt boots, wordlessly expressing our gratitude to the hotel administrator. After all, she might not have let us in, or, after she let us in, she might have turned us out again. But we stayed, and it was as if the place next to the hot radiator had been especially reserved for us and our bundles of future calfskin. Apparently she saw socially useful people in these midnight wanderers. And so she saved our lives while she broke the house rules.

Now the simplest task remained: to get to the furrier. Both of us, young and strong, once again warmed by our dream, bent under the still-damp bundles, set off for the renowned address. Actually, there was no address. There was only Sysoev's wonderful memory, and we had barely walked along Lenin Street and crossed Kirov Street when that wonderful memory kicked into action.

"It's like this," Sysoev said. "Here we turn right at the church." We turned. "Now we walk wa-a-ay down to the light blue fence, like she said, two blocks, and there'll be a water pump." And there it was: a pump covered with a crust of ice appeared before us. "At the pump we turn left and go straight until we get to a store." We passed a store that hadn't opened yet. "Now, let's see, at the store we turn right and walk wa-a-ay up to those trees." We walked, we panted, we stopped to catch our breath. We tried to joke, pretended that we were having fun, that it was all a lark: the night, the Oka, the ice run, the hotel. In the frosty morning air you could clearly catch the scent of tanned hides. No one was awake yet—there was no reason to be. We were the only ones keeping vigil in this world, inexorably moving toward our great goal. And suddenly it appeared before us around a bend; it appeared, and for a moment we stood still.

"Well, now, Shalch," Sysoev said, panting, "this is it. Here's the house." He gushed, "Of course it's here, where else would it be? I'll go and check it out."

He walked away as I leaned against a tree and cooled off over the bundles, hot sweat dripping down my high forehead. I imagined a miracle. What if it happened: Say the furrier had a supply of tanned hides, and he simply traded those for ours, and we wouldn't have to wait again. . . .

In about five minutes Sysoev came out, grinning broadly.

"We hit the nail on the head," he said. "He's waiting for us. Well, Shalch, you'll have your calfskin."

He dragged the bundles to the house by himself along with a deposit, and then we were free.

"We'll get the hides at the end of April," Sysoev said, laughing, when he returned. "Just get together the rest of the money, Shalch."

"Once we sew the coats, why don't we go to Moscow?" I asked.

"Why not?" he gushed. "Let them get a look at us. . . ."

How I survived until the end of April I can't tell you. Of course I battled my affliction honorably and persistently, but the insanity (which, by the way, wasn't insanity at all), the yearning that had gripped me, was hardly appeased. My dried-out soul, like a dry throat, demanded its own, and all my efforts to make peace with it, to calm it, to comfort it, to pacify it, came to naught. God alone knows how I got through it. Why did this happen to me? What can I say? The times were hard for most people. I recall being stoical. No one spoiled me in childhood, and the inclination of my soul was somewhat different. Why, then, did I yearn to look so fashionable? It couldn't be because I felt . . . that I . . . that people like me . . . that is, we . . . It couldn't be because we . . . Who did I want to look like? Seem like? Be? As God is my witness, I was contemptuous of sharp dressers. What did I yearn for, then? My parents were out *there*. And although the sins of the father . . . and so on, all the same the sorry reflection of disaster lay on me. Was I perhaps possessed just by the thought that I could transform myself into someone handsome and imposing?

I don't know.

To top it all off, on the eve of May Day I spent a sleepless night. In the morning the whole school was to congregate for a holiday meeting. The evening before, I looked over my only suit. It was an old suit of my uncle's that had been given to me when I came home after the war. It was noticeably the worse for wear since my student days. The pants were torn and frayed at the cuff and the jacket was stretched out of shape and shone on the back and at the elbows. In despair I had a mind to throw myself at Marya Petrovna's feet and beg her, a woman, to use her agile little hands to make my only clothes suitable for the festivities, but I had thought of it too late—it was already after midnight. Certainly nothing terrible would have happened. My students and colleagues, used to such deprivation, would not have caused me shame. In fact, they would have gazed at me with sorrow and compassion, and, for all I know, might even have taken up a collection to uphold my reputation as an attractive young teacher of Georgian parentage with urban tastes and a love of beautiful things. . . . So I clenched my teeth, put my shoulder to the wheel, took the scissors and a needle and thread in hand, and got to work. How I managed to handle the old, raveling material that no longer wanted to live, I don't know. It tortured me, it offered up the wrong places to be cut, the seams got lost in the folds and slipped away, and the needle went in far from where it should have. But by morning I emerged the victor, and when I steamed the threadbare fabric with an iron, it had nobly lost its sheen, and an almost completely new suit hung before me. I hadn't gotten a minute's sleep, but the success was uplifting. Do we need much? What more do you need if you feel like a human being? You who are so proud and unfettered: go to your classroom, to your deck, into the storm, to your death. . . .

And so at the very beginning of May, when the festivities had already died down and everything around was turning green, and the awful March ice run looked like child's play, and my impenetrable coat hung on a nail, no longer needed—on one such day Sysoev looked in on me. With feigned horror, as always, he surveyed my room and said, rubbing his hands together, "Well, Shalch, get ready. Tomorrow we're up at first light, we say our prayers, and we head out," and he laughed, happy that he had brought the long-awaited good news.

Again we traveled to Kaluga, this time unburdened under the May sun. I saw that the road was in fact beautiful, not the highway itself, but its setting: that classic central Russian landscape, with forests right out of a fairy tale and valleys cloaked in a light haze. Traveling was a joy, and even the prospect of spending the night in the musty hotel corridor didn't depress me, especially since my hopes were so high. It turns out, I thought, that it isn't so hard, after all, to wait for something, to overcome impatience. It's worth suffering a bit now and then, I thought, as we bounced over the bumps in the open flatbed.

We crossed the bridge, which had been put up again after the horrifying ice run. Now it proudly creaked under the trucks, and the yellow water of the Oka, already receded, amicably lapped against the pontoons, and the early evening was tender and kind.

"Now, Shalch," said Sysoev, chuckling, "let's retrace our steps."

And we jauntily marched down Lenin Street under trees turning green, crossed Kirov Street, reached the church, turned to the right . . .

"We better go faster," Sysoev said, "it'll get dark and then just try and find . . ."

Before us appeared the familiar light blue fence. From there we walked two blocks, as we were supposed to, but . . . the pump wasn't there.

"Wait a minute," Sysoev said, "I remember in two blocks . . ."

"We've already gone four blocks," I said, trying to contain my rising agitation.

"Hey," Sysoev said to a passerby, "shouldn't there be a pump here?"

"A pump?" the man said. "There's never been a pump here. There's one over on that street, parallel to this one, actually on the corner, but there never was one here."

"We counted the blocks on the wrong street," I said.

"For God's sake," Sysoev said, dumbfounded. "Then what about the light blue fence?"

"Maybe there's a blue fence over there too," I said. "Let's go to that street, Semyon Kuzmich, and if there's a pump, then that's the street."

We ran over. It was quickly getting dark. I wasn't worried—I was in a frenzy. On the parallel street we finally found the pump. We looked around to be sure, but now we couldn't see the blue fence. We ran back along that street two blocks, then three, four . . . to a painted fence, but you couldn't tell the color anymore. It might have been light blue, but it could also have been green, or brown. A fat woman stood by the wicket gate.

"Evening," Sysoev said, "I just can't seem to make out what color your fence is."

"What's it to you?" she asked.

"Well, you see, we got into a fight about what color it is."

"Well, it's dark blue."

"Maybe light blue?" I asked, encouraged.

"Why light blue?" She got angry. "Dark blue is dark blue."

We stepped away.

"You know, Shalch," Sysoev said heartily, "we'll have to return to Lenin Street again and then come back once more, good and careful this time. You and me, we took it too easy. I mean, it's spring, it's warm, here we are, already here, we took it easy. . . . But it's not so easy."

We went back to the Hotel Oka and slowly walked back the other way. When we crossed Kirov Street it was already dark. The infrequent streetlamps were little help. We got to the church, where we turned right. So far, so good. Finally the light blue fence showed up, the real one. Even in the dark its blueness was clearly visible. Slowly, stealthily, we walked two blocks, and . . . the pump was standing in its place! We touched it, caressed it. Water dripped from its spigot. Now it was easier: just turn left and walk to the store. We walked, but there was no store to be found. Instead of a store there was a tidy little square. The street was deserted. We stood, breathing heavily.

"We should have at least written down the address," I said, annoyed. "Complete idiots."

"Don't worry, Shalch," Sysoev said dourly, "we'll find it."

"Maybe we ought to go to an information booth," I asked. "What's his last name?"

"God knows." Sysoev laughed nervously. "His name is Stepan Egorovich, that's all I know."

Suddenly we heard hurried footsteps and a man emerged from around the corner.

"Hey, there," Sysoev said joyfully, "just a minute, my friend . . ."

When he saw us the man darted to the side.

"Now don't get scared," Sysoev implored. "Where is it, the store that used to be here?"

The man took a few steps back.

"Hey," Sysoev complained, "we're asking you a question, what's with you?"

"Ask at an information booth!" the man yelled, and ran down the street.

"What the devil," Sysoev said, "are we lost, or what?"

"Let's try again," I suggested, without much hope, "all the way from the hotel."

But that was utterly ridiculous, and we decided to head for the train station and sit out the night there.

At the station the dimly lit restaurant worked around the clock. The only train for Moscow was leaving in an hour, and the merriment was at its very peak. Actually, "merriment" is a slight overstatement: it was noisy, clattering, rollicking, drunken. It smelled of burned oil and last year's cabbage. Tobacco smoke hung over the tables. . . . No, I remember it that way because now I don't like station restaurants, the drunken doormen and waiters, and the constant frenzied activity: from the train to the table, from the table to the train. Now I don't like them. But then, apparently, I did. But what would you expect? After the village, my damp, cold room, the yellow light bulb hanging from the ceiling—suddenly this hall, and the people, and the clatter of trays, and you can order whatever you want, change your mind, lounge, joke around, survey the hall and the people at neighboring tables scornfully or, just the opposite, smile sweetly at everyone. I pay—you serve me. No one knows anything about me. Just like in a bathhouse—everyone is equal. If only I had money. Now I don't like station restaurants. Now there isn't any need to prove myself, to try to look a certain way. But then, although it was the same—the stench, the clatter and frenzy, the drunken doorman—it was a carnival to me. And through the open door, beyond the clouds of smoke, you could see the familiar portrait in a gilded frame on the wall. Sysoev's idol stood in the middle of an endless plain, early in the morning, and looked off into the distance over our heads.

For a long time the doorman refused to let us in—just like that, for no particular reason. We took no offense and pitifully crowded the door, hunching lower and lower, smiling unctuously at him, laboring under the weight of our own hunched backs. He humiliated us for a long time, but the more he did, the more we stared longingly at the restaurant tables where we could sit and stretch out. Finally he relented, and we went into the hall. Now you can stand on your rights, as they say, and demand that people do their jobs properly. But at that time such jokes were dangerous: after all, we could clearly see how the militiaman with his raspberry-colored cap band amicably patted the doorman on the shoulder as he went by, as if they were in-laws, or relatives, or maybe even brothers. . . .

We ordered a small carafe of vodka and cutlets with noodles for each of us.

"So, Shalch"—Sysoev sighed, settling back—"who says life's bad?"

I nodded to him in agreement because I felt just fine.

We drank. The light got brighter. . . . I walked up to the door of the restaurant without hunching over. I was wearing a black leather coat and a light gray cap, and the doorman flung open the door ahead of me. I patted him on the shoulder. . . .

I finished my cutlets and wanted a liqueur with my coffee. Now I can't stand liqueurs, I find the cloying liquid revolting, but then liqueur with coffee seemed so high-class, so refined, so aristocratic— just imagine it with cutlets made out of God-knows-what and noodles that glued your insides together!

So I ordered liqueur with coffee. I was brought a glass of liqueur and a cup of black swill, but all the same . . . Sysoev had a good laugh and moved the carafe of vodka closer to him. At that very moment two people, a man and a woman, came up to our table and sat in the empty seats. They were well into the bottle, especially the woman, but they immediately ordered a half liter and two bowls of sour cabbage soup. The woman stared at me for a long time, then uttered with difficulty, "Mustaches," revealing black teeth.

"Hush up," the man said to her, and explained to us, "I'm taking her to Archangelsk, to cut timber."

"Her alone?" I asked in amazement.

"Of course not," the man snorted. "I recruited a bunch of them. Now I'm taking them up there. And who would you be?"

"We're locals," Sysoev said, and nodded in my direction, "and he's Georgian."

"Georgian?" the man said in amazement.

"Uh-huh," said Sysoev, and nodded again, this time at the portrait.

The woman slept, her head on the tablecloth. The man drank a shot of vodka and suddenly began to cry.

"Hey," Sysoev said, "what's the matter with you?"

"I want to write him a letter," the man said, "to straighten things out. . . ."

"What's the problem?" I asked.

"You won't . . ." The man began to cry again. "We got saboteurs in the boss's office . . . you know what I mean?"

"Write a letter, write a letter," Sysoev said, and nodded at the portrait in the gilded frame, "he'll give them hell."

"Of course," I said.

"I don't know how," the man whimpered. "How do you write a letter like that? Where do you start? I don't know how. I'd say the wrong thing. . . ."

"Let me write it," I offered. "You give me the facts, every little fact, and I'll write it all down."

"He'll do it," Sysoev said, "he's Georgian, he graduated from the university."

I no longer remember exactly how it all came about. He mumbled something, and I wrote it down. What do I need this for? I thought, but I kept on writing until I heard someone say over my head:

"Your papers, citizen."

The militiaman in the raspberry cap held out his palm. The woman slept. The man watched, wild-eyed. Sysoev turned red and said quietly, "I got to go to the can, I'll be right . . ."

I placed all I had on the militiaman's wide palm. He grabbed my notebook and ordered me to follow him.

"Don't touch him," the man squeaked, "don't touch him, I tell you . . ."

And I was taken away.

In the duty room sat a captain with a flaccid yellow face. The militiaman laid out my papers in front of him and said, "This citizen,

Comrade Captain, was sitting with a drunk, asking him questions and writing things down. He himself wasn't eating or drinking anything."

"Well?" the captain asked.

"What do you mean I wasn't eating or drinking anything?" I said, weakening. "I ate cutlets with noodles and drank a liqueur—"

"What were you writing?" the captain asked.

"You see—" I said.

"Put him in there," the captain said, and nodded at a side door.

I went into a small dirty room that had one cot. The door slammed shut and the lock clicked.

Six square meters. A dim light bulb over the door. Bars on the window, beyond the window the May night. Beyond the door—an indifferent officer, a stranger to me. A few minutes ago I wanted to be somebody. Was that really so unfair? Why, oh, why did I need that idiotic leather! I deceived myself, I thought, playing a game with that village inveigler. I didn't believe it, but I played along and now look where it's got me. . . . When they find out that my parents . . . then they'll smile knowingly and unkindly . . . I, of course, will repeat like a magical incantation the expression he once said that the sins of the father aren't visited on the son . . . but they also say that an apple doesn't fall far . . . and you've got to take that into consideration, since it's folk wisdom, too, and the people are never wrong. . . . Now, in our times, a young man in a similar situation would ask with the smirk of a member of society who has nothing to fear, "And why exactly can't I write whatever I want?" What would that tired captain have answered him? So he got out a notebook, so he wrote something down. So what? That's now . . . but then . . . A short jacket, the devil's own mustache, a glass of liqueur, and drunken delirium about some kind of saboteurs—all of this when, as we all knew, hundreds and thousands of undercover spies were poking around among us, writing things down, eliciting information, poisoning us, blowing things up. . . . In horror I remembered how, in a lecture on the perfidy of foreign intelligence agencies, the speaker had said, "For example, a Western agent will sit in a restaurant nursing a drink without eating anything. You can't help but notice it."

If only I had stayed in my village and not given in to Sysoev's provocations, none of this would have happened: not the frenzy, not the longing, not the torturous road in the flatbed of a truck, not the boat ride through ice floes, not the humiliation in the hotel, not that horren-

dous liqueur and those drunken, ugly faces, not the barred windows and
the prospect of a forced trip somewhere far away, for a long time, forever. . . . "Where are your parents?" "You see . . ." And that would be
it. Because pitiful words are no match against a well-entrenched stereo-
type. Why did I need that cursed coat?

Dawn came. I think I was crying. Quietly, to myself. I still hoped
that a miracle would happen: The tired captain would forget about
everything, hear me out indifferently, wave his hand, and I would dash
into the street, run to the Oka, take the first truck that came along back
to the village, back home, make myself some soup out of young nettles
and millet, go to bed, and wake up in another world.

At that moment in the anteroom there was a crash, a crack, and
then a hoarse voice yelled, "Don't touch him, I tell you!" They were
dragging and pushing someone through the door, but he stood his
ground and yelled, "Where's mustache? What did you do with mustache!" It was that Archangelsk recruiter, rip-roaring drunk. He was
looking for me and was ruining me once and for all, in his dim consciousness confusing my feeble mustache with that other one, and he
was ruining me, ruining me and sentencing me to a long trip, that
drunken bastard. . . .

"Shut up, you bastard!" I shouted through my tears, but no one
could hear me, and there was no longer any point in hoping for a
miracle.

It got light quickly outside the window. The May morning soon
dawned in full, and the steps of happy pedestrians rang out. If it hadn't
been for that calfskin! Then the door creaked open and I was summoned into the anteroom to the duty officer. I resolutely walked over
with a gurgling cry in my throat: "Comrade Captain, I beg of you . . .
it was all a misunderstanding! Honest, I'm not guilty! He's the guilty
one, that drunken bum, that blabbermouth. . . . Ask any of our . . . I
wanted to have a leather coat made. . . . Like an idiot, I was waiting
until morning . . . I thought . . . It was Sysoev who put the idea into
my head, and then he ran away. Honest, honest, I beg you!" But I
didn't manage to shout any of this.

A young lieutenant I hadn't seen before sat on the other side of the
barrier. He twirled my papers and asked indifferently, "Sleep it off?"

"I didn't sleep," I said, and smiled pleadingly.

"Cot too hard?" he asked, snorting disdainfully.

Through the window I could see the platform: Passengers stood
around; flowers bloomed on the lawn; I could see a sign for bread.

"All night I thought about how improperly I behaved," I said.

He handed my papers to me!

"Now what?" I asked in disbelief.

"Drink less," he said. "Now get out of here."

I ran from the station to the pontoon bridge in something like ten minutes, not looking back once. Sysoev was sitting on a fresh log on the bank of the Oka. I sat down next to him, breathing hard. We didn't say anything. He was drawing a little house in the sand with a twig. When he finished he erased it and started in again, this time with greater precision. I started to draw too.

Time passed that way. There were no vehicles going our way. More people wanting to travel appeared.

"What happened, Semyon Alekseyevich, did you get scared?" I asked, not looking at him.

"Get scared—what for?" he said through clenched teeth. "No way . . . Now I'm waiting for a truck."

We were again silent.

"What did they say to you there?" he suddenly asked, erasing the house he had just drawn.

"Nothing," I said. "They gave me back my papers and that was it."

"Sure, that was it." He laughed. "They didn't by any chance take your name down?"

"What if they did?" I whispered.

"No reason," he said. "You'll see. . . ."

"The duty officer changed," I said hurriedly, "some young lieutenant, and he didn't ask me a thing. Just 'get out of here,' so I left. At first I was scared, you know, when I thought that they'd ask about my parents—one thing leads to another—and then, I thought, this is the end. . . ."

"What do you mean, the end?" he said contemptuously. "Do you think they can't get to the bottom of things? You got awful worked up, like you were guilty of something. . . ."

"Why are you using that tone with me? Like we were strangers!" I said in amazement.

"Well, we're not all that well acquainted," he said, looking off down the road. "I don't really know you well at all."

Before I had a chance to answer, a truck rolled up, like a chariot that would take me far from here to a place where nothing could touch me. I got into the flatbed and sat on some kind of sack. Sysoev still sat and continued to draw his house.

"Hurry up!" I shouted, without much hope.

"You get going," he said without raising his head. "There's a lot left to do here in Kaluga."

And I rode off.

My friendship with Semyon Alekseyevich ended. He didn't invite me over and I didn't look for an invitation. He forgot about the leather. I didn't ask. Later I found out from a knowledgeable person that we had preserved the hides wrong, and they were sure to have gone bad in that length of time without processing. That information thoroughly consoled me. I didn't regret the money. Perhaps if I had turned up at the station in a black leather coat—who knows where I'd be today. But in my crude jacket like everyone else's, my boots worn down at the heels . . . what would you expect of me? You wouldn't expect much, would you, now?

October 1985

Translated from the Russian by Michele A. Berdy.

THROUGH THE FIELDS

Lyudmila Petrushevskaya

I never met him again; once and only once we traveled together to someone's distant dacha, in a workers' village. We had to walk about four kilometers through a forest and then through a bare field, which may, in fact, have been pretty at any time of year, but on that day was awful. We stood at the edge of the forest and couldn't bring ourselves to go out into the open space, there was such a thunderstorm. Lightning struck the clay earth of the path, and the field was strangely bare. I remember those mounds of clay, the bare, absolutely bare, broken earth, the cloudburst, and the lightning. Perhaps something had been planted in this field, but at that moment nothing was growing, and our feet slid every which way, buckled, and twisted in this exposed bare field, because we had decided to take the shortest route and go straight across. The way led steeply upward, and hunching over for some reason, we laughed wildly. He was a very taciturn person, from what I remembered of him on previous group outings of this kind—birthdays, trips, and the like. At the time I still did not know the value of silence, didn't appreciate silence, and tried my best to get Vovik to open up, all the more so because we had an hour-and-a-half train ride, just the two of us, alone among strangers, and it was uncomfortable and somehow embarrassing to remain silent. Looking at me with his kind little eyes, he grinned and said almost nothing. But that was all right; it could have been endured were it not for the cloudburst that greeted us at the station. My head, my freshly washed and curled hair, my made-up eyelashes—everything was ruined, everything, my light dress and my bag, which later shriveled and faded—in short, everything. Smiling foolishly, Vovik hunched his head into his shoulders and raised the collar of his white shirt. A drop immediately formed on the tip of his thin nose, but there was nothing that could be done. For some reason we began to wander in the rain through the clay; he knew the way—I didn't. He said that the straight route was closer, so we started across that cursed field through which the lightning gamboled, leaping now close to us, now farther away, and we jumped over the waves of clay earth. We didn't remove our shoes; evidently we were embarrassed in front of each other. I don't know. At that time any manifestations of my natural state embarrassed me and most of all my bare feet, which seemed to me the incarnation of unsightliness on earth. Later on I met women who felt the same way and never went barefoot, especially in the presence of the men they loved. One even went to such extremes to hide her feet that when she got married she deserved her husband's remark "What ugly feet you have!" But others were not concerned in the least by crooked or hairy or long or hairless feet—not in the least. And they turned out to be right, but then, on that day, we walked on the cursed soles of our shoes, slipping and sliding, a hairbreadth from death, and had a wonderful time. We were both twenty years old. Glancing around shyly, good-naturedly, he walked at a distance of about one and a half meters from me; later I found out that lightning can kill two people if they are walking side by side. It was not shyness, however, that kept him from offering me his hand; on that day his fiancée was waiting for him at the dacha, so he didn't offer me his hand out of youthful zeal to serve his love and her alone. But we laughed terribly as we rocked on those waves of earth, and covered all over with clay, we hit it off somehow. Those four kilometers through the clay in the rain dragged on for a remarkably long time: There are times in life that are very difficult to live through and drag on endlessly—hard labor, for example, or sudden solitude or a marathon. We endured those four kilometers together. At the end, when we reached the porch, he even helped me climb up the steps, and accompanied by the astonished laughter of the assembled group and the constrained exclamation of his fiancée, we entered the warm home, still cackling. Everything had gone to hell—his and my clothing, our shoes, our hair; a drop still hung from his nose, but there was not a single person dearer to me than he. I vaguely surmised that I had been lucky to meet in the course of my life a very good and faithful man; the treasures of his soul together with the drop hanging from his nose touched me to the point of tears. I was distraught and didn't know what to do. They showed us to different rooms in this empty, dusty summer house, still not inhabited by summer guests. They changed my clothes and his, too, led us back, and gave both of us half a glass of vodka—how marvelous! At the table he glanced in my direction now and then, smiling foolishly, sniffling, and warmed his hands on a mug of tea. I knew that none of this was mine and never would be mine, this miracle of kindness, purity, and what have you—even beauty. His friend took charge of him; they settled down to a game of chess—even his fiancée was waiting for him. I was not waiting, however, for I was warming my soul after the long and difficult path of my life, realizing that tomorrow and even today I would be torn away from the warmth and the light and thrust out again to walk alone through the clay field in the rain. And that's how life is and one must become stronger, everyone has to—not just me, but Vovik, and even Vovik's poor fiancée, because a person shines for only one person once in his life and that is all.

1983

Translated from the Russian by Stefani Hoffman.

WHAT SHOULD I TELL
THE CROW?

Valentin Rasputin

As I was leaving early in the morning, I promised myself that I would return that evening without fail. My work was finally coming along, and I was afraid to interrupt it, afraid that even after two or three days away from it I would lose everything I'd pulled together with such difficulty as I was getting into the right frame of mind for work—by reading and reflection, through long and agonizing attempts to find the voice I needed, one that wouldn't stumble over every phrase but, like a specially magnetized string, would attract to itself the words required for a full and precise resonance. I couldn't boast of "a full and precise resonance," but some things were turning out right; I sensed it, and for that reason I tore myself away from my writing table this time without the enthusiasm I usually felt on those occasions when I had to go into the city.

A trip to the city takes three hours from door to door and just as many back. So that I wouldn't change my mind or be detained there, God forbid, I went straight to the bus depot when I got to the city and bought a ticket for the last bus that evening. Almost the whole day lay ahead of me, during which I could both attend to business and spend some time, as much as possible, at home.

And everything went fine, everything proceeded according to plan until the moment when, having finished rushing around but still not slackening the pace I'd set, I stopped by the nursery school at the end of the day to pick up my daughter. My daughter was overjoyed to see me. She was coming down the stairs, and when she caught sight of me she gave a start and stood stock-still, her little hand gripping the railing, but then, that was my daughter: she didn't race toward me or hurry at all but, quickly regaining control of herself, came up to me with intentional deliberateness and restraint and reluctantly let herself be hugged. Her willfulness was showing, but I saw right through that inborn if still not hardened willfulness; I saw what an effort it took her to restrain herself from throwing her arms around my neck.

"So you've come?" she asked like a grown-up, and began hurriedly putting on her coat, glancing at me frequently.

We were too close to home to make a real walk out of it, so we went past our apartment building to the river embankment. The weather was warm and quite summerlike for the end of September, and it had been this way for some time now without any visible change, rising each new day with the regularity of what seemed like an unseasonable gift of grace. It was even pleasant just to be out on the streets, and all the more so here, on the embankment along the river, with the uneasy and pacifying power of the water's eternal movement, the unhurried and unheard footsteps of sober, cordial people, the soft voices, and the luminosity of the waning day, low in the slanting sunlight but full and warm and thus disposing one to harmony. This was the sort of magical hour that occurred with great infrequency, when it seemed that throughout the whole throng of strolling people, their souls, disliking solitude and having gathered here at an appointed time, led each person and spoke for each one.

We walked for about an hour, and contrary to habit, my daughter didn't take her little hand out of my hand but pulled it away only to point something out or to gesture when words alone would not suffice, and then she'd slip it back into mine. I couldn't help but appreciate this: it meant she had truly missed me. Last spring, when she turned five, she'd somehow changed a great deal all at once—and not for the better, in our view, because she revealed a stubbornness that had gone unnoticed until then. Apparently considering herself sufficiently grown-up and independent, our daughter didn't want to be led by the hand like all other children. We'd have to struggle with her even in the middle of a raging intersection. Our daughter was afraid of cars, but, jerking away her little shoulder, which we'd grab out of desperation, she would still try to walk at her own pace. Blaming each other, my wife and I argued over which of us could have passed on to our little girl what seemed to us such fierce stubbornness, forgetting that neither of us, of course, could have done it alone.

And now all of a sudden such patience, obedience, and tenderness . . . My daughter was chattering away, finding plenty to tell me as she talked about nursery school and questioned me about our crow. At Lake Baikal we had our own crow. We had our own little house there, and our own hill, a rocky cliff rising almost straight up from the house. Our own little spring spurted out of the cliff, ran through our yard alone in a burbling stream, then disappeared back underground beneath the wooden planks near the gate, and never again appeared for anyone anywhere. In our yard stood our own larch trees, poplars, and birches and our own large bird-cherry bush. Sparrows and titmice would congregate in this bush from all over the neighborhood, then rise up and head for our water, our spring (the wagtails would fly in a long arc from the fence), which they seemed to choose because it matched their size, height, and taste, and on hot days they'd splash around in it without fear, bearing in mind that after their swim they could feed on bread crumbs under the mighty larch growing in the middle of the yard. The birds would gather in great numbers, and even our Tishka, the kitten I'd picked up on the railroad tracks, became resigned to them, but we couldn't say that they were our birds. They'd fly in and, after eating and drinking, they'd fly off somewhere again. But the crow was truly ours. The day my daughter arrived at the beginning of the summer, she spotted the shaggy cap of its nest high up in the larch. I'd been living there for a month by then and hadn't noticed it. A crow kept flying about, cawing as crows do—so what? It never once occurred to me that this was our crow simply because here, in our midst, was its nest and because in this nest it was raising its young.

Our crow, naturally, had to be special, unlike all other crows, and so it became. We learned to understand each other very quickly, and it would tell me everything it saw and heard while flying over regions far and near, and then I would relate its stories at length to my daughter. My daughter believed them. Maybe she didn't actually believe them; like many others, I'm inclined to think that we aren't the ones who play with children, amusing them any way we can, but that they, as purer and more sensible beings, are the ones who play with us to deaden the pain of our existence. Maybe she didn't actually believe them, but she listened with such attention, she waited with such impatience for me to continue when I was interrupted, and her eyes shone so, betraying a complete uncloudedness of soul, that these stories began to give me pleasure too. I began to notice an excitement in myself that I picked up from my daughter and that in some amazing way made us equals, as if bringing us together on the same level, despite our age difference. I made things up, knowing that I was making them up, and my daughter believed them, not paying any attention to the fact that I made them up. Yet, in what seemed like a game, there prevailed between us a rare harmony and understanding that did not arise from the rules of any game here, but seemed conveyed from someplace out there where they alone exist. Conveyed, perhaps, by that crow. I don't know, I can't explain why, but for a long time I've lived with the certainty that if a link between this world and that actually exists, then only crows can fly from one to the other, and I've been watching them for quite some time with secret curiosity and fear, trying and yet afraid to comprehend why only crows can do this.

Our crow, though, was completely earthly and ordinary, having none of these dealings with the other world, good-natured and talkative, with inklings of what we call clairvoyance.

I had stopped at home that morning and learned a thing or two about my daughter's recent activities, if you can call them activities, and now I related them to her as if I had heard them from the crow.

"It flew to the city again the day before yesterday and saw that you and Marina had a fight. Naturally, it was very surprised. You were always such good friends, wild horses couldn't drag you apart, but then all of a sudden you behaved like the worst barbarians on account of a stupid little thing—"

"We-e-ll, but what if she stuck her tongue out at me?" My daughter lashed out immediately. "Do you think it's very nice when people stick their tongues out at you, huh? Is that very nice, huh?"

"It's disgraceful. Of course it isn't very nice. Only why did you stick your tongue out at her, then? It's not very nice for her either."

"Did the crow see me stick my tongue out or something?"

"Sure it saw you. It sees everything."

"But that's not true. Nobody could've seen me. The crow couldn't have either."

"Maybe it didn't actually see you, but it guessed right. It knows you inside out, so it didn't have a hard time guessing."

My daughter took offense at being known "inside out," but, uncertain about whom to blame for this, me or the crow, she fell silent, further dismayed because something extremely secret had somehow been found out. A bit later she admitted that she had stuck her tongue out at Marina from the doorway when Marina had already left. My daughter wasn't capable of concealing anything yet, or, rather, she didn't copy us and conceal every trifle—those little things we could disclose and thus make life easier—but, as they say, she kept her own counsel.

Meanwhile, the time was approaching for me to get ready to leave, and I told my daughter it was time to go home.

"No, let's walk some more." She wouldn't give her consent.

"It's time," I repeated. "I have to go back today."

Her little hand trembled in mine. My daughter didn't so much speak as sing out:

"Don't leave today." And, as if that settled it once and for all, she added, "There."

And now it was my turn to tremble: this wasn't simply a request, the kind children make at every turn—no, it was a plea uttered with dignity and restraint but with her whole being, which cautiously staked out its legitimate claim over me, not knowing and not caring to know the generally accepted rules of life. But as for me, I was already more than a little corrupted and oppressed by these rules, and when the rules of others, established for everyone, fell short, I would make up my own, just as I did now. Giving a sigh, I recalled the promise I'd made to myself that morning and stood my ground:

"I have to, you understand. I can't stay."

My daughter obediently let herself be turned toward home and escorted across the street, and then she broke free and ran on ahead. She didn't even wait for me at the entrance to our building, as she always did in such situations; when I got up to the apartment she was already occupied with something in her corner. I began packing my knapsack, continually going over to my daughter and trying to start up a conversation with her; she'd become reticent and her replies were strained. It was all over—she was no longer with me, she'd withdrawn into herself, and the more I'd try to get close to her, the further she'd retreat. I knew this all too well. My wife, guessing what had happened, made the most sensible suggestion under the circumstances:

"You can catch the first bus in the morning. And be there by nine o'clock."

"No, I can't." I became furious because this really did make sense.

I still had some hope of getting a proper send-off. When it comes to parting, this is the way it's done in our family: no matter what might have happened, be kind enough to put all bad feelings, just and unjust, behind you and say good-bye with an unburdened heart, even on the most ordinary and nonthreatening occasions. I finished packing and called my daughter over.

"Good-bye. What should I tell the crow?"

"Nothing. Good-bye," she said with a certain glibness and indifference in a voice that sounded too grown-up for her, and looked away.

The streetcar came immediately, as if on purpose, and I arrived at the depot twenty minutes ahead of the bus. I could have spent those twenty minutes walking with my daughter, you see; that probably would have been sufficient for her not to notice my haste and nothing would have come between us.

Then, as if someone wanted to teach me a lesson, I ran into a string of bad luck. The bus pulled in late—it didn't simply pull in, but lunged into view, screeching and grinding around the corner as if to say: Look how I've rushed—all ratty-looking and scratched up, with half the front door torn off. We got on and then sat there after mounting this skittish bus, suspiciously quiet beneath us as though it were about to buck again, while the driver, looking in at the dispatcher's office, vanished inside and didn't reappear. We sat there for ten minutes, then fifteen, inhaling the smell of the sacks of potatoes piled on the backseat; we were a silent lot, feeling sluggish at the end of the day, and no one let out a murmur of complaint. We sat mutely, content simply to be sitting in our places. How little, I've noticed on more than one occasion, our people need: scare them by saying there won't be a bus until morning and a furious outcry will erupt, until everyone is in a complete stupor, but rush the same bus in, load it up, and let it stand there until morning—and they'll remain satisfied and believe that they've gotten their way. Here the principle of one's rightful place is apparently at work: your place can be occupied by no one else and given to no one else but you, and whether this place takes you anywhere or not isn't really that important.

My common sense did indeed tell me to get up from this place that wasn't taking me anywhere and go back home. My daughter would have been overjoyed! She would never have let on, of course, that she was overjoyed and, true to form, she wouldn't have come up to me right away, but then she would have latched on to me and not left my side until bedtime. And I would have been forgiven, and so would the crow. And how fine and warm the evening would have turned out, one to recall over and over again later on, during my days of solitude, to warm myself beside, stirring up and then soothing my soul, to make me feel tormented with joy by its full and happy conclusion. Our days don't coincide in time with the days allotted us for our activities; time usually runs out before we manage to finish, leaving the ends of the things we've begun and abandoned sticking out in an absurd way. It is not the sin of conception that hangs over our children like a great weight from their very first hours but the sin of what their fathers left undone. This day could have become uncommonly complete, consummated in all respects, and, like a seed, it could have been the source of other days just like it. When I speak of activities, of their completeness or incompleteness in terms of days, I don't mean all activities but only those in harmony with the soul, which gives us a special assignment, apart from ordinary work, and holds each of us accountable.

And I was prepared to stand up and get off the bus, fully prepared, but something held me back. The place where I'd been sitting such a long time held me. It was conveniently located, a window seat on the right-hand side where oncoming vehicles wouldn't disturb me. And then the bus driver finally came running up almost at a sprint, demonstrating again that he was in a hurry. He quickly counted us once more, checked the itinerary, and stepped on the gas. I became resigned, and I even rejoiced that the chance to decide whether to go or not to go had been taken away from me. We took off.

We took off, all right, but we didn't get very far. Nothing else could possibly have been expected from our bus and from our driver. The driver, a small, fidgety, crafty little guy, resembled a sparrow—the same hopping and bobbing, the same jerkiness and lopsidedness in his movements, but with a craftiness that could be seen not only in his face, where it shone through openly, but also in his whole physique, and when he sat with his back to us it was clear even from behind that this guy would survive in any situation. I began to wonder why he'd stayed so long in the dispatcher's office: perhaps this wasn't his route, and this wasn't the bus that was supposed to make this run, but because there was something in it for him, he'd talked somebody into switching and then talked the dispatcher into it—and there we sat again, a mere two blocks out of the dispatcher's sight, while our driver hopped around like a sparrow in the middle of the street with a pail in his hand, begging enough gasoline to make it to the gas pumps. That meant another stop; I began to worry in earnest about whether the ferry would wait for us as it normally did. We were already terribly late. It would be the last straw if, after enduring all this for the sake of being able to work in the morning, I had to spend the night in full view of our cabin on the other shore of Lake Baikal, and not simply spend the night, but be in an agony of suspense the whole time waiting for the morning ferry and thus spoil the entire coming day. And I still could have gotten off here, but I didn't get off here either. "Spitefulness, boy, was born before you were," my grandmother often used to say in such situations. In this case, though, it wasn't just spitefulness, but some other trait I'd acquired from earlier spasmodic attempts at building my character that still echoed in me from time to time. My character hadn't grown any firmer, of course, but the direction in which it had been bent sometimes manifested itself in the most unexpected fashion and made its own demands.

We just barely made it to the gas pumps at last, and from there we continued on our way. I was afraid to look at my watch; let come what may. It grew dark right outside of town; the woods, which hadn't lost a leaf yet, fell sweepingly away from where I was sitting like a solid black curtain. There turned out to be no lighting inside the bus—it would have been strange if there had been—but at least the headlights worked well: we rode in darkness and everyone dozed. The bus, meanwhile, was making a dash for it, as if it were hurrying home itself; glancing out the window in my semislumber, I saw the roadbed quickly slipping back and kilometer markers flashing by. The wind began to blow through the half-missing door, and the closer we got to Baikal the more we could feel the bus clank and sputter in infernal bursts under the driver's feet whenever he shifted gears, but beyond that we noticed little and differed little from the sacks of potatoes piled up in back.

Good luck: this is not when you actually have good luck, but when, compared with bad luck, things change for the better. In this case it was impossible to designate the degree of divergence. I was so overjoyed when I saw the lights of the ferry as we approached that I didn't pay attention to the fact that it wasn't the *Babushkin*, the ship that functioned as a ferry from April through January and was equipped to handle passengers as well as cargo, but a small motorboat, barely visible at the base of the pier. Still going full speed, the driver hit the brakes sharply, making us feel that we were living people after all, and was the first to hurriedly jump out; he bent down over the boat, shouting something and waving his arms until they understood what he wanted, and then rushed back to hurry us along.

A rumbling sound was coming from Baikal, and quite a powerful one. The air, however, was completely still, even dead—that meant that Baikal had been stirred up somewhere to the north and that this billow had been driven for dozens upon dozens of kilometers, but even here it was moving with such force, delineating fiery streaks of foam time after time under the gentle new moon, and moving with such a roar that the night grew windy and chilly from the feeling of cold that

rose up inside you. The poor little boat kept bobbing up and down next to the pier as if it were trying to leap on top of it. We were almost an hour late, and the boat's crew, four or five young guys (it was impossible to get an exact count), hadn't wasted any time: they were all at least three sheets to the wind. The driver nimbly carried the sacks of potatoes off the bus and handed them down, and the crew stumbled about and shouted in confusion as they took them, and you got the feeling that they were tumbling down right along with the sacks. The other passengers dispersed, and only we, the three unfortunate figures who faced crossing this Baikal in this boat with this crew, huddled together, not knowing what to do. The crashing water and the still air: it gave you sort of an eerie feeling—as if out there, beyond the end of the pier, was the beginning of another world. From out there, from the nether regions, the guys yelled at us, and after setting our sights and taking aim for a long time, in the last throes of gloomy foreboding, we awkwardly began to jump into the boat. I jumped first. From down below I could make out the driver's voice over the crashing water, cheerfully ordering the crew not to pull any tricks and to wait while he parked the bus, and I calmed down: we wouldn't perish with that guy along.

When I later recalled the return trip from beginning to end, and the boat ride in particular, I thought of it not as something awful or unpleasant but as something unavoidable that had occurred under all these conditions and in exactly this sequence only because of me, to teach me some kind of lesson. What lesson? I didn't know and perhaps I won't know anytime soon, and it's not really the answer that's important here but the feeling that I was to blame. These weren't accidents of chance. It seemed to me that even the people who were traveling with me suffered and faced risks only on my account. The last half hour, when we were crossing from one shore to the other, was, of course, filled with risk—there's no denying it! This half hour barely left a trace in my memory or my feelings. As our little boat alternately plunged into the water and leapt into the air, the guys in the deckhouse, and the bus driver along with them, let out one and the same cry of delight while I, wet and chilled to the bone, sat on a sack of potatoes that kept sliding around underneath me and apathetically waited to see how it would all end. I remember that we couldn't get close to the pier for quite a while, and that by the time we did I'd already regained my senses; I remember that when we finally caught hold and began climbing up onto dry land, one of the four or five brave lads rushed after us to collect forty kopecks from each of us for the ride. A crowd of people were waiting for our bus driver, and they greeted him onshore with a lot of noise and affectionate profanity, and then they immediately led him off somewhere.

The day had exhausted me so that, once I got to my cabin, I didn't bother to make any tea or even to unpack my knapsack but just collapsed into bed. It was already past midnight. At the last moment, when I was just on the verge of falling asleep, it suddenly struck me: Why, for what possible reason, was he bringing potatoes from the city out here, to the country, when everybody else, on the contrary, takes them from here to the city, the way they should?

I don't know if this is true of anyone else, but I lack a sense of complete and indivisible integration with myself. I don't have the feeling, as one is supposed to, that everything inside me matches up from beginning to end, that everything down to the smallest detail merges in a single whole so that nothing comes loose anywhere and nothing sticks out. Something in me is constantly coming loose and sticking out: either my head will start to ache, and not with a simple pain that you can get rid of with pills or fresh air, but seemingly because it is suffering from having been acquired by the wrong person; or I'll catch myself with a thought or feeling that never should have been in me in the first place; or I'll get up in the morning healthy and well rested without the slightest desire to go on living; or some other thing. Such things don't happen to a normal person, of course; they are characteristic of people who are either accidental or substitutes. Concerning "substitute" people, I've given the matter particular thought: let's assume that someone should have been born, but for some reason (not for us to know) he lost his turn to be born, and then another person was quickly summoned from the next row to take his place.

And so that person was born, differing in no way from the rest, and grew to adulthood; it never occurs to anyone in this huge populace that something about him isn't quite right, and only he suffers—the further along he gets, the more he suffers—from his involuntary guilt and from his not matching that place in the world that had been set aside for someone else.

Similar ideas, no matter how foolish they might seem, have crossed my mind more than once in moments of discord with myself.

And this leads to my other abnormality: I'll never get used to myself. Having lived a good number of years, I discover with continuing amazement when I wake up every morning that I am really me and that I exist in reality rather than in someone else's recollections and imaginings (of things that might have come before or after me) that happen to have reached me. This occurs not just in the mornings. I have only to fall into deep thought or, on the contrary, to drift off in a pleasant absence of thought when suddenly I lose myself, as if I'm flying on ahead to some border region from which I have no desire to return. This not being inside myself, this straying from home, happens quite often; I involuntarily begin to keep track of myself, to be on guard so I'll stay in place, inside myself, but the whole tragedy lies in my not knowing whose side I should take, which one of them contains the genuine "me"—the one that waits for itself with patience and hope or the one that makes futile attempts to run away from itself? Does it run away to find something different, yet kindred and all its own, someone with whom it would make a complete and successful match? Or is it waiting to resign itself to its own likeness and to the impossibility of remedying anything even one iota? For "I" must be in one of them, the primordial, fundamental "I," so to speak, the one to whom something could have been added later rather than the one who would simply serve as an addition to someone else's incompleteness.

The morning after my trip to the city I got up late. I hadn't closed the shutters on the windows the night before, and the sunshine tortured me even in my sleep; I lay there half asleep under its onslaught, tormented by wanting to wake up and not being able to. Everyone is well acquainted with this helpless state: you seem right on the verge of forcing your way through your oppressive body toward a means of escape where you can regain consciousness—but no, at the last minute some force hurls you back. Each time I'm in this situation I experience terror at the vast expanse that must be overcome in order to approach the line between wakefulness and sleep, and that's not all—once you've reached it, you have to calculate your final move in such a way that the oncoming gust won't pull you under again. There, in this numb state of consciousness that you can't control, everything has different dimensions: it's as though it might take a whole lifetime to wake up.

Somehow I managed to open my eyes—I opened my eyes and instantly felt my indisposition as though I could see it in front of me. A stifling emptiness in both my chest and my head weighed me down, something I knew all too well to just brush aside, for it came from the type of disharmony with myself that I've been trying to explain.

But, oddly enough, I wasn't the least bit surprised at my condition, as if I should have known about it in advance but for some reason had forgotten.

The sunshine that had seemed strong and bright to me in my sleep lay on the floor of the room like a faded, washed-out spot; the window frames quivered in it like a barely noticeable, deeply sunken shadow.

My cabin was unpretentious: a small kitchen, a good third of which was taken up by the stove, and a small front room or parlor with corner windows on two sides, both with a view of Baikal across the road. The third wall, the one near the cliff, had no doors or windows and always gave off a coolness and a faintly discernible smell of rotting wood. Right now this smell was coming through more strongly than usual—a sure sign that the weather was taking a turn for the worse. And sure enough, as I was getting dressed, the spot of sunshine on the floor vanished altogether; perhaps I hadn't dreamed that the sun was bright after all, for it may well have been when it came up, but since then the sky had clouded over. It was still; after my agonized sleep I didn't realize right away that the stillness was absolute, which almost never happens in this bustling place where my cabin is located, next to the railroad tracks and the pier. I listened again: stillness—like on a day of celebration for old folks, if there were such a thing—and this put me on guard, and I hurried outside.

No, everything remained in place—the railroad cars that had stood on the siding not far from the house since spring, a long double line of them going nowhere, and the big heap of dry cargo on the lakeshore across the way with the motionless arm of a gantry crane poised above it, and an old woman sitting on a log by the road with shopping bags at her feet, observing me in silent reproach, not comprehending how it was possible to get up so late. . . . Baikal was growing calm. Here and there on its surface a small wave would still tremble and break, then glide away before reaching the shore. The air dazzled the eye with the hazy brilliance of the ruined sunshine; the sun itself found it impossible to show through in any one place, and it seemed to spread across the whole smoky-white, drooping sky and to shine from all directions. The morning coolness had passed by then, but the day hadn't warmed up yet; it looked as if it never intended to warm up, being occupied with some other more important change, so it was neither cool nor warm, neither sunny nor cloudy, but somehow in between the one and the other, somehow oppressive and nondescript.

And once again I felt such restlessness and lucklessness inside myself that I almost went back to bed without doing a thing. Sleep, whose grip I hadn't known how to break, by now represented a longed-for liberation, but I knew that I wouldn't fall asleep and that in the attempt I might get even more worked up.

I sometimes managed to get the better of myself in these situations. . . . I couldn't recall how this came about—by itself or with the help of my conscious efforts—but now, too, something had to be done. With exaggerated vigor I began lighting a fire in the stove and making tea, unpacking my knapsack in the meantime and carrying packages and canned goods out to the pantry. I love these moments just before my morning tea: the fire flares up, the teakettle starts to snuffle, and the tea concentrate, giving off a most agreeable aroma, languishes in the weak heat at the edge of the stove as it waits for the boiling water, while a breath of fresh air drifts in through the open door and goes back out again, as if it had gotten burned on the stove. In these moments I love to be alone and, keeping pace with the flaring fire, to savor my own ripening thirst for tea, my long-suffering and pleasant readiness for the first sip. And now the tea is brewed, now it's poured, the mug is giving off a fragrant, intoxicating steam, a violet haze hovers low over the hot, dark brown surface in a concealing, mysteriously stirring film. . . . Now, at last, the first sip! . . . You can't help but compare it to the solemn stroke of a bell sounding forth in your lonely world, proclaiming the full advent of the new day, and, interrupted by nothing, continuing to ring until it reaches multiple reverberations, like a resonating echo. And the second sip, and the third—these are stentorian signals of the general readiness of the powers that were exhausted during the night. Then begins the nearly hour-long, work-related tea drinking, which gradually sneaks up on you and adapts itself to the business at hand. To start with, there's a lordly, superficial sidelong glance: What's this that you came up with yesterday? Will it do or not? Does it hit the mark or does it miss? You seem to have no interest whatsoever in yesterday's work; you simply happened to remember that you'd been doing something. . . . This is attention focused in the right direction but still wandering. You drink your tea unhurriedly, with each sip pondering more and more deeply some vague and aimless idea that is lazily groping around in a complete fog for something unknown. And suddenly, heaven knows why, the first reciprocal idea will flash in this fog like an image, dim and flickering, which later will have to be discarded, but once it flashes it will indicate where to continue looking. Now you're getting close, you move from one table to the other, grabbing your mug of tea, and for the sake of routine you still look over your old work while its continuation impatiently begins to make itself heard inside you.

This time nothing of the kind happened to me. Even moving around required effort. I took pleasure in drinking my tea, as always, but it didn't help me in the least and didn't cheer me up; the causeless, cold weight had no intention of retreating. Out of stubbornness I settled down at the table with my papers anyway, but with the same effect as a blind person looking through binoculars: not a single ray up ahead and a solid gray wall all around. I sat there for half an hour like a perfect statue with a brick for a head, and then, thoroughly detesting myself, I got up.

Something seemed to squeak with malicious joy behind my back when I walked away from the table. . . .

Fretting, I wandered around stupidly and aimlessly—first I'd go outdoors and listen carefully and peer at something without knowing myself what it was, then I'd go back into the cottage again and stand next to the burning stove, torturing myself until I felt faint from the heat, and then I'd go back outside. I remember that I kept trying to figure out how such a complete and ancient stillness had built up and where it had come from, although by now the morning's earlier stillness was no more—by now something banged from time to time over on the dry cargo, a strong voice accustomed to commanding was giving orders through a megaphone somewhere on the water, and a motorcycle had roared past two or three times. But the air was growing softer and deader, as if the day were taking cover, trying to wrap itself up more tightly and guard against an alien spaciousness, and sounds died away and got stuck in the dense air, reaching the ear faintly and despondently.

After suffering like this for an hour or so and sensing that I wouldn't find any relief, I locked up the cottage and decided to go wherever my feet would take me. They took me through the gate and down the dry, well-beaten path along the railroad tracks, and in no time I had gone far beyond the town, to those sonorous and joyful spots along the shores of Baikal that remained sonorous, joyful, and fully distinguishable in any weather—in summer and winter, in sunshine and rain. But even here I could now feel almost tangibly how the day was sinking lower and lower and how much more tightly it was drawing itself in from the edges. Baikal is never without wind; it's as though it were breathing— calmly and evenly at times, a little more heavily at others, and sometimes with all its might, when you're lucky if you manage to find a place to hide. . . . A breeze was blowing now, too, but it seemed to fluctuate, as if it were trying to pick up speed and yet kept getting bogged down. . . . The sun was finally overcome and was fading even from the atmosphere. Baikal was a solid deep blue.

I stood on the bank awhile trying to choose which way to go, down to the water or up the hill, without the slightest desire to go in either direction, and because the descent to the water was easy at this point, a gentle slope, while the hill was steep, as the hills are almost everywhere, abruptly rising to full height out of fear of Baikal, and because it appeared especially steep here, I began to climb, trying to breathe in rhythm with my steps in order to make my breath last over a greater stretch of the hill. Traversing the bare, rocky scarp, kicking gravel loose, I managed to reach the grass that poked out like long white tufts of hair from under the soil, which was still sparse and also white, and I turned to look back. The low sky circled above me, its broad rim curving downward toward Baikal—it was somehow completely faded and colorless, preparing for something from one end to the other but not yet ready. The wind was a little fresher at this altitude, but the breeze wafting from the rocks and the earth was deep-seated and dry, hastening to give off warmth as if it, too, had a purpose in mind. I went farther and over the next change of terrain came to a long and narrow winding glade that had been cleared to make a hayfield—the hay had long since been cut and carted away, and the glade seemed somehow very sad and solitary in its forlorn, harvest-home spentness. Feeling sorry for it, I sat down on a rock there and began to look down.

The sky continued to circle slowly and soundlessly, descending closer and closer all the time and acquiring a dry, smoke-colored, cloudless skin. Beyond the hill, beyond the sparse trees on the summit, there was no more sky, only a gray and unpleasant gaping void. The whole sky had girded itself tightly and come to a halt over Baikal, repeating both its contours and its color exactly. But now even the water in Baikal, submitting to the sky, started moving in slow and regular circles without splashing against the shore, as though someone had stirred it up like water in a tub and left it to settle.

The circles made me dizzy. Soon I could only poorly comprehend what I was, where I was, and why I was here, and I had no need of such comprehension. Much of what had troubled me only yesterday and today and had seemed important was unnecessary now and slipped away from me with great ease, as if this were an inevitable stage in

some fixed sequence of renewal whose time had come. It wasn't renewal, however, but something else, something that was happening in
a larger world, a world distant from me in breadth and height, in
which I found myself by sheer accident and whose mysterious movement had inadvertently swept me up too. I felt a pleasant liberation
from the recent morbid weight that had tormented me so; it had totally
disappeared, as if mentally I had half risen and straightened up inside,
and, trying the feeling on for size, I somehow knew that this still wasn't
a complete liberation and that something even better was yet to come.

I sat there without moving a muscle, watching the dark glow of
Baikal before me with a diffuse significance that seemed to anticipate a
special moment, and I listened to the hum rising from the depths as
though it came from a bell that had been tipped over and aimed at the
sky. You could sense anxiety and alarm in it and in the water's movement—whether the anxiety and alarm were dying down or, on the
contrary, gathering strength was not for me to know: the instant in
which they were born stretched out for me into a long and monoto-
nous existence. And it wasn't for me to know whose force it was, whose
power—the sky's over the water or the water's over the sky—but I saw
quite clearly that they were in an animate and divine subordination to
each other. In divine subordination—for what reason, over what?
Which side has height and which depth? And where is the boundary
between them? Which one of these equal expanses contains the consciousness that knows the simplest of the secrets, simple yet beyond us,
of the world in which we are caught?

These questions, of course, were all in vain. Not only are they impossible to answer, they're even impossible to formulate. Questions,
too, have boundaries that should not be crossed. It's the same as the sky
and the water, the sky and the earth, existing in an eternal continuum
and subordination to each other—which of them is the question and
which is the answer? After using every ounce of strength to approach
them, we can merely freeze in helplessness before the inexplicability
of our conceptions and the inaccessibility of the adjacent boundary
lines; we are forbidden to step over them and send back our voices, no
matter how faint and tentative they may be. We should mind our own
business.

I tried to ponder these matters further and to listen, but my consciousness and feelings and vision and hearing kept growing dimmer
and dimmer in me like a pleasant depression, receding into a kind of
universal nerve center. And I kept growing stiller inside, more and

more tranquil. I had no sensation of myself whatsoever; all inner movement had gone out of me, but I continued to notice everything that was happening around me, taking it in all at once and at a great distance around, but I did nothing more than notice. It was as if I had merged with the single nerve center that serves everything and remained inside it. I didn't see the sky or the water or the earth, but an invisible road was suspended in the deserted, luminous world and led off horizontally into the distance, with voices—now faster, now slower—shooting along it. The only way you could determine that a road existed was by the sounds the voices made—they came from one direction and whirled off in another. And strangely enough, they sounded completely different when approaching than when leaving: harmony and a faith happy to the point of self-oblivion could be heard in them before they got to me while beyond me they sounded almost like a grumble. There was something in me that they didn't like, something they objected to. I, on the contrary, felt more agreeable and lighter with every passing moment, and the lighter I felt, the fainter the departing voices became. I was already preparing myself and somehow knew that soon I, too, would begin to race off along this purifying road as soon as I was ready, as soon as it unfolded before me in reality, and I was impatient to be off. I seemed to hear an unbearable summons from the direction in which the road led.

Then I came to and saw that a lone spider's web hung swaying before my eyes. The air still hummed with the same voices (I hadn't lost the ability to hear them yet); they had encircled me, forming an edifying round dance of farewell. I was sitting in a completely different place and, judging from Baikal's shoreline, it was a long way from the previous one. Next to me three birch trees were sadly tossing down their leaves just like fortune-tellers as they played some game. The air was absolutely still; it is in just such motionlessness, when everything, it seems, is left only to its own devices, that more things die away and vanish than in a wind, which is supposed to die away; this is the tranquillity of a cautious, divine presence gathering in its harvest. How joyful it must be for a free soul whose time has come to die in the autumn, in that radiant hour when the expanses unfold! . . .

And, regaining consciousness, I again discovered that I was a long way even from the last place, the one with the birch trees. Baikal was nowhere in sight—that meant I'd managed to cross the hill and descend almost to the bottom on the opposite side. It was getting dark. I was standing up—either I'd just arrived or I'd gotten up to go farther.

But how I'd come, where I'd come from, why I'd come here—I had no idea. Somewhere down below a river flowed noisily over some rocks, and without actually seeing the river, I could see its course by its noise, lively and intermittent yet continuous—I saw where it turned and where it went, where it beat against which particular rocks, and where it grew still for a short time, trembling in foamy ripples. I wasn't the least bit surprised by this kind of vision, as if this were just the way it was supposed to be. But that wasn't all: I suddenly saw myself rising from my previous place beside the birch trees and heading up the hill. I continued to stand on the spot where I'd just discovered myself, clutching a thick bough that stuck up from a fallen larch tree for verification, and at the same time I was walking step by step, glance after glance, picking a handy trail; I palpably sensed every movement and heard every sigh I made. I finally drew near the place where I was standing next to the fallen larch and merged with myself. But even this didn't surprise me a bit, as if this, too, were exactly the way it was supposed to be; I only felt a certain excessive satiety inside that prevented me from breathing freely. And now, completely united with myself, I thought of home.

By the time I approached my little cottage it was already completely dark. My legs barely held me up—from the looks of it, all the crossings, those I remembered and those I didn't, had actually been made on foot. I found a jar in the grass by the little spring and set it under the stream of water. And I drank for a long time, returning to myself once and for all—to what I was yesterday and to what I'd be tomorrow. I didn't feel like going inside, so I sat down on a log and, rooted to the spot from fatigue and from a peculiar spiritual fulfillment, I merged with the stillness, darkness, and immobility of late evening.

The darkness grew thicker and thicker, the air became heavier, and the damp earth gave off a sharp, bitter smell. I sat there in a mellow state and watched the red light from the little lighthouse flash on the retaining walls across the way, and I listened to the voices borne by the spring, the incoherent, wordless voices of friends who had died, trying to the point of exhaustion to tell me something. . . .

O Lord, have faith in us: we are alone.

I was awakened in the middle of the night by the patter of rain on the dry roof, and I thought with pleasure that now the rain, which had been building up and anticipated all day, had set in, and yet, heaven knows why, I once again began to feel such anguish and sorrow inside that I barely refrained from getting up and tearing around the cottage. The rain fell faster and harder and I went back to sleep in this anguished state, to its sound, suffering even in my sleep and realizing that I suffered. And throughout the rest of the night I thought I heard the crow cawing loudly and insistently time after time, and it seemed to be walking along the low earthen insulating wall in front of the windows and tapping its beak on the closed shutters.

And sure enough, I was awakened by the cry of the crow. The morning was gray and wet, it was raining incessantly, and drops large and white as snow were coming loose from the trees and falling off. I got dressed without lighting a fire in the stove and headed for the port dispatcher's office, where you could make phone calls to the city. For a long time I couldn't get through—the connection kept being made and then broken—and when I finally did get through to my home, I was told that my daughter had been sick in bed since yesterday and was running a fever.

1981

Translated from the Russian by Gerald Mikkelson and Margaret Winchell.

THE DEVIL'S WHEEL IN KOBULETI

Mikhail Roshchin

In Memory of A.

On the Kobuleti beach* in August there are so many people there's nowhere for an apple to fall, but by September, when the children are sent off to school, it's already quiet and empty. Without its human crowds the beach itself is revealed—"its beauty infinite and its infinity beautiful," as the poet said—as is the town, with its elegant two-story houses and their formal outer staircases (so that every man can feel like a prince as he descends) and a main street that is "the longest in Europe," as the residents of Kobuleti like to point out. But the promenade that follows a rise above the beach is longer still. The local residents come here now to stroll, and for the first time all summer they can at least see each other; earlier they dissolved into the vacationing masses. The promenade is especially lovely: people sit peacefully, stroll, admire the sunsets; children play underfoot. All in all it's a wonderful time of year. The sun rises later and sets earlier, but it doesn't leave the sky all day, and you can still sunbathe. Sometimes clouds move in and there's a downpour, or the rain may murmur all night long, but then the sun comes out again and it's dry. Fog, rainbows, those luxuriant crimson sunsets that people come to look at as if they were going to the opera, and the blindingly white moon. A cool wind blows under relic pines: during the summer it was refreshing, but now you have to pull

* Kobuleti is a resort on the Black Sea in the Soviet republic of Georgia. —Trans.

on a sweater. In the café on the promenade girls turn tiny white demi-tasse cups upside down and tell fortunes in the coffee grounds. At the snack bar you can finally get shish kebab or even mullet without standing in line. In the gardens black figs burst on their branches. The smoke and scent of roasted chestnuts linger on your fingers. A gynecologist from Tbilisi and a dentist from Moscow are seated at a table together in the Intourist Hotel. The velvet season. Peace and quiet.

By the way, about the Intourist. Several years ago this sixteen-story spaceship landed on the native Kobuleti shore and no one has been able to decide whether it fits in. Not really. This Intourist has been nothing but a headache, although, of course, no one wants to be inferior to Sochi or Marseilles. Perhaps in the future dozens of these buildings will be strung along the thread of the Kobuleti beach, stifling and crowding the little old houses and, like gigantic pumps, sucking money out of tourists' pockets. Maybe—but thank God we won't be here to see it. For the time being an emissary from the future still feels out of place here. During the day the Intourist holds itself up proudly, squaring its brick-colored shoulders, but at night it dissolves into the darkness, glimmering in muted lamplight, sorrowfully reaching for the sky, longing to fly.

In the hotel—foreign music and foreign speech. Czech brewers and hairdressers, Polish miners, elderly Hungarian ladies, Dresden students—everyone comes to the warm sea. Sometimes there are Finns, Greeks, Swedes. Although why, one might ask, does a Greek need Kolkhida* now? But they come: a youth with the face of Apollo, in white shorts, holds hands with a Georgian girl; young, sweet, with enormous eyes and a shock of black hair, she wears a long skirt to hide legs that aren't very shapely. His name is Jason, hers Medea.

And then suddenly the Americans arrived. You wouldn't believe what went on in Kobuleti! It was like something out of a Daneliya comedy.[†] Scruffy palms were dug up from tubs and fresh ones planted. In one night a fence was put up around the foundation pit that had been dug five years earlier for a swimming pool (What do we need a swimming pool for when we're right next to the sea?) and had long

---

*Kolkhida (Colchis) is the Greek name for Georgia. According to legend, Jason and the Argonauts came to Kolkhida in search of the Golden Fleece. Jason married Medea, daughter of the native king. —Trans.

†Georgi Daneliya is a contemporary Georgian film director known for such popular comedies as *Mimino*. —Trans.

been overgrown by brambles. At dawn a yellow-black beetle-bulldozer crawled around the courtyard, scraping away the mounds of old cement still left over from construction and filling in the puddles. The gynecologist and the dentist were immediately moved to another hotel, even though the gynecologist insisted he had spent some time in America himself. The administrator raised his voice to the German students. Stately waitresses were brought in from the capital. Responsible-looking men in big caps stood in the marble lobby, twirling their key rings as they deliberated day and night among themselves, while sweaty maids, unacquainted with deodorant, dragged bundles of fresh linen past them across the slick floor and loaded them into the elevators. On Thursday, the eve of the Americans' arrival, to the horror of the hotel administration, the elevators went out of service. According to the conventions of this genre, the Americans should have been taken past the hotel and put up someplace else. But no, they came. About eight of them. At night. No one saw them. And no one saw them leave. And that was the last stroke, the last gasp of the departing, noisy summer. After the Americans, absolute quiet descended.

The old writer was wheeled in a wheelchair along the promenade by an extremely youthful woman. She looked like a girl—she could have been his granddaughter, but everyone who sat or strolled in the evenings above the sea already knew that she was not his granddaughter, nor his daughter, nor his private nurse. And everyone, of course, was shocked by this couple. The women whispered among themselves and shook their heads. They had arrived in Batumi by steamship; sailors had carried him to shore down a rickety gangplank. They then traveled an hour by taxi, while Niko—the son of his old friend—who had come to meet the writer, drove another car carrying an English folding wheelchair with glittering spokes. Niko was young, flustered, wearing a tie; he looked like his father, the kind Givi. Good Lord, how young the writer once was himself on this very shore—could it have been that long ago? It seemed like yesterday, and Eteri, Niko's mother, was young, and what a whirlwind swirled around him then: friends, poets, women, a singer with his guitar, fishermen, sailors—after the war he had written his famous play about navy men, and they hadn't forgotten it. He himself had been through the war and had capsized near Murmansk in a destroyer that was escorting an English convoy. That's the way it was, it all happened, all of it, and officers in white tunics, their gold shoulder straps ablaze, also walked along the Kobuleti beach, crunching the pebbles underfoot.

Now no one was left and nothing remained. Only the children of old friends, whom he had seen when they were babies. Givi had died years ago; for a long time afterward the writer couldn't forgive himself for not going to the funeral—he had been traveling abroad. And then he bought a house on a completely different shore, on the Baltic. He moved there with his wife, his grown daughter, and his grandchildren. His fame grew, and he ran away from it so he could work. But . . . in his old age he suddenly abandoned everything again, walked out—just like Pushkin's Aleko*—and, as if in punishment, he became paralyzed. Three months in the hospital and now—nothing: no home, no family, no archives, no books, no friends. Now—a wheelchair, illness, a scarf around his neck, his guardian angel at his side, and love, new love, which made him happy. Oh, it's no wonder people say that life is the best playwright and the most dangerous gambler, and you never know what card you'll be dealt, how the tables will turn. You look back: Lord, that was just a year ago? And now what—where am I, who am I, with whom?

And why—what was the point of such subtle discrimination? To deprive the musician of his hearing, the artist of his vision, the silver-tongued of his speech? Oh, he was a master teller of tales, like no one else, always able to find just the right word; he inspired himself when he spoke, like a nightingale. That's how all his works took shape—out loud: he would recite them and check them a dozen times, and then it was only a matter of sitting down and writing them out. But how much he had not written down, how much he had prattled away, prattled out, cast upon the wind, playfully—he could thank friends and students for putting on paper at least some of it.

Everyone remembers him on his feet, inspired, gesturing—a cigarette in one hand and a glass of dry white wine in the other, always tan by March, thin, with a suntanned bald spot and gray curls trailing artistically behind, with some ultrachic detail of clothing, perhaps a white jacket that no one else had yet, or a kerchief around his neck, a scarf or a blazer with gold buttons that even the captain of a Spanish clipper ship would envy. He never stayed in one place for more than a month; he loved planes and gliders, fast scooters, and those seconds in hockey when both five-man teams come together and tear toward the goal. He was perpetual motion, a rolling stone, a poet, and now, if you

*The hero of Pushkin's poem *The Gypsies*, who leaves civilization to join a band of nomads. —Trans.

will, he'd been shot down like a bird in flight. "For what?" he would ask himself, and then answer, "For everything."

Now he was ashamed of everything he had written; it seemed to him that his life consisted of mistakes and that at least four times he had taken completely different paths than he should have. He was good at and delighted in seducing and attracting—men fell in love with him, believed in him, and followed him, especially young writers, directors, and artists. Now he included this among his sins too: he hadn't taught them right, the right things. And as far as women were concerned— here it's better to say nothing at all. To say nothing and turn instead to that young creature, a student, a girl from a Moscow suburb who sent him her innocent poems for review a year ago—that's how they met. Whoever might have seen her the evening of their arrival, after a turbulent, emotional day, their meeting with Eteri, heavier now and old, in eternal mourning, with a black scarf around her gray head—how she wept as she embraced him!—the long dinner, sad toasts, the plush album of faded amateur photographs in which they all stood, arms around each other, all young, alive, in love with one another, the sun in their eyes, a palm tree shading their heads like a green fountain. The photographs remain, and the palm tree remains, but the people are gone; the people have died or grown old, and an unseen horror scratches at the heart: you're standing in that line too.

"No, my knight, you're the same, you're young!" Eteri said, brimming with tears. (There was a time when they called him "our knight in tiger's skin"* because he once cavorted on the beach in just that costume, although it was made out of sheepskin.)

But finally the two of them were alone, in "his" half of the house, on the open terrace entwined with grapes—dense, black clusters like small balloons, richly dark against the green—the terrace protected from the wind and sea by the house itself. She was with him constantly. They hadn't been apart for even a day the whole year. She alone understood his mumbling and the occasional word he struggled to form like an infant; she alone was able to take care of him without causing him the torture of shame, somehow learning how to feed him, dress him, comb his hair, and put up with everything. Thank God she had grown up in a poor, simple family with lots of children. Besides, she felt guilty. If only even one of the people who condemned her and whispered about her had been struck by the simple thought: who feeds

*The title of an epic poem by the Georgian writer Shota Rustaveli. —Trans.

him and how, who tends him, who dresses him in that fine shirt and ties his tie, who is responsible for his well-cared-for and even elegant appearance in that shining wheelchair, with a gray lap robe over his knees, a sweater or shawl thrown over his shoulders, in a white hat during the day and a dark cap in the evening? If people only thought about it a bit they would stop gossiping. But then again, do people ever stop? And how does she live with him, the poor thing—why?—what for? Why does she put up with it, why does she push the heavy wheelchair in front of her over the potholes in the pavement?

Meanwhile, the cripple, as often happens with cripples, was in the most powerful spiritual turmoil—unusually powerful even for him. It was reflected on his face, in his fervent and animated gaze. Everyone who met them on the promenade was struck by the gentleness of her face and the ardor of his gaze—penetrating, bright, alive, full of interest in everything, and reacting to everything. *Everything*: an infant in an old woman's arms; a late fluttering butterfly; elderly foreign tourists with identically dyed and curled gray hair; schoolchildren in blue uniforms and red ties wandering on the beach after classes; the girl from Moscow at the Intourist in a baseball cap who was too spontaneous to hide her pity as she looked at them—pity and delight at understanding their relationship. She was probably in love with someone too. He tried to smile in response and thought he was smiling and even winking, but that was the side of his face that remained lifeless.

It's not surprising that his gift of observation, his ability to analyze, synthesize, and create had not disappeared. And neither had his yearning to create. He had new ideas—what to create and how. Without an outlet, all this became even more acute. We'll presently describe where these tremendous powers were mainly channeled, but he had enough for petty matters and trifles as well. He paid no attention to his illness whatsoever. He accepted it like a bolt of lightning; he decided that there was nothing he himself could do about it and that he didn't have time for treatment, which was useless anyway. However odd it might seem, he hardly suffered at all. He had left all his suffering behind the walls of the clinic. Really, now—wait to get better, put all his energy into it? Ridiculous! Especially since he *felt* wonderful. Happiness had not abandoned him.

Was she gentleness incarnate? You could say so. From afar she certainly seemed like an angel. If his eyes burned with open yearning, then hers were downcast more often than not. The world didn't interest her. But neither could you say that she knelt before him, palms pressed together at her breast and wings unfurled behind her. Her entire figure was covertly active and tense. She constantly moved ahead, watching from above: How was he, did he need anything? She looked around him: Was there any danger to him? . . . When they stopped to rest she would unabashedly look only at him, unless he directed her attention to something with his eyes or his weak right hand. She looked at him with a covertly joyful and loving gaze—the kind people have in mind when they say "they can't take their eyes off each other." And it was true. Although you might wonder what there was to look at for this very young, good-looking, slender, and very well dressed girl (you just couldn't call her a woman: she was so young and everything about her appearance and demeanor so girlish). But she looked, and no one could question her sincerity. It was simply astonishing. If she had been less reserved, less modest, if she had at least gone to school in the capital and could have expressed her feelings more boldly, she would have looked at him with open adoration. And she was not interested in the Apollo-like youths, the swarthy Jasons, or the fair-haired Swedes who came from far away, or the proud local Kolkhida youths, each of whom had a small, but authentic, piece of the Golden Fleece. They straightened up like springs at the sight of her figure in the loose, billowing white clothes that were fashionable that summer, with a muslin scarf tied smoothly around her head, tipped to the side, and knotted at her temple—that was her evening wear—or in a sleeveless T-shirt, white shorts, and sandals during the day, her cap cocked at an angle, lifted like a bubble, with a red button at the top of the crown. The young men snorted and stomped in place like horses.

People whispered, then they got used to it—she was very convincing. Besides, rumors began to seep out of Eteri's house, where the sounds of young life had been extinguished long ago (Niko was a shy boy). Once again (people saw for themselves) taxis arrived from the bazaar laden with baskets, Eteri was in command of the summer kitchen, the postman delivered newspapers and telegrams, and the sound of the old piano and the laughter of a young woman, a normal laugh, could be heard. Judge for yourself, but you could feel it: the people who moved in weren't wretched or depressed, but happy. And fat Eteri, with her weak heart and ailing legs, breathing heavily, would nod her head in the early evening and confirm: Yes, it's true, but then he was always like this, our knight, I remember, of course; yes, they're happy people, see for yourself.

What else would you expect? That's the way it should be. He had wanted to come here, he had thought of it himself as he was going over in his mind the places where he had lived especially fully and happily. He remembered this shore where he had once played so hard and worked so easily and so much—doing a month's work in a day— where he had loved so much that happiness had taken his breath away, where he was only healthy and tireless, wild and high-spirited—oh, those were the days! He called that living the good life. If you get up, brush your teeth, take a shower, and get dressed, all the while singing or whistling without even noticing, and then you suddenly notice or your wife says, "Look at your father singing today!"—that's what living the good life means. It means that everything's going just fine, things are rolling along as they should, your conscience is clear, you're happy with people and they're happy with you. That's the way to live, by God: singing and whistling as you go. Some people have their burden to bear, some serve fools, some just aren't happy with themselves—that's their concern. But we forge the work we love and put all our strength into it. In the end people are grateful—why not sing? If you're bat- tered, beaten down, if your nerves are shattered, if you're twisted inside out, crushed—that's sad, but it's not the end. It's still not the end— weren't there plenty of times when you were at the helm and the end loomed and flashed right in front of you? But it's not the end: the soul is still alive, it's not the end yet, you're alive, man is tenacious and keeps on wriggling like a worm. The main thing is, as Pushkin said, "May God grant that I not go mad"—anything but that, I could take anything but that, that would be the last straw, the limit. Now I can still control what I do, but then—chaos. God forbid. The image of the insane Maupassant, crawling around the hospital ward on all fours, constantly came to mind.

No, no, we're alive, the mind burns still hotter and brighter than ever, and my angel is with me—what a gift of fate before the final cur- tain. And won't you read to us, my soul, from the Book of Job before bed? That's what his eyes said and his right hand trembled, the hand that was even learning, little by little, to hold a pencil, only, to be sure, if she steadied it from above with her own hand, as light and weightless on his as a hovering butterfly, and moved it over rough wallpaper, which was the only kind of paper strong enough to withstand the jerk- ing pencil. In this way he indicated the book, in this way he reached over to her knee, and she understood. Yes, read the book of the Bible that has become so popular in the last half of the twentieth century, the book about the unfortunate but steadfast Job, to whom God gave everything and from whom He took everything away to test him: well, man, how much can you bear? . . .

She read, faltering, virtually illiterate and understanding very little— she had never held a Bible in her life. But he would indicate to her that she wasn't reading it right, that she had to reread it and understand, that there wasn't anything difficult about it. She caught on and gradually became inspired. Her modest poetic gift at least gave her a sense of word and rhythm; and besides, she wanted so badly not to seem foolish before him. And so she struggled and grasped the beauty and meaning of the ancient verses. . . . They loved each other and tried for each other—it was as simple as that.

He didn't come here only for himself: he brought her with him as well. So that she would see, see through his eyes, the splendid shore celebrated by poets, Mother Kolkhida, the mountains: snow-covered mountains that gleamed white in the distance like clouds, and dark ones that were lower and closer, a secretive blue, and closest of all, green foothills as round as sheep, covered with tea bushes. There the mountains and the sky, here the sky and the sea. The sea sparkling in the sun, like a tub with a splashing child, or gloomily crashing against the shore in a storm like a heavy green bottle. Coastal pines affecting whimsical, decadent poses. The moon's round, questioning face when it's full and no one can sleep. It has a rapturous light: it's full, it has passed through phases of loss and want. Poor Eteri moans in her sleep— please take a good look at her doughy face, leave me for a second, it's the face of kindness itself, eternal feminine kindness, the greatest virtue. You must see everything and understand everything as best you can, like me, so that you can take it with you forever, take it away, as my last, perhaps, gift. I could give you nothing better.

He can't work, he can't write, but he can't help creating. Such is the nature of his God-given gift—the rules have been laid down: be generous, sensitive, talented; show good taste and a sense of proportion; be an artist; be able to comprehend another better than oneself. He creates, transforming his gift into the pure gift of love. He creates it every day, tirelessly, wholeheartedly, in rough drafts and in clean copies, in fragments, in torrents—better in clean copies right away because there is no time, but then all the more strongly, certainly. No false or badly crafted lines. No repetition, no mistakes; it's a new game, and you have to move like brilliant chess players—making the best of all possible moves. All of his experience, his powers, his strength, his consummate professionalism, his illness itself, and the sorrow of parting—everything goes into the work. A whirling waterspout twists, a storm cloud is filled with a gigantic electrical charge, the entire surface of the water is warmed by the sun—what for? To put one poor girl with her inexperience, her trust, her pure heart at the very center? "Let in the maid, that out a maid/ Never departed more," as Ophelia sang. Stop—she has enough for a long while. But he keeps going further and further, and so far he has enough strength to conquer his own self.

He wants to enrich and develop her mind. He tries, but he still doesn't know it's impossible in so short a time, and unnecessary besides. It's just his own icing, that's all it is—icing, not the essence. A woman always knows the essence. He revels, he is involved in the wonderful process of creation. She understands only one thing: he is involved and it's with her, for her. And you can't say that his labor was in vain, even though it might seem as if there is nothing to show for it, no visible result. But that's like telling a mother cooing to her infant that it's pointless talking to him, singing to him, smiling at him, or even entrusting her tears to him—he doesn't understand a thing anyway. No, it's not in vain! The secret of their closeness deepens every day: his every word and every glance, his every touch is an expression of the titanic labor of love that flows from his half-mad, intelligent eyes, drenching her in gentleness—no, she wouldn't trade that for anything! His love flows and flows, it's a sea of love; and her love is perhaps only a river, but they flow together and she floats in this sea more easily than in the real one—it's warm and transparent, and she's no longer afraid. She throws open her arms and floats on her back; she dives and splashes, her body slender and buoyant and weightless, like the body of a fish in water. One slap of the tail and she's on the surface, another and she's underwater. She's completely free and open, the water penetrates her, its salt sticking to her lips. Later she falls asleep in an instant, without knowing how, in weightlessness, in suspension, in a slow drift to the bottom—sinking like a sleeping fish.

She's an excellent student, a devoted listener, an ingenuous spectator who believes and feels that everything is true, that no one would lie to her. That's why she's so trusting, so at peace now and free, so responsive to his affection. That's how it was at first, she came to realize. Now it's more and more often the case that she, too, is talented and versatile and frequently amazes him with some gesture of response or appeal that he hasn't seen before. Musician and instrument, composer and performer, sculptor and sculpture—they attain harmony and loftiness, purity of composition. And not only in the sexual side of their relationship, but in the unity of spirit they have forged, in their flawless understanding of each other, in their fusion into one. What happiness this is: to give everything and to receive everything.

Now it's evening. A long and full day is behind them and an equally full evening with much to do lies ahead. She wheels the now-heavy chair in front of her along the uneven asphalt and stone slabs of the promenade. He moves his eyes as energetically as before, but she knows that he is already tired, although he would never admit it; his head and his whole figure have listed to the side. And she is tired too. Darkness has fallen quickly, and cool air has descended like dew. Yes, there is much to do ahead: the return home, where Niko will greet them; the new excitement of supper; the assimilation of the day's impressions; then television, another bath, changing his clothes, giving him his medicine, sleep and insomnia, when he will call to her and she will curl up next to him, because everything that has built up between them all day and evening must come together and be unleashed in private. Afterward he still won't fall asleep, disturbed by the moonlight, and through her youthful sleep she will feel it and wake up often, ask after him. He will give her a sign—go back to sleep, sleep—but tears glisten in his eyes like moonlight.

All her strength goes to him—such was his ability to capture and conquer her—but all of her strength is sometimes not enough. Today something is bothering her. She quickens her pace a bit, senses that something's troubling him, too, and suddenly feels tired herself. Eteri said that the weather was changing, and perhaps that's it, but there is still something else worrying her. What is it? . . . She doesn't like these moments, because at one time she was viciously warned about everything in anonymous letters and phone calls. Her fear for him was stored away in her subconscious, and he taught her not to fear and always to be ready for anything. But the fear still exists, apart from her will and consciousness, and in such moments of fatigue her heart grows cold and skips a beat. And she suddenly thinks realistically about how hard it is to make a simple phone call from Kobuleti.

No, she knows that he's healthy, healthy, however strange it may seem; the illness deprived him of movement, but it left his heart and mind even stronger, just as an amputee becomes inordinately strong. Like him, she is more afraid for his mind, which is so active, afraid of an inevitable new stroke, with its unpredictable consequences. She had already heard her fill of stories about people destroyed by strokes who lie unconscious and motionless for years. He laughs—he's a fatalist and a gambler. Sometimes they play cards or she lays out a hand of patience* for him, and he is always thrilled by the unexpected way the cards fall. He tells her with a gaze, laughing, one of his favorite phrases: "That's the hand I was dealt." He always accepted both wins and losses with equal dignity.

But he's a greedy thing, always getting carried away, always ready to recoup his losses. Nothing is enough for him. Like now: they are already on their way home, it's time, it's grown damp and they're tired, but she hears a mumbling demand and, following his gaze, she sees that he's indicating the direction of the park. What for? What do you want? . . . He's become animated, he's smiling, asking: Take me there. She turns the wheelchair.

We forgot to tell you: Kobuleti has yet another tourist attraction, the Park of Culture and Recreation, pride of the local authorities. True, the entire shore is one big park, but it's for recreation; what about for culture? And the residents of Kobuleti did their best to rival Tbilisi and Moscow. Is there a carousel? There is. Swings? There are. Bumper cars? There are bumper cars too. Let our children have fun! And there is even a "devil's wheel," excuse me, a Ferris wheel. You can see everything from the top. Of course it isn't higher than the Intourist, where the upper decks open onto a great expanse, as from a helicopter. But if you're looking at the Intourist, all you want to do is climb to the stars, while on the "wheel" you actually can. . . . The season isn't over yet in the park and the rides are still running, although there's hardly anyone left by about nine o'clock. It's empty; only one couple is riding the chain carousel, colliding in the air and laughing, and two or three others have gotten on the wheel. For them alone it squeaks and turns, completing the circles in the dark—all its garlands of lights have been turned off and only three ordinary naked light bulbs burn, wresting segments of metal construction from the darkness and indicating the movement of the wheel in their revolution through space. But thanks to the darkness, when you're sitting at the top in a swaying car, you can see the bright stars, the moon that seems to have come closer with a plumage of little clouds flying around it, and as you press together tightly in light and giddy fear, you can melt into a kiss.

---

*A card game similar to solitaire. —Trans.

In the absence of visitors, all the rides were operated by a young, sarcastic, lazy demon disguised under the Georgian name of Shotik and a Kobuleti residence permit. He wore a T-shirt with faded letters in English announcing I LOVE—although whom exactly I LOVE was completely faded and washed out—and a jacket with sleeves rolled up to show the lining. With a gangster's swagger, he went back and forth, tearing off tickets that looked like tram fares. The pocket of his jacket hung to the side with the change he had collected. Smirking, he looked up to where the swings were colliding and flying apart with the sound of laughter, like metal milk cases being tossed in a van by the deliveryman, and where an invisible girl aerialist was yelping in the dark. A cigarette dangled from his lips at the corner of his mouth like Azazello's fang.*

He began to ask, demand, mumble to this fellow: I want to go there, up there! She objected, she didn't want to—how could they? She was terrified of heights, never would have dared to ride on such a thing—her middle ear could barely endure riding up and down on elevators—what was the point? What for . . . But no, he was insistent: he wanted to, and that was that. And this demon, this Shota, snickered and said, "Listen, what's the matter with you? If Grandpa wants to go for a ride, let him, I'll take him myself!" How it all happened, in two minutes, was really strange: Shota stopped the wheel, lifted him with ease, and carried him into the car. She even helped. His fervent and happy gaze told her not to be afraid for him, that he really wanted to—one or two turns and that would be it. And she translated to the demon: "One or two turns and no more, please, I'm so nervous."

"What are you nervous about?" the demon muttered. "How can it hurt him? It can't get any worse for him."

He whistled, and another little devil, his younger brother, came running out of the darkness. He stood near the switch handle that stuck out of a rusty box, his white teeth gleaming, and then, in an instant, the whole hulking wheel, which seemed hellishly gigantic to her in the dark, began to squeak, shuddering metal began to grind, the unpainted, numbered cars began to swing and squeal on their hinges, and it took off and floated away. The demon bent over him and held him, and he sent her a cheerful greeting with his eyes. His hand moved

---

*Azazello is one of the demons in the novel *The Master and Margarita*, by Mikhail Bulgakov. —Trans.

as if to wave, so in reply she also began to wave farewell and made herself smile. But under her white scarf her eyes showed dread and alarm: something had happened, she didn't know what, she couldn't make sense of it, she wasn't prepared; where was he going, what for, how did this happen?

The demon stank of tobacco and sweat. He twisted his mouth into a smile, and as the car rose higher he kept speaking, breathed right into the old man's ear as he bent over him. "Isn't it beautiful? . . . The moon? . . . The sea? . . ." They slowly floated up above the pines, above the roofs, above the road, with its streetlamps and headlights, above the park, where an illuminated pool with a mosaic of colored fish and an octopus suddenly came into view and glowed. The sky opened up, blue-gray in the moon's brightness, and there was the moon itself, the stars, and the light-hued clouds. He could see the leaden sea and ash-gray mountains, human dwellings glowing white.

"Look, look!" the demon whispered to him. "Remember!" The car suddenly shook and stopped at the very top. It began to sway and squeak, as did the other cars hanging below it. The boy on the ground had turned off the switch on purpose so that they could sit and look around awhile. This trick was reserved for the most honored guests— so the demon had ordered it. Now he whispered, "Look. Remember."

And he saw: ocean waves rolling, a hurricane whistling; trimmed palm trees sticking up like matchsticks; a camel floating on red dunes, his bells jangling; a white helicopter flying around the white Taj Mahal; his daughter Nastya standing next to the ice-covered frame of a well in Egorievo; nailheads shining on the old stage of the Moscow Art Theater; low clouds and snow over Chicago; the old bookshop on Lubyanka; First Lieutenant Misha Kuznets, hit by heavy shrapnel; the errata of his four-volume set; Milka in a short mink coat with her hair nearly clipped off; the Swedish king at the premier of his *Metamorphoses*; the view from the window in Maiori; the little window of the bindery where he had apprenticed; the border patrol boat on the Amur; the great neurosurgeon Roger Cartier, entering the operating room, white hands raised as if in surrender; Galina Ulanova, curtseying deeply, handing him a bouquet of roses in full bloom. . . .

And the entire night, the entire world, his entire life screamed at him: "Here! Take it! What is power over one poor girl and the warmth of one small hand to you? Where are you? You've already conquered her, what next? The whole world is waiting for you to conquer it, don't stop. . . . For once in your life be charitable and let her go! What will she do without you later—she is already poisoned by your love, let her go! Once again you're thinking only of yourself and not of others. . . . What do you want, tell me? Anything is possible as long as you're alive, and you don't believe in an afterlife. Save yourself in this life and take it all. Look, look, here they are, still rushing by: the stone cell in Garni, where a man sat and wrote for thirty years;* the great books; Chopin's piano; Eugene O'Neill's house in Connecticut; *City Lights* on cassette; a clean ream of paper; and—do you want it?—a new word processor, we'll redo it with Russian letters, you barely touch the keys and it writes all by itself, you see it on the screen, you can make corrections instantly and a printed page immediately drops out. . . ."

"No! I don't need anything! I don't need anything else, my world is her. Nothing on earth could replace our spiritual bond for me. She doesn't know, she might not know, what and who she is to me—but I know. Maybe it's not her, maybe there could have been someone else to put my heart to the test: Is it alive or not? Can it feel or not? But it's her, her hand, her eyes, the bloom on her cheeks . . . to love and devote—"

"You're lying, lying! You have wants, you want everything—to love and take—but you simply can't anymore, so you thought up your own little Everest, and you're climbing it three steps a day—well! well! well!—and you seem to be alive, and seem to be involved in conquering the summit. But look—Master Bocharov is flying off Everest in a hang glider: he climbed up on his own two legs, now he's flying with his own two arms! . . . Well? . . ."

"Get away from me! Let me go!"

"You're lying! You want it!"

"Go away!"

"Then we'll take her. . . ."

"Take her?"

He nearly threw himself over headfirst. He didn't see anything right away except the moonlit crowns of the pine trees. And then he looked around: on the weakly lit, well-trodden square stood only his empty wheelchair, forlorn and gleaming.

---

*Garni, located outside Erevan in Armenia, is the site of a Greek temple dating to the third century B.C. This seems to be a reference to Narekatsy, a ninth-century Armenian mystic. —Trans.

His heart stopped beating in horror. How could he have left her there, forgotten her, for the sake of the devil's wheel? His heart contracted and blood didn't reach his brain—how could he have? . . .

"Come now, one more loss, there have been plenty of losses in your life," the demon said, smirking. "You'll survive this one too."

"No!"

The blood didn't reach his brain, and horror shot through the lucky man like an electric shock.

. . . But she was in her place. She, too, had taken a step to the side, but only in her imagination; she imagined it and was hurt, how could it be? Just like that he had traded her for the devil's wheel, floated away in a stranger's arms, in a ridiculous child's toy, sick, helpless, but happy, thrilled by the new experience that excluded her momentarily. Where had he gone? Why? And she had been left behind in confusion, alone, in the emptiness that had instantly formed around her without him. How could it be? That's how it will happen in an instant: he flies away, and she's left on earth, alone. No, that's not it, and she knows it, but then how could he cut himself loose and fly away, without her? He'd abandoned her, he was consumed by another idea, one unknown to her. What idea? About what? What attracted him so? How could he have so quickly entrusted himself to another, left her, almost run away, casually said good-bye? Is that how it will happen one day: When he's healthy again, a complete stranger to her, happy, with the lights of the Ferris wheel in his impenetrable eyes, will he go off without a backward glance? And she'll remain, bewildered and hurt, and the little devil will be off to the side but with her still. . . . She came to her senses, looked around, and saw herself: in some idiotic park, in a strange town, on the very edge of the country—why? What for? . . . There's the road, "the longest street in Europe," the cars with their clean headlights shining—I've got to run away, hail a cab, get in, and—to the station, to the airport, away, wherever.

Only in her imagination did she take this step, but he couldn't see her from above. Only in his imagination did the possibility (or impossibility) of losing her occur to him, but his mind couldn't bear it.

"Le-e-et m-m-m-"

It creaked, it started downward, into the blackness—where are you?—and everything disappeared.

"What's he saying, what's he saying? I don't understand," his wife cried, wiping her face, red and swollen from tears, with a towel the same shade of raspberry. "What do you want, what?" she seemed to ask him, but she turned away, trying not to look, fearing the end. This had been going on for nearly a year, and every day could be the last.

"De-de-de . . . Kob . . . be . . ." Something incomprehensible gurgled in his contorted throat, but his eyes asked for understanding.

His two doctors, already aloof, conferred together briefly. His friends stood frozen in the corners. Only the young nurse moved about—very pretty, her lab coat gathered tightly at the waist, a stiffly starched white cap coquettishly clipped to her hair. She leaned over him on the side opposite the raspberry lump of his wife, gave him an injection, tenderly asking him to bear it. The arm was yellow and already covered with needle marks, but the girl's clean, slender, unmanicured fingers were lively on the almost lifeless arm. They had just found the girl the day before and persuaded her to come for 150 rubles. She had come that morning. When he caught sight of her a certain animation, a spark flickered in the eyes of the dying man, and he shouted to himself happily, "Kobuleti! The devil's wheel!" and laughed.

No one understood.

1987

Translated from the Russian by Michele A. Berdy.

STEPANIDA IVANOVNA'S FUNERAL

Vladimir Soloukhin

Do any of us know where we will die? What with the new fashion to die in hospitals and not under your own roof. True, one's own roof is a rarity these days, at least in big cities, but there are those places we call home, even if they are state-owned. Places with close friends, family around. For what transgressions should anyone be left to spend that last hour alone among the bare, gray, suffering-disease-and-death-ridden walls of a faceless and terrifying hospital ward?

Over the last few years Stepanida Ivanovna's life had fallen into the following routine. For the summer we would drive her out to Olepino. Although the house had been so altered through renovation that it might almost have been someone else's, the windows and, better yet, the window bench and the porch (when we would half-carry her outside) looked out onto familiar Olepino: lindens, white willows, water wells, and even a church. The fence had been dismantled to make a cow shed, and inside the basilica was the abomination of desolation, hog fodder, and dank sheepskins, but Stepanida Ivanovna would never see any of that thanks to her limited mobility (one leg had given out entirely), while the exterior was still soothing to the soul, even if in one corner the torn metal roofing flapped shamefully in the wind. The main thing was that the cross was where it should be, you could breathe a sigh of relief, you could cross yourself.

She would sit it out in Olepino as long as possible, until the Feast of the Protection, when, like it or not, it was time to trundle back to winter quarters. Slowly, laboriously, we would slide her onto the front seat of the Volga. The main difficulty lay in getting her stiff, diseased leg inside the car. Although Stepanida Ivanovna was quite shriveled and almost weightless, someone still had to grasp her under the arms and lift her up high inside the car so that the bad leg would fit, then find a comfortable place and position for the leg, and then lower the passenger down onto the seat. After that, no moving until Moscow. No getting out, no stretching, no changing positions, nothing but wriggling back and forth on the seat to try to relieve the numb spots. Stepanida Ivanovna had a peasant's patience. If she'd endured the preceding fourscore and three years, she'd endure the four hours to Moscow.

The agreement was that while in Moscow she lived at my place. And essentially she did. But her three daughters in Moscow and a fourth (the eldest) in Minsk would sense her restlessness, and there were frequent trips from place to place. A few weeks at Katyusha's, then a few weeks at Klavdiya's . . . The road from Moscow to Minsk was not onerous—only one night's sleep on the train in more comfortable conditions, for that matter, than on the front seat of the Volga from Olepino to Moscow.

It's not acceptable to talk about such things—not among yourselves, not even to yourself—but we all understood that the time was approaching, and, most likely, each of us secretly tried to guess where exactly—in Olepino or in Moscow—it would happen. It would have been best in Olepino, for even if Stepanida Ivanovna had died on the moon, we'd still have buried her in the family's village cemetery. Right next to Alexei Alexeyevich, close to Alexei Dmitrievich, Granny Vasilisa, Dmitry Ivanovich, Alyona, and Marfa, and all our other various, now nameless, ancestors. And what better place than in Olepino, in the family home: no need to hire a bus, no unnecessary carrying and jarring (from the sixth floor down a narrow staircase), everything simple and natural.

Stepanida Ivanovna died in Minsk.

I set off that same evening. In the coming day I would have to solve some complex problems: buying a coffin, having it zinc-coated (but first I'd have to get the zinc), loading the coffin into an airplane, and having it flown to Moscow. There my brother, Nikolai, would meet the plane with a bus, aboard which Stepanida Ivanovna would continue her final journey from Moscow to Olepino.

Death had not changed her in the least. She lay clean, white, at peace, like all old women who have lived out their time and expired quietly, as if they'd simply fallen asleep. Death had yet to smooth out her facial features, to efface her look of preoccupation, expectation, questioning, in short, the stamp of her earthly existence. Strange as it might seem, it was only now that I noticed the little gold wedding band on her motionless, dead hand; only now did I see how all the washing, mowing, potato digging, and various other chores that had spanned her long life had worn the ring down to almost paper thinness and in places to wirelike narrowness.

Immediately, as is usually the case, while still at the door, I was told the details of her last hour by Klavdiya, the very details that fill our days to overflowing, but to which no one pays any attention as long as the days pass uneventfully, but which, when something does happen, instantly assume the proportions of omens, freeze in place, and remain that way forever, just as a film frame freezes on the screen when the projector ceases its whir.

"'Mama,' I say, 'would you like some tea or milk?' And she says, 'A little condensed milk would be nice. . . .' You know yourself you can't get condensed milk anywhere. So I made her tea with milk. She had her breakfast, wanted to take a nap, I fluffed her pillow. . . ."

I reserved a seat on the airplane and made arrangements for the freight. I had feared red tape, but in the end this turned out to be the simplest of all my tasks, not because it was easy to get a ticket for the evening of the same day, especially with that kind of baggage, but because all the other tasks would exceed even my most pessimistic expectations. It's possible that the ensuing pages may ring with inappropriate (given the situation) satirical intonations, but what is to be done if at times reality actually does imitate an endless, more-bitter-than-humorous satire? In any case, I have not added or removed a thing, but set it down here exactly as it was. You should also keep in mind that time has passed, some of the details have faded, and the rage I felt during those days, which would have sufficed to overthrow half the government, has now dissipated.

Never in my life had it been my lot to visit a funeral service office. At the very sight of a store bearing the sign FUNERAL SUPPLIES, I cross to the other side of the street. But it is fair to assume that if anywhere in the human community particular tact ought to be exercised, additional vexing headaches minimalized, and automatic attention to detail accorded, it should be here, first of all, in this most sorrowful, but (alas!) most essential sector of the service industry.

Back in the village the procedures were well known. Ivan Vasilievich, the best of Olepino's carpenters, would arrive on the spot to take measurements, and within about two hours a freshly planed, strong pine box would be delivered to the hut. Actually, Ivan Vasilievich himself went to his grave a long time ago, and I don't know who performs this doleful obligation for him now.

I don't know, either, how similar procedures are handled in other large cities, say, in Paris, Copenhagen, Vienna, or in some tiny Saulgau near Munich. But I assume that the relatives and friends of the deceased simply dial the phone number of the appropriate agency, list everything that's needed for the funeral, and that by the desired time at the designated place all this will be done for them with the utmost meticulousness.

The occasion brings to mind that relatively recent rivalry between two provincial Russian companies described in Il'f and Petrov's scathing, but—there's no denying it—witty novel: "And their materials ain't no good, durn it, and the finish is worse. What's more, the tassels ain't thick enough, durn it!"*

"Who cares about the tassels and the finish, it's going to be zinc-coated anyway," I thought on my way to buy a coffin for Stepanida Ivanovna. Klavdiya had explained how to get to the Minsk funeral supplies store, and I set off early on the morning of the eleventh of May 1967, that is, exactly one half century since the Great October Revolution.†

At first sight I was unpleasantly shocked by the crowd outside, and by the emptiness inside. Experience immediately suggested what was the matter. Pushing my way through the crowd, I noticed a woman writing something with a black grease pencil on the palm of another woman. Squinting, I managed to discern the number: 78. Still not accepting the possibility of catastrophe, I entered the store and found absolutely nothing: no people and no supplies. But still stubbornly refus-

---

*Ilya Il'f and Evgeny Petrov, *The Twelve Chairs*, trans. John H. C. Richardson (New York: Vintage, 1961), p. 10. —Trans.

†Not long ago I saw—and in retrospect quote here—an ad for a Russian funeral service in Paris. I think it offers a pretty good idea of how these things are done in other places: "Our funeral service scrupulously fulfills all orders exactly, according to former practice in Russia. Our service stocks clothing for the deceased. Russian-style coffins. Nuns available to read the Psalter. Refrigeration and transport and shipping provided. We carry wooden Orthodox crosses for the grave. We will ship and receive the deceased to and from all corners of the earth. Orders may be placed in person, by phone, by telegraph, and by messenger service within the territorial boundaries of France. Orders for memorial monuments also accepted. Special prices for fellow countrymen. Night guard."

ing to accept monstrous reality, I thought to myself that there was no reason coffins had to be kept on display, that they were probably stored someplace out back, and that here all you did was pay and get a receipt.

Timidly I asked a person who appeared to be an employee of the store, "Excuse me. My mother has died. We need a coffin, but—"

"No coffins."

"What do you mean, no coffins? Excuse me, but how can we bury—"

"The coffins should be here around one o'clock. First come, first served."

I dashed out into the street toward the woman who was writing numbers in grease pencil, numbers that were astronomical, you might say, given the situation. And yet even the most bitter and dismal circumstances can hold a ray of light. To my joy, to my exultation, there turned out to be two lines in front of the store: the first, which was very long (and to which the number 78 I had seen earlier applied) was for memorial wreaths, while the second, which was considerably shorter than the first, was for coffins. I, for example, was number eighteen in the second line. There was reason to rejoice. I had managed to overhear that usually no more than fifteen to twenty coffins came in with each shipment. That meant that if I in fact had been number seventy-nine, I would have had to stand in line for four days. But now there was hope that I'd get a coffin today. Let them stand in line for wreaths for four days. I can do without wreaths. What will they want next, wreaths! No, all I need is the most basic, the most ordinary . . . all I need is a pine coffin. And there's hope that I'll be able to buy it today. Wouldn't that be a coup! My mother just died? Sorrow and mourning? A bitter lump in my throat since the day before? A quiet, genteel conversation appropriate to the circumstances? Oh no, no! On the contrary, rejoice, rejoice and exult, damn it, because you'll have your coffin by one o'clock this afternoon! It could have been a lot worse; you could have been delayed, arrived half an hour later, like that guy over there in the sports cap, the one with the broad face and submissive blue eyes who's thirty-fourth in line.

To be perfectly frank, the delay suited me just fine. Because if I had gotten the coffin right away, that very moment, where would I have taken it? After all, it was still a mystery to me where in a city like Minsk you could have a coffin zinc-coated, where you could get the zinc, or how you went about it. The next hour brought me a whole slew (seven or eight, to be exact) of bitter disappointments. I stopped at several workshops and spoke with roofers and metalworkers, called factories and warehouses, and tried to hunt down a tinsmith. . . . All this only to be convinced that in Minsk, the capital of Byelorussia, it is essentially impossible to have a coffin zinc-coated. In no way do I intend this as an insult to the residents of Minsk, it's not their fault; in other cities—even in the capitals, including Moscow—the order probably would have been no easier to fill.

Giving up was out of the question, there could be no retreat, so I braced myself for one last-ditch effort. I turned what you might call legalistic, and in retaliation for the whole devastating series of rebuffs, I initiated an equally energetic series of phone calls. Petrus Brovka, Pyotr Glebka, Maksim Tank, and Yanka Bryl—laureates, deputies, academicians, the most influential people in all of Byelorussia—joined forces in "Operation Coffin" to help their Moscow colleague. An hour later I found out that my case had been taken up by a minister—of what ministry I no longer recall—and half an hour after that I was instructed to proceed to the marketplace, where, in a distant, isolated corner, I found the shop of a certain self-employed craftsman who—at the personal request of the minister!—had agreed to do everything I needed to get done.

One o'clock was approaching, and I had to rush back to the store to get the coffin. Confident that I would be able to buy a coffin (that confidence having been reinforced by a high-placed phone call to the director of Funeral Supplies), I hailed an empty truck on the street, bargained with the driver, and drove off with him to the store.

There were still no coffins. The driver of the truck was nervous and wanted to leave, but I had paid him well and had given him the money in advance. At least that sector of the front had been stabilized.

In an effort to alleviate the tedium, I perused a large gray display, or, rather, bulletin board—a plywood board covered with fabric, like those used to exhibit photographs of front-rank workers. It read, "Samples of Custom-Made Memorial Monuments." What amazed me was that the spacious board (it could have accommodated about fifty samples) was totally blank except for one lone, faded photograph in the lower right-hand corner illustrating a depressing gray, squat, poorly made, and formless concrete grave marker. Lord, do what you must so that no such monument ever stands on my grave! And why bother displaying a sample if it's the only one and there's no choice anyway?

I'd long ago come to realize that for several decades now the entire country has been operating on a variation of the ration system, extending, without exception, to all facets of life. Walking into a store, a person buys not what he or she would like to buy but what's in stock. The selection, as a rule, is very limited, if there is one at all. Little wonder that in our society the word *handout* has replaced the word *sell*.

The word *handout* conceals profound meaning. Everyone understands that handouts are not simply handed out but handed out for money. But they're still handouts—as they can only be in a system of strict daily limitations, a ration system—the absolute minimum.

Say you'd like to buy something of your own choosing for dinner: fresh beef tenderloin, liver, tongue, tripe, pigs' feet, chicken giblets, pork, mutton brains, veal, sweetbread, oxtail, steak, filet, suckling pig, goose, turkey, quail, grouse, cow's udder, rabbit. . . . You try twenty stores in a row and in each and every one you find exactly the same thing, if you find anything at all: either second-rate beef labeled choice, or mutton, or, more likely, beef or pork kidneys. That's all you have to choose from. And that's in Moscow, the capital. In outlying cities, not to mention provincial towns, you won't find even that.

Say you wanted to buy some mushrooms (in our densely wooded country mushrooms are no rarity), and you ask yourself what kind of mushrooms you'd like most: milk agarics, coral milky caps, black-spotted milky caps, mock oysters, Russula, golden chanterelles, Steinpilz, brown mushrooms, or meadow mushrooms? Or, perhaps, truffles? Or, perhaps, marinated Caesar's mushrooms? You make the rounds of the entire city, and either you don't find any mushrooms at all or everywhere you go you find only one variety, the variety that was shipped in today, the one that's being "handed out." More often than not it will be marinated mock oysters.

Sure, from time to time first one, then another variety of mushroom may appear briefly on the counters. Sometimes there's even beef liver, turkey, or goose, but never are you offered a choice. At times you may be able to obtain, say, tripe or even marinated saffron milkcaps (though both the former and the latter at once is unlikely), but you will never be able to buy what you really crave, what you crave that very minute. Nor are you in a position to plan your purchases, because you are forced to make do with "handouts."

But food is matter of a lower order. Let's take something a bit more refined—let's go to the flower stores. . . . Today they have only chrysanthemums for sale. No matter how much you might want to buy orchids, or roses, or primroses, or hyacinths, or carnations, or irises, or tulips, you can't, you're rationed here as well.

Do we really need to stop and consider everything that lies on the spectrum between beef tongue and orchids? Every one of you—if you would only stop running for a moment, give your head a good shake, and take a sober look around—will agree with me that the ration system has permeated our entire life—from metal sheet roofing to women's winter coats, from shoes to sweaters, from books, records, films, and news information to cars, razor blades, furniture, housing, colors of fabric, and varieties of tea.

And so I'd known for a while that we've all been on a kind of diet, but it had never occurred to me that the "ration principle" extended to such things as memorial wreaths, coffins, and grave monuments. I also had no idea that the next day I would run up against an even more monstrous limitation, a limitation I am unable to accept to this day. . . .

At long last the coffins were delivered. My turn came. What I saw before me was a loose construction of damp, poorly planed boards of incredible weight and length.

"Excuse me . . . ah, you know . . . my mother was a tiny old woman, not very tall, and light as a bird. This thing here's for a weight lifter. . . ."

"One-meter-ninety. Citizens, all coffins come in standard sizes. Today we have only one-meter-nineties."

"But I don't need a meter-ninety coffin!"

"You don't? . . . Then step aside and get out of the others' way."

"No, no, don't misunderstand me, I'll take it! I just wanted to say—"

"You can talk about it at home. With your dead mama, hee-hee. If you're taking it, hand over your money."*

I'm not going to regale you with what it took to get this incredible coffin zinc-coated or what it weighed afterward, and I'll also spare you the details of where and how I managed to find someone who could solder it shut—it turned out at the last minute that Stepanida Ivanovna could not be placed on the airplane until the coffin was soldered shut. . . .

At eleven that evening, totally exhausted, I finally arrived in Moscow. My sisters and my brother, Nikolai, were already waiting for me with the bus. Straight from the airport, in the middle of the night, they set off for Olepino (in that kind of bus, a five- to six-hour drive), while I

---

*Just a reminder that the events described here took place in 1967. Nowadays, at least in large cities, there supposedly are funeral service agencies.

begged off to go sleep at home, proposing to drive out in my own car the next morning and be there by noon.

I could have shown up even later, since, basically, the time of the funeral depended on me. But I still faced a trip to another village, where a functioning church had miraculously survived, to fetch Father Sergius, a wizened old man with a very oily, grayish-yellow, skinny braid. . . .

All times and all peoples have shared a respect for the last request of the dying. True, in times of occupation, invasion, barbarism, terrorism, and plunder, one could hardly, of course, place any stake in having one's last request fulfilled. But all civilized peoples throughout history have held the last request of the dying sacred.

And even if Stepanida Ivanovna hadn't expressed her last earthly wish, we, her children, would have known that she was to lie only in Olepino and that she—a deeply religious, passionately devout Orthodox Christian—was to be buried according to church ritual, that is, from her point of view, as befits a human being.

Different people have different ideas about what kind of burial befits a human being. The ancient Slavs would place the deceased in a wide-bottom boat and burn the corpse along with the boat. Ancient Egyptians would mummify the body. Hindus (certain sects, at least) preferred to leave the body to be pecked apart by birds. Tell any of them that they're going to be interred and they'd die prematurely from grief. If someone considers birds preferable to worms, then to deprive them of the burial they want would be callously cruel, tantamount to telling you or me that after our deaths we will be thrown on the trash dump where crows and stray cats scavenge.

In the Moscow writers' organization we have our own ritual. When a writer dies the tables in the restaurant in the Oak Hall—where only the night before we had put down no small quantity of tea and other, stronger libations—are quickly cleared, a few tables are pushed together, and the coffin is placed on top of them. Indeed, as it is written: "Where stood a table of bounty now stands a coffin cold. . . ."* Following the speeches—on behalf of the secretariat (if the deceased was prominent), on behalf of the Party committee, or just on behalf of friends—the coffin is carried out, the floor is swept, the tables are returned to their places, and before long someone fresh off the street

---

*From Gavriil Derzhavin's (1743–1816) poem, "On the Death of Prince Meshchersky." —Trans.

comes into the restaurant and orders up two hundred grams of vodka, never even suspecting that only an hour ago it had been the scene of a solemn farewell ritual. The waitresses hustle, glasses clink, and a disconnected murmuring fills the air.

If the deceased was very prominent, the corpse is displayed on the stage in the Great Hall, which only the day before had witnessed an Arkady Raikin* performance and tomorrow would boast a Brigitte Bardot film. The speakers in this case are a rank higher, perhaps even Fedin† himself. When he dies Fedin will probably be laid out downtown in the Hall of Columns (as was Fadeev,‡ for example), where again, just the day before, the Piatnitsky Folk Ensemble might have performed. And the speakers will be even more eminent—from the Central Committee, from the government, from the Moscow Party Committee.

And there you have it, a ritual. Tell any of the currently hale and hearty members of the Soviet Writers Union: When you die we're going to give you a church service, and they'd be outraged, they'd protest. And rightly so. As far as they're concerned, that would be the height of cruelty.

Throughout all of Russia tens of thousands of churches have been closed, but millions of elderly people who would like to be buried in— as they see it—a manner befitting human beings, remain, awaiting the final call. The fact is that millions of perfectly innocent people have been denied the fundamental prerogative of funeral rites. Just one more howling cruelty, just one more "ration" in an innumerable depressing series.

But I have a car and I am determined to honor my mother's last wish. And I will go to the village of Snegirevo and fetch Father Sergius so that he can perform Orthodox Christian burial rites over my mother's remains. . . .

---

*Arkady Raikin (1911–88), the most celebrated of Soviet satirical comics. —Trans.
†Konstantin Fedin (1892–1977) established his literary reputation with the novel *Cities and Years* in 1924. After a brief association with the experimentalists of the 1920s, he gradually moved into more conservative ranks and became a strident opponent of literary and political dissidence. —Trans.
‡Aleksandr Fadeev (1901–56) is remembered principally for his 1945 epic about guerrilla resistance to German occupation during World War II, *The Young Guard*. Regarded as Stalin's literary henchman, a reputation he acquired as secretary of the Writers Union between 1939 and 1954, Fadeev was ostracized during the de-Stalinization campaigns of the "thaw." He committed suicide in 1956. —Trans.

Upon entering the house I saw that it was full of people, that the coffin had been unsealed, and that Stepanida Ivanovna lay in the front corner. Thus, having flown on a plane (for the first time ever), having been jostled all night in a bus, she had, you might say, finally arrived. The last four hundred meters she'd float on white cloths draped over the pallbearers' shoulders, float past our garden, past the long-abandoned plot, past the potato patch where she'd spent so many hours crawling on her knees, digging and fumbling through the cold autumn ground with stiff, frozen fingers searching for potatoes, past the rye yet to come to ear, along the edge of the steep hill down to the river, until she reached the familiar pine grove about which so many Olepino generations had remarked, "We're all headed there."

Nikolai and I also would have offered our shoulders, but apparently it is not a son's station to carry his mother's coffin.

Each time another of the close relatives assumed a place near the coffin, the sobbing and wailing would rise with renewed force. Above these sounds of grief rustled the congregation's murmurings of satisfaction when—straight from behind the wheel, straight from four hours of blurred white lines—I stood on the threshold under the low-hanging lintel. He made it. That means it'll start soon. How long does it take from here to Snegirevo by car? An hour round-trip.

It's not directly relevant to the matter at hand, but on the way there I decided to take a shortcut through the woods (seven kilometers instead of twenty), but failed to consider one little sweatpit (as we call them) camouflaged by the May grass; here the car started to spin its wheels and dug itself into the mud. It took an hour and a half to get it out. First I tried to do it myself by breaking off branches and throwing them under the wheels, then, losing hope, I walked to the nearest village and got a truck to pull me out of the mire. None of this would be relevant to the matter at hand, except for the resulting shortage of time and my frayed nerves, which in turn affected the nature of my conversation with Father Sergius, making me even more determined and insistent.

To tell the truth, Father Sergius didn't say no when I first spelled out my request. It was only later, after he had collected all his things—cross, censer, chasuble, and books—and after we had reached the open door of the car, that he suddenly asked, with no illusions, by the way, as to what my answer would be:

"You do have authorization from the regional administration?"

I came that close to losing it, that close to asking what do you mean more authorizations, but his question had so taken me aback that it

took me a full three or four seconds to recover. The delay was pro-
pitious. It was just long enough for Father Sergius to explain:

"One is supposed to have written authorization."

It's all you can do to refrain from uttering a string of obscenities after
that. If this were happening in some vanquished country where the
occupying forces held the local population under such tight restraints,
under such oppression that they even forbade the people to bury their
dead according to their own customs without first obtaining permission
from those same occupying forces, then maybe it might have been possible to understand. But I can't imagine that such occupying forces
exist on this earth, or that there exist any people on this earth who
would submit to such oppression.

A wavering abyss gaped beneath my feet. Through my mind raced a
feverish stream of images. What now? Put off the funeral until tomorrow? Dash off to the regional center for authorization? Bury Stepanida
Ivanovna just like that, like cattle, the way the elderly are buried nowadays? Dash off to the regional center to hire that loathsome funeral
wind ensemble? My conscience would allow none of these. Especially not after one more image came to mind, a vision of myself going
straight to that all-too-familiar office in that all-too-familiar institution
tomorrow morning and retroactively obtaining that monstrous piece
of paper, a disgrace to any government, and delivering it to Father
Sergius. And so, without batting an eye or allowing my voice to falter,
and staring with innocent blue eyes straight into the inquiring eyes of
the priest, I lied:

"You see, Father Sergius, there were a lot of problems with the
transportation, but I called the regional administration and they gave
me permission. I'll bring you the written authorization tomorrow."

The priest believed me (a writer, after all!), and we set off for Olepino, this time by the longer, safe route. My delay, as might have been
expected, had caused alarm among those waiting for the funeral, and
even more people had arrived. On our appearance, slender wax candles
were passed from hand to hand, and a minute later dozens of golden
lights flickered and fluttered in the air around Stepanida Ivanovna. It
smelled like church. Volunteers immediately came forward: Vladimir
Sergeyevich Postnov with his besotted bass, Aunt Polya with her oc-
togenarian, but still pure, untainted alto, and others who'd almost
forgotten how to sing and were just glad for the chance to sing again.
Exultation in the vale of tears.

Once some guests had gathered at my Moscow apartment. I put on a recording of the Orthodox High Requiem, and for the next half hour no one uttered a single word, not a single remark. When the last note had faded, one of the guests—a man of unquestionable candor and candidness—blinked back a tear and said, "Well? It wouldn't be so terrible dying, it wouldn't even be terrible lying in the grave, if such words and such singing saw you off. . . ."

Vladimir Sergeyevich and Aunt Polya could not equal the impression created by the harmonious Paris choir, but then this was no dinner party but a real funeral. Stepanida Ivanovna lay as if alive in her coffin, the candles flickered, and glancing around, I saw that people were weeping and sobbing. Not, I think, for Stepanida Ivanovna (her time had come, it was inevitable, and we're all headed there), but for something they had remembered, something they had recognized, something they had lost that had been taken away from them and almost forgotten but had been returned to them at least for this one day. "For dust thou art, and unto dust shalt thou return," the volunteer choristers chanted painstakingly, "neither sorrow nor lamentation, but life everlasting . . . the Lord's handmaiden, the deceased Stepanida . . . and grant her remembrance everlasting. . . ."

In days past, the church bell would begin to toll as the body was carried from the home. Its heavy bronze reverberations would resound far out into the countryside. Each succeeding note would linger and linger. And the sound of the bell would descend over the people walking toward the cemetery again and again—forty times, was it? And thus the slow tolling of the bell would accompany the funeral procession to the grave, announcing to all the mournful hour of burial. The plowman in the field, the woman bent over her scythe, even the chance passerby would stop, make the sign of the cross, and, if only for one minute, be spiritually joined with her for whom the bell tolled.

Nowadays it's the rare place where you'll hear a bell. We marched to the cemetery pines in doleful silence, although Father Sergius—who also, apparently, missed the ritual—would constantly stop, turn to the procession, and again and again recite words of prayer. Then clods of earth thudded on the hollow wooden lid (at this point my sisters began wailing and the women of Olepino renewed their sobbing), and soon only a reddish clay mound remained among the May wildflowers, and we all trailed off—not shoulder to shoulder as we had walked on the way there, but in little groups, some of us alone—back to the village.

I drove Father Sergius back to Snegirevo and asked what his customary fee for this type of service was.

"Three rubles," Father Sergius answered meekly.

I held out four tens.

"Why are you giving me so much money? And why exactly forty?"

"It costs forty rubles to hire the regional wind ensemble for a funeral. Why should I pay you any less?"

But I had another reason, one I wasn't telling Father Sergius: My deception and the sinking feeling in my heart that at the regional administration tomorrow things might not go so smoothly after all and that some difficulties might be in store for Father Sergius.

"My humble gratitude. You won't forget about the authorization from the regional administration, will you now?"

"How could I forget about that!"

On what did I base my optimism, on what did I pin my hopes? On the fact that to date the regional administration had never once turned me down. True, I didn't appeal to them very often. You don't want to disturb people or, worse, incur indebtedness unless it's an emergency. But still, when we were renovating the house and needed (for hard cash) a few materials (roofing metal, lumber, and cement), when we needed spare parts for the car, or when the chairman of the collective farm would talk me into going down to the regional administration to request something on behalf of the collective, I would go and ask, and never once had I been turned down. On one occasion, for example, I had asked for two kilometers of water pipe, and before long the village had its water pumps.

Tikhon Stepanovich—head of the regional administration and in all respects a fine person—and I had gotten to know each other back in the days when he worked in the Iuriev-Polsk area. We met several times at the Kositsyns' and became, if not friends, at least close acquaintances. Later, even after Tikhon Stepanovich got promoted and transferred to the regional administration, our relationship continued. That's why the chairman of the collective, when he needed something desperately for the farm, instead of going directly to Tikhon Stepanovich, would come to me first, hoping that I would go and do the talking and get it all worked out. I tried, however, not to abuse the relationship and appeared in the regional administration only in exceptional situations.

Well, the situation this time was certainly exceptional.

As usual, Tikhon Stepanovich began by reproaching me for never calling or coming by.

"And take you away from business?" I objected. "As if I didn't know that even if there were forty-eight hours in a day and three Tikhon

Stepanoviches, there would still be too much to do and too little time to do it in."

"That's true." Tikhon Stepanovich laughed. "And how are things at home? My son, Shurka . . ."

"Everyone's fine, healthy. But I just buried Stepanida Ivanovna yesterday . . ."

"Why didn't you call? We would have sent the regional wind ensemble. I know what an ensemble they've got over in Stavrovo."

"She didn't want a wind ensemble."

"Who didn't?"

"Stepanida Ivanovna."

"But she's dead! . . . So, how did you bury her, then?"

"That's what I came to see you about. . . ."

Our conversation was constantly interrupted by telephone calls, and right in my presence Tikhon Stepanovich reeled off important orders, coordinated regional organizational activities, and reprimanded several managers. That, I had noticed long ago, was his style: Don't put anything off, not even for ten minutes, no less until tomorrow. Hearing out each successive request, then replacing the receiver, he would immediately spring into action: He'd press the buttons of a machine that allowed him to talk to any member of the regional administration just as if the person were right there in the room, or he'd call in his secretary and ask her to get so-and-so on the phone. Calls went out to factories, warehouses, distant regions, state farms, regional tractor stations, and then and there—be it in a field, an office, or a workshop—the responsible person would be found. The telephone calls multiplied, branched out, coursed through the entire region, and came back until the problem found a solution. Consequently, my retelling of yesterday's events took a great deal more time than the matter essentially required. But I still managed to convey how it had been my mother's last request and how, as her son, I had had to accede to it. More than that, it had been my filial obligation.

I kept waiting for Tikhon Stepanovich to cut short my tortured explanations and to say that none of this mattered and that there was nothing to worry about. But the longer I spoke, the more flushed and morose Tikhon Stepanovich grew. I barely made it through the final, constructive (so to speak) part of my speech before my interlocutor disappeared, replaced by a mere listener. Not even a listener, really, but a person in authority hearing out what for him was a very unpleasant request.

"The deed's done, Tikhon Stepanovich. I ask for only one thing, that the priest not be punished. I deceived him, and he trusted me. I alone am to blame. But I didn't know that things were that strict."

"You've gone and done it now!" Tikhon Stepanovich darkened after hearing me out, and, true to form, he reached for his machine.

He was just about to push the appropriate button when he reconsidered and picked up the phone instead. This could mean only one thing: He didn't want me to hear the other end of the conversation.

"Alexander Ivanovich? Hello . . ."

That meant he had reached the regional undersecretary for Orthodox Christian affairs. "Under" was "under," but obviously at some remove as well, otherwise Tikhon Stepanovich's speech would have contained more declarative indicatives and fewer careful interrogatives.

"So, how are things on the church front? Everything in order? . . . I see. . . . I want to ask you about a certain case. Tell me, what would you do with a priest if he went to another village to preside over a funeral? Say he was asked, and he upped and went. . . . Categorically forbidden? Uh-huh . . . Forfeit his parish? Uh-huh. And what if he also accompanied the processional from the house to the cemetery? . . . I know, I know, it's impossible. But what if it happened? . . . Uh-huh. That means any outdoor religious ceremonies? . . . Uh-huh. Anywhere in the entire country? . . . I see, I see."

Tikhon Stepanovich never talked this way on the phone, asking over and over, repeating the other person's words as if he were hard of hearing or didn't catch what was being said. Usually he listens in silence and then hands out the orders. He was obviously repeating certain of Alexander Ivanovich's phrases for my benefit, so that I would sense the total absurdity and irresponsibility of my behavior, so that I would recognize my guilt. I did recognize it, but nevertheless the thought that what was done was done and that no Alexander Ivanovich—no matter how loudly he might curse over the phone—could do anything to change it filled my heart with calm, even joy. Then I realized that this wasn't the first time I'd rejoiced in those sorrow-filled days. I'd rejoiced when I succeeded in buying the coffin, I'd rejoiced when I found someone to zinc-coat it, then to solder it shut. I'd rejoiced when they loaded the coffin onto the plane, I'd rejoiced when Father Sergius agreed to go to the funeral, and I was rejoicing now. By and large, my earlier rejoicing had been for me, for being spared even more trouble, but this time, the last time, it was for Stepanida Ivanovna, and it was joy pure and simple.

Tikhon Stepanovich continued his conversation.

"In the house? Probably he officiated in the house too. . . . People? Probably the whole village. They didn't bury her at night, after all. . . . Where was the Party organizer of the collective farm? You don't believe it? You think I'm putting you on? Now you listen to me, Alexander Ivanovich. In the village of Snegirevo you've got a priest named . . . [inquiring glance in my direction] . . . Father Sergius or something. . . . Right. Yesterday, this priest drove out to Olepino and presided over a funeral. First he conducted a service in the house. Then he accompanied the processional out to the cemetery and performed rites over the grave. Again, 'It couldn't happen!' It happened. You listen to what I've got to say. You know we've got a writer living in Olepino? . . . Ah-ha, you know each other. Even better. Yesterday he buried his mother, Stepanida Ivanovna, and brought that—that . . . blast him! . . . Father Sergius . . . to the funeral. Well, we can't punish Vladimir Alekseyevich. He's got his own authorities in Moscow, the Writers Union. They'll know what to do without us. Besides, his mother left him a last request—to be buried by a priest. So he, as her son, fulfilled her last request. . . . No, you listen, listen. From our point of view, of course, this is an outrage, but you know those writers. . . . Vladimir Alekseyevich told him that he had authorization from us. Well, there was no time. All in all, of course, it's an outrage. So here's my personal request to you: Don't punish the priest too severely and don't take away his parish; give him a reprimand or a warning, reprove him for it. You know how to handle these things. That's my personal request. Vladimir Alekseyevich is sitting right here; he sends his regards. . . . Good. Well, so long, that's all for now."

Tikhon Stepanovich replaced the receiver.

"This time, as an exception. But next time . . ."

"There won't be a next time, Tikhon Stepanovich. I've only got one mother, Stepanida Ivanovna. And we buried her yesterday. . . ."

"Of course, what am I saying. Sorry. Have you seen Kositsyn lately? How's he doing? How about going fishing one of these days?"

1967; first published 1987.

Translated from the Russian by Diane Nemec Ignashev.

FIRE AND DUST

Tatyana Tolstaya

Where is she now, that lunatic Svetlana, nicknamed Pipka, about whom some people, with the nonchalance of youth, used to say, "But I mean, is Pipka really human?" and others, exasperated: "Why do you let her in? Keep an eye on your books! She'll walk off with everything!" No, they were wrong: The only things assignable to Pipka's conscience are a light blue Simenon and a white wool sweater with knitted buttons, and it was already darned at the elbow anyway. And to hell with the sweater! Much more valuable things had vanished since that time: Rimma's radiant youth; the childhood of her children; the freshness of her hopes, blue as the morning sky; the secret, joyful trust with which Rimma listened to the voice of the future whispering for her alone— what laurels, flowers, islands, and rainbows had not been promised to her, and where is it all? She didn't begrudge the sweater; Rimma herself had forcibly thrust Svetlana into that little-needed sweater when she threw the insane girl, half dressed as always, out into the raging autumn one cold, branch-lashed Moscow midnight. Rimma, already in her nightgown, shifted impatiently from one foot to the other in the doorway, pressing her shivering legs together; she kept nodding, advancing, showing Svetlana the door, but Svetlana was trying to get something out, to finish what she had to say, with a nervous giggle, a quick shrug of the shoulders, and in her pretty white face black eyes burned like an insane abyss and the wet abyss of her mouth mumbled in a hurried dither—a hideous black mouth, where the stumps of the teeth made you think of old, charred ruins. Rimma advanced, gaining ground inch by inch, and Svetlana talked on and on and on, waving her hands all about as if she were doing exercises—nocturnal, night-owl, unbelievable exercises—and then, demonstrating the enormous size of something—but Rimma wasn't listening—she gestured so expansively that she smashed her knuckles against the wall and in her surprise said nothing for a moment, pressing the salty joints to her lips, which seemed singed by her disconnected pronouncements. That was when the sweater was shoved at her—you'll warm up in the taxi—the door was slammed shut, and Rimma, vexed and laughing, ran to Fedya under the warm blanket. "I barely managed to get rid of her." The children tossed and turned in their sleep. Tomorrow was an early day. "You could have let her spend the night," muttered Fedya through his sleep, through the warmth, and he was very handsome in the red glow of the night-light. Spend the night? Never! And where? In old man Ashkenazi's room? The old man tossed and turned incessantly on his worn-out couch, smoked something thick and smelly, coughed, and in the middle of the night would get up and go to the kitchen for a drink of water from the tap, but all in all it wasn't bad, he wasn't a bother. When guests came he would loan chairs, get out a jar of marinated mushrooms, untangle rats' nests of sticky tinned fruit drops for the children. They would seat him at one end of the table and he would chuckle, swing his legs, which didn't reach the floor, and smoke into his sleeve: "Never mind, you young people, be patient—I'll die soon and the whole apartment will be yours." "May you live to be a hundred, David Danilich," Rimma would reassure him, but still it was pleasant to dream about the time when she would be mistress of an entire apartment, not a communal one, but her own, when she would do major remodeling—cover the preposterous five-cornered kitchen from top to bottom in tile and get a new stove. Fedya would defend his dissertation, the children would go to school—English, music, figure skating. . . . What else could she imagine? A lot of people envied them in advance. But of course it was not tile, not well-rounded children that shone from the wide-open spaces of the future like a rainbow-colored fire, a sparkling arc of wild rapture (and Rimma honestly wished old man Ashkenazi long life—there's time enough for everything); no, something greater, something completely different, important, overwhelming, and grand clamored and glittered up ahead, as though Rimma's ship, sailing along a dark channel through blossoming reeds, were on the verge of coming into the green, happy, raging sea.

In the meantime, life was not quite real, it was life in anticipation, lived out of a suitcase, slipshod, lightweight—a pile of junk in the hallway, midnight guests: Petyunya in his sky-blue tie, the childless Elya and Alyosha, and others; Pipka's nocturnal visits and her outrageous conversations. How hideous Pipka was with those black detoothed stumps—yet lots of people liked her, and often at the end of a festive evening one of the men couldn't be accounted for: Pipka had whisked him away while no one was looking—always in a taxi—to her place in Perlovka. That was where she holed up, renting a cheap little wooden shack with a front yard. At one time Rimma even worried about Fedya—he was flighty and Pipka was crazy and capable of anything. If not for those rotten stumps in her hurried mouth, it might have been worth thinking about not allowing her into the family home. Especially since Fedya often said mysteriously, "If Svetlanka would just keep her mouth shut, you could actually talk to her!" And she was forever trembling, half dressed, or dressed topsy-turvy: crusty stiff children's boots on bare feet in the middle of winter, her hands all chapped.

No one knew where Pipka went, just as no one knew where she actually came from—she had simply shown up and that was that. Her stories were outrageous and confused: It seems she'd wanted to go to drama school and had even been accepted, but in a market she met some pickled-garlic merchants and was gagged and taken off to Baku in a white Volga with no license plates. There they supposedly ravished her, knocked out half her teeth, and abandoned her, naked, on the seashore in a pool of oil. The next morning, she claimed, she was found by a wild mountain man in transit through Baku; he carried her off to his hut high in the mountains and held her there all summer, feeding her melon from a knife through the cracks in his shack, and in the fall he traded her to a visiting ethnographer for a watch with no hands. Still completely naked, she and the ethnographer, who called her Svetka-Pipetka, which is where she got her nickname, holed up in an abandoned watchtower, dating back to Shamil's time, that was covered with rotten Persian rugs—the ethnographer studied their patterns with a magnifying glass. At night eagles defecated on them. "Shoo, shoo, damn you!" Pipka would act it out, racing around the room with an indignant expression, frightening the children. When winter came, the ethnographer left to go higher into the mountains, and at the first snowfall Svetlana descended into a valley where the people calculated time by the lunar calendar and shot at schoolmarms through the school window, publicly marking the number of casualties with notches on a post in the center of the bazaar. There were more than eight hundred notches; the Regional Department of Public Education couldn't manage—several pedagogical institutes worked exclusively for this valley. There Svetlana had an affair with the local store manager. But she quickly dumped him, finding him insufficiently manly: Instead of sleeping as a Caucasian horseman should, on his back in a *papakha* fur cap with a sword at his side, fiercely displaying his wide, muscular shoulders, the local store manager would curl up, snuffle and whimper in his sleep, shuffling his legs; he explained in his own defense that he dreamed of gunfire. Toward spring Pipka reached Moscow on foot, sleeping in haystacks and avoiding the high roads; several times she was bitten by dogs. For some reason she went through the Ural Mountains. But then geography gave her even more trouble than her private life; she called the Urals the Caucasus, and placed Baku on the Black Sea. Maybe there really was some kind of truth in her nightmarish stories, who knows. Rimma was used to them and hardly listened; she thought her own thoughts, surrendering to her own unhurried daydreams. Almost nobody listened to Pipka anyway—after all, was she really human? Only occasionally some newcomer, enthralled by Pipka's nonsense, by the disgorged fountain of tales, would exclaim in joyous amazement, "Boy, does she ever lay it on! A thousand and one nights!" That was the type Pipka usually carried off to her semifantastic Perlovka, if it actually existed: Was it really possible to believe that Svetlana was employed by the owners to dig troughs around the dahlias and that she ate fish-bone meal along with the chickens? As always, during a simple gathering of friends, amid the noise and chatter and clatter of forks, a dreamy somnolence overtook Rimma, marvelous dream-visions real as life appeared, pink and blue mists, white sails; the roar of the ocean could be heard, far off, beckoning, like the steady roar that issued from the giant shell gracing the sideboard. Rimma loved to close her eyes and put the shell to her ear—from those monstrous, salmon-colored jaws you could hear the call of a faraway country, so far away that a place could no longer be found for it on the globe, and it smoothly ascended, this country, and settled in the sky with all of its lakes, parrots, and crashing coastal breakers. And Rimma also glided in the sky amid pink, feathery clouds—everything promised by life will come to pass. No need to stir, no need to hurry, everything will come all by itself. To slip silently down dark channels . . . to

listen to the approaching roar of the ocean . . . Rimma would open her eyes and, smiling, look at her guests through the tobacco smoke and dreams—at lazy, satisfied Fedya, at David Danilich swinging his legs—and slowly return to earth. And it will start with something insignificant . . . it will start bit by bit. . . . She felt the ground with her legs, which were weakened by the flight. Oh, the apartment would have to be first, of course. The old man's room would be the bedroom. Baby-blue curtains. No, white ones. White, silky, fluffy, gathered ones. And a white bed. Sunday morning. In a white peignoir, her hair flowing (time to let her hair grow out, but the peignoir had already been secretly bought, she couldn't resist) . . . Rimma would stroll through the apartment to the kitchen. . . . The aroma of coffee . . . To new acquaintances she would say, "And in this room, where the bedroom is now, an old man used to live. . . . So sweet . . . He wasn't a bother. And after his death we took it over. . . . It's a shame—such a wonderful old man!" Rimma would rock back and forth on her chair, smiling at the still-living old man: "You smoke a lot, David Danilich. You should take care of yourself." The old man only coughed and waved her away, as if to say, Never mind. I'm not long for this place. Why bother?

How lovely it was to float and meander through time—and time meanders through you and melts away behind, and the sound of the sea keeps beckoning; time to take a trip to the South and breathe the sea air, stand on the shore stretching your arms and listening to the wind. . . . How sweetly life melts away—the children, and loving Fedya, and the anticipation of the white bedroom. The guests are envious; well, my dears, go ahead and envy, enormous happiness awaits me up ahead— what kind, I won't say, I myself don't know, but voices whisper, "Just wait, wait!" Petyunya, sitting over there biting his nails, is envious. He doesn't have a wife or an apartment, he's puny, he's ambitious, he wants to be a journalist, he loves bright ties, we should give him ours, the orange one, we don't need it, happiness awaits us. Elya and Alyosha are also envious, they don't have any children, they've gone and gotten a dog, how boring. Old man Ashkenazi sitting there, he's envious of my youth, my white bedroom, my ocean roar; farewell, old man, it will soon be time for you to leave, your eyes shut tight under copper coins. Now Svetlana . . . she envies no one, she has everything, but it's only imaginary, her eyes and her frightful mouth burn like fire—Fedya shouldn't sit so close—her talk is crazy, kingdoms rise and fall by the dozens in her head all in one night. Fedya shouldn't sit so close. Fedya! Come sit over here. She's spinning her yarns and you're all ears?

Life was happy and easy, they laughed at Petyunya, at his passion for ties, said he was destined for a great journalistic future, asked him ahead of time not to put on airs if he traveled overseas; Petyunya was embarrassed, and he wrinkled his mousy little face: What are you talking about, guys, let's hope I make it through the institute!

Petyunya was wonderful, but sort of rumpled, and, moreover, he tried to play up to Rimma, though only indirectly, to be sure: He would slice onions for her in the kitchen and hint that he, frankly, had plans for his life. Oh-ho! Rimma laughed. What plans could he have, when such incredible things awaited her! You'd be better off setting your sights on Elya, she'll dump Alyosha anyway. Or else Svetka-Pipetka over there. Pipetka was getting married, Petyunya said. To whom, I'd like to know?

It was soon discovered to whom: to old man Ashkenazi. The old man, feeling sorry for Pipka's little feet in their children's boots, for her frozen little hands, distressed about her nighttime taxi expenses, and all in all succumbing to a teary, senile altruism, conceived the idea—behind Rimma's back!—of marrying that vagrant who blazed with a black fire and of registering her, naturally, in the living space promised to Rimma and Fedya. A scene complete with sedatives ensued. "You should be ashamed, shame on you!" cried Rimma, her voice breaking. "But I've got nothing to be ashamed of," answered the old man from the couch, where he lay amid broken springs, his head thrown back to stop the flow of blood from his nose. Rimma applied cold compresses and sat up with him all night. When the old man dozed off, his breathing shallow and irregular, she measured the window in his room. Yes, the white material was the right width. Light blue wallpaper over here. In the morning they made up. Rimma forgave the old man, he cried, she gave him Fedya's shirt and fed him hot pancakes. Svetlana heard something about it and didn't show up for a long time. Then Petyunya also vanished and the guess was that Svetlana had carried him off to Perlovka. Everyone who ended up there disappeared for ages, and when they returned they were not themselves for quite some time.

Petyunya showed up one evening six months later with a vague expression on his face, his trousers covered to the waist in mud. Rimma had trouble getting anything out of him. Yes, he had been there. He helped Pipka with the work. It was a very hard life. Everything was very complicated. He had walked all the way from Perlovka. Why was he covered in mud? Oh, that . . . He and Pipka had wandered around Perlovka with kerosene lanterns all last night, looking for the right house. A Circassian had given birth to a puppy. Yes, that's what happened. Yes, I know—Petyunya pressed his hands to his chest—I know that there aren't any Circassian people in Perlovka. This was the last one. Svetlana says she knows for sure. It's a very good story for the "Only Facts" column of the newspaper. "What's got into you, are you off your rocker too?" asked Rimma, blinking. "Why do you say that? I saw the puppy myself." "And the Circassian?" "They weren't letting anyone in to see him. It was the middle of the night, after all." "Sleep it off," said Rimma. They put Petyunya in the hall with the junk. Rimma fretted, tossing and turning all night, and in the morning she decided that "Circassian" was a dog's name. But at breakfast she couldn't bring herself to increase the lunacy with questions, and, anyway, Petyunya was glum and soon left.

Then all of a sudden Svetlana had to move her things from Perlovka to some other place right away—figuring out the geography of it was useless; it had to be by taxi, of course, and for some reason Fedya's help was absolutely essential. Hesitating a bit, Rimma let him go. It was ten in the morning, so it wasn't very likely that anything could . . . He returned at three that night, behaving very strangely. "Where were you?" Rimma was waiting in the hall in her nightgown. "You see, there were a lot of complications. . . . We ended up having to go to Serpukhov, she has twins in the Children's Home there." "What twins?" Rimma shouted. "Tiny ones, about a year old, I think. Siamese. Their heads are joined together. Karina and Angela." "What heads? Are you out of your mind? She's been coming here for ages. Have you ever noticed her having a baby?" No, of course he hadn't noticed her having a baby or anything like that, but they really did go to Serpukhov, and they did drop off a package: frozen hake. That's right, hake for the twins. He himself stood in the cashier's line to pay for the fish. Rimma burst into tears and slammed the door. Fedya remained in the hall, scratching at the door and swearing that he himself didn't understand anything, but that they were called Karina and Angela—of that he was sure.

After that Pipka disappeared again for a long while, and the episode was forgotten. But for the first time something in Rimma cracked— she looked around and saw that time kept flowing on, yet the future still hadn't arrived, and Fedya was not so handsome anymore, and the children had picked up bad words on the street, and old man Ashkenazi coughed and lived on, and wrinkles had already crept up to her eyes and mouth, and the junk in the hallway was still just lying there. And the roar of the ocean had grown muffled, and they hadn't gone to the South after all—everything had been put off until the future, which just didn't want to arrive.

Troubled days followed. Rimma lost heart; she kept trying to understand at what point she'd taken the wrong path leading to that far-off, melodious happiness, and often she sat lost in thought; meanwhile, her children were growing up and Fedya sat in front of the television, not wanting to write his dissertation, and outside the window either a cottony blizzard blew or an insipid city sun peeked through summer clouds. Their friends grew old, it became harder for them to get themselves going, Petyunya had completely vanished somewhere, flashy ties went out of fashion, Elya and Alyosha got another unruly dog and there was no one to leave it with evenings. At Rimma's job new co-workers had appeared, big Lucy and little Lucy, but they didn't know about Rimma's plans for happiness and didn't envy her; rather, they envied Kira from the planning department, who had a large, expensive wardrobe, who exchanged hats for books, books for meat, meat for medicine or hard-to-come-by theater tickets, and spoke in an irritated tone of voice to someone on the phone: "But you know perfectly well how much I love jellied tongue."

And one evening, when Fedya was watching television and Rimma was sitting with her head on the table listening to the old man coughing on the other side of the wall, in burst Pipka, all fire and flame, rosy-cheeked, looking younger, as sometimes happens with insane people, and smiling, her blazing mouth full of sparkling white teeth. "Thirty-six!" she shouted from the threshold and banged her fist on the top of the doorway. "Thirty-six what?" said Rimma, lifting her head from the table. "Thirty-six teeth!" said Pipka. And she told the story of how she got a job as a cabin boy on a steamer bound for Japan, and since the steamer was already overstaffed she had to sleep in a cauldron with the meat and rice, and the captain had rendered her honor but the captain's assistant had rent it; and a rich Japanese man fell in love with her on the way and wanted to arrange their marriage by telegraph without delay, but they couldn't find the right Japanese characters and the deal fell apart; and then—while they were washing the meat-and-rice cauldron in some port or other—she was kidnapped by a pirate junk and sold to a rich plantation owner, and she spent a year working on Malaysian hemp plantations, where she was bought by a rich Englishman for an Olympics memorial ruble, which, as everyone knows, is highly prized among Malaysian numismatists. The Englishman carried her off to misty Albion; first, he lost her in the thick mist, but then he found her, and to celebrate he footed the bill for the most expensive and fashionable set of thirty-six teeth, which only a real moneybags could afford. He gave her smoked pony for the road and now she, Pipka, was finally going to Perlovka to get her things. "Open your mouth," said Rimma with hatred. And in Svetlana's readily opened mouth she counted, fighting vertigo, all thirty-six—how they fit in there was beyond comprehension, but they were indeed teeth. "I can chew steel wire now. If you want, I'll bite off a bit of the cornice," the monster started to say, and Fedya was watching with great interest, but Rimma began waving her hands: That's all, that's it, it's late, we want to sleep, and she thrust taxi money on her, and pushed her toward the door, and threw her the volume of Simenon. For heaven's sake, take it, read a little tonight, only just leave! And Pipka left, clutching the walls to no avail, and no one ever saw her again. "Fedya, shall we take a trip to the South?" Rimma asked. "Absolutely," Fedya answered readily, as he had done many times over the years. That's all right, then. That means we will go after all. To the South! And she listened to the voice that still faintly whispered something about the future, about happiness, about long, sound sleep in a white bedroom, but the words were already difficult to make out. "Hey, look—it's Petyunya!" said Fedya in surprise. On the television screen, under palm trees, small and sullen, with a microphone in his hands, stood Petyunya, and he was cursing some kind of cocoa plantations, and the black people passing by turned around to look at him, and his huge tie erupted like a pustular African sunrise, but there wasn't a whole lot of happiness to be seen on his face either.

Now Rimma knew that they'd all been tricked, but by whom and when, she couldn't remember. She sorted through it all day by day, searching for a mistake, but didn't find any. Everything was somehow covered with dust. Occasionally—strange to say—she felt like talking it over with Pipka, but Pipka didn't come around anymore.

It was summer again, the heat had arrived, and through the thick dust the voice from the future once again whispered something. Rimma's children were grown, one had married and the other was in the army, the apartment was empty, and she had trouble sleeping at night—the old man coughed incessantly on the other side of the wall. Rimma no longer wanted to turn the old man's room into a bedroom, and she

didn't have the white peignoir anymore—moths from the junk in the
hall had eaten it, without even looking at what they ate. Arriving at
work, Rimma complained to big Lucy and little Lucy that moths were
now devouring even German things; little Lucy gasped, holding her
palms to her cheeks, and big Lucy grew angry and glum. "If you want
to outfit yourselves, girls," said the experienced Kira, breaking away
from her telephonic machinations, "I can take you to a place. I have a
friend. Her daughter just got back from Bahrain. You can pay later. It's
good stuff. Vera Esafovna got seven hundred rubles' worth on Saturday. They lived well over there in Bahrain. Swam in a pool, they want
to go again." "Why don't we?" said big Lucy. "Oh, I have so many
debts," whispered the little one.

    "Quick, quick, girls, we'll take a taxi," said Kira, hurrying them.
"We can make it during lunch break." And, feeling like schoolgirls
cutting class, they piled into a cab, inundating one another with the
smells of perfume and lit cigarettes, and whirled off down hot summer
side streets strewn with sunny linden-tree husks and patches of warm
shadow; a southerly wind was blowing, and through the gasoline fumes
it carried the exultation and brilliance of the far-off South: the blazing
blue heavens, the mirrorlike shimmer of vast seas, wild happiness,
wild freedom, the madness of hopes coming true. . . . Hopes for what?
God only knows! And in the apartment they entered, holding their
breath in anticipation of a happy consumer adventure, there was also a
warm wind fluttering and billowing the white tulle on the windows and
doors, which were opened wide onto a spacious balcony—everything
here was spacious, large, free. Rimma felt a little envious of this apartment. A powerful woman—the mistress of the goods for sale—swiftly
threw open the secret room. The goods were rumpled, heaped up in
television boxes on an ever-rising double bed, and reflected in the mirror of a massive wardrobe. "Dig in," ordered Kira, standing in the
doorway. Trembling, the women buried their hands in boxes crammed
with silky, velvety, see-through, gold-embroidered stuff; they pulled
things out, yanking, getting tangled in ribbons and ruffles; their hands
fished things out while their eyes already groped for something else, an
alluring bow or frill; inside Rimma a vein twitched rapidly, her ears
burned, and her mouth was dry. It was all like a dream. And, as happens in the cruel scenario of dreams, a certain crack in the harmony
soon emerged and began to grow, a secret defect, which threatened to
resound in catastrophe. These things—what is this anyway?—weren't
right, they weren't what they seemed at first. The eye began to distin-

guish the cheapness of these gaudy, fake gauze skirts hardly fit for a corps
de ballet, the pretentiousness of those violet turkey-wattle jabots, and
the unfashionable lines of those thick velvet jackets; these were throw-
aways; we were invited to the leftovers of someone else's feast; others
have already rummaged here, have already trampled the ground; someone's greedy hands have already defiled the magical boxes, snatched up
and carried off those very things, the real ones that made the heart beat
and that particular vein twitch. Rimma fell on other boxes, groped
about the disheveled double bed, but neither there, nor there . . . And
the things that she grabbed in despair from the piles and held up to
herself, anxiously looking in the mirror, were laughably small, short,
or ridiculous. Life had gone and the voice of the future was singing for
others. The woman, the owner of the goods, sat like Buddha and
watched, astute and scornful. "What about this?" Rimma pointed at
the clothes hanging on coat hangers along the walls, fluttering in the
warm breeze. "Sold. That's sold too." "Is there anything—in my
size?" "Go on, give her something," Kira, who was propped up against
the wall, said to the woman. Thinking for a moment, the woman
pulled out something gray from behind her back, and Rimma, hurriedly undressing, revealing all the secrets of her cheap undergarments
to her girlfriends, slithered into the appropriate openings. Adjusting
and tugging, she inspected her mercilessly bright reflection. The warm
breeze still played about in the sunny room, indifferent to the com-
merce being conducted. She didn't exactly understand what she had
put on; she gazed miserably at the little black hairs on her white legs,
which looked as if they'd gotten soggy or been stored in dark trunks all
winter, at her neck, its goosey flesh stretched out in fright, at her flat-
tened hair, her stomach, her wrinkles, the dark circles under her eyes.
The dress smelled of other people—others had already tried it on.
"Very good. It's you. Take it," pressured Kira, who was the woman's
secret confederate. The woman watched, silent and disdainful. "How
much?" "Two hundred." Rimma choked, trying to tear off the poisoned clothing. "It's awfully stylish, Rimmochka," said little Lucy
guiltily. And to consummate the humiliation, the wind blew open the
door to the next room, revealing a heavenly vision: the woman's young,
divinely sculpted daughter, suntanned to a nut-colored glow—the one
who had come back from Bahrain, who darted out of swimming pools
filled with clear blue water—a flash of white garments, blue eyes; the
woman got up and shut the door. This sight was not for mortal eyes.

The southerly wind blew the refuse of blossoming lindens into the old entryway, warmed the shabby walls. Little Lucy descended the stairs sideways, hugging the mountain of things she'd chosen, almost crying—once again she'd gotten herself into terrible debt. Big Lucy kept a hostile silence. Rimma walked with her teeth clenched: The summer day had darkened, destiny had teased her and had a laugh. And she already knew that the blouse she'd bought at the last minute in a fit of desperation was junk, last year's leaves, Satan's gold, fated to turn into rotten scraps in the morning, a husk sucked and spit out by the blue-eyed Bahrain houri.

She rode in the saddened, silent taxi and said to herself, Still, I do have Fedya and the children. But the comfort was false, feeble, it was all over, life had shown its empty face, its matted hair and sunken eye sockets. And she imagined the long-desired South, where she'd been dying to go for so many years, as yellowed and dusty, with bunches of prickly dry plants, with spittle and scraps of paper rocking on brackish waves. And at home there was the grimy old communal apartment and the immortal old man, Ashkenazi, and Fedya, whom she knew so well she could scream, and the whole viscous stream of years to come, not yet lived but already known, through which she would have to drag herself as through dust covering a road to the knees, the chest, the neck. And the siren's song, deceitfully whispering sweet words to the stupid swimmer about what wouldn't come to pass, fell silent forever.

No, there were some other events—Kira's hand withered, Petyunya came back for visits and talked at length about the price of oil, Elya and Alyosha buried their dog and got a new one, old man Ashkenazi finally washed his windows with the help of the Dawn Company, but Pipka never showed up again. Some people knew for a fact that she'd married a blind storyteller and had taken off for Australia—to shine with her new white teeth amid the eucalyptus trees and duck-billed platypuses above the coral reefs, but others crossed their hearts and swore that she'd been in a crash and burned up in a taxi on the Yaroslavl highway one rainy, slippery night, and that the flames could be seen from afar rising in a column to the sky. They also said that the fire couldn't be brought under control, and that when everything had burned out, nothing was found at the site of the accident. Only cinders.

1986

Translated from the Russian by Jamey Gambrell.

LOVE IN MUSTAMÄGI

Arvo Valton

When Mihkel Jürimäe, a mechanical engineer at the Ilmarinen * Factory in Tallinn, parted from his family, he left everything, down to the very last item, to his wife. It happened on an ordinary workday morning: His wife threw him out irrevocably after they had spent the entire night clarifying their relationship and characterizing each other. They did not envision themselves as their life partner saw them, and this lack of communication made further cohabitation impossible.

Mihkel Jürimäe knew no better way to celebrate this event than to get to work at eight-thirty. As he walked down the stairs, out the gate, and onto the street, an old suitcase was hurled at his feet from the third-floor window. This took place on Kunderi Street, where they lived at the time, and the corner of the suitcase got dented. Mihkel Jürimäe picked up the suitcase because he had always taken his wife's wishes into account, more or less, and walked to the trolley stop. As he passed through the factory gate he felt self-conscious about the suitcase, but he didn't explain anything. Only at the end of the workday did he ask his coworker Guido Ooter whether Guido could take him in for the night. Guido Ooter was a bachelor; he had a one-room apartment and he stipulated that if he were to bring home a girl, Mihkel Jürimäe would either have to leave for that period of time or remain absolutely quiet behind a screen.

That's how Mihkel Jürimäe became an inconvenience to his co-

---

*Mythical smith in the Finnish epic the *Kalevala* who forges the sky vault and the *Sampo*, a magical device that is the source of all bounty. —Trans.

worker, which troubled Mihkel a great deal. The factory management understood his situation and placed him near the top of the list of applicants for apartments. Technologist Volmer Tomp advised him to offer a bribe, but Mihkel Jürimäe couldn't manage this because our officials are loath to accept bribes very readily.

Mihkel Jürimäe tried to be as discreet as possible with regard to the coworker who had provided him shelter and he spent many nights dozing in Baltic Station, where, in fact, he witnessed numerous novel aspects of life, but his work capacity suffered as a result. Under the circumstances Guido Ooter was unable to take a wife and had to make do with chance chicks, which was hazardous to his health. Fortunately, he was of an energetic nature and tirelessly investigated possibilities for getting Mihkel Jürimäe an apartment.

Chance came to his aid. A distant relative of Mihkel Jürimäe's died, leaving behind a one-room cooperative apartment in Mustamägi.* Mihkel Jürimäe was asked to the funeral and was, in fact, very saddened by his relative's death because there is always something unjust about death, whether you believe in God or nature. It wasn't he who thought about his relative's apartment but Guido Ooter, whose mind, in its time off from work and love, dealt solely with the problem of finding a place for Mihkel.

The direct heirs of the deceased emptied the apartment, removing even the curtain rods and chandeliers. They didn't need the apartment—they had one of their own—and trying for it would have meant a great deal of fuss. Naturally, Mihkel Jürimäe had no right whatsoever to the apartment, but with Guido Ooter's prodding, he joined the ranks of applicants for the newly available place. Guido Ooter made very skillful use of his many connections and gradually Mihkel Jürimäe moved up, becoming applicant number one. Of course, in our society the decisive factor is not connections but the law; nevertheless, in some undefined circumstances connections can be of help in interpreting the law. And the circumstances involved in obtaining an apartment are almost always undefined.

Thus not a year had passed before Mihkel Jürimäe was the legal owner of a small private apartment, on a cooperative ownership basis, of course. The heirs had left behind a wobbly, faded stool that no one

*A large development of high-rise buildings on the outskirts of Tallinn; the equivalent in English is "Black Hill." —Trans.

had coveted. Mihkel Jürimäe pounded three nails into the stool and it then could withstand long periods of sitting.

And that's just what he did. The first day he sat his apartment owner's rear upon the stool in the middle of the room and looked at the walls. He did this for a long time and very thoroughly, and finally he was overcome with sadness because he had attained his happiness through the death of a person near to him, one who had visited them in the country sometime during Mihkel Jürimäe's childhood and had brought him a rubber dog as a present.

But Mihkel Jürimäe's life wanted living; he bought an iron bed with nickel knobs in a secondhand store. He made this choice because his coworkers, after discussing his problems, couldn't reach an agreement on whether dark red or poison green was the fashion. Mihkel Jürimäe didn't want to be fashionable or unfashionable, he simply liked a mattress with springs. And he also liked what Tovio Kelp, from the marketing department, who came to his housewarming along with the others, had said: Mihkel Jürimäe is a man who does as he himself thinks best.

He grew accustomed to his new daily routine. From time to time he felt troubled about the past, but at other times he contemplated with curiosity what might lie ahead. Essential household items gradually accumulated in the room, and in the place of honor stood the old gray suitcase, which his wife had packed—well in advance, apparently— with his yellow-spotted underwear, old shaving kit, woolen scarf, socks, a medal he had once received for saving someone from drowning, a bundle of letters, and other odds and ends. Sometimes he came into the room in his muddy shoes, stomped from corner to corner with relish, and there was no one to say an angry word to him. Then he would take a pair of old undershorts, fit only for use as a rag, and wipe the floor clean.

And then a woman came into his life.

Maire Looke lived her life of solitude and constant yearning in Mustamägi at 249 Friendship Lane. She considered herself a respectable girl with firm principles, which was why she had grown overripe. The young men whom she had known wanted everything too quickly, and that, in Maire Looke's opinion, left nothing of the wondrous mystery that made it possible to get through life. So men found her snippy and nothing to write home about, whereas Maire Looke's soul longed for true love.

It was Maire Looke's custom to pine away at her window in the eve-

nings. She would stand there and watch people. Her coworkers—she
worked in the Red Dawn stocking factory and earned quite a decent
salary—were all of the same cast and there was no mystery to them.
Besides, they were mostly women, except for an occasional male elec-
trician, fitter, or stoker.

But the people who walked past her building were mysterious, and
Maire Looke could make up personalities, fates, interesting relationships, strange domestic situations, and purposeful lives for them. At
first she paid more attention to passersby, who quickly disappeared
from view. Some of them grew familiar to her, were included in her
coterie of acquaintances—they were even given nicknames, such as
Red Hat, Idler, and Cheerful.

An entirely different relationship bound Maire Looke to the inhabitants of the cooperative building facing hers. Each window had its own
specific people; there was no need to give them names. They were
more permanent than the passersby, whom Maire Looke didn't care
about much once she got a taste of looking into the windows; she kept
only a few friends.

The windows of the facing building were far enough away for her to
keep an eye on many lives, but an abundance of details wasn't important to Maire Looke because she had a vivid imagination. There were
families who led ordinary and boring lives—perhaps those were the
ones deemed happy. In others there were parties, fights, and lives lived
passionately, overtly. Maire Looke liked to invent whole novels about
the things she had seen; it gave her satisfaction.

At first Maire Looke would stand in the dusk and eye the lit windows, most of which were covered with heavy curtains. Only the
movements of shadows or of an occasional fleeting figure through a slit
in a curtain could be seen. Daytime offered more, when children and
elderly people were drawn into the light; they opened windows and
lived their lives with great conviviality. With time a characteristic new
to Maire Looke manifested itself at these evening window sessions: She
often forgot to turn off the light in her own room as she stood at the
window, a waiting silhouette. With bitter self-irony, Maire Looke
thought: Well, she's now a spinster who wants to display herself to others
in the hopes that a prince will be taken by her melancholy figure.

One night, in the window opposite hers, Maire Looke saw a man
who was just tall enough and just sad enough. This man caught her
attention because the window at which he appeared had remained an
engima the entire time that Maire Looke had lived in her Mustamägi

apartment. The last few months even the curtains had been gone; the lifelessness had been absolute. And now, suddenly, a man appeared at that lifeless window. Maire Looke's instinct told her unerringly that this was a single man who was just starting to get his life together. Not too young and not too handsome, not too conceited and not too sociable. All these qualities implied that they should notice each other. The man was new here. Maire Looke could build her dreams and hopes only on someone new—in her mind everything from the past was fixed and assigned its proper place.

The reader who has had occasion to glance through books before will immediately grasp that this man was none other than Mihkel Jürimäe. Life is multifaceted, repetitive in its renewal, and in fact seems rather drawn out, but repetition is frowned upon in a literary work: Every gun must fire, chance occurrences must mesh with one another, characters must meet and pass through life's junctures within a few pages. Such is the law of a literary work, and scarcely anyone purposefully wishes to break that law. If mention has been made here of a man and a woman, then every perceptive reader immediately knows what is going to happen, and the only matter of interest is just how it will all take place.

So Maire Looke and Mihkel Jürimäe stood at their respective windows, a bit at an angle to each other, and from there to a certain feeling couldn't be too far away.

A poor, honest, and beautiful young woman, whose only wealth is her rich inner life, meets a moneyed gentleman of noble birth whose life up to this point in upper-class—but for him distasteful—society has gone awry and who can now find consolation only in the nearness of a pure soul. The highly educated but poorly paid engineer maintains his authority in the eyes of the irrevocably unemancipated working girl with the secure job and the good income.

For many nights Mihkel Jürimäe had noticed a woman who stood at her window for hours and looked out. He had tried to guess who in their building the woman's glance might be directed at, but to no avail. One night when it became lonely in his empty room, he also went and stood at the window to banish empty, troubling thoughts. And so it inevitably happened that they noticed each other and began gazing at each other intentionally. Mihkel Jürimäe now felt that it would be impolite for him to be the first to leave the window, so he stood valiantly until the woman finally decided it had been long enough. Later on that same evening the woman's shadow flitted past a few times and

Mihkel Jürimäe knew that there beyond the window was a living person with her own activities and thoughts. The following evening Mihkel Jürimäe felt a strong urge to stand at the window, but he restrained himself.

Finally the woman appeared at her sentry post, and then there was nothing for the Ilmarinen engineer to do but take up his position as well. To his satisfaction, he noticed that the woman was now looking intently in his direction and only sometimes, for a brief moment, turned her gaze toward the other windows, as if carrying out a routine inspection.

Evening after evening they stood facing each other this way, and by the end of each workday, as one put her machine in order and the other concluded his creative thinking, they were already filled with anticipation of their evening vigil.

One night the woman didn't appear at the window. Mihkel Jürimäe could not read or work; he constantly jumped up to look at the familiar window. Only now did he realize, once and for all, that this woman had entered his life. Quite late in the evening the window lit up. Mihkel Jürimäe was already in bed reading, a vague feeling of injury gnawing at his heart, and as a punishment, he decided not to go to the window. The woman's shadow moved quickly; he could see how she turned down her bed, then apparently took something from the kitchen and had a bite to eat. When she came to the window for a moment, Mihkel Jürimäe couldn't keep up his stubbornness for long; he got out of bed, then hesitated over whether or not it was proper to show himself to the woman in his pajamas. But before he had a chance to decide, the woman had disappeared from the window, and the light soon went out in her room.

Confusion raged in Mihkel Jürimäe's soul. He said to himself, "What's that stranger of a woman to me? Let her live as she wants." But he could feel that what he was saying wasn't sincere. The thought even crossed his mind that she had come home with a suitor, and a furious jealousy gripped his heart. But then she wouldn't have come to the window at all, and with the wisdom of experience, Mihkel Jürimäe decided, Let's wait it out and see what happens next. To his joy he noticed that, contrary to expectations, this decision did not bring him peace of mind.

So it continued for an entire week; the woman came home only late at night, and then Mihkel Jürimäe realized she was working the second shift. He would never have thought such a realization could bring him so much joy.

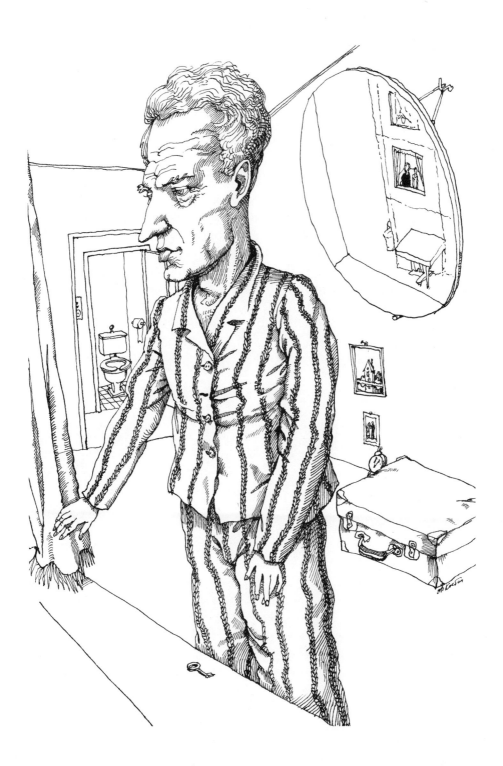

The next week they stood faithfully at their respective posts again. Fate had given them the gift of love. They had the feeling that they couldn't survive without those evening hours, without seeing each other.

But this new burst of feeling in Mihkel Jürimäe was mixed with a certain bitterness, and from time to time old hurts and disappointments forced themselves to the surface, doubts about himself and about all women, about the possibility of happiness; he was a bit over forty and thought that love couldn't be his anymore. Sometimes he was filled with an inexplicable jealousy toward all the men whom the woman from the opposite window might have known, talked with, shook hands with, and then there was struggling and raging inside him, he thought about his new love with deep scorn, called her ugly words, even went to the window to show his wrath. But if the woman opposite him stood there happy and sad, seeing no one but him, then Mihkel Jürimäe relented completely and his feelings were hurled to the opposite extreme: The entire world, all of his thoughts and goals, were channeled into the single path that united their glances. This intense emotional life tired him, though at times he thought that precisely because of it he was a living human being and not a robot from the Ilmarinen factory.

Maire Looke's feeling was pure, unperturbed. This man, obviously older than she, had not said even one vile word to her, as other men did, those who wanted her every once in a while out of loneliness or the thrill of the hunt. He hadn't clouded Maire Looke's image of him in any way, but stood at the window solely for her, and from the very beginning had eyes for no one else. There had to be some kind of catastrophe in his past, a tragic event. Maire Looke felt this clearly and vividly pictured various scenarios. The catastrophe had broken the man, but it had also led to a renewal: His life force sprouted fresh shoots and the plant of his life was filled with love's juices for Maire Looke. She couldn't have imagined a more ideal man, so Maire Looke yielded to her feelings with complete rapture. As she saw it, she was truly in love for the first time in her life, and no reality clouded the feeling. She opened everything within her to that man in the window, she had no regrets about revealing the most secret, dark corners of her soul to him. Maire Looke now had a man, her one and only, for life, the choice had been made, it could no longer be otherwise. And Maire Looke didn't deliberate, hesitate, or weigh, she didn't require a single formality or condition. In this man lay her future life, her posterity, her concerns, and the fulfillment of motherhood.

And in fact Maire Looke was glad that she felt this way, glad that she was a genuine Estonian woman with a beautiful soul for whom a man was not a means of self-affirmation, glad that she herself was free and worthy of respect, and that she surrendered to her feelings of her own free will, not out of a sweet fear in the face of power, not out of calculated designs to set her life up, and not to satisfy petty vanity. She surrendered purely, without question, without demand, following only the call of her heart.

This nightly contemplation signified life and love to both of them; it contained so many nuances a bystander would have overlooked. It had its own tiny caprices, rushes of love, gratification, sometimes little tiffs as well, forgiveness, and all-conquering reconciliation. Even when Maire Looke worked the second shift, they still found time to stand for a little while, despite the late hour, and then they were only silhouettes to each other, which added diversity to life and prevented their mutual attraction from waning.

One day Marie Looke felt nauseous, and a presentiment filled her with joy. The bad days ceased. Maire Looke waited a couple of weeks and then went to the women's clinic on Pärnu Road. She was told that she would become a mother, and a pregnancy chart was filled out. She now went around proudly all day, an involuntary smile perpetually lighting up her face.

She was unable to keep the secret to herself for very long. One evening, as they stood facing each other, Maire Looke pointed at her stomach and smiled at the man. Her heart ached with anticipation of Mihkel Jürimäe's reaction to this. At first he seemed to be startled—perhaps most men react this way, even when they want to have children with their beloved. Then Mihkel Jürimäe smiled back at her. The smile was a bit forced, perhaps, but Maire Looke didn't condemn him for it—a little drama was inevitable in the initial flood of feeling. Now Maire Looke smiled with the well-meaning superiority of a mother-to-be and showed him how much she loved her one and only man.

Mihkel Jürimäe had been startled at first, perhaps out of a sense of responsibility for another human being, something he hadn't felt for a long time. While a sketch of a blast engine on a desk in Ilmarinen's construction department was lifeless and abstract, the young woman and her future child were an entirely different matter. But life experience helped Mihkel Jürimäe quickly overcome his fears—after all, he was becoming a father at an age when a man, tormented by thoughts of extinction, longs for posterity and feels a need to bring his precious genes into being.

During the pregnancy Maire Looke changed rapidly. She was as happy as before, but the first few months she was nauseous a great deal and often had to leave the window. Mihkel Jürimäe would smile at her understandingly and encouragingly; he knew of no other way to help the woman.

In her last months of pregnancy Maire Looke's face became splotchy, but with her innate naturalness, she was not embarrassed to let the man see her this way. Wasn't her suffering his concern as well? Let him have his share of it.

Once, just before Maire Looke went on maternity leave, as she was returning home from work with a gait grown heavy, she couldn't restrain herself: She went into the third entrance of the cooperative apartment house and studied the roster of names. The occupant of the center one-room apartment on the fourth floor was listed as Mihkel Jürimäe. And that is how Maire Looke found out her beloved's name. At home she wrote it in large letters and put the paper on the radio. And to herself she repeated, "Mihkel, Mihkel, Mihkel." In Maire Looke's opinion, there was something incomparably beautiful in that name, like old-fashioned music.

During the final days it became difficult for Maire Looke to stand at the window with her large stomach; she put a chair there, but sitting was even more burdensome. Thus she alternated between sitting and standing, and smiled from time to time at her sweetheart, who kept watch faithfully in his room, but the woman's thoughts were now more with the child drumming in her stomach.

During one such evening hour the pains began. When they subsided Maire Looke rang the doorbell of neighbors who had a telephone and presently an ambulance drove up to Building 249.

Mihkel Jürimäe's heart pounded, for an instant he went numb, then he kneaded his fingers. He was afraid for her, although his reason told him that this was all so natural, life and birth. The woman was led to the ambulance, and it took her away.

That night Mihkel Jürimäe couldn't shut an eye. He thought about the woman, wanted to suffer with her, but from time to time peculiar pale green visions appeared before his eyes that had nothing to do with either giving birth or the future.

He may have dozed off after all, because in the morning, after a cool shower and coffee, he felt completely fresh, and when he went to work distinct problems demanding solutions preoccupied him. They didn't leave him for a second, not even during the department meeting; that day he didn't add a single useful jot to his computations.

In the evening it made no sense for him to stand at the window, although he did so for a moment out of habit; an inexplicable emptiness filled his being. Everything that had been churning inside him for more than a year now was tied to this woman, to her window, but today she was in a safe place, in the hands of attentive doctors, and her room was empty. Mihkel Jürimäe walked around the apartment for a little while, then went out, paused before Building 249, eyed his own window, and tried to experience what the woman must have felt looking at him.

The next day was payday at Ilmarinen. Mihkel Jürimäe bought an armful of carnations at the flower shop, looked around timidly, stuck the flowers in his black briefcase, and went to the maternity clinic on Sakala Street. In the reception room he studied the roster of names and realized with amazement that he didn't know his beloved's name. He read the beautiful names of valiant Estonian women who had given their tiny nationality the gift of new citizens; it was like a joyful round dance, with gaily colored folk costumes flashing by, but he didn't know how to distinguish his one and only among them.

Alas, men are not particularly astute in matters of this kind, but Mihkel Jürimäe did, nevertheless, dare to explain to a woman in a white uniform, who was carrying packages into the wards, that he didn't know the name of the woman to whom he wanted to give the flowers, couldn't she help him in some way? The woman on duty naturally wanted to answer that it was possible to find someone here only by her name, but after she had listened to the man's stammering for a little while and eyed him observantly, she perceived his bewilderment and, for an instant, was seized by the patronizing compassion that women sometimes feel for the pitiable male sex, so she decided to help him. Fortunately, she had a good imagination, as all real women do, and didn't start asking who or how but quickly came up with a moving scenario in her mind: The man had helped a woman who had to be transported to the maternity clinic directly from the street. She asked the man when the woman had been brought to the hospital. Mihkel Jürimäe was able to answer precisely to the hour.

After a long wait the woman in the white uniform returned, and the man learned that at least three women had been brought in at that time. Now the man could give the woman's address, even her building number; the package deliverer thought the matter solved and allowed him to leave the flowers with her. In response to the question, did he want to send a note along as well or at least a name card, Mihkel

Jürimäe hesitated for so long that the woman on duty didn't have time to wait, she had other packages to deliver as well, and she disappeared behind the door where anyone not giving birth was forbidden to go.

Mihkel Jürimäe wandered to the trolley stop full of strange feelings, but Maire Looke received an armful of beautiful carnations, which filled her with joy and soothed the new mother's agitation over the fact that her little daughter had not yet been brought to her to breast-feed.

Soon Maire Looke came home in a taxi. Mihkel Jürimäe was working at the time. In the evening when, out of habit, he looked toward what he assumed would be an empty window, the woman appeared there. She was exactly as she had been before, but stayed for only a brief time, since there was always something she had to do elsewhere. Mihkel Jürimäe understood this and wasn't the least bit angry.

And then she came to the window holding a tiny bundle in her arms, but from that great distance Mihkel Jürimäe could only make out a colorful blanket. Nevertheless, he tried to smile joyfully at the woman for having shown him the child.

After that Maire Looke appeared at the window with the child from time to time, and once she even suckled the child, but became startled and drew the curtain.

When the time came to name the child, and the Bureau of Family Status asked who the child's father was, Maire Looke said clearly and definitely, "Mihkel Jürimäe," but she could give no more information about him, neither his date of birth, nor his place of work, nor anything else. The girl was registered as Inge Looke.

For Mihkel Jürimäe those days were filled with tense thought. His life was, and yet it wasn't, in order. He had a woman and a tiny bundle, and at the same time no one pestered him with needs. He came to the window when he pleased, and the fact that he came every day, as if it had been agreed upon, was his own business, and merely attested to the freshness and steadfastness of his feeling, to his need for a companion, for mutual affection. Wasn't this the ideal marriage men sometimes dream of—to be sure of someone and free at the same time? But once in a while it seemed to him that something was missing. This was particularly true when he lay in bed in the morning on his days off, when his body longed to be touched.

On the next payday Mihkel Jürimäe dropped a quarter of his salary into a mailbox in the fourth entrance of Building 249. And when Maire Looke was offered a subsidy as an unwed mother, she refused it proudly, announcing that the child's father supported her.

The marriage continued. Soon two women appeared at the window facing Mihkel Jürimäe's, one growing older, the other tiny at first, then growing, becoming ever more beautiful, the kindlings of womanhood.

And sometimes the fifty-year-old man had a wondrous longing to see these two women, his own kin, up close, and even touch them with his hand.

1974; first published in Russian 1985.

Translated from the Estonian by Ritva Poom.

THE DETAILS OF
NIKITA VORONTSOV'S LIFE

S. Yaroslavtsev*

> "These are not thoughts," replies the artist. "These are
> fleeting moods. You saw for yourself how they would
> spring up and disappear. Such moods are like soap
> bubbles—they are good only for the astonishment and
> amusement of stupid little kids like you, Your
> Worship."
>
> Dmitry Pisarev

The Bachelor Party

It so happened that on a rainy June evening in the year one thousand
nine hundred and seventy-eight the telephone gave a loud ring in the
apartment of Alexei T., a writer quite well known in the Cultural Section of the Party's Central Committee. When he picked up the receiver, Alexei T. was pleased to discover that the caller was his very
oldest friend, Varakhasy S., now an investigator for the municipal
public prosecutor's office. Roughly the following conversation took
place between them:

After an exchange of the usual not-terribly-decent greetings dating
back to their student days, Varakhasy asked:

"Is your family still in the South?"

"They're coming back in a week," replied Alexei. "Why?"

"Here's why! I sent my women off to Yalta too. Three hours ago.

*S. Yaroslavtsev is the pseudonym of Arkady Strugatsky.

Maybe we can get together? Have a little bachelor party, just you and I. Like in the old days?"

"Right now?"

"Why wait? What an opportunity!"

Alexei T. turned to look at the wide-open window, beyond which rain was falling, splashing, coming down in torrents from the low, cloud-covered sky.

"It is a great opportunity, of course," he said. "Only it's absolutely pouring. . . . And I haven't got a thing in the house and by now the stores—"

"Hush, hush, hush!" Varakhasy began to shout. "I have everything! Just get on over here! And don't be afraid—you won't melt. . . ."

And so they met in the kitchen of a cozy three-room apartment on Bezbozhny Lane, and cans of food were opened (something exotic in tomato sauce and oil), and boiled potatoes sat steaming, and a salami of Finnish origin was sliced into thin petals, and two bottles of vodka were brought out with the promise that if they weren't enough, then something else would turn up too. . . . What more do old friends need? This is what we must do sometimes when the time is right— send the wives and kids packing to the azure shores while we ourselves bask a bit in an asphalt-and-concrete-slab paradise!

After the first round they talked this over, Alexei T., the writer, whose hair was wet and who had put Varakhasy's robe on over his bare body, and Varakhasy S., the investigator, who was wearing shorts and an unbuttoned shirt, as they looked affectionately at each other across the table to the accompaniment of splashing and other water noises from outside.

After the second round, having laid waste to half the can of some-thing in tomato sauce and smearing butter on a potato, Alexei T. de-clared that for the majority of people, generally speaking, the nine-teenth century and even the eighteenth would have completely sufficed, but they found the twentieth century horrible and incomprehensible, and they simply couldn't accept it. After swallowing the potato he even put forth the supposition that no matter what was said out there in Siberia, the people constructing the Baikal-Amur Main Line Rail-road were in essence, deep down inside, driven by the very same motives as Yermak Timofeyevich and Semyon Dezhnyov, the first Cossack explorers.

They polished off the third round, and Varakhasy acknowledged that he was prepared to agree with this to some extent. He suggested that they just take the example of his mother-in-law. The old woman had lived through World War I, the Revolution, the Civil War, ruin and famine, then the purges, then the Great Patriotic War, and so on. She belonged to the generation that bore the entire brunt of the monstrous blow of the twentieth century. And naturally, how could she understand it and how could she help but be horrified? Yet on the other hand . . .

After the fourth round Varakhasy offered to illustrate his point with a graphic example and he turned on the splendid color TV sitting on a special stand in a corner of the kitchen. Apparently some kind of variety show from abroad was on. Germans were performing. A dozen girls wearing brassieres of extremely elaborate design and long bloomers with lace hanging down below the knees were swinging their fannies around a young man in a checked suit who was singing about love. Ah, the German mentality, unchanged since Bismarck's time, brazenly well-intentioned! Frivolous girls in bloomers and vulgar men in checked suits, while behind them—a somber ugly mug under a tall metal helmet. *Hab' Acht!** And bulging soldier's eyes, like a cat's when it's defecating on chopped straw!

Alexei T. began to growl with hatred, and Varakhasy quickly turned off the TV. He admitted that this was not a good example, and he opened the second bottle. But still, he said stubbornly, there are many people who live and think in twentieth-century terms, and these people are becoming more and more numerous every day, and as the end of the twentieth century draws near their number is increasing ex . . . expo . . . basically in a geometric progression.

("Exponentially," he uttered at last, pouring the fifth round. "Hell, I've completely lost my train of thought. What were we talking about?")

Holding his shot glass in front of him like a candle, Alexei T. gloomily proclaimed that the most sickening thing in the world was the worship of power. That was precisely what made an invading enemy loathsome. A gang of thugs attacking a defenseless passerby on the street—they were invading enemies too. Here's to their destruction! To console him Varakhasy immediately described how they had put an end to a group of thugs that had been on the rampage in Sokolniki Park for a long time, but Alexei T., not to be outdone, told Varakhasy how they had caught an employee of the Foreign Commission of the Writers Union stealing some bottles from a banquet table.

Melancholy was relentlessly approaching, and after the sixth round Alexei T. asked Varakhasy to sing. Varakhasy did not refuse; he had

*Be on guard! —Trans.

been wanting to sing for some time now. He went to his study to get his trusty old seven-stringed guitar and said as he got comfortably settled:

"I'll sing you a new song. A lawyer I know sang it at a party a month ago. I liked it very much. It's in Ukrainian, but almost all of it is understandable. Here, listen."

And he began to sing softly in a low, pleasant voice:

> "Let us hurry
> From afar to this place
> Where they know how
> To wait for us forever. . . .
> Wherever you are, my friend,
> Wherever you are, my friend,
> Remember, remember:
> Even the cranes fly back to the house!
> More and more seldom
> Do we write letters
> And we even send
> Holiday greetings in haste.
> But the years are behind us,
> The years are behind us—
> Like bridges, like bridges
> That we can no longer cross. . . ."

This song was strangely beautiful, and it seemed to possess a certain magic, but then, Varakhasy had an excellent ear, and his guitar had a melancholy, insinuating tone, and even the water noises outside seemed to have died down a bit. Alexei T. coughed and asked:

"One more time, please."

Smiling, Varakhasy leaned toward him with the bottle, but he shook his head, covered his glass with the palm of his hand, and repeated:

"One more time."

And Varakhasy sang it one more time, then grabbed the bottle again and threw his friend a questioning look, but Alexei T. shook his head again and said:

"Not right now. Let's switch to tea instead."

Varakhasy set his guitar down and put the teakettle on the stove. Alexei T. actually had tears in his eyes; he cleared his throat hoarsely and said in a constricted voice:

"How true it is . . . 'But the years are behind us . . . like bridges that we can no longer cross. . . .' And basically how sad it is."

And they became cruelly aware that they were already past fifty and that their youthful optimism, their belief that the best lay ahead, would never return, and that the paths of their lives had already been determined long ago, down to the very end, and that these paths could not be changed by their free will but only by worldwide disaster, which would then mean an end to all conceivable paths. It was sad, of course. But on the other hand—the time to take had passed, the time to give back had come.

"Don't be down in the dumps," Varakhasy said gently in Ukrainian. "Let me sing your favorite song instead."

And he sang Alexei's favorite song and then one more favorite, and he sang "Capricious Horses" and "The Submarine," and he sang "On the Road to Smolensk" and "Your Honor, Lady Farewell."

Then they drank a lot of very strong tea (both approved of nothing but the strongest), and Alexei T. described his latest adventures with the literature of their homeland. This was a sweet sore spot with him, his joy and his suffering, his hobbyhorse, and he shouted vehemently:

"What the hell is this? Every bureaucratic, half-baked literary expert wants to give me orders on what I should write about and what I shouldn't! My own knowledge is a hundred times greater than his, and I have perhaps a million times more feelings. Well, I think, just wait, you son of a bitch! And I wrote to the Central Committee, to the Cultural Section. . . ."

Varakhasy listened and kept adding tea to their cups. He found it interesting and somewhat funny. When Alexei fell silent, puffing, he shook his head and said as he always did:

"Yes, old buddy, you lead a turbulent life, no doubt about it."

To which Alexei T., as always, muttered:

"I'd rather it weren't so turbulent."

The friends remained silent for a while. It was already well past midnight; not a single light shone in any of the windows in the apartment building across the way. The downpour had abated, and the sky seemed to have become clear. Suddenly Alexei T. said with a spasm in his throat:

"'But the years are behind us . . . like bridges that we can no longer cross. . . .'"

Varakhasy looked at him quickly, and Alexei T. gave a broken sigh and wiped his eyes with the sleeve of his robe. Then Varakhasy said:

"Listen, man of letters, you don't want to sleep yet, do you?"
Alexei T. dismissed the idea with a feeble wave of his hand.

"Why would I want to sleep?"

"Are you sober?"

Alexei T. became attuned to himself—he stuck out his lips and gingerly rolled his eyes together toward the bridge of his nose.

"I think so," he said at last. "But we'll fix that right now."

He reached for the vodka, but Varakhasy stopped him.

"Wait," said Varakhasy S., investigator for the municipal public prosecutor's office. "There's no rush. First I want to show you something."

He left the kitchen, his bare feet making no sound, and returned a minute later with an official red office folder. Alexei T., the writer, was thoroughly familiar with these folders—produced at the Voskhod Factory, product code 81-53-72, item number 3707 r, priced at 60 kopecks, fastened with white ties. Alexei T. said uneasily:

"What's this? Have you become addicted to the writer's craft too? Then I'd better read it at home, with a clear head—"

"No-o," responded Varakhasy, undoing the white ties. "This is something else, something a bit more curious. . . . Here, take a glance at this."

From the folder he extracted an all-purpose notebook with a black oilcloth cover of very grimy appearance and held it out to his friend. Alexei T. took the notebook with two fingers.

"What's this?" he inquired.

"Just take a look, take a look," said Varakhasy.

The black oilcloth was covered with patches of a whitish film highly repulsive in appearance, although it was completely dry. Alexei T. lifted the notebook to his nose and sniffed cautiously. As he had expected, the notebook smelled. To be more exact, it had a slight odor. The devil only knew of what—some kind of mold.

"Don't go turning up your nose at it," said Varakhasy with a certain amount of irritation. "Man of letters. Open it and start reading from the first page."

Alexei T. sighed and opened the notebook to the first page. An inscription was printed boldly in the middle of it in unpleasant blue-gray ink: THE DIARY OF NIKITA VORONTSOV. The pages of the notebook were ruled into small squares, like graph paper, and the letters, drawn painstakingly and not very skillfully, were each three squares high.

Alexei T. turned the page. It really was a diary. "2 January 1937. I've decided to keep a diary again, starting today, and I hope I won't quit anymore. . . ." The ink was pale. Possibly faded. The handwriting was neat but unsteady, like an adolescent's. It was written with a fine-tipped, steel fountain pen. Alexei T. said with displeasure:

"Listen, this is interesting, of course—a boy's diary from '37—but certainly not at two o'clock in the morning!"

"Just read it, read it," said Varakhasy in a somewhat tense voice. "It's only seven pages long."

And Alexei T. began to read with an air of condescending obedience, whistling soundlessly, but on the third page, approximately in the middle, he stopped blowing, raised one eyebrow, and glanced at Varakhasy.

"Keep reading!" Varakhasy shouted impatiently.

The entries stopped precisely on the seventh page. Alexei T. leafed ahead. The succeeding pages were blank.

"Well?" asked Varakhasy.

"I don't get it," Alexei T. admitted. "What is this—the notes of a madman?"

"No," said Varakhasy, smiling. "Nikita Vorontsov was no madman."

"Aha," said Alexei T. "Then I'll read it once more, if I may."

And he began to read it a second time.

The Diary of Nikita Vorontsov

An entry probably made with a bulb-tipped fountain pen tilted slightly to the left, neat but unsteady adolescent handwriting, ink faded to a reddish-brown:

2 January 1937. I've decided to keep a diary again, starting today, and I hope I won't quit anymore. This morning Serafima and Fedya took Svetka and went off somewhere to visit Fedya's relatives. I went to see if my best friend, Mikael Khachatryan, could come out, and first we played "Battle of the Battalions." Then we started fooling around and had a snowball fight. Mikael carelessly hit me in the face and nearly broke my glasses. We played until lunchtime, when we went to Mikael's and had lunch. After lunch we locked ourselves in his room and argued about girls. Mikael said that he would always be true to Silva Stremberg, and I confessed to him that I'm now in love with Katya Mikhanovskaya. Mikael said that anything is possible, he likes Katya, too, because

she's pretty and blond, but he will still love Silva no matter what happens to her, otherwise he'd be a traitor. We had a falling-out, and I went home. I'm home alone now and I started a diary. In the future I must keep a diary without fail.

3 January 1937. Yesterday my family got back late, Fedya was very drunk, Serafima was cussing, and Svetka was whining and asleep on her feet. Serafima and Fedya went to work in the morning while I lay around in bed till ten o'clock and read *The Roof of the World*. A great book. I would have read even more, but Svetka woke up and started whining because she was hungry. We got up and had breakfast, and she went off to see her girlfriends. I read a little more, but then I started getting kind of bored, and suddenly Mikael showed up. He said that yesterday he'd been a little hasty. In short, we made up. I must honestly confess that I like Mikael very much. He's my best friend. We went out to play and made an agreement to sign up for a boxing class but not tell anybody about it, and one fine day we'll meet up with Murza and his Fascists, and God have mercy on them! After lunch I lit a fire in the stove and told Svetka scary stories. I left the light off on purpose. It's very funny how scared she gets but still asks me to tell more stories.

4 January 1937. I wanted to lie around again in the morning and read a little, but Svetka got up at eight o'clock just as if this weren't vacation at all. I had to get up and feed her. In a fit of anger, I cuffed her on the back of the head. How many times have I vowed not to do that! She doesn't start bawling, you see, she just sticks out her lips and looks at you with those round eyes. I can't stand it. I had to tell her a fairy tale and also take her out with me to play, and after we played I had to take her with me to Mikael's. What didn't I do! And the way Susanna Amovna, Mikael's mother, clucked over her, the way she combed her hair, stroked her, stuffed her with all kinds of delicious things—it was enough to try the patience of a saint. But we were actually better off. We managed to play a fierce game of chess as well as figure out the Amateur Chemist set that Mikael's father bought yesterday. Tomorrow we're going to do experiments.

An entry probably made with the same bulb-tipped pen but not tilted, firm printing, the same reddish-brown ink:

testing testing testing

there is no way for me to die

some are taken up, some down, but I am taken back again, start all over from the beginning

I shall die 8 (eight) June 1977 (seventy-seven) at 11:15 P.M. Moscow time.

An entry made with the same pen, hasty cursive with splatters and scratches on the paper, the same reddish-brown ink:

Sashka Shkryabun (summer '41, went to Kiev with his parents, missing)

Boris Valkevich

Sara Iosifovna

Kostya Sherstobitov (wounded at the Drut, June '44; married Lyubasha from Medvedkovo, fall '47)

Grishka the Wild Boar, sapper

2d. Lt. Sirotin

Sgt. Pisyun

Gromoboev, coward

light mach. gun. with a wart on his eyelid (+near Bolychovo)

Foma, well-equipped with a full soldier's bag

Mariana, first-aid instructor (+at the Ruza near Ivanovo)

Battalion Commander Chereda (+at Yadromin?)

obsessively neat gun layer (Ilchin? Ilmin? Ilkin?)

Kapitonov (shop supervisor in '55)

Styosha (son will die, suicide, look into it)

Belsky, smokeless technology, patent (several formulas, hastily sketched blueprint)

Tosovich, karate

Verochka Korneyeva, *she* is Vorontsova, *she* is Neko-chan

Firm printing again in the same reddish-brown ink:

It's useless. Memory.

I shall rise from the dead 6 (six) January 1937 (thirty-seven) on the night of the sixth and seventh in bed. Watch out! Don't thrash around! Lying motionless, count to a hundred, then turn over onto your stomach, hang your head over the edge of the bed, open your mouth, and inhale and exhale deeply several times, sticking out your tongue.

Svetka's bed is on the left, Fedya and Serafima are across the hall.

An entry made with a dull pencil, huge letters all over the place, barely legible:

New Year's, New Year's
I wonder, has Gurchenko been born yet?
Dark braids, a pensive gaze
Sexual-alcoholic excesses at age fifteen
Ah, what are you! Oh, what are you saying! Oh, where are you going! Oh, why are you doing this! Ai! Oh.
Vorontsov! Stop that chattering!
Three fifteen six twelve, and here's an ice-cream bar for Svetka
Ai-yai-yai, Galina Rodionovna!
A slipup. Last time it was: I'll remain here a little longer with you, Galina, if I may. . . . But now it's blunt: Do what you want, but I'm going to stay here with you. However, I stayed then and I stayed now. And the time before that, too, it seems. A convergence of different versions.
But this time Bonaparte, but this time Bonaparte crossed the border!
Ai-yai-yai, Galina Rodionovna!

An entry in high-quality black ink, obviously a fountain pen:

21 August 1941. I'm hiding my diary in its usual place until '46.
All quiet on the Western Front again.
Oh, have mercy on me just this one time! Why do you wish to toy with me like this!

An entry made with a low-quality steel fountain pen, low-quality violet ink:

9 April 1946. My whole life, 31 years, still remains. Let's live it up!
Grisha the Wild Boar, a sapper, was crushed by a tank near Istra. And his whole family has perished; there's no one to give his medal to.
Fedya, as always, was killed in '42 during the retreat from Kharkov. Serafima has wasted away, she's nothing but skin and bones. But Svetka has developed into the most beautiful filly.

The Killing on Granovsky Avenue

Alexei T. closed the notebook and carefully placed it on the edge of the table.

"An odd style," he said prudently. "What can it mean—'killed, as always'? Listen, this isn't . . . a hoax?"

"No," replied Varakhasy. "But is that all that surprises you?"

"N-no, of course not. . . . Listen, are you sure this isn't a hoax?"

"I'm sure. Unfortunately, I'm sure."

"Why 'unfortunately'?" Alexei T. was surprised.

"Because, dear fellow, I'm not a man of letters but an investigator for the public prosecutor's office, and I don't like insoluble problems in real life."

The friends fell silent for a while. It had grown completely light outside; the sky above the facing building had become clear and turned a pale light blue. And it was still, still with the distinctive stillness of the white nights in June.

"All right," said Alexei T. "You get your way. You've shaken me up. You can be satisfied. Now, if you'll allow me, it's my turn. May I ask questions?"

"If you wish," said Varakhasy S., investigator for the municipal public prosecutor's office. "Ask me anything. Even questions I can't answer."

It was obvious to the naked eye that he was pleased. Alexei T. collected his thoughts.

"So," he said. "First of all. Who is this Nikita Vorontsov? Or no, first tell me how this little notebook ended up at the public prosecutor's office. That will be more interesting."

"If you wish," Varakhasy consented, and told him the story.

Late in the evening on June 8 of last year a murder was committed on Granovsky Avenue. The witnesses, Jane Doe, a retired woman, and John Doe, an elderly artist, who had been walking their dogs nearby, described the incident this way. On the sidewalk beneath the windows of a sixteen-story monstrosity five hulking young men were tinkering with a motorcycle. The motorcycle was making an awful roar, and half-naked men and women had already begun to lean out of the windows and shout indignantly, and by then the witnesses, according to them, were all ready to go up to these young men and reproach them for disturbing the peace and quiet when suddenly an elderly man wearing a white linen suit and carrying a cane appeared from somewhere, approached the group of motorcyclists, and said something. It was probably about the noise the group was making. Immediately all five hulking young men closed in menacingly around the elderly man. The witnesses did not hear their discussion—the roar of the motorcycle drowned everything out. They only saw how the elderly man placed his cane on the chest of one of the young men who was crowding him more than the others; next came an exchange of inaudible retorts, after which the elderly man lowered his cane, but the young man swung around and shoved a fist into his face with great force. Then, as if on purpose, the motorcycle fell silent. The elderly man, toppled by the punch, fell straight back like a stick, and in the ensuing silence they clearly heard his head strike the edge of the sidewalk with a crack. And, strictly speaking, that's how it all ended. The hulking scoundrels stood there indecisively for about half a minute and then, convinced that their victim was not moving, they rushed off in all directions without a word except for one young man, who hung around the ill-fated motorcycle. After a minute the brutally tortured motorcycle started up again, and he raced off too. Only then did the witnesses, dumbfounded with surprise and horror, simultaneously run over to the elderly man. He lay stretched out on the asphalt with his arms spread apart and his eyes wide open. He was dead. And only then did the weak-sighted old woman recognize the man as a neighbor from her section of the apartment building; he lived in a two-room apartment on the sixteenth floor.

"That was . . . him?" said Alexei T., half certain, tapping the diary with his fingers.

"Yes, that was indeed Nikita Sergeyevich Vorontsov," said Varakhasy. "Here's an interesting detail, a curiosity, if you will. The female witness testified that a few minutes before the incident her dog, a regal poodle named King, had whined and strained at his leash, trying to drag his owner to the place where the tragedy was about to occur. And the male witness, on the contrary, recalled that his dog, a mongrel mutt named Agate, had tried to pull his owner away in exactly the same manner. But this, of course, has no bearing on the case."

"Bastards," said Alexei T., thirsting for retribution. "But at least they caught them, didn't they?"

"That very night," Varakhasy readily replied. "And they fell apart on the spot. They weren't inveterate criminals, after all, just badly brought-up imbeciles. Perhaps there's something else of interest to you?"

"Please excuse me." Alexei T. suddenly snapped back to attention. "Go on."

"Well, sir," Varakhasy went on, "they gave this case to me—I was still working in that district then."

The case seemed crystal clear. The testimony of the witnesses and of the extremely frightened friends of the defendant agreed completely with the testimony of the defendant himself, whose enormous fist had smeared tears and snot all over his unshaven mug, which was twisted with horror and grief. Reckless manslaughter, Article 106 of the Criminal Code of the Russian Republic, up to three years in the camps or up to two years of correctional labor. A few formalities remained to be carried out.

Because the dead man had lived alone, Varakhasy first of all made an inspection of his apartment, according to regulations, with the object of compiling an inventory of his things, his furniture and so on. During the inspection, incidentally, a few items were discovered that clearly did not belong to the dead man: in the hallway—women's slippers and shoes, size thirty-four; in the bathroom—a coquettish women's dressing gown on a hook, perfume, lotions, and sundry feminine bric-a-brac on the vanity; in the bedroom—a couple of women's nightgowns. But most important—in one of the locked writing-table drawers, buried under layers of licenses, diplomas, certificates, decorations, and other important documents, this very same diary had turned up in a tightly sealed envelope of thick paper. Varakhasy glanced through it quickly right there, at the table, and then went over it twice, attentively reading the contents of the notebook, which smelled slightly of mold, put it back in the envelope, and stuck the envelope into his briefcase.

He sealed the apartment and returned to his office at the district public prosecutor's. The coroner's report was already lying on his desk. Varakhasy read it and groaned. The crystal-clear case had become muddy. Falling after a hard punch in the face, Nikita Sergeyevich Vorontsov had indeed hit the back of his head on the edge of the sidewalk and fractured his skull, and this actually could have served as the cause of instantaneous death were it not for one circumstance. To wit: Even the punch in the face (on the right cheekbone—the hulking imbecile was left-handed), not to mention the blow to the head against the concrete curb, had taken place at least five or six seconds after the onset of Vorontsov's clinical death. The hulking imbecile had struck a man who was already dead.

"How's that?" said Alexei T., startled. "If I understood you correctly, Vorontsov was standing up—"

"Well, so what if he was standing? He'd died but hadn't had time to fall over. Stranger things than that happen! That's not the point."

"And what did he die of?"

"I don't recall," said Varakhasy impatiently. "It said in the report, but I've forgotten now. Something like an acute heart spasm. That's not the point, I tell you!"

"Yes, yes, forgive me. Please go on."

"I will. Can you imagine my position?"

"I certainly can. It's one thing if they knocked a man off his feet and he fell down and was killed. And it's quite another if they hit a corpse. Not a pretty deed either, of course, but is it a crime? Right?"

Varakhasy gave a loud laugh.

"Approximately," he said. "To make a long story short, the most uninteresting and tedious scribbling lay ahead of me. I got right to work on it without losing a second of valuable time. And then, when I came to the old concluding sentence . . . uh . . . 'Comparing the testimony of the witnesses and the coroner's findings, it is possible to establish with sufficient certainty that clinical death occurred at 11:15 P.M.—'"

"Stop! Stop!" exclaimed Alexei T., and he grabbed the notebook from the table. "When did you say this happened?"

"On the eighth of last June, in the year one thousand nine hundred seventy-seven," replied Varakhasy, grinning.

Alexei T. found the right page in the notebook and read aloud in a breathless voice:

"'I shall die on the eighth of June in the year one thousand nine hundred seventy-seven at 11:15 P.M. Moscow time.'"

"That's just the way I grabbed this very notebook then too," said Varakhasy. "Rather interesting, isn't it?"

"I'll say! Well, then what?"

"Then . . . All right, I'm an old hand—I don't keep secrets from my boss. I showed this little notebook to the prosecutor to get his reaction. It was just what I'd expected—'a fake, a madman, chance coincidence, don't try to pull my leg, what's the matter, don't you have any other cases?' And I decided to try to unravel this mystery on my own. In a private capacity, so to speak, but with discretionary use of my official position."

"And rightly so!" Alexei T. exclaimed enthusiastically.

"Right or not, I don't know. But I just had a feeling that this little matter was opening up onto an abyss that not a single human eye had ever glanced into before. And I began, as you yourself can understand, with the biography of the deceased."

The Biography of Nikita Sergeyevich Vorontsov

Nikita Sergeyevich Vorontsov was born in Moscow in 1923. His parents died when he was three years old, and he was left in the care of an older sister (by their father's first marriage) named Serafima, who was then twenty and worked at a factory called the Hammer and Sickle (formerly Guzhon's). And this Serafima was obviously a kind young woman: Although a three-year-old boy complicated her life terribly, she did not palm him off onto an orphanage but put him in a nursery school and later, when he was a little bigger, she placed him in day care at the factory.

A year after that Serafima married Fyodor Krivonosov, who worked in the same shop she did, and three years after that their daughter, Svetlana, was born. From the looks of it, Nikita loved his niece, and he also had an excellent relationship with Fyodor.

The family occupied two rooms in a huge brick apartment house on Andronievskaya Street, in a communal apartment whose dimensions are unbelievable by present standards. Even now a couple of old folks still live there who remember Serafima and Fyodor, and Nikita, and Svetlana, but I didn't succeed in ascertaining anything specific about Nikita from them: Everything became too jumbled in their poor memories during the stormy years that followed.

Nikita graduated from high school in 1940, and although he was an excellent student and just barely fell short of getting straight A's, he did not wish to continue his studies and began working at the renowned Hammer and Sickle Factory under the supervision of Fedya, who by that time had become a foreman.

Then the war broke out.

Nikita volunteered immediately. He was apparently a splendid soldier and did not spare himself: two wounds, shell shock, an Order of Glory, three Red Stars, two medals "For Valor." When the war ended he was in Mukden—

("Where? Where?" Alexei T. asked him to repeat.

"Now it's called Shenyang," Varakhasy S. explained.

"Where is that?"

"Why, it's in China! In Manchuria!"

"A-a-ah . . . Yes, yes, of course. Forgive me.")

Nikita was discharged in the middle of '46 and went back to his native Andronievskaya Street. Things were bad there. Fyodor had been killed. Serafima was living with some jerk of a major from the war commandant's office and was drinking pretty heavily. Svetlana had gotten mixed up with a gang of thieves or hoodlums.

Without wasting any time, Nikita first of all went back to work again at the factory, in his old shop, quickly made himself at home there, and then sized up his family situation and silently rushed into battle. First he brutally beat up the jerk who was ordering Serafima around like a servant. There could have been a good deal of unpleasantness, but the major was a married man and a Party member and he hushed the matter up. Shortly after that he returned to his quarters on the base, alluding to an order from his superiors, and then he completely faded away for good. And the unhappy Serafima must have reproached Nikita bitterly!

Or perhaps not so bitterly, because Nikita then turned his full attention to his niece. And he managed to bring her around, to separate her from her dangerous friends, and by hook or by crook to get her a job at the factory as an accounting clerk—she had quit school back in '44 after just barely making it through the mandatory seven years.

But all these are details and perhaps superfluous at this point.

In 1947, Nikita enrolled in night school at the Moscow Institute of Steel and Alloys, graduated in 1952, and was assigned to his shop as the engineer in charge of one shift.

In 1955, Serafima died of a heart attack. In 1956, Svetlana got married and volunteered to go work in the North. Nikita Vorontsov was alone. Here it is appropriate to note that he remained that way, a bachelor, to the end of his days. Judging from several facts, this was through no fault of the women.

In 1957 he was transferred from the Hammer and Sickle to one of the top-secret research institutes. In 1972 he got an apartment on Granovsky Avenue and left the old nest on Andronievskaya Street.

He died late in the evening on June 8, 1977. He was fifty-four years old.

"That's all?" asked Alexei T., somewhat disappointed.

"That's all, if you don't count the details," replied Varakhasy. "Do you want to see what he looked like?"

"Yes, of course."

Varakhasy took a photograph out of the red folder and handed it to his friend. It was a standard six-by-nine-centimeter photo. An ordinary face, probably unremarkable in any way, of an elderly man. Receding hairline, thinning hair neatly combed straight back. Rather deep-set eyes half veiled by puffy lids. Sharp creases along the sides of a dry, tightly closed mouth. Clean-shaven. What else? Ears slightly protruding. A gray jacket over a black sweater buttoned to the top. An absolutely ordinary man.

"It's a pity that his eyes hardly show," said Alexei T., returning the photograph.

"Uh-huh," responded Varakhasy. "You hit the nail on the head. It's a real pity."

"Why is that?"

"As one lady put it, Nikita Sergeyevich's eyes were terrifying, wise, and melancholy. And other people who knew him unanimously confirm that he had a strange gaze. Although unanimous, they expressed themselves in different ways, it's true—"

"Sure," said Alexei T. "I understand. But now get on with it . . . all the details."

It was already light, the sky had become a piercing blue, and pink reflections of the rising sun were falling on the upper stories of the building across the way.

The Details About Nikita Vorontsov

"As I've already informed you," said Varakhasy S., "I decided to try to unravel this mystery and I went about it according to all the rules of our art. I visited the military registration and enlistment office, the Hammer and Sickle Factory, and that top-secret institute. I studied his biography in the most thorough fashion possible, you might say, and just imagine, absolutely nothing turned up there that might shed any light at all on the peculiarities in the diary. That is, he actually did go to the front with his unit at the end of August '41, he actually did see combat west of Moscow and cross the Drut River three years later, and five years ago he and a certain Belsky received a patent for some kind of smokeless technology. But this didn't bring me one step closer to unraveling the mystery.

"All right, these things happen. The time had come to concentrate on our hero's closest surroundings—his friends, relatives, acquaintances, and so on—to ascertain the details of his private and even highly personal life. As an honest man I must confess that, strictly speaking, I had no right to do this, but the dead feel no pain, and by then I couldn't stop. I sensed, I just sensed that something vast, something almost global, lay hidden behind this little mystery. . . . But you will see and you can judge for yourself.

"I interrogated about twenty people. The majority of them had nothing interesting to report. He was a good fellow, a sociable guy, an outstanding expert in his field, such a sweet, kind man . . . that type of thing. He liked and knew how to drink; when he told stories you'd split your sides laughing; he would often take on the authorities and stick up for those who had been wronged; he practically dragged so-and-so out from under a court action; he got so-and-so a place for his kid in a special children's sanitorium by practically beating it out of the All-Union Central Trade Union Council itself; he wasn't afraid of anything; he asked for nothing for himself; he publicly slapped a good friend in the face for brutish behavior toward an older female technologist. Well, he did pinch someone now and then, that can't be denied. To make a long story short, he was simply an angel in the flesh. Apropos of this, I ran across a certain Bobkov, who used to be a self-defense instructor but is now a drunk with an offended, scornful expression on his face. Nikita Sergeyevich took lessons from him in the mid-fifties and was his best student. As Bobkov put it, 'With him, with Nikita, even if you had to eat shit, he'd snatch it right out of your mouth. That's the kind of guy he was.'

"And only five people gave me any truly valuable information—but alas, it only deepened the mystery. If, of course, you regard it in the same old way, from a prosecutor's commonsense point of view. Here's who these people were."

(From his red folder Varakhasy took out several sheets of paper fastened together with a massive paper clip from his office.)

"Vera Fominichna Samokhina, née Korneyeva, age forty-six, a chemical technologist and coworker of Vorontsov's at the top-secret institute; met him in 1958.

"Valentina Mirlenova Samokhina, Vera Samokhina's daughter, age twenty-four, employed at the Patent Library; met Vorontsov in 1974 and became his lover.

"Svetlana Fyodorovna Panikeyeva, née Krivonosova, age forty-seven, housewife, Vorontsov's niece.

"Mikael Grikorovich Khachatryan, age fifty-four, retired captain senior grade, school friend of Vorontsov's.

"And, finally, Konstantin Panteleyevich Sherstobitov, age fifty-five, an employee of the Mytishche Machinery Plant, wartime friend of Vorontsov's; met him in '42 in a reserve regiment.

"Well, sir, that's it. I taped all the conversations and afterward, naturally, I erased the ones I didn't need, but I did keep the recordings of my conversations with these five and even made excerpts from them, whatever seemed most interesting to me. It would take too much time to play all the tapes one after another, so why don't I read you the excerpts and make comments when necessary. All right?"

(Alexei T. hurriedly began to nod his head, indicating that yes, it was fine with him, then poured some vodka into their glasses, polished his off, and washed it down with cold tea, after which he said in a lowered voice:

"Go on, read.")

"Okay," said Varakhasy, who likewise polished off his vodka and likewise washed it down with cold tea. "Let's start reading. We'll go right to Vera Fominichna Samokhina. I was drawn straight to her by that entry in the diary, remember? 'Verochka Korneyeva, *she* is Vorontsova, *she* is Neko-chan.' I'll read the transcript:

"'We met at some party. I don't remember anymore if it was somebody's birthday or some holiday. It's hard to say—a quarter of a century has gone by! But on the other hand, I remember as if it were yesterday that he sat almost opposite me at the table and looked at me constantly. I saw this out of the corner of my eye, that he was looking at me constantly, but whenever I looked at him, he'd already managed to lower his eyes. Well, I was twenty-six then and, sure, men didn't ignore me, but it was still flattering. But that's not the point. Later, when they moved the table aside and started dancing, he asked me to dance, and that's when I looked him straight in the eye for the first time. It was like an electric shock went through me. No, no, don't think it was anything male/female. . . . His eyes were somehow so . . . terrifying, as if they were wise and melancholy or something. I mean the eyes themselves were ordinary, gray-green, but the way he gazed. . . . I decided right away—no, this knight in shining armor is not for me. He was perfectly cheerful, spoke of interesting things, told jokes quite well, and one or two women were openly after him. But we didn't look each other in the eye anymore.'

"'Was your husband also at this party?'

"'N-no . . . Oh, no, he'd stayed home with Valka. She was just a little kid then, three years old, maybe four. And that's when the strangest thing happened. I was tired, and I'd also gotten pretty drunk, and I

sat down on the couch to rest. And Vorontsov immediately sat down
beside me. He sat down next to me—I remember it very well—folded
his hands in his lap, and said to me softly without looking at me,
"Don't worry, Vera Fominichna, everything will turn out all right with
your tonsils." I just stared at him. I actually did have something wrong
with my tonsils, ever since childhood, and in recent years I'd always
been meaning to have them removed and couldn't bring myself to do
it, but how could he possibly have known about this? I asked him,
"How do you know about my tonsils?" Then he leaned toward me and
said practically in a whisper, "That's not all I know about you, Vera
Fominichna. For instance, I know that you have a charming birthmark on—" And he named, pardon me, a place on the body that you
don't even show your husband very often. I froze, my mouth fell open,
I didn't know whether I should slap his face or just what I should do,
but he got up and left. He left the party altogether.'

"'But do you have a birthmark?'

"'That's just the point, I do. And on that very spot!'

"'And everything turned out all right with your tonsils?'

"'Everything went splendidly. Believe it or not, I somehow instantly
stopped being afraid and went in for the operation literally the next
week. And I came out of it with flying colors. Tell me, Inspector. I see
that you are concerned with Vorontsov even after his death. Do you
also think he was some kind of sorcerer or clairvoyant?'

"'And what do you yourself think, Vera Fominichna? I never looked
him in the eye when he was alive, you see, but you spent nearly two
decades with him at least, side by side in the same institution, you
probably associated with each other, talked with each other. What kind
of impression did you form?'

"'I don't even know what to say. To tell you the truth, we never associated with each other after that. Except in our work. And if we ran
into each other in the hallway or at the snack bar—"hello," "hi," that
was it. Though of course . . . two whole decades have gone by, all
sorts of things happened during that time, a lot has been forgotten, but
I see him at that party as if it were yesterday.'

"'And he didn't speak to you once after that?'

"'Not once. He probably sensed . . .'

"'What?'

"'Why, Inspector, I was afraid of him, you see! I feared him like the
plague. The way children fear the bogeyman. When Valka told me
she'd taken up with him, I trembled for a week with fear and grief. It's

funny to recall now, but I was even straining at the bit to file a protest with the Party committee, with the police, God knows where else.
It's a good thing my husband held me back. That would have been
great—an old scoundrel seduced a poor little girl, but the poor little
girl happened to be twenty-three. . . .'

"'By the way, how did Valka take Vorontsov's death?'

"'You know, she took it surprisingly calmly. Not a word, not a
tear . . . It's possible she didn't love him all that much.'

"'Possibly . . . Tell me, Vera Fominichna, did anyone ever call you
by this nickname—Neko-chan?'

"'Neko-chan? No, this is the first time I've ever heard it. What is it?'

"'It's a Japanese word. It means "kitty."'

"'Kitty . . . When I was a child my mama called me "Kitty." . . .'"

"That's all from Samokhina," said Varakhasy. "Are you impressed?"

"Yes, I am," said Alexei T. "I wonder where that birthmark of hers
was located?"

"Degenerate," said Varakhasy with disgust.

"Sorry. I was only kidding. Keep reading."

Varakhasy rustled his papers.

"And next we come to Samokhina's daughter," he said. "Valentina
Mirlenovna. A charming individual, let me tell you. Well, sir, she was
the first one I talked to; she came to me herself—she appeared with a
request to retrieve her things, which were still in Vorontsov's apartment. So we talked for a while. I'll read the transcript:

"'How did we become acquainted? Very simply and altogether quite
by accident. In October . . . no, in November of last year my boss
instructed me to do a quick review of a reference book on the Austrian
system of licensing patents. And I didn't know a word of German—I
studied English in college—but this was my first real assignment at
work, and pride played a part in it too. Well, I surrounded myself with
dictionaries, started plugging away at the text, used up one day, then
another, and was still on the first page. No, I thought, I won't get anywhere this way. I began to think about what to do. I went down the list
of all my friends and acquaintances—as luck would have it, nobody
knew German. Some knew English, some knew Spanish, one even
knew Esperanto, but not a single one knew German. Then I decided
to drag my parents into it—maybe they knew of somebody. I went to
them and—it was a Saturday, I remember—my mother had company,
two couples from her institute. This is the situation, comrades, I told

them. Help a poor child. I need an expert in the German language right away. Why, nothing could be simpler, they cried. Our Vorontsov, Nikita Sergeyevich, knows German perfectly. And Uncle Seva got out a notebook on the spot and gave me his home phone number. My mother kicked up a fuss. Don't you dare bother the man, she said, but they pelted her with arguments, saying that Vorontsov was a good guy, that he'd think nothing of it, and so forth. Well, I went out into the hallway, to the telephone. I called him, identified myself, and told him the reason why I was invading his privacy. He was silent for a few seconds and then said softly, very calmly, "I'll be glad to help you, Valka. I'm not busy. You can even come over right now . . ." and he gave me his address. And I went to see him then and there.'

"'And did he help you?'

"'He didn't help me—he did the whole thing himself. When I went to see him after work two days later, as we'd agreed, the review was all ready—two typed copies, everything in order. I started to thank him, but he shook his head and said, "Don't, Valka. It's in my own interest for you and me not to work today but to drink champagne. . . ." And at that moment his eyes were unusual—sad and somehow shining—I've never seen such eyes on anyone else. That's probably the moment I fell in love with him. Okay, I'm a decisive person. I picked up the receiver right in front of him and called home to tell them I would be spending the night with a girlfriend. . . .'

"'Love at first sight, so to speak. . . .'

"What's this—irony?'"

(Varakhasy interrupted his reading.

"I've already told you," he said, "that this girl proved to be a charming individual. And she talked to me willingly, as if she'd just been waiting for an opportunity to speak out. But when I joked about love at first sight, her face became violently distorted. That is, I say 'distorted' while in fact it remained beautiful, only different somehow.")

"'What's this—irony?'

"'No irony intended, Valentina Mirlenovna, God forbid. . . .'

"'You didn't know him. What's more, nobody knew him, not even his closest friends. I was the only one who knew him, probably because he was the first man in my life. I loved him to distraction. Although from that very night I knew, I sensed, that this happiness would not be mine for long. . . .'

"'Did he tell you that he was going to die soon?'

"'That's nonsense! He couldn't have told me that. He was healthy, he was completely healthy and affectionate beyond words. My mother was never as affectionate with me as he was. Only once . . .'

"'What?'

"'Not long before . . . Well, about two weeks before his death he suddenly said to me out of the clear blue one night—I'd already drifted off to sleep—he said loudly and clearly, "We must part soon," and I asked him through my drowsiness, "Why?" And he replied, "Because you must go on, but I must go back, Neko-chan. . . ."'

"'Excuse me, what did he call you?'

"'Neko-chan. That's what he called me sometimes. He'd been in Manchuria once and fallen in love with a Japanese woman there, and she'd taught him to call her that. It's a term of endearment. Neko-chan. I liked it very much when he called me that.'"

"Now we come to a man," said Varakhasy. "Konstantin Panteleyevich Sherstobitov, former army buddy of Vorontsov's. He told me a lot of curious things, and I copied out parts of many of his stories, but I'm not going to read everything, just a small excerpt. Listen."

"'. . . Over there, on the other side of the Drut, is where they got me. We'd torn across the Drut, but as soon as we came out onto a precipice—bang-bang, and I didn't remember a thing. I was already in the medical battalion when I came to. Half my leg was completely gone, it ached—I had no strength, I was weeping, but what could you do? All right. And then, an hour before they sent me to the rear, Nikita showed up. Alive and well, all covered with dust, grinning from ear to ear, his left arm in a sling—they'd hit him, too, but it was a light wound, and he'd stayed in formation. How he'd forced his way through to me I don't know, I couldn't say. Well, we hurriedly exchanged a few words about this and that—our new battalion commander, it turned out, had been killed too—we kissed each other good-bye, and then he stuck a folded piece of paper into my hand and said to me, "You do just what I've written down here, and don't you forget," he said, "or else after our victory I'll find you myself, and even though you're disabled now, I'll knock your nose out of joint for old times' sake." And he ran off. Well, I unfolded the piece of paper and read it. I don't remember now exactly how it was worded—many years have gone by—but the message went like this—that in the fall of '47, when I marry Lyubasha from Medvedkovo, I should invite him to the wedding without fail. That was it.'

"'And what did you think then, Konstantin Panteleyevich?'

"'What did I think . . . At the time I'd never even heard of any Lyubasha from any Medvedkovo. The first thing I thought then was that Nikita simply wanted to cheer me up this way, as if to say, never mind, life goes on, even without a leg you're a great guy, don't hide in the shadows, we'll meet again after the war. But then I recalled all sorts of incidents with him, the ones I've already told you about, and you know, Inspector, I'm not going to hide the fact that my spirits rose. But I confess that later on, while I was lying around in hospitals, I somehow sort of forgot about all this. And I mislaid that note, and I ended up suffering quite a bit—they performed two more operations on me, you see. In short, I only thought about it four years later, in the summer of '47.'

"'Please tell me about it.'

"'All right. This has an interesting ending. I was already working at the Mytishche Plant. Once I stayed late in the shops—I was working overtime—it was the end of August, the evenings were already dark, and what's more, it had been raining constantly. Well, I was hobbling home, and it was awfully dark and awfully muddy, and the whole street was nothing but potholes! And the wooden sidewalk hadn't been fixed since before the war. And I fell crashing into some pit. And I jammed my stump right into the ground. Lord, did I see stars! I sat there, I couldn't get up, I just moaned now and then. And suddenly there was this gentle voice above me—"What's the matter, sir? Are you hurt?" I looked up—there was a white dress next to a gate. "Yes, young lady," I said. "And how could I avoid it when you've dug foxholes by your house and I have only one leg!" To make a long story short, she helped me up, took me to her room, made me sit down on her couch, and began fussing over me. And she said in passing, "The street out there is certainly in bad shape, only this house isn't mine. I'm just renting a room here," she said. "I live in Medvedkovo." "And what's your name?" I asked. "My name is Lyuba." There! It was like lightning flashed in my head—I remembered everything all at once.'

"'And did you get married?'

"'Of course we did. What else could we do? And what's more, let me tell you—we've lived happily together for thirty years, raised two sons—'

"'Did you invite Vorontsov to the wedding?'

"'Absolutely! I found him through the address bureau, he was living somewhere on Bolshaya Andronievskaya Street then, I visited his place once or twice afterwards. Yes, he was at my wedding, all right. . . .

Only here's what came of it. The day before we were supposed to go to the registry office, I stupidly told Lyubasha the whole story—'

"'Why do you say "stupidly"?'

"'It turned out to be a stupid thing to do. During the wedding Lyuba kept sizing him up and every now and then she seemed to shudder or something. True, he probably didn't notice anything. He was jovial, he kissed us, drank heartily, ate, shouted "the wine is bitter—sweeten it with a kiss!" Only sometime after that Lyuba and I had a discussion about him, and she said to me, "If you love me," she said, "stay away from him." I was awfully surprised. "Why?" I asked. "He has an evil eye," she said, "a sinister eye." I laughed at her, I tried to shame her, I even got mad, but she wouldn't budge. She kept repeating the same thing—"If you love me . . ." Well, what could you do with her? I saw Nikita a couple of times behind her back, and then our paths just went in different directions.'"

Alexei T. took the diary again and found the entry: "Kostya Sherstobitov (wounded at the Drut, June '44; married Lyubasha from Medvedkovo, fall '47)."

"An ordinary case of clairvoyance," he muttered sarcastically, and put the diary back on the table. "Keep reading."

"Next," said Varakhasy, "with your permission we come to one more man. Mikael Grikorovich Khachatryan, retired captain senior grade, childhood friend of Vorontsov's. I'll read the excerpt:

"'So Nikita is dead. . . . Ah, so many people are dying all around! My mama just died too. True, she was almost eighty. . . . I'm sorry to hear about Nikita, very sorry. Of all the males in our class, he and I were probably the only two still alive—the war gobbled up the rest. . . . So you want to know about him during our school days. . . . Hmm . . . Please forgive my curiosity, but why does this interest you?'

"'I'm actually interested in whether you noticed any sort of peculiarities, incongruities, even abnormalities in the character, habits, or opinions of Nikita Vorontsov when he was a schoolboy.'

"'Hmm . . . It's quite likely that Nikita really was a strange boy to some extent. Hmm . . . We were great friends . . . wild horses couldn't drag us apart, as the saying goes, but frankly speaking, I was sometimes rather afraid of him. He acted somehow too grown up, too much at attention, if you understand what I'm trying to say, too reserved. And if he let himself go, it was just plain terrifying!'

"'I'm afraid I don't quite follow.'

"'I'll give you a couple of examples that should make it clear. Hmm . . . There was this gang of ruffians in our school, about ten delinquents under the leadership of a certain Grishka-Murza. I don't know what they didn't like about Nikita and me, but they started picking fights with us. Wherever they ran into us, they'd pick a fight. They'd take our lunches and our pocket money, they'd tear off our caps and throw them somewhere. You yourself know how it is with adolescents. Primitive cruelty. Hmm . . . Nikita and I put up with this for about two years, maybe even three. . . . I don't recall. We didn't rat on them, of course, and besides, ratting on them would have been useless. And then one day they ran into us on the way home from school and got down to business. What did we usually do? We'd shield ourselves somehow or other, then try to slip away quickly and take off as fast as our legs would carry us. And suddenly Nikita turned around and dished out a blow to Grishka-Murza himself, right on the bridge of his nose. I swear to God I could even hear the crunch. This was completely unexpected, and they froze. But by then Nikita had kicked one of them in the groin, grabbed another one by the hair and smashed his ugly mug against his raised knee, done something else to a third one. . . . Hmm . . . They came to their senses and went for him all in a pack. They'd forgotten about me, and I was completely beside myself, you know, everything went dark before my eyes, and I yelled inarticulately so the whole street could hear. They beat Nikita up pretty badly then, but they themselves suffered losses too. Fortunately some passersby came running up. Hmm . . . Yes. And so from that day on Nikita himself began to lie in wait for them one by one and beat them up. I was there sometimes. It was horrible. It was . . . It was incredibly cruel, skillful, and, I would say, businesslike. That is, he didn't fight the way boys usually fight—he didn't try to insult them with his blows, to humiliate them, to simply demonstrate his superiority. Hmm . . . He fought as if he were doing some job. He began right off the bat with Murza, attacked him in the school lavatory and spent one whole recess period working him over in a terrifying and businesslike way. All those rules boys have—"stop at the first sign of blood," "no hitting in the breadbasket," "no tripping," "lay off someone who's down"—all this he ignored. After only a minute the unlucky Murza was lying on the tile floor wheezing while Nikita worked on him with his fists and his shoes, any way he could. We froze in horror, and nobody dared to interfere, not even the boys in the upper grades. I swear to God, the only other time I ever saw such icy cruelty after that was in the movie theaters, in gangster movies!'"

(Here Varakhasy interrupted his reading again.

"It's striking," he said with a smile, "how tenaciously the boy stays alive even in elderly men! A retired colonel, in his fifties, yet he got so carried away that I began to feel his fear vicariously. He opened his eyes wide, waved his arms around, jumped up to demonstrate with his feet how our Nikita regaled this Murza with kicks. . . . He went on telling the tale in this fashion for a long time, we won't dwell on it, everything here is quite clear, so let's skip ahead to the next part. I'll continue reading.")

"'I see, Mikael Grikorovich. Well, what about the other example?'

"'What other example?'

"'You promised to clear things up with a couple of examples. You've given one. What about the second one?'

"'Hmm . . . The second example . . . I didn't actually have another one in mind. . . . Only please understand that what follows is more like impressions I have, since I saw almost none of it with my own eyes, so to speak. Hmm . . . To make a long story short, after a certain point I began to notice that Nikita acted with unusual boldness around girls. You know what adolescents of fourteen or fifteen are usually like—yearning to do things that are bad for them . . . spying on girls and snickering while they suffer hot and cold flashes, and for the most part it's generally just futile daydreaming. Then all of a sudden Nikita became extremely brazen. And I'm almost certain that something happened between him and one of the girls in our class. . . .'

"'I see. Mikael Grikorovich, you said "after a certain point." Do you recall a little more precisely when that was?'

"'Yes, I do. I can tell you exactly when. Nikita had an attack, some kind of brain disorder. He was a healthy boy in general, not sickly, and then all of a sudden he took to his bed, lost consciousness, and lay there with a high fever for several days. He'd gone out in the cold without a cap or something . . . or he'd bumped his head. I don't remember anymore. And he began to show signs of all these peculiarities, as you and I call them, shortly after this illness!'

"'And when did this happen?'

"'I remember exactly when. During winter vacation when we were in seventh grade. I remember it because he and I began to be fascinated by chemistry during that vacation. I myself lost interest in it

when we were in eighth grade and became addicted to electrical engineering while Nikita actually went on to become a chemist.'

"'Who is Galina Rodionovna?'

"'Galina Rodionovna? Galina Rodionovna . . . Hmm . . . Somehow I don't recall.'

"'She might also be from your school days.'

"'Ah! Galina Rodionovna! Yes, yes, yes, of course! We had a teacher
by that name, an Englishwoman. She came to us right out of college.
By the way, Nikita's English was absolutely flawless. . . .'"

Alexei T. threw the diary on the table and said wearily:

"Who else have you got left?"

"We've come to the last figure," Varakhasy S. responded. "Svetlana
Fyodorovna Panikeyeva, née Krivonosova, the niece of our Vorontsov
and his sole heir."

"And was there anything to inherit?"

"I'll say! He left behind quite a good library, furniture, some
clothing. If you remember, she'd gotten married in due course and
gone off with her husband to the North, but at the beginning of the
sixties they came back loaded down with tons of money and a whole
pack of kids. Well, sir, she turned out to be a simple, unpretentious
woman, although let me tell you, at the age of forty-seven she's still
very, very— All right, that's neither here nor there, of course. Now
I'm going to read you just one small quotation, which I find the most
interesting."

"Go ahead. I'm listening."

"'Even as a little girl I realized that he had a gift for knowing the
future. Nikita loved me, he loved me very much and he used to play
with me, and he'd read books to me and sing when I was sick. I was
often sick as a child. And sometimes the songs he sang me you
couldn't possibly have heard from anybody at that time, and I heard
them again only as an adult and many years after the war. "Hey,
Roads," he sang, "Dust and Fog," "Black Cat," "Hear the Boots Thun-
dering." And he had a thorough knowledge of the war, that it would
take place and when, and what it would be like. I remember once
when he was singing me one of his favorite songs, which I liked a great
deal, too, although I didn't understand very much of it, of course. He
was singing "Oh, rotten war, what have you done . . ." And then Papa
walked in on us. And Nikita didn't like to sing in front of anybody,
only me, but he didn't stop—he sang it to the end. Papa listened to all

of it and said, "What are you singing about, Nikita?" He answered, "About the war, Fedya. I'm singing about the war." "What war, for heaven's sake?" "The one that will begin next year, and many people will lay down their lives for it." "Why, shame on you for saying such things," Papa said. And I saw that Nikita was looking at him and there were tears in his eyes. . . .'"

Alexei T. watched until the sheets of paper fastened together with a paper clip and the all-purpose notebook with its moldy oilcloth cover had been put into the folder, and he turned his gaze to the window. Beyond the window a bright sunny morning reigned supreme.

"Well, how does this strike you?" asked Varakhasy S., tying the white ties.

"How about you?" asked Alexei. "Did you unravel the problem?"

"I won't hide the fact that, yes, I do indeed have an idea or two. . . ."

Alexei T. grimaced mockingly:

"A clairvoyant? A time traveler?"

"No-o, a clairvoyant—that, old buddy is . . . That's banal. Now, a traveler—that's closer to the mark."

"Might as well lead with diamonds if that's all you've got."

"Let's discuss it a little," Varakhasy S. proposed. "If you're not tired, of course."

"All right," Alexei T. consented. "Only first we'll finish off this manna from heaven."

And he reached for the bottle, which held about two more shots, three at most.

The Discussion

If you carefully compare all the facts (Varakhasy S. reasoned), then a paradoxical picture emerges, to wit: Nikita Sergeyevich Vorontsov lived a great number, an indeterminate number, of lives. Romantic literature contains well-known characters who live several lives—suffice it to recall only Jack London's Wanderer, who rushed from epoch to epoch in his straitjacket like someone with diarrhea rushing from crapper to crapper. A pretty sight, no doubt about it. But Nikita Vorontsov's case is completely different. It would be more accurate to say of him that he lived not a great number of lives but one and the same life a great number of times. And from the looks of it, this was painful, depressing, and tiresome enough. Not for nothing, not for nothing does the old song go (in the words of the common folk): "Better forty different things than one thing forty times." . . .

Yes, Nikita Vorontsov actually was a time traveler, only not by his own will and within highly restricted boundaries. And this is how it worked. Vorontsov lived just fine until the evening of June 8, 1977. At 11:15 P.M. Moscow time some force stopped his heart and instantly transported his consciousness forty years back, to the night of January 7, 1937, where it took root in the brain of the adolescent Vorontsov and, moreover, took root with all the experience, all the information accumulated during the forty years he'd just lived, completely supplanting, incidentally, everything that the adolescent Vorontsov had known and remembered until that night. Then Vorontsov again lived just fine until the evening of June 8, 1977, and again that same mysterious force killed his body and transported his consciousness back in time, a consciousness enriched, by the way, with the experience and information of another forty years . . . and so on and so forth.

And this happened to him repeatedly a great number of times, a number unspecified and perhaps even incalculable. It's possible that Nikita Vorontsov lived a thousand and one lives. It's possible that during his recent lives he'd already forgotten when it happened to him for the first time. And it's possible that there never even was a first time. . . . (Only don't spread your hands in helpless bewilderment and roll your eyes: Science as a form of human imagination can come up with many variations, of course, but nature can come up with an incalculably greater number.)

It should be taken into account that all these lives could not, of course, coincide in every detail. Too many things arise by chance during each lifetime; there are too many situations requiring choice and too many variants of such situations within these social microcosms. In one life Vorontsov might have married Vera, let's say, in another— Cleopatra, in a third—Roza, while in a fourth life he might have abstained from this business altogether and given himself a rest from family burdens. We may even suppose that at some point he was overcome by depression and hanged himself way back before the war, or that at some point he was blown to bits by an enemy shell, or that at some point he perished in a plane crash long before his time was up. But no matter when his life was interrupted and no matter what the circumstances, he invariably returned to the night of January 7, 1937 and began the next forty-year period all over again.

There is no sense in asking such questions (Varakhasy S. continued, raising his thick index finger) as how and why all this happened to Vorontsov and why to Vorontsov in particular. Science has not yet surmounted these heights and will not surmount them, one would think, in the near future. For here we are concerned with the nature of time, and time is a subject in which any one of us is no less competent than the greatest academician. It is possible that the hypothesis put forth by Varakhasy S. does not correspond to the true state of things in the universe, but just let anyone try to refute it! It is particularly senseless to roll your eyes blankly, move your lips, and count on your fingers. To try to imagine how the innumerable realities of Nikita Vorontsov correlate with our sole reality is a futile endeavor. Here we are dealing, beyond all doubt, with higher manifestations of the dialectics of nature that are as yet unknown to us; the human brain cannot encompass them at present, especially the brain of a fairly ordinary man of letters, so there is no reason to exert yourself or else, God forbid, your navel might come undone. You must simply accept as a given: It is the fate of Nikita Vorontsov time and again to cross the bridges "that we can no longer cross. . . ."

Here Alexei T. interrupted his friend. He inquired whether it was by accident that he had been treated to this fine song precisely today.

Varakhasy S. assured him that it had turned out that way completely by accident.

Then Alexei T. wrapped his robe more tightly around himself, stood up, and began to speak. He said that he was not going to pretend that the strange details of Nikita Vorontsov's life had not made an impression on him. He did not even intend to deny the position that Varakhasy S.'s hypothesis was striking in its boldness and unusualness. Being nothing but a fairly ordinary man of letters, he, Alexei T., was nonetheless prepared to guarantee that this hypothesis would elevate Varakhasy S., investigator for the municipal public prosecutor's office, to the very summit of science's Mount Olympus and seat him squarely between M. Lomonosov* and A. Einstein.

On the other hand (Alexei T. continued), a careful comparison of all the facts also permitted the formation of a hypothesis with a completely different thrust. Varakhasy S. would not pretend that the strange details of Nikita Vorontsov's life could not have been fabricated to

---

*Mikhail Vasilievich Lomonosov (1711–65)—Russian scholar, scientist, and poet, considered the founder of modern literary Russian. —Trans.

startle his friends, not to mention cute little law interns. Varakhasy
would not even deny the position that modern specialists in crime de-
tection would have no trouble manufacturing a moldy little notebook
and filling up a few of its pages with faded ink. And although fairly
ordinary, but a man of letters nevertheless, he, Alexei T. was prepared
to guarantee that this practical joke would elevate Varakhasy S., investigator for the public prosecutor's office, to some side ridge of literature's Mount Olympus and seat him squarely between B. Munchausen* and K. Prutkov.†

Having said this, Alexei T. sat down, crossed his legs, and looked at
his friend with the utmost condescension.

Varakhasy S. nodded his head several times, deep in thought. Then
he frowned and scratched behind one ear. And then he began to speak.

"Well put and convincingly stated," he said. "Good strong irony
there. The style wasn't bad either. I especially liked the location between Munchausen and Prutkov. Hmm?"

"Well, I was exaggerating, of course," Alexei hastened to say. "In
the heat of the controversy, so to speak. They, of course, didn't lower
themselves to such abstruse language."

"Abstruse language?" Varakhasy was surprised. "I see that you don't
know what real abstruse language is. But you writers would have everything simpler. The way you and your ilk paint a picture—'Vasyatka
stuck his feet into his father's boot and began lumbering outside.
Arishka darted out of the john with a squeal: "Ho-ho-ho! The trac-
tors've already started granulating the soil for the winter crops, but you
guys just keep screwing around!"'"

"Lomonosov!" Alexei T. snapped.

"And this coming from you, of all people," Varakhasy S. parried
coolly. "F. Abramov."‡

The friends fell silent for a while. Then Alexei T. growled angrily,
"Hand over the diary."

He flipped through two or three pages and became engrossed in
reading. Varakhasy cleared the table and began to wash the dishes.

"Should I put on the teakettle?" he asked.

*Baron Munchausen (1720–97)—German soldier, hunter, and raconteur of tall
tales. —Trans.
†Kozma Prutkov—fictitious author created by several nineteenth-century Russian
writers in order to parody contemporary social and literary trends. —Trans.
‡Fyodor Alexandrovich Abramov (1920–83)—a leading Russian writer in a contemporary school that depicts Soviet rural life. —Trans.

Alexei did not reply.

"I say, should I put on the teakettle?" Varakhasy yelled.

Then Alexei slammed the diary shut, threw it on the table, and rubbed his face hard with the palms of his hands.

"Sit down and listen," he said abruptly.

Varakhasy returned to the table, and Alexei, gazing over his head with eyes slightly puffy from the sleepless night, began:

"An interview between N. Vorontsov, wanderer through time, and writer and journalist Alexei T.:

"'Tell me, what do you experience during resurrection?'

"'Pain. And then several days of horror and depression.'

"'Why horror and depression?'

"'Because universal evil, universal stupidity, and the war lie ahead of me each time, and I must inevitably go through all of it.'

"'Inevitably? Each time?'

"'Yes. These are basic circumstances. They form the permanent background of every life.'

"'And didn't you ever try to prevent them? To warn somebody, write letters, come forward and speak out somewhere?'

"'I used to. A very long time ago, probably a thousand years back. I remember it very vaguely now. No, nothing came of it. I even had to commit suicide. One time I rotted away in a concentration camp. Three times I was executed by firing squad, and once I was killed right on the street with metal rods—it took them ten minutes or so and was excruciatingly painful. In all centuries, you know, people have burned clairvoyants—and eyewitnesses, too, for that matter—at the stake. . . . And I was a clairvoyant and eyewitness rolled into one. No, I've always known that one person can do nothing, but sometimes I simply couldn't hold back.'

"'I understand. This concerns circumstances that are, as you put it, basic. But under ordinary, everyday circumstances . . . I, for example, had I known in advance, would have saved my father. I'd simply not have let him leave the building that day, I'd have locked him in the apartment. . . .'

"'That's useless too. Everyday circumstances usually vary with each life. What happened to your father?'

"'He was hit by a truck.'

"'Well, in another life that truck might not have encountered your father. It might have gone by a minute later, or it might even have been demolished a whole month before that and become scrap metal.

In my last life I married Verochka Korneyeva, but in this one I met her after she'd already gotten married and had a daughter.'

"'But her birthmark . . .'

"'The birthmark evidently arises out of circumstances that are also part of the basic scheme even though they are not political.'

"'Forgive me, we've digressed. So, on a personal level it is impossible to warn anyone about anything, to keep them from disaster, to ward off misfortune?'

"'It's useless. Judge for yourself. I warn Fedya, the husband of my sister, Serafima, that he will be killed near Kharkov. What is he supposed to do, desert? Ask to be sent to another front? Blow his brains out to spite the prophecy? Not to mention the fact that he, of course, doesn't really believe me. And not to mention the fact that he's been killed near Kharkov only in my last five lives while for two hundred years before that he regularly died a completely different death.'

"'Knowledge without power—that's probably a heavy burden.'

"'True. At times I feel that it is unbearable. Sometimes I would love to die for real, like other people.'

"'But there are also many joys connected with your situation, you know!'

"'Yes, of course, and rest assured that none of you takes as much delight in your joys as I do in mine.'

"'Elaborate on that if you will.'

"'I won't go into detail. You wouldn't understand me anyway.'

"'Wine, love, travel?'

"'Those are pleasures, not joys. You and I have the same pleasures. Our joys are different.'

"'Tell me, was it accidental that you didn't destroy your diary just before your death?'

"'No, it wasn't. And the way I arranged my own death was no accident either.'

"'Meaning . . .'

"'My diary was not supposed to fall into the hands of my venerable sweetheart/niece but into the hands of Varakhasy S., investigator for the municipal public prosecutor's office.'

"'Thank you. Until we meet again in your next life.'"

"How did that strike you?" said Alexei T. smugly.

"Extremely uneven style," responded Varakhasy S. "It's obvious immediately that no human being wrote that. It started out pretty well but ended up like crap. Or, rather, the voice, lo and behold, is that of a man, not a boy. If you would spend a little more time—"

God knows what advice Varakhasy intended to give his friend, but right then the doorbell rang. Varakhasy went out into the hallway and came back unfolding a telegram.

"'Arrived, settled in,'" he read out loud. "'Kisses for our beloved husband, papa. Sasha, Glasha, Dasha.'"

Varakhasy gave a delectable yawn and stretched.

"That's splendid," he said. "Let's go to sleep. I'll make up a bed for you in my study if you have no objection. It's nice, isn't it, that we don't have to go to work today. And our little bachelor party turned out wonderfully well, don't you think?"

"Yes, wonderfully," Alexei agreed.

He, too, gave a delectable yawn and snapped his mouth shut suddenly, clicking his teeth. His whole body shuddered.

"You know," he said in a hoarse whisper, "I'd rather go to the devils in hell than back in time. . . ."

Varakhasy remained silent. Perhaps he didn't hear him.

September 15, 1983
Moscow

Translated from the Russian by Gerald Mikkelson and Margaret Winchell.

PROSE

Sergei Zalygin

Do you know anything about a writer named Gustov? Have you ever heard of him? No, you don't know of him, haven't heard of him. The name's unfamiliar to you? His first name, by the way, is Vladimir. Vladimir Ivanovich. A simple name, down-to-earth, not like Arnold, Ricardo, Askold, Ruslan, or Svyatopolk. And his name's not Onufry either. . . . Nothing like that—Vladimir Gustov, short and simple.

But are you sure you don't know anything about him? Are you sure you've never heard of him?

He's apparently one of the young ones.

Why "apparently"?

Because even he himself doesn't know. These days it's a complicated question: Is a writer still young at forty or not? Is he already middle-aged? (For some reason nowadays people often say "fortyish.")

Of course people who know about the contemporary literary process by hearsay will immediately begin to cite examples. First Lermontov, then Dobrolyubov, Pisarev, then Pushkin and even Gogol. (After all, they were also "fortyish.")

But those who stand closer to the business, to the contemporary literary process, will say "At forty a prose writer is still a child, is just beginning to cut his teeth."

Doctors say that if a baby cuts its teeth very late, it's bad, it's very painful and indicative of abnormal development. But doctors say all kinds of things! If you listen to doctors, you might as well up and die.

At forty a contemporary prose writer still has his baby teeth; he's just being weaned from the breast—from literary commissions that work with the "young," with the eternal beginners.

At forty a prose writer is just cutting his creative and other teeth and he is learning to toddle from one chair to another, from one editor's desk to another.

Now, as for Vladimir Ivanovich Gustov: He's on his second marriage and pays alimony and holds the position of senior engineer in the design department of the Water Canal concern, and in the past year his relationship with his second wife (Lyudochka Gustova—a nice woman on the whole, also a plumbing engineer, in the budget department) has grown complicated. In our country, you see, people are fond of the expression "a complex person." They say that about Gustov, too, and tell me, how can a complex man have simple relations with his family and with the labor collective? And, for your information, Gustov served his stint in the army long ago, in the far Far East to boot, what we think of as the very end of the earth, and he's already got some work experience, has a reputation in the design department for being a brain, knows a bit about chess, and much, much more, but as far as literature is concerned—he's nothing! A little seed. A crumb. No one's ever heard of him. No one anywhere.

Only I know him. Because I am he.

So, since nobody knows about me, I'm unique.

I'm unique because you won't find another identical Vladimir Ivanovich Gustov anywhere.

I'm unique because no one else has written what I've written in prose. You'll find better, but you won't find the exact same lines.

I'm unique because I know I'm unique.

Now we've been properly introduced, haven't we? If so, I'll tell you more. Now that we've met, I'll go on. I'll say, Being a writer, a real one, above all means having a sense of yourself as unique. As singular. It's not necessary for the unique and singular writer to be better, smarter, loftier, more talented, more penetrating than all others, not at all, that's not the point at all. The point is that a writer must express his uniqueness, no matter what it is. That's the long and the short of it.

Here's how it is: A child is born, but what's important is that he was born to a *writer*; someone dies, and what's important is that he wasn't just anyone, but someone close to a *writer*; a brick falls on a writer's head, his last thought is, Why did the brick fall on a *writer's* head and nowhere else?

Egoism? Call it what you like—egoism, egocentrism, vanity, a crazy idea, eccentricity, absurdity, comedy, tragedy—whatever you like, but that's the way it is. It's that way and no other.

You'll ask me, How do I know?

That's the whole point! I don't know how, but somehow and for some reason I know everything about literature, about literary creation. Everything there is to know. And no matter what I've heard about the subject, no matter what I've read, it turns out that I'd already known it all long before. Long, long ago, from time immemorial. And I also know every work of prose on my own, and no one can fool me on the page of a book, or onstage, or on television, or on the radio. Everything I know about literature I know by myself: the big names and the relics and the multivolume collected works that are republished every six or seven years in Russian and other languages and the extensive reviews and the prizes—they're nothing to me. Because I know it all myself! I even find it funny if someone tries to twist me around his little finger on this question, to buy me cheap. But that's impossible. Neither cheap nor dear, no way. And I only wonder, What do writers published in eight volumes think about? Doesn't it even occur to them that among their readers there might be some as all-knowing as Gustov? Vladimir Ivanovich?

And the conversations between more or less venerable writers and the young . . . What's the point? What's the point if I feel that my interlocutor, my instructor is less interested in me than in himself? If in this respect we are equal? In the striving to become established in literature, to become a great writer. He wants to become one, and I want to become one, we're just at different stages in the process, that's all. I'm at the first stage, and he's at the second, that's all. . . . Not much of a difference. He, of course, might receive something for successful work with the young, some compensation, and I don't, I can't, but as you probably realize, that's not the point. The point is there should be a real difference between us, there should be a truly great writer before me, in relation to whom I would truly and sincerely feel like a child.

That's what I find missing in literary communication, in which, after all, I have considerable experience: conferences of young writers, the Youth Literary Union . . .

I wish a really great writer would talk with me and talk just like an equal and I wish I would feel the inequality between us only while reading his book, at night, when I'm one on one with his book, agitated and distressed: Tomorrow I have to get up early, and I can't fall asleep, can't forgive myself for the fact that I'm a child, that during the day I talked with him as an equal, as an adult. But the opposite happens: In our communication during the day there was no question of his absolute superiority, and then I picked up his book, leafed through it, read snatches—Lord! Where was it, that superiority? Why did I, fool that I am, seek out this meeting myself? This humiliation? Therein lies the offense! The true offense!

I live in the midst of what they call the "thick of life." He's only heard about it, but all the same it's not I who's published but he, who knows much less about life than I do! I'm the one who knows, but luck is on his side. Where's the justice? Where is my uniqueness?

They tell me, a beginner—and I truly believe it, believe it with all my heart—that literature has always devoted itself to truth, beauty, and justice. Wonderful! I believe, believe and even unite all three concepts into one—justice. That's what I think, that's how I perceive it.

But in the life of literature itself there is so much injustice that I am forced to ask, How can literature reflect justice if the conditions of its own life are so unjust?

And so, despite my faith, I'm beginning to have doubts. I don't know how my faith and these doubts can coexist in me. But I know that my doubts, too, are nothing more than my knowledge of literature, of how it works.

I seek, I try to find justifications for literature, as I would seek them for myself if I had to stand and be judged—had to face the highest judgment of my life. "An actress?" I ask literature. "After all, an actress doesn't play herself! She herself may be very, very kind yet play a villainess! She herself may be irreproachably moral and serve in the temple of art—in the theater—which is up to its neck in squabbles and quarrels! And what if, on the contrary, a villainess plays a very, very good heroine?"

Doubts . . .

"But after all, aren't doubts also in the nature of literature?" I comfort myself.

I really find it difficult to live—I don't have the heart for anything and everything. I don't have enough heart for all the faith and all the doubts. And because my heart isn't big enough to hold it all, it grows empty. That's it, there's no middle ground—all or nothing. But after all, of all people on earth, a writer should have enough heart! If he doesn't, he has no right to live. He should have the heart! I know that a painter can paint for himself alone—get a little easel and, on his days off, set himself up on the shore of a lake (or river or reservoir) and paint landscapes for himself to his heart's content. Afterward he can hang his landscape over his bed or in the vestibule. When guests come, they'll ask, "Did you paint that yourself? Really? It's not bad, not bad!"

All the more so in music—a person can play the piano or the balalaika for himself, for his friends, and he'll get all the satisfaction he needs from it, and he's not looking for anything more.

And in drama it's possible to limit oneself to an amateur group. Quite possible.

Even in poetry there are any number of homegrown and domestic poets. How many of them there are today among scholars, representatives of the exact sciences; they write verses—and they're not bad—they get together, read their "own" poetry to one another—also not bad. This suits them perfectly.

But in prose—not at all. It's not the same in prose! There's none of that do-it-for-yourself, and never in my life have I met a prose writer who wrote stories or novellas for his own satisfaction, for a narrow circle of friends and acquaintances. In prose, if you've written something, you'll have no peace until it's published, until it's become the property of many thousands of people. Perhaps it's not a property at all, perhaps it's something dubious and even unnecessary to anyone, but here the reckoning is different: Once it's published, then it's necessary, absolutely essential to everyone, something without which mankind would perish tomorrow. And it all begins here—when everyone is fighting for his place in the sun, and that place is the pages of books and journals. That's what it is, this accursed prose: Who thought it up? How perfidious it is! Whoever has seriously made it in prose expects to get ten of his books published a year! And to get his children published! And his friends and acquaintances! And . . . he gets it! And what about all the others? They also want it!

Prose demands solitude while it's being written, but as soon as it's finished—give it the reading masses, it can't do without them for a minute, it desires compensation with interest—oh, with what interest!—for its initial solitude.

Absurd?

Quite possibly, but that's the cross that must be borne. Those are the conditions—you have to accept them. You didn't move a mountain when you squeezed some little story into some little newspaper, but it nonetheless seems to you that you did just that—moved a mountain, that almost every passerby recognizes you on the street: "Ah, that's him, the one who . . ."

"Who made me happy"—that, it seems, is what every passerby is saying.

And no one anywhere will be able to dissuade you from this, not even the editorial staff of the newspaper for young people that published you. Although they think the opposite, that it was they who made you happy. The editor in chief and the deputy editor in chief and the director of the section and the literary consultant and even the typist Yulechka—all of them staunchly believe that you are unconditionally beholden to them for life.

But even that doesn't bother me, and I make my appearance at the editorial office as if it were seventh heaven. And whoever doesn't understand this, whoever is not in seventh heaven, but only in sixth, is a fool and very nearly my personal enemy.

At that moment I completely forgot that the editor in chief—in his enormous glasses, with a very loud voice and a very quiet disposition, who is always on the lookout for someone to suck up to and makes it his business never to forget anyone's birthday—isn't thinking about me at all. He's no longer young, he should have been transferred somewhere else a long time ago, and he's thinking about this transfer, about it alone, and not about me at all.

I forgot that the deputy editor in chief, a tennis buff, a well-built young man (in the summer he wears a multicolored cap; in the winter, a multicolored knitted cap) who has close but mysterious connections with journalists in the capital, is thinking about nothing but these connections. Besides, it was he and no one else who killed my three previous stories, and, as far as I can tell, he took a certain malicious pleasure in killing them. Now, when my fourth story has nonetheless been published, he, of course, is more than willing to take the credit.

A small digression on a phrase I used in my brief characterization of the deputy editor, specifically, "connections with journalists in the capital":

I often think, If only I had close acquaintances in the journals of the capital! If I did, I wouldn't have gotten involved with these potbellied provincial small fry. Not with the editor in chief, not with the deputy editor, not with any of them ever!

But I have no one in the capital.

Almost no one—I have Alex Plitochkin, but I can't even say for sure whether I have him or not!

He sometimes answers my letters (which I write nonchalantly, without any ulterior motives, without asking Alex for favors) and tells me that he has spoken about me, about my talent, with "certain people," but who those "certain people" are I don't know. Nevertheless, having "certain people" just in case isn't a bad thing, it's even a good thing.

It's the kind of thing that brings me back once again into the circle of humanity. After all, humanity also pins its hopes on some sort of "connections" in this world, on "something" and "someone," so why shouldn't I?

Why can't I dream about connections? And even better—about such of my own personal abilities that need nothing and no one, only themselves?

Why can't I dream about collected works? With commentaries. With a volume or two of correspondence . . .

And so now I'm writing not only another story but also a piece about how I wrote that story, about the domestic and other circumstances in which it was written. Could it be that it might help? What if I send all of this to some editor along with the story so that he knows whom he's dealing with!

So that he knows beyond a shadow of a doubt!

Well, this is a short digression, nothing more.

The next person I visit in the editorial office of *Youth* is the director of the art and literature section.

I've forgotten that the director of the section, my true fan and well-wisher on the whole, an excellent chess player, probably because he looks like a rook—fatter on the bottom, thinner on top—told me last Tuesday, "Here's the situation. Vova, my dear friend, we'll publish you, but . . . but don't bother us for six months, no manuscripts, understand? That will be better for both of us, understand?"

I haven't forgotten the literary consultant, but try not to notice him. He envies me. He, a pip-squeak with a little mustache and just off the school bench, thinks that he writes mu-u-uch better than I do and that they should publish him instead of me. "My friend," he often says to me, "you shouldn't think that working at a newspaper is a piece of cake for a writer. In fact, my friend, do you know what kind of attitude the editorial board has toward its own? An obscene attitude, yes! The editor orders you to write something, you do everything just right—they praise you, toss you a bone, but your own work will never cross the threshold. Take your own work elsewhere. As far as your own work is concerned, you might as well kill yourself. Nobody cares! That's how it is, my friend, that's how things stand. . . . I just wanted you to know, to understand, my friend!"

The typist Yulechka—some important personage's daughter, no doubt, who could have done better, a swell girl all in all, a good sport and full of spunk—rejoices in my success. True, her sincere joy is clouded for me by the fact that I know that Yulechka rejoices in all correspondence as long as she and no one else typed it on her Ufa typewriter.

But after all, the point isn't in what I forgot and what I remember, not to whom and how I said hello and spoke, or whom I went to see and in which rooms, the point is: Today I am an AUTHOR!

An author, authorship . . . Today it seems to me that if I weren't an author, my life would be completely senseless, impossible. It seems that if the deputy editor, the tennis buff, were once again to pull, to kill, my story, I wouldn't survive it, I would die. But this also gives me a feeling of happiness—after all, I'm alive, alive! I made it! I walked along the edge of the abyss and here I am—alive!

Then, as I'm leaving the editorial office with a stack of today's issues of *Youth* in my briefcase, I begin to think seriously and realistically.

And, if you like, tragically.

Yes, yes, if I understand literature—and I do understand it!—I can't help but know that my little story is so-so. Crap. Whether it exists or not doesn't affect literature one way or the other. This little story not only does not confirm my talent but even contradicts it. And at this point I begin to feel that, together with my briefcase, I am sinking to the bottom, to the bottom of myself and of the whole surrounding world.

I have to save myself somehow, to come back to the surface.

And a short time later I do resurface. I rejoice in being an author just like any other member of the literary union associated with *Youth*, just like them, but I suffer and have doubts—not like them at all, completely in my own way.

None of my colleagues has such doubts; they couldn't.

Which means?

It means that all the same I'm somehow different from them—the beginners, the promising ones, tomorrow's geniuses who are still unacknowledged today, the ones everyone is sick and tired of, whom nobody needs. . . . I'm different! And it means that there's hope. Because if you're in no way different from twenty of your friends and comrades, it means you're a nobody, all doors are closed to you, you won't go further than anyone else, others will go further than you.

And you know—it helps, and now I'm no longer going to the bottom but to my Water Canal. Two hours late—I asked for two hours' leave and have been gone for four.

It's not a good situation, but then, unlike many, many others, I know and feel very keenly what literature is.

It's true, I have no one to talk to about this, to explain my understanding ingelligently.

Absolutely no one!

As I've already said, earlier for such occasions I had a reliable friend at hand, the journalist Alex Plitochkin. He listened attentively, without interrupting and without imposing stories about himself on me!

A rare occurrence?

Rare, but completely explicable: Alex, although a journalist, had never even thought of becoming a writer. Lucky man!

And because he didn't think about it, he became one (almost). He contrived to go to Moscow, get himself a residence permit, and become corresponding secretary of a "thick" literary and artistic journal in the capital. How about that!

And how hard it is for me now without a friend! A friend who listens to you, listens and listens and doesn't interrupt.

So here it is: I know, for example, that nowadays you can no longer surprise anyone with a so-called artistic image. . . . No matter what kind of character a prose writer might create, there's sure to have already been one like it in literature. No matter how improbable the character might be, you'll find a still more improbable one in real life, and imagination here is powerless.

Events are a different matter. Events are still a subject for literature, provided that they are mythologized. Though contemporary, they must be mythic, contemporary but parables. Without this—and by themselves events are of no interest to anyone—there are so many of them, real events, taking place in the world every day, every hour, they are subject to such inflation year after year, that nowadays they aren't worth anything anymore, five kopecks a bundle if anything at all.

And only if a parable can be extracted from an event, if it can be transformed into a contemporary legend—well, then it's a different matter, then it can still attract the reader to the artistic work. The reader prefers documentary works, memoirs, or investigations of social questions to events without legends.

And the most important of today's writers have realized this, know it and do it—they write legends.

Laksness—remember his *Nuclear Power Plant?* What is it if not a legend, completely in the spirit of an Icelandic saga, only contemporary?

Camus—remember *The Plague?*

And Gabriel García Márquez—all of his work is like that. Isn't *The Autumn of the Patriarch* a legend and a parable? And *One Hundred Years of Solitude?*

The greatest contemporary writer will be the one who creates a *Divine Comedy* for the twentieth century.

What if Vladimir Ivanovich Gustov were to create this *Comedy!* What if it were he! Well?

At Water Canal I immediately sensed that in my absence an emergency had arisen. And once again I immediately sensed that it was my fault it had happened.

As it was I arrived at Water Canal late, arrived I myself don't know in what condition—sad or joyous, cowardly or brave, modest or brazen, intelligent or foolish, and now an emergency on top of it all!

My fault! I have to do something, to clarify something, and to conduct myself somehow.

I conduct myself thus:

"Hello, Mikhail Andreyevich! Hello, hello!"

"Well, there he goes again," quietly says Mikhail Andreyevich, our group leader and generally an okay guy. And loudly he says, "The explication for tower seventeen, S. district? Well? Don't you have anything to say?

I really don't have anything to say, I don't understand what's going on.

"You don't understand? No? What do you understand? Novels? Honorariums?"

I hold my ground:

"Hey, what honorariums? A thousand or two a month comes my way, that's all. . . ."

So, that's what's going on: A month before, I had drawn up a project for an interbuilding distribution network in residence tower number 17 in the S. district, and I had not transferred the explication—the general calculation of the fittings, of all sorts of joints, tees, sockets—onto Whatman paper. . . . I had forgotten.

I rushed to my drafting table—some drafting table, a real monstrosity, homemade, but for some reason I love it, this drafting table, my work station. In the drawer I immediately found the explication on two sheets of bluish paper, but now they were useless, they really hadn't been transferred onto Whatman paper. . . .

Of course Vladimir Ivanovich Gustov, the senior engineer, was to blame, but it's amazing: What were the others thinking of? What had Mikhail Andreyevich been thinking of when he signed the sheet without the explication? What had the bookkeepers been thinking of? It's perfectly obvious: A sheet without an explication is not yet a sheet and not a project. It should be returned that very moment to the executor, that is, to me. No one returned it. . . . And so what was I occupied with until the end of the workday? I was writing an explication for the chief engineer, I went to the bookkeepers, I went to the supply department, and no matter where I went—everywhere they looked at me as if I were crazy.

But after all it's also craziness to let a sheet pass without the explication, and I wanted to speak with my colleagues sincerely and as equals—as one lunatic to other lunatics, as a loony to other loonies, as a muddler to other muddlers, but no one recognized this equality. No one! And I alone—quite alone was a lunatic, a loony, and a muddler, I alone—and no one else!

One big, big face with many eyes of different colors and different expressions looked at me alone with amazement. There was bewilderment in them, there was anger, there was blame, goodwill, but too much curiosity. There was scorn.

But I didn't look at them, at all of those faces in one face. I looked at the floor, at the ceiling, at the windows, only not at them. And this is what's strange: They all stared at me and didn't see me, while I didn't look at anyone but saw them all. . . .

Isn't this also literature? Doesn't it have all the characteristics of literature?

And here's what else.

They say that the artist, the artistic nature, always has two lives: one—personal, everyday; the other—creative, constructive. There are two tissues in the organism of the artist: the cellular, mechanical "tissue" and the spiritual "tissue." And everyone agrees with this view.

But I don't agree, no! Spiritual tissue couldn't be directly connected to cellular, to mechanical tissue, it couldn't be. It couldn't be that, say, the feeling of love or artistic imagination is connected just like that, directly, to the skeleton of my organism. No, they are incompatible! They have completely different properties. One tissue should have the strength of iron, the other—lightness, improbability. How could they be connected to each other? So different and having completely different functions?

No, there absolutely must be a third tissue as well—a connective one. When I began to suspect this I consulted the Great Soviet Encyclopedia and found out that this is "the tissue . . . that fulfills the support, trophic [nourishing], and protective functions." The protective—that's the most important.

And as far as I myself am concerned, the whole problem lies in the fact that I don't have a connective tissue. No protective one.

I'm at a loss: How can you do without it? If I were to restrict myself to Water Canal and nothing else, no place else, and had complete and eternal order in drafts and explications and nothing else! . . .

It was possible once. It was, but I let the opportunity slip, and there's no way back, as if there had never been a possibility at all. And, when you stop to think, Why the hell? you grab your head: Oh God, oh God, oh God—what blasphemy! What a blasphemer! What a traitor to art and literature!

And so I waited for the bell ending work. I heard the bell, heard it and decided to wait another five minutes or so, so I could leave the office alone. Five minutes turned out to be too long—after a minute or two there wasn't a soul left in the whole office, but I sat out the five minutes as I had planned anyway and then walked to the bus stop.

And I went home on the bus. I went home to my family.

My own family: Vovka and his mama, Lyudochka Gustova. (In our family, as in the story, there is a big Volodya and a little Volodya.)* What can I say about little Volodya? He's a poor student but a good kid. A good little calf with big eyes, affectionate, carefree, and you can't believe a single one of his promises. He'll say, "Tomorrow I'll get up at six-thirty. Don't wake me—I'll get up by myself, honest!" But rest assured he'll sleep through until ten and won't even be surprised. What's the big deal? The whole day's still ahead of him. But the whole day will pass for him in exactly the same way: He was planning to do this, that, and the other thing, but accomplished nothing; he'd read something, phoned someone, watched something on television, but as for getting anything done, forget it.

"Well, and so what if I didn't get anything done? What is it, the last day of my life? Tomorrow will be another day and the day after tomorrow and the day after that and so on. What is there to feel sorry for?"

It's very likely that he'll still be a little calf in ten years. And in twenty. And his whole life.

*Both Vovka and Volodya are nicknames for Vladimir. —Trans.

One day I asked him:

"Vovka! What'll you do if I die?"

He answered me:

"Please, don't lie . . ."

"Well, what if I abandon you. What if I finally get sick of you and up and abandon you . . ."

"Again, don't lie . . ."

I thought and thought and asked:

"What'll you do if I become a great, great writer? If I write many, many books. And publish all of them. And in many editions?"

"I'll buy a bicycle!" said Vovka. "First. And then—a motorcycle!" And he asked, "You're not lying again, are you? If you're not, then I'll buy a car."

That's my Vovka. It's not tragic yet, and I'm content with that. And he couldn't care less about literature, he doesn't want to know about it, and, believe me, that's also for the best.

Well, and Lyudochka Gustova, she knows very well what she'll do if I become a great writer, if I write many, many books and publish them all.

That's her dream, but to her credit be it said, it's a secret dream. She would never allow herself to say aloud to anyone, "When my Volodya becomes . . . I'll . . ."

No, no, she knows that it's a dream, an unrealizable dream, that she has to resign herself to it as best she can, that she's lucky: Others have to resign themselves to the fact that their husbands are unfaithful, that they drink, that they're lazy, while all her husband does is write. . . . Is it so hard to resign oneself to that? It's possible, necessary, and it even has certain advantages. It gives one a certain sense of superiority: "I quietly, calmly, and wisely accept my husband's eccentricities, which means I'm smarter than he is, which means I'm not obligated to him, but he to me. . . . My husband's first wife couldn't take it, she walked out, but I won't walk out—which one of us is better? There you are. . . . Who's the real wife, and who's not up to it? There you are. . . ."

That's her logical proof of her rightness, of her superiority.

I emphasize: logical.

Furthermore I emphasize: After the business with the explication, when I sat it out after work in the empty office at my drafting table for five minutes, I also had to do this in order to go home alone, without Lyudochka Gustova.

That's how we've worked it out: She doesn't stop by for me if I linger after work at my drafting table; instead, I stop by for her in the budget department. If I don't stop by, she knows that I want to go home alone, she knows that either I'm in a bad mood because I've again suffered some adversity or unpleasantness or worry on the literary front, or I've simply had a brainstorm and I'm hurrying to jot down a page or two of my prose, or, on the contrary, I'm in a good mood, carefree, and I want to play chess with Mikhail Andreyevich.

In the first, second, and third cases each of us goes home alone, it's better that way. And again, it's more logical, and we're the envy of all the other married couples who work at Water Canal—misunderstandings constantly arise between them because of the absence of such coordination.

Lyudochka Gustova and I never have such misunderstandings, and everyone credits this to her self-control, to her irreproachable ability to manage family relations. As one, that is, together with Lyudochka, the entire Water Canal collective forgives me my literary diversions.

And so now I know for a fact: For a day or two there will still be a lot of talk about the business with the explication, and then all will be forgiven me. Yes, with such a wife you won't go wrong! With her it's like being in Christ's bosom, and you don't even have to try to prove this to anyone—like in Christ's bosom!

Well, that's it, and as I was riding home on the bus—alone—I was thinking about the plot of my new story.

The one that was published today in *Youth* and because of which I hadn't filled out the explication—that one is trash, but the one I'm thinking about as I ride home alone, hanging on to the strap in the bus—this one is really something.

Is really something important.

So . . .

One spring a passenger plane makes a forced landing in the uninhabited steppe.

That's how it begins: The steppe, the plane, near the plane a crowd of passengers who have lost their heads, who are already condemned to something. They are trying to figure out what. They press close to one another, whisper, weep, and curse, and only one young woman in a green dress walks away from the crowd into the steppe.

She walks away and thinks that this is what she has to do—the time has come to walk away into the uninhabited steppe. She has always, all her life, walked away from people, you see. . . .

Two million seven hundred thousand three hundred and sixty-seven people have passed her by on squares, on streets, and in the subways of various cities, in trolleys, in buses, in trams, and she has passed by them. . . . Perhaps more than two million seven hundred thousand three hundred and sixty-seven, but for some reason it seemed to her that it was precisely that many, no more and no less. . . . It could have been the population of a whole country, but now she can't remember a single one of them, and of course none of them ever remembered her. . . .

And so she walks off, walks away from the other seventy-three passengers—she feels obliged to walk away, feels the logic of walking away, the obligation, and is amazed that no one feels this obligation except her.

The more so as she is the only one in a green dress, and the steppe is also very green, and right before the eyes of the frightened crowd the woman disappears into this bright color, as if into a fire, and the crowd near the airplane sighs with relief—it seems to the crowd that the steppe, the whole surrounding expanse, having accepted this sacrifice, will become more benevolent and will help save all the rest.

Each person in this crowd has also passed by millions of passersby, passed through his or her past history, through his or her stormy present, but no one, not one of them, even thinks of that now.

But once the plane is repaired, once it has again taken off into the air, none of the passengers remembers the woman in the green dress who walked away into the green steppe. . . .

Indeed, to remember would mean to speak up, to speak up would mean to search for the woman in the steppe, to search would mean to remain longer in that green, beautiful, but uninhabited steppe. . . .

Wouldn't that make a great plot? And why shouldn't it be brilliant?

Well, of course, it's a strange piece—strange for the author, let alone the editor.

And while I was riding home on the bus, I also thought about the role of biography in a writer's work.

Take Tolstoy and Gogol, for instance.

The mighty, long-lived Tolstoy. His numerous ancestors made a significant impact on our history, his numerous descendants left their mark as well, and he seemed to spend his whole life getting used to his own life, vast and sprawling, to his experiences at different ages, to the experiences of those close to him, and his immense works arose out of these experiences. After all, even *War and Peace* could quite aptly be retitled *War and Family*.

And Gogol?

He didn't even have a biography, and himself was a sickly, neuras-thenic little man who saw little on the earth, experienced little, never fell in love (just had some trifling flirtations, it seems). He wasn't a father, didn't have a family, couldn't do anything practical, didn't know how, but nonetheless—what grandiose images he created! Taras Bulba! Even Tolstoy doesn't have one like that! And Chichikov! What enter-prise, what a sharp wheeler-dealer! And Sobakevich! And Nozdrev! And just try to find in all of world literature as jovial a rascal as Khlestakov!*

The question arises: What role does biography play in a writer's crea-tive work? Perhaps none? Perhaps in principle, theoretically, a writer doesn't need a life at all, is only hindered by it, and the best, the ideal variant is not a writer per se, but some kind of creative substance that lives no other life but the creative?

Indeed, what use has an ideal for life? To mangle its idealness? To squander itself in vain and to no purpose?

But here's the heart of the matter: Both Tolstoy and Gogol were to an equal degree martyrs to literature, its slaves. Moreover, voluntary ones, and, after all, voluntary and even enthusiastic slavery is the worst kind. Well, yes, one was a slave because of the richness of his life, the other—because of its poverty.

Here I also think: Where is the cause that would make me a slave of literature too? A true, groveling, and submissive slave?

Where is it? Is it possible it doesn't exist? And never will?

Yes, no matter how strange it might seem, I often (and now all the more often) remember my first, truly unsuccessful marriage, my first wife, Fainka, our awkward, lengthy, and indecisive divorce. Which I can in no way seem to forget. Why can't I? But, you know, it's prob-ably because in that whole situation I acted rather nobly. That's it—not just rather nobly, but simply nobly, and isn't your own nobility, after all, something you don't tend to forget? When there's no need to prove it to anyone, when for a long, long time, perhaps to the very end of your life, only you yourself need it, no one else? When you are completely aware of where your nobility came from?

I realized that I had deceived Fainka, and that's where the nobility came from—out of that deceit.

*Taras Bulba is the hero of a story by the same name; Chichikov, Nozdrev, and So-bakevich are characters in the novel Dead Souls; and Khlestakov is the protagonist of the play The Inspector General. —Trans.

I had at length and ardently explained to her, to this young, sweet, and oh-so-credulous girl, what a writer I was, how wonderful, how unusual, well, and she of course believed me. It goes without saying that I told her "I will be," but, after all, if I will be, it means I already am—without "I already am" what kind of "I will be" can there be, where would it come from?

And so declarations of "I will be" and no declarations of love at all became our love. And what a bright, what a lively and precious love! No matter how hard Fainochka and I looked around us, no one else had such a thing, such light, such all-consuming kindness toward each other. Now I think we realized from the very beginning that all of this was our invention, a dream, but can't a dream be love? And so we dreamed, we looked at the stars, at the sky, at the earth, at the grass beneath our feet, together trying to memorize all of it, to commit it all to memory for the pages of my (our!) future story, future novella. Today we looked around ourselves silently, and the next day we related to each other what each of us remembered—what colors, what smells, what sounds, what objects. In the trolley bus we would listen with all our attention to the conversations of other people, to their words and phrases, catch the plots in these conversations and then relate them to each other, embroidering them with our own imaginations—who would have thought it!

That's the kind of literary union Fainochka and I had!

When we got married we continued to relate little scenes, plots, stories, novellas, and novels to each other, but for some reason not a single story or novella, let alone a novel, appeared. Instead, Svetlanka appeared—in other words, we had a daughter, a baby. And life for three began in one room of a communal apartment.

I won't talk about that; everybody already knows what it's like, even those who have never experienced it themselves. It's just what you'd expect: Every night you sit on the edge of the bathtub, a piece of cardboard on your knees, a sheet of paper on the cardboard—you can write all you want! Write *War and Peace* if you want to—who will mind? Nobody will mind. All genres are in your power, just go ahead and wield it.

And then I couldn't lie anymore, and I honestly confessed to Fainka, I don't have any "I will be." None—and that's it.

And Fainka flew off the handle: How could that be? Where did it go? Why had it been and wasn't anymore? If it wasn't there anymore, what had taken its place?

And when I couldn't answer a single question, she began to scorn me, and what abilities she turned out to have in that sphere—in the sphere of scorning a man! There were moments when she even amazed herself: "How can I be so spiteful?"

A banal story?

It would have been completely banal and dreadfully boring, there would have been no reason to tell it, if not, I repeat, for my nobility, which at this point came into play. There were minutes when Fainka asked, even begged, "Promise, Vova, again! Promise just a little bit!"

But I remained silent.

When she asked for the last time, "Promise," I knew it was the last time, she knew that I knew—and all the same I remained silent.

And as for the fact that Fainka, charmer that she was, even with Svetka on her hands, wouldn't remain unmarried for long, there could be no doubt of that. Her "I will be" wasn't the same as mine, it was certain.

And now that she has another family and well-groomed children and a full-size apartment, and doesn't pick fights with anyone, doesn't make spiteful remarks, even she herself has turned out to be very good: She remembers that she owes all of this to my nobility. I've run into her a number of times—she remembers.

Well, and me? To whom am I obliged?

I owe it all to literature. I swear! To that same accursed prose. All the same it put something into me, some nobility, helped me see things clearly. I realized that before many, many people could come to understand through my works that literature lives in me and has always and inevitably lived in me, it first had to live in me alone, I didn't even have the right to talk about it with anyone. Not with Fainka, not with Lyudochka, perhaps only with myself, and even that in a whisper, in the timid hope that someday I would become its slave.

What am I saying—slave! Slavery of this kind is only a prelude, a foreword.

One must get to the roots, that is, to the epilogue. And such is the epilogue . . .

Did Tolstoy, did Gogol really end in slavery? No, they ended in failure. . . . Tolstoy ran away from home; Gogol burned his manuscripts and died a horrible death.

The more examples, the more alluring the dream: If only I, too, Vladimir Gustov, might experience such failure! If only I, too, might!

And still people ask me all the time: Where do you find your subject matter? Subject matter! My God, there's as much of it as you like! Without even speaking of your own family relationships, the family relationships of all your friends and acquaintances—they are such fascinating subjects, it takes your breath away! And relations at work? And the relations of each person with the surrounding world? If the truth be told, you don't know how to get away from subject matter!

The whole matter lies in the form. To give form to the content of a story, a novella, a novel—that's the problem!

Most people think it's a literary problem, a problem of art.

But it's nothing of the sort. It's a problem of our existence, of our whole life. There's as much life as you could ever want, and full of content, and we, people, search and search for a form for it all. . . . So the problem of form and content isn't a literary problem at all, not at all. There has never been and perhaps never will be a more universal problem.

Hares have it good: They have complete harmony between the form and the content of their life. And sparrows have it good. And hippopotamuses! They evolved long ago; they don't wage wars among themselves. Each knows his unchanging place in this world and therefore isn't tormented by creativity.

But I am tormented. Too much. And I envy Gogol. Look whom I've chosen to envy, look whose failure—a truly unattainable height.

I envy greatly, and at the same time I trivialize, trivialize, and that's how I want it to be—it's so tempting and necessary for me to talk about myself, about what a writer I am, what a personality, what an individual, and what stands behind this signature:

Vladimir Gustov, Senior Plumbing Engineer

Alex! My friend!

Here's the thing, here's my question: I am sending your editor in chief a wonderful story, almost a novella—"Forced Landing."

Either I understand nothing about literature and am completely without talent, or "Landing" is a wonderful story. Please, explain this to your editor in chief!

Explain it to him clearly, and so you'll have evidence at hand of the fact that he is dealing with a real, one-hundred-percent bona fide writer, I am also sending along an epistle in which I discuss some of my views on the subject of prose. Maybe it will help? After all, the editor in chief should know whom he's dealing with.

Life's pretty good.

I bought Vovka a bicycle. What conclusions should be drawn from this fact?

1. We live pretty well.

2. We are physically and morally healthy.

3. We possess the requisite conditions for survival, that is, time (to buy a bicycle—these vehicles are now rarely available, you have to search and search) and space (around our house, where Vovka is already riding his bicycle).

If only you could print my "Landing" in the November issue! That would be an event! Every year on November 10 I call F. That's the day we got divorced. We congratulate each other on our day of liberation.

Now, imagine that along with my congratulations I inform F. about my publication and advise her: "Read it! You must read it—among the heroes (heroines) of 'Forced Landing' you will certainly recognize yourself! Besides, I think that we thought up the plot of this story together, in two voices, way back in our youth."

So don't forget, Alex, about your editor in chief!

Yours,
Senior Plumbing Engineer Vl. Gustov

My friend Volodya!

You know how I feel about you, with what unchanged warmth, and I had a talk with my editor in chief for one hour and seventeen minutes (1 hr. 17 min.).

I explained to him that we were dealing with the outstanding prose writer Vladimir Gustov, that he could assure himself of this by comparing "Forced Landing" with the universally recognized and celebrated novels of such authors as A——v, B——v, C——v, D——v. . . .

I asserted that it was a crime to turn down—for the fifth time in a row—the works of V. G——v (Vladimir Gustov).

My editor in chief scratched his head, sighed, and seemed to be shuffling his feet under the desk, but he didn't throw me out (we're both fans of the army soccer club, the Torpedo soccer team, and Karpov).

Then my editor said, "Well, all right, all right . . . The journal isn't made of rubber. They've promised to increase the size by sixteen pages, when they give us the extra pages, then we'll print him. . . ."

And at that point I placed before him your letter about prose in general—isn't that what you'd call it?—and said that I wouldn't leave his office until he read this "epistolary legacy."

He read it, scratched his head, sighed, but didn't seem to be shuffling his feet under the desk anymore.

Then he said, "Well, all right, all right . . . We'll see, we'll see. . . ."

That's the news. Nothing more.

My best to Vovka (he hasn't broken the bicycle yet?) and Lyudochka (she still hasn't left you, you bore?).

Your friend,
Alex Pl.

From the editor's desk
(Outgoing correspondence)
Dear Comrade Gustov!

Your story needs a great deal of revision, if there's any point in revising it at all.

To begin with, the plot is extremely improbable. Really, now. You write that a certain airplane makes a forced landing in the desert and in addition loses contact with the outside world, and the passengers, not knowing where they are and what awaits them, each sets forth his own version of their predicament, these presumably being versions of the very existence (or end?) of all contemporary humanity.

Yes—no more and no less, all humanity!

It is a very confusing and implausible situation.

And the woman who for some reason walks off alone into the steppe? This fact must be explained—is she right in the head?

How strange, unreal, and unconvincing!

The style of your story could also stand improvement. What, for instance, could "winning by losing" mean? You are, after all, writing for the mass reader, how would the average reader understand this? On the other hand, an expression like "the gray sky" is too hackneyed and trivial. Well, and what do you mean by a "motley airport" or a "corrugated field"? And what kind of word is "schizzy"? Not only isn't it in the regular dictionary, it's not even in the orthographic dictionary. Or when you write, "They went into the crosslike building." What does "crosslike" mean, why invent words? Write in plain Russian, "They went into the cross-shaped building."

Wishing you creative success in the future,

> Literary consultant,
> member of the Writers Union,
> A. Kulebyakin

P.S. It's true, your accompanying letter, to which you gave the awkward title "A Few Words About Myself and My Prose," interested the editor in chief.

Dear Vladimir Ivanovich!

Unfortunately, we cannot publish the story "Forced Landing." You have probably already received a detailed letter on this subject from our consultant.

But the letter you sent along with the story, to which you gave the not altogether successful title "A Few Words About Myself and My Prose," and in which you seemingly are not addressing the editorial board but are speaking in general about your attitude toward prose, this letter drew the attention of the editor in chief and he proposes publishing it under the title "Prose" (with "A Story" in parentheses).

We ask you to inform us whether or not you would allow such a publication. Do you want to see it under your own name or under a pseudonym?

Please respond as soon as possible.

> Assistant Editor of the Prose Section,
> O. Khudyakov

> [And added in the handwriting of the
> editor A. Plitochkin:] ("O! Khudyakov")

Alex! Friend!

What is this, even in your eyes I'm not a writer?

I can make judgments about literature, the judgments can be published, but what about the story?

What about "Forced Landing"?

No chance?

I expect an immediate reply. By telegram.
Besides you, there's no one to give me an answer.

> Yours,
> Vl. Gustov
> Plumber? Engineer? Prose writer?

1985

Translated from the Russian by Catharine Theimer Nepomnyashchy.

BIOGRAPHICAL NOTES

Andrei Vasilievsky

ANDREI G. BITOV (b. 1937), a native of Leningrad who now lives in Moscow, began his literary career in the early 1960s. Over the years he has evolved from a young writer quite typical of his time into one of Russia's most original voices. He is a short-story writer, a novelist, a critic, a literary scholar, a travel writer, an ecologist, an essayist, and a poet. Critics point out Bitov's fundamental "dilettantism" (in the best sense of the word), for he writes about the most diverse subjects, from architecture to problems of versification and translation. He developed a keen awareness of the seriousness of ecological problems, as seen in "The Birds, or New Information About Man" (1976), before these issues became matters of universal concern. The year 1987 has been called the "year of Bitov." The journal *Novy Mir* published two of his works, the novella "The Man in the Landscape" and the nearly fifteen-year-old novel *Pushkin House*, several chapters of which were published earlier as short stories. Published in the same year were the novella "The Symmetry Teacher," part one, the phantasmagorical story "Pushkin's Photograph (1799–2099)," which is included in this collection, and an essay about Dostoevsky. He was interviewed in the newspaper *Literaturnaya Gazeta*, made appearances on television, and traveled abroad. From an author for a relatively small audience of "gourmets," he is turning into a rather popular, almost fashionable figure, and this, too, is a kind of test that Bitov will yet have to endure.

ELCHIN, whose full name is Elchin Ilyas ogly Efendiev (b. 1943), is an Azerbaijani writer and critic who lives in Baku. His first stories were

published in the early 1970s. The critic Lev Anninsky has described
Elchin's short stories as "psychological études painted in watercolors
on a rough, natural canvas." He paints real, trouble-ridden life with
gentle and subtle irony, and critics have noted the influence not only
of Chekhov and Bunin on his work but also that of the satirists Mikhail
Zoshchenko and Mikhail Bulgakov. He writes about his native Azerbaijan, organically blending the poetry of antiquity and the charm of
the old patriarchal system with modern life. In addition to novellas and
short stories, Elchin is the author of a historical novel, *Makhmoud and
Miriam* (published in Russian, 1985). Set in the sixteenth century, it
tells the tragic love story of a young man and woman—legendary heroes of a medieval Azerbaijani epic—who became the victims of national and religious discord. Elchin's prose has been translated into
English, French, German, Arabic, Farsi, and many other languages.

I. GREKOVA is the pseudonym of Elena S. Ventsel (b. 1907). The
pseudonym derives from *igrek*, the Russian word for the variable "y."
The mathematical allusion is by no means accidental as Elena Ventsel
graduated from the department of mathematics at Leningrad State
University in 1929. She holds a doctorate in the technical sciences,
has been a professor for many years, and is the author of a number of
books on higher mathematics. In her fiction she often depicts the life
of the Russian scientific intelligentsia. The novella "On Probation"
(1967), published in *Novy Mir*, was subjected to biased criticism for its
truthful portrayal of a collaboration between scientists and the military.
In "No Smiles" (written in 1970, but first published in 1986), the story
that appears in this volume, she gives a candid account of the ordeal
and the consequences of such criticism.

By 1967 VALENTIN P. KATAEV (1897–1986) had long been one of the
most highly regarded writers in the Soviet Union. He was showered
with awards and his books were constantly republished. His novella "A
Lonely White Sail Gleams" (1936, and the film by the same name,
1937) had become a classic of Soviet children's literature. Almost every
Soviet schoolchild is familiar with it as well as his story "Son of the
Regiment" (1945, and the film by the same name, 1946; U.S.S.R.
State Prize, 1946), which is about an orphaned boy during World
War II. It seemed that his place in literary history was firmly estab-
lished, but an entirely new stage in Kataev's long career began with the
novellas "The Holy Well" (1967), "Grass of Oblivion" (1967), and

"The Cube" (1969). The writer jokingly referred to his new style as "mauvism" (from the French *mauvais*, "bad"): "When everyone has learned to write 'well,' great masters intentionally write 'badly.'" This was, of course, the openly ironic remark of a true professional, a master. Among the works of Kataev's "new" prose we should also mention the novella "My Diamond Wreath" (1978)—his reminiscences of Mikhail Bulgakov, Mikhail Zoshchenko, and Boris Pasternak—and "Werther Has Already Been Written" (1980), which describes with unusual candor for its time the Red terror in Odessa during the Civil War. The story selected for this volume, "The Sleeper" (1985), was, like all Kataev's later works, published in *Novy Mir* and was one of the last he wrote before his death. He was named a Hero of Soviet Labor in 1974 and was appointed a foreign member of the renowned Goncourt Academy in 1976.

VIKTOR V. KONETSKY (b. 1929) graduated from the naval academy and is an avid sailor to this day. Most of his books are fictional chronicles of naval voyages and they comprise a multivolume "travel" novel, *In Search of Good Hope*, begun in 1968. In essence the author himself, as he changes over time, is the hero of his own prose, and his work occupies a place all its own in contemporary Soviet literature. Konetsky has written scenarios for many films, including the lavishly produced and popular Soviet comedy *Striped Voyage* (1961). By the writer's own admission he believes in the necessity of restoring Russia's image as a great sea power. But *None of Us Takes the Beaten Path* (1987) was probably the last of Konetsky's naval chronicles to be written in his traditional manner—"Too much repetition," the author feels. The story included in this volume, "Cat-Strangler Silver" (1987), reflects certain new tendencies in his work that he will no doubt develop more fully in the future. "It's getting harder and harder to write," Konetsky has said. "The desire to harangue didactically, to raise one's fists at every injustice is overwhelming."

VLADIMIR S. MAKANIN (b. 1937) graduated from Moscow University in mathematics (1960) and then went on to receive a degree in screenwriting and direction (1967). His fiction is widely read and even more widely debated. Critics argue about whether Makanin's prose lies outside the established ethical values of classic nineteenth- and twentieth-century Russian literature or is in its own way a development and a refraction of that tradition. The basis for this argument is the author's

pointed severity, mercilessness, and lack of illusion toward his characters and toward human nature in general. As critic I. Rodnyanskaya
puts it, Makanin is not a psychologist but a "social anthropologist"
concerned with portraying types who are characteristic of contemporary society but who were, before him, somehow outside the scope of
Russian literature (for example, the novella "The Precursor" [1983],
about a strange doctor who is either a charlatan or a prophet or a mentally ill man and who tries to save his unhappy fellowmen). *The Swiftly
Flowing River* (1983), the title of one of Makanin's many short-story
collections, alludes to a key image in his work: life as a swift river that
sweeps every swimmer away in its powerful current and reduces all of
man's good intentions to naught.

As recently as 1984 the Georgian writer REVAZ A. MISHVELADZE
(b. 1940) was known as a "young" author, yet today it is hard to imagine the contemporary Georgian short story without him. Unlike many
of his fellow Georgians, Mishveladze bases his writing not on myth or
parable or fairy tale but on the joke or anecdote. Consequently, most
of his works are short, sometimes exceedingly short, and many are
highly dramatic. They heighten life's collisions to a kind of paradox
and often involve striking plot twists. Mishveladze is intrigued by man
and it is no accident that many of his stories have characters' names as
their titles. His preferences are always obvious and his sympathies
easily detected. He sides with those who are good, honest, sincere, and
kind, but such people, as a rule, are unlucky in life. Mishveladze is
drawn to unusual human types—eccentrics, simpletons, "holy fools,"
"saints"—and tends to idealize them to a certain extent. The Georgian
national character leaves a distinct mark on Mishveladze's work and
his stories are filled with inimitable Georgian humor, proverbs, and
slices of everyday Georgian life.

"I am a lucky man—I have always done what I wanted," BULAT SH.
OKUDZHAVA (b. 1924) once said. Just about everyone in our country
knows him, first and foremost as a poet who sings his verses to his own
guitar accompaniment. Okudzhava had to travel a long road of official
nonrecognition, even of active hostility, but all the while his songs
were spreading throughout the country on casette tapes and were being
performed by amateur singers. Several books of his poetry have been
published and he is also a talented prose writer. After the novella
"Good Luck, Schoolboy!" (1961), with its sincere and fresh depiction

of a young soldier at the front (Okudzhava himself served at the front), elicited sharp criticism for "de-heroization," he began writing historical prose, which might more accurately be called historical fantasy, based on material from the nineteenth century: *Poor Avrosimov* (1969; republished as *A Gulp of Freedom*, 1971), *Merci, or the Adventures of Shipov* (1971), *The Dilettantes' Travels* (two parts, 1976–78), and *A Meeting with Bonaparte* (1983). Okudzhava is of Georgian descent, but he lives in Moscow and writes in Russian. A number of his relatives and close friends were victims of Stalin's terror, and in "The Girl of My Dreams" (1986) he tells the story of his mother's return from one of the camps. The story selected for this collection, "The Art of Needles and Sins" (1985), captures the atmosphere of fear and suspicion in the early 1950s with sad humor and hope for a better future.

LYUDMILA S. PETRUSHEVSKAYA's (b. 1939) works have had a strange history. They have been the subject of much discussion and debate, but few have been published or staged. She is a playwright, a prose writer, a screenwriter, a poet, and an author of fairy tales. Each of her infrequent publications evokes lively interest among both the general reading public and the critics. Until recently even sophisticated critics perceived her plays as "problematic." Today, as *perestroika* proceeds, allowing theaters to establish their own repertoires, Petrushevskaya's name is appearing on theater bills more and more often. She is a keen observer of contemporary morals, and the language of her plays treats the prevalent "corrosion of speech" as a symptom of intellectual and social impoverishment and decay. Petrushevskaya does not flatter her contemporaries; love and compassion are revealed paradoxically in her work through pity and ruthlessness, which is evident in *Love*, staged in 1975, *Cinzano*, *Smirnova's Birthday*, both staged in 1977, and *Music Lessons*, staged in 1979. Petrushevskaya's short stories are unusual for their laconism and are virtually without analogue. Her "long" short story, "A Circle of One's Own," written in 1979 but published only in 1988 in *Novy Mir*, was not accepted by some readers and critics because of its seemingly excessive gloominess. The renowned Soviet director Yu. Norstein made a full-length animated film of Petrushevskaya's scenario *Fairy Tale of Fairy Tales* (1979), which was received with great acclaim in the Soviet Union and abroad. It was awarded a prize at the All-Union Film Festival, the Grand Prix in Zagreb, the Grand Prix in Lille, first prize in Ottawa, a prize in Oberhausen, and a medal from the International Union of

Journalists. In 1984 a jury of film critics from various countries named *Fairy Tale of Fairy Tales* the best film in the archives of animation.

He hasn't written a great deal, but every new work by VALENTIN G. RASPUTIN (b. 1937) becomes a major event for, without exaggeration, the entire Soviet reading public. Most literary journals felt it their duty to comment on his stories "Money for Maria" (1967), "Borrowed Time" (1970), and "Live and Remember" (1974; U.S.S.R. State Prize, 1977). Critics have noted Rasputin's deep spirituality, his penchant for contemplating nature, his sensitivity to the surrounding world. But in "The Fire" (1985), his last major work, he directly addresses current social and moral issues: What is happening to us? What is going on in our homeland? Perhaps his best-known story is "Farewell to Matyora" (1976), which relates the devastating effects of the construction of the enormous Bratsk Dam on the inhabitants of the little village of Matyora. They are forced to abandon the village forever, the place with which their entire lives and the lives of their ancestors have been connected. "I could not help but write 'Matyora,' the way sons . . . cannot help but bid farewell to their dying mother," the writer commented. The Soviet director Elem Klimov made a film, *The Farewell* (1983, screenplay by Larisa Shepitko), based on the story. In a television interview Rasputin, who lives in Siberia, admitted that he relishes solitude and that contact with people is trying for him. This does not stop him from being an effective public figure, however. His speeches in defense of nature, the cleanup of Lake Baikal in particular, and the preservation of the nation's historical and cultural legacy have earned him the respect of his readers. People of the most diverse convictions heed his words and some regard him as a spiritual leader. On his fiftieth birthday (1987) Rasputin was awarded the title Hero of Socialist labor—a rare honor since this title is usually bestowed on people of much more advanced age.

"I think of myself as a prose writer, but I'm thought of as a playwright," MIKHAIL M. ROSHCHIN (b. 1933) has complained, although at first glance he has no grounds for complaint. Roshchin's plays have been lovingly staged by the finest Soviet directors. Popular actors have performed in them and they have generated considerable interest abroad. They have been mounted in the United States, Japan, West Germany, Finland, and other countries. Such plays as *Valentin and Valentina* (1971), *The Old New Year* (1973), *The Echelon* (1975), and *Hasten to*

Do Good (1979) have earned a permanent place in the repertoires of theaters all over the Soviet Union. Roshchin the dramatist writes more sharply, more dynamically, but also more straightforwardly than Roshchin the prose writer. One is struck by the open conventionality of many scenes, the clearly expressed authorial presence, and the way everyday details build up at times into fantastic exaggerations. Roshchin the prose writer, strange as it may seem, has cultivated a completely different style. His lucid, tranquil, realistic manner harks back to the tradition of classic Russian literature, especially to Chekhov and Bunin. Roshchin himself has stressed the connection with Bunin in his story "Bunin in Yalta" (1970), which is a kind of declaration of love. Mikhail Roshchin is actively involved in *perestroika*, especially in the theater. In 1987 the publication and staging of two of his most controversial plays became possible—*Mother-of-Pearl Zinaida* and *The Seventh Labor of Hercules*.

The poet, essayist, and prose writer VLADIMIR A. SOLOUKHIN (b. 1932) is one of the most widely read authors in the Soviet Union, although opinions of his work vary. His early works, *Vladimir Country Roads* (1957), *Letters from the Russian Museum* (1966), and *Searching for Icons in Russia* (1969), are prime examples of the genre known as lyric prose. They combine the authenticity of travel essays, the authorial freedom of letters and diaries, the directness of journalism, and the poetic quality of landscape painting. Soloukhin's prose is directed against the consequences of scientific and technological progress and the urban way of life, although the author lives in Moscow. He was born into a peasant family in the Vologda region and to this day speaks with a northern Russian accent. Soloukhin was one of the first Soviet writers to raise the issue of preserving monuments of antiquity. He has spoken out bitterly against the "unconscionable negligence" that has been shown toward ancient churches and old Russian icons. He fervently advocates national self-awareness for the Russian people and decries artificial "internationalism." *A Time to Gather Stones* (1980)— the title of one of his collections—is clearly symbolic. Soloukhin's books, as a rule, are written in the first person and there is a strong vein of "enlightenment" in his work. He loves to talk—not without self-admiration, it must be said—about what he has seen, what he knows, and where he has been. Everything he has written is based on personal experience, whether the subject is gathering mushrooms, fishing, collecting icons, or recuperating in an oncology clinic.

TATYANA N. TOLSTAYA (b. 1951), a philologist by profession, comes from a renowned literary family. She is the granddaughter of the writer Aleksei N. Tolstoy and the daughter of the prominent scholar Nikita A. Tolstoy. Her first story was published in 1983 and since then some two dozen have appeared in various periodicals. Her first collection of works, *On the Golden Porch*, came out in 1987. Tatyana Tolstaya's talent is indisputable. Her writing is odd, whimsical, stylistically refined almost to the point of foppishness, shot through with literary currents, especially those of the 1920s, nurtured on a diversity of literary sources, and rich in "bookish" associations. She has a relentlessly keen eye and tends to identify with all the insulted, weak, old, young, and sick of this world, with everyone "who was not taken to the holiday celebration." "I write not about the 'little' man, but about the average man," she has said. Her outspokenness on many issues has made her a rather controversial figure, but this has not alienated the many admirers of her writing.

ARVO VALTON, the pseudonym of Arvo Yu. Vallikivi (b. 1935), is an Estonian writer who lives in Tallinn. He gained national recognition as one of the authors in the collection *Estonia's Young Prose* (published in Russian in 1978). The short story included in this volume, "Love in Mustamägi," is quite representative of Valton's prose. As a rule his works resemble parables; they are multilayered and emotionally charged. He is noted for combining everyday details, realistic in the extreme, with fantastical situations that give the illusion of being credible in context. Valton must be read carefully for his prose is saturated with meaning and it takes only a moment's distraction to miss something essential. Some critics have reproached him for rationalism and inordinate complexity. His novellas and short stories shatter ingrained stereotypes and prejudices, and he boldly explores the alienation and loneliness of people, primarily city dwellers, in the modern world. At the same time Valton's respect for man—for the toiler, the builder, the creator—is immutable.

S. YAROSLAVTSEV is the pseudonym of Arkady N. Strugatsky (b. 1925), who is best known for the works he coauthors with his brother Boris. The Strugatsky brothers are by far the most popular science-fiction writers in the Soviet Union and their stories are widely translated. Even though their subject matter might seem far removed from everyday life, their works mirror the spiritual evolution of Soviet society. When they began their careers in the late 1950s, the Strugatskys shared the euphoria of the "thaw" that occurred after the landmark Twentieth Party Congress in 1956. Their early works were rather naive, full of enthusiasm for technological progress, faith in a radiant future, and in man's creative abilities. Soon, however, irony, alarm, skepticism, and satiric elements crept into their writing. From the utopian *The Return. Midday. 22nd Century* (1962), they moved toward the anti-utopian *Predators of the Age* (1965). Their most popular work among young people is the novella-fairy tale "Monday Starts on Saturday" (1965). Perhaps their most important work is the philosophical novel *Snail on the Slope* (parts one and two, 1966–68). Satirical criticism of bureaucracy (*The Tale of the Troika*, 1968), the problem of man's encounter with the unknown, and reflections on the price of progress are themes that occupy a special place in the work of the Strugatsky brothers. Andrei Tarkovsky, the late Soviet director, made the film *Stalker* (1980) based on the Strugatskys' book *A Picnic on the Curb* (1972). The brothers have been awarded many national and international prizes, including the Campbell Award (United States) in 1977.

SERGEI P. ZALYGIN's (b. 1913) first book of short stories came out in 1941, but for the next twenty years he stubbornly resisted becoming a professional writer, even though he joined the Writers Union. He graduated from the hydromelioratization department of the Omsk Agricultural Institute and has worked as a hydrotechnical engineer, a surveyor, and a hydrologist at an Arctic hydroelectric station. His novella "On the Irtysh" (1964), about the injustices of Stalin's collectivization of agriculture, propelled him into the front ranks of contemporary Soviet writers. For his novel about the partisans in Siberia during the Civil War, *Salt Valley* (parts one and two, 1967–68), he was awarded the U.S.S.R. State Prize in 1968. Zalygin's urban novel, *The South American Variant* (1973), generated discussions about the consequences of the emancipation of women. And his novel *After the Storm* (part one, 1980; part two, 1985) anticipated today's debates about the meaning of Lenin's New Economic Policy of the 1920s. He wrote a study of Chekhov, *My Poet* (1971), and several collections of his journalism and criticism have been published. His short stories have been gathered in the collections *Festival* (1980) and *First-Person Stories* (1983). Sergei Zalygin is now editor in chief of *Novy Mir*, the country's leading literary journal, and head of the recently formed organization

Ecology and the World. His fight to prevent the implementation of enormous projects fraught with serious ecological consequences, including the diverting of northern Russian and Siberian rivers to the south, has won him a well-deserved following. He is a devoted and active participant in *perestroika* and was named a Hero of Socialist Labor in 1988.

Translated from the Russian by Steven W. Nielsen.

FIRST PUBLICATION INFORMATION

Andrei Bitov, "Fotografiya Pushkina (1799–2099)," *Znamya*,
   No. 1, 1987.
Elchin, "Avtomobil'naya katastrofa v Parizhe," translated into Russian
   from the Azerbaijani, *Druzhba narodov*, No. 10, 1985.
I. Grekova, "Bez ulybok," *Oktyabr'*, No. 11, 1986.
Valentin Kataev, "Spyashchii," *Novy mir*, No. 1, 1985.
Viktor Konetsky, "Koshkodav Sil'ver," *Znamya*, No. 5, 1987.
Vladimir Makanin, "Antilider," *Ural*, No. 6, 1983.
Revaz Mishveladze, "Voprositel'nyi i vosklitsatel'nyi znaki," translated
   into Russian from the Georgian, *Literaturnaya Gruziya*, No. 5, 1987.
Bulat Okudzhava, "Iskusstvo kroiki i zhit'ya," *Znamya*, No. 3, 1987.
Lyudmila Petrushevskaya, "Cherez polya," *Avrora*, No. 5, 1983.
Valentin Rasputin, "Chto peredat' vorone?" *Nash sovremennik*,
   No. 7, 1982.
Mikhail Roshchin, "Chertovo koleso v Kobuleti," *Ogonyok*,
   No. 5 (January), 1987.
Vladimir Soloukhin, "Pokhorony Stepanidy Ivanovny," *Novy mir*,
   No. 9, 1987.
Tatyana Tolstaya, "Ogon' i pyl'," *Avrora*, No. 10, 1986.
Arvo Valton, "Mustamäe armastus," *Looming*, No. 2, 1974.
S. Yaroslavtsev, "Podrobnosti zhizni Nikity Vorontsova," *Znanie—sila*,
   Nos. 6–7, 1984.
Sergei Zalygin, "Proza," *Znamya*, No. 8, 1985.